Business Continuity and Disaster Recovery for InfoSec Managers

Computer Security and Computer Forensic Related Book Titles:

Rittinghouse & Hancock, *Cybersecurity Operations Handbook*,
ISBN 1-55558-306-7, 1336pp, 2003.

Rittinghouse & Ransome, *Instant Messaging Security*, ISBN 1-55558-338-5, 432pp, 2005.

Rittinghouse, *Wireless Operational Security*, ISBN 1-55558-317-2, 496pp, 2004.

Ransome & Rittinghouse, *VoIP Security*, ISBN 1-55558-332-6, 450pp, 2005.

De Clercq, *Windows Server 2003 Security Infrastructures: Core Security Features*,
ISBN 1-55558-283-4, 752pp, 2004.

Erbschloe, *Implementing Homeland Security for Enterprise IT*,
ISBN 1-55558-312-1, 320pp, 2003.

Erbschloe, *Physical Security for IT*, ISBN 1-55558-327-X, 320pp, 2005.

Speed & Ellis, *Internet Security*, ISBN 1-55558-298-2, 398pp, 2003.

XYPRO, *HP NonStop Server Security*, ISBN 1-55558-314-8, 618pp, 2003.

Casey, *Handbook of Computer Crime Investigation*, ISBN 0-12-163103-6, 448pp, 2002.

Kovacich, *The Information Systems Security Officer's Guide*,
ISBN 0-7506-7656-6, 361pp, 2003.

Boyce & Jennings, *Information Assurance*, ISBN 0-7506-7327-3, 261pp, 2002.

Stefanek, *Information Security Best Practices: 205 Basic Rules*,
ISBN 0-878707-96-5, 194pp, 2002.

For more information or to order these and other Digital Press
titles, please visit our website at www.books.elsevier.com/digitalpress!
At www.books.elsevier.com/digitalpress you can:
•Join the Digital Press Email Service and have news about
our books delivered right to your desktop
•Read the latest news on titles
•Sample chapters on featured titles for free
•Question our expert authors and editors
•Download free software to accompany select texts

Business Continuity and Disaster Recovery for InfoSec Managers

John W. Rittinghouse, Ph.D., CISM
James F. Ransome, Ph.D., CISM, CISSP

ELSEVIER
DIGITAL
PRESS

AMSTERDAM • BOSTON • HEIDELBERG • LONDON
NEW YORK • OXFORD • PARIS • SAN DIEGO
SAN FRANCISCO • SINGAPORE • SYDNEY • TOKYO

Elsevier Digital Press
30 Corporate Drive, Suite 400, Burlington, MA 01803, USA
Linacre House, Jordan Hill, Oxford OX2 8DP, UK

∞ Recognizing the importance of preserving what has been written, Elsevier prints its books on acid-free paper whenever possible.

Library of Congress Cataloging-in-Publication Data
Application Submitted.

British Library Cataloguing-in-Publication Data
A catalogue record for this book is available from the British Library.

ISBN-13: 978-1-55558-339-2

ISBN-10: 1-55558-339-3

For information on all Elsevier Digital Press publications
visit our Web site at www.books.elsevier.com

05 06 07 08 09   10 9 8 7 6 5 4 3 2 1

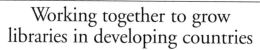

Contents

Foreword

Foreword by Mr. Paul Kurtz

Paul B. Kurtz is currently the executive director of the Cyber Security Industry Alliance. Most recently, Paul was special assistant to the President and senior director for critical infrastructure protection on the White House's Homeland Security Council (HSC), where he was responsible for both physical and cyberspace security. Before joining HSC in 2003, Kurtz served on the White House's National Security Council (NSC) as senior director for national security of the Office of Cyberspace Security and a member of the President's Critical Infrastructure Protection Board, where he developed the international component of the National Strategy to Secure Cyberspace. Previously, he was a director for counter-terrorism in the NSC's Office of Transnational Threats from 1999 to 2001. Prior to his White House work, Kurtz served in several bureaus in the State Department, specializing in weapons of mass destruction non-proliferation policy and strategic arms control. He also served as political advisor to Operation Provide Comfort in Incirlik, Turkey and as science attaché in Vienna, Austria. He participated in several arms control inspection teams, traveling to Iraq and North Korea. Kurtz received his Bachelor's degree from Holy Cross College and his Master's degree in International Public Policy from Johns Hopkins University's School of Advanced International Studies.

Planning for recovery from a disaster is now commonly recognized as an essential component in the management of risk. Businesses today have become accustomed to planning for commercial risks, such as the sudden failure of a critical parts supplier, an unexpected debt or liability, labor strikes, or the discovery of a serious fault in a retail product. Planning for a terrorist incident is, in many ways, very similar. Nearly one in five businesses suffer a major disruption every year. Business continuity planning is a means of ensuring that essential functions of your business survive a terrorist incident, natural disaster, or other disruption. It is crucial for any business or organization to plan its survival following the loss or denial of access to buildings, a significant number of staff, their IT systems, important records and information, or myriad other assets they depend upon to operate successfully.

I have learned in my career that one can never plan enough to mitigate all of the effects of a disaster. I have been privileged to participate in strategic planning for many unforeseen events; such experiences expose the magnitude and scope of devastation and destruction with which people close to the event must contend. In the middle of such unforeseen events, there is little one can do to stop an explosion, a volcano, flood, fire, or myriad other things that we see happen every day in our instant-news environment. What one must realize is that the distinguishing factor between coping successfully with such events or being totally overwhelmed and unable to cope at all is the amount of planning and preparation that takes place before the event occurs. This, of course, does not mean preparation and planning will insulate those who take such steps from the explosion's effects, or from the waters of a flood, but it does mean that their likelihood of preventing greater damage or of lessening the effects of damage is greater than that of someone who did nothing. While no amount of planning can magically defray the effects of a disaster, planning and preparation can help reduce the after-effects and aid in recovery after such events.

In *Business Continuity and Disaster Recovery for InfoSec Managers*, Drs. Rittinghouse and Ransome present a thorough, well-structured explanation of the need for taking such preventative measures. They have carefully crafted a presentation of the material that is crucial to help any organization develop a set of contingency plans that will assist in the recovery process. The book is clearly business oriented, and from the very first page, the authors emphasize the need to understand what can happen and why the organizations that survive such events are the ones that have prepared for their mitigation and recovery. They candidly point out that organizations that fail to do so generally do not survive the effects of an event.

In Chapter 1, they present the issue of planning, distinguishing between the contingency and continuity planning processes and explaining each facet of planning that an organization must undertake to create a successful Business Continuity Plan. They even cover the steps necessary to organize a project team to build the plan. In Chapter 2, the process of risk assessment is covered thoroughly. It is impossible to cover every conceivable aspect of business risk assessment in any book, but the authors have presented a cogent approach for businesses that allows planning teams to look at what is possible for them and perform an impact analysis from that perspective. A very complete coverage of business impact analysis is presented.

I am reminded of the old adage that "on ounce of prevention is worth a pound of cure" when I think of the things that could have been done in nearly any circumstance you read or hear about today. The focus of Chapter 3 in this book are ways to develop strategies that mitigate the effects of an unforeseen event. This section covers preventative measures that can be taken and preventative controls that can be implemented to reduce the impact of an incident to an organization. Having the foresight to prepare for such unforeseen events is not just good business practice these days, it is often required by law.

Chapter 4 of this book shows how to prepare for emergencies and what steps must be taken to facilitate a recovery process. In any event, there are really two stages of recovery that take place. First, when the event occurs, an organization must recover from the immediate threat of that event. Second, after the event, an organization must recover business operations. The focus of Chapters 5 and 6 deal precisely with those two stages of recovery and provide the reader with an insightful look at how organizations should be prepared to respond.

There is no amount of contingency planning in any organization that will be effective without proper training and periodic testing. Drs. Rittinghouse and Ransome provide a complete and concise approach organizations can leverage to develop testing, auditing and training programs in Chapter 7. Strategic audits and recurring training often differentiate organizations that recover successfully from organizations that never quite seem to get back on their feet. Even those organizations that do manage to stand up operations again often have suffered great losses in the process, and can never really regain momentum in the marketplace or leadership in the industry after they suffer a catastrophe. It drives home the need for continuing maintenance of the strategic plans an organization invests its money to build. Business Continuity Planning should be considered a strategic investment in any organization, and I think *Business Continuity and Disaster Recovery for InfoSec Managers* is an investment every organization should make to learn how to properly prepare and plan for disaster.

Paul B. Kurtz

Executive Director of the Cyber Security Industry Alliance

7/20/05

Introduction

Introduction: Business Security 101

An area that is typically overlooked in most corporations today is the need to introduce the executive management team to the business continuity planning and management process. With senior management buy-in and direction from the top, this process delivers confidence to all stakeholders (e.g., customers, employees, suppliers, the local community, and even the environment) that plans are in place to avert or recover from catastrophe. The speed of business has changed, and there is very often little time to allow for a gradual recovery. The emergence of ecommerce and the lack of loyalty among customers have changed the need for recovery to one of ensuring continuous availability. The BCP/DRP (business continuity planning/disaster recovery planning) process described herein includes an assessment of availability and shows you how your plan should be structured to meet customer expectations. The BCP/DR plan is key to organizations for which 24/7 availability is critical.

Initially, BCP/DRP was important for organizations to ensure compliance with regulatory requirements. Since September 11, 2001, it has become critical to protecting their customer's interests and corporate value. Without the value and the confidence of their investors, most companies would be vulnerable in today's highly competitive marketplace. For that reason, contingency management is an important process necessary to ensure business survival. Of course, there is typically a marked contrast between what managers perceive the threats to their companies to be and what their continuity plan addresses. We will discuss ways to address these issues and show you how to develop and manage your BCP in this book. First, however, a short overview is in order.

The State of the BCP and Network Disaster Recovery Industry: Where Are We and Why?

The events of September 11, 2001 resulted in Chief Information Officers (CIOs) scrambling to implement business continuity and disaster recovery planning. Such business continuity investments appear to have been only a spike after that dreadful date. Unfortunately, business continuity has continued to slide downward on the priority scale when CIOs and senior management are forced to make tough business choices in today's instant-on, ever-changing business environment. Gartner analyst Roberta Witty estimated as late as July 2003 that even after the terrorist attacks on the United States, less than 25% of large enterprises had comprehensive business continuity plans [1].

We all know that disasters can result in large monetary losses, legal ramifications, loss of customer confidence, and, in some extreme cases, the company's existence. Organizations therefore need to have plans to recover their assets, which include people, facilities, business applications, processes, and IT systems, so they'll be able to return to normal business operations as soon as possible. This requires sensible business continuity and disaster recovery plans, and sensible management that takes the contingency plans seriously. Disasters requiring these types of plans can be caused by natural events such as floods, fires, and earthquakes, or by systems-related causes, such as network problems and power or telecommunications failures. Human and malicious causes, such as hackers, viruses, terrorism, disaffected employees, and theft, also require planning and preventative measures.

Historically, BCP has resided in the Information Technology (IT) department of most organizations. For this reason, most companies have some disaster recovery alternatives in place for their IT systems. The most common disaster recovery alternative used is offsite data storage, in which data is backed up on a regular basis onto a tape or disk and kept at a remote location. Although several other technology alternatives for IT recovery are available, such as hot and cold sites, electronic vaulting, shadowing, mirroring, and disk-to-disk remote copy, all of which we will discuss later in this book, they are not used by as many corporations as you might think. In this tough economic environment, it is very tempting to cut resources for BCP. Many enterprises mistakenly view BCP as an insurance policy for which they will likely never have to place a claim.

However, we all know that disasters can happen at any time and any place, and it is recommended that CIOs make contingency planning a high priority in their organizations. CIOs should implement business continuity plans, get buy-in from executive-level management, and require business and IT managers to work together on the contingency planning process. They should look into implementing limited business continuity plans. In fact, although contingency planning is important for any business, it may not be practical for any but the largest organizations to maintain fully functioning plans in the event of a disaster. With the cooperation of executive management, CIOs should allocate budget and time for contingency planning. Until the early 1970s, most companies had no serious form of contingency or continuity planning at all. Major disasters were rare, and companies relied on insurance to protect them against asset losses. Business complacency was shattered, however, by the OPEC oil embargo. This event showed U.S. corporations they were vulnerable to external events beyond their control. In addition, dealing with the rest of the world suddenly became riskier with the emergence of terrorism and global cultural conflict. At the same time, and closer to home, the U.S. financial sector realized they were becoming more and more dependent upon new computer technology and recognized the catastrophic impact that nonavailability might have on a financial institution's ability to function. The regulators put considerable pressure on the financial sector to develop contingency plans to protect clients' funds. The computer industry saw this as an opportunity to sell more equipment. If the loss of a data center could put survival of the business at risk, then surely it would be a good idea to duplicate it in a location that could not be affected by the same disaster. Disaster recovery developed to encompass the replacement of facilities and property lost due to fire, flood, earthquake, or other disasters.

The emergence of business continuity planning was not about computer disaster recovery. It was about a new way of managing a business, viewing the continuation of business functionality in all circumstances as a key responsibility. Recovery of computer systems was simply part of the technical implementation of the overall business strategy. In general, disaster and emergency plans are written on the basis of recovery after an event. Business continuity is a process of anticipating that things are beginning to go wrong and taking planned and rehearsed steps to protect the business and shareholder interests. It is about coordinating and integrating all the planning processes across all departments, and presenting a confident image to the outside world. Business continuity planning has progressively developed to a point where today it takes an holistic view of an organization. Examination into the causes of most major disasters has found that there are several incidents or circumstances that, when combined together, led to the eventual disaster.

Business continuity planning is about prevention, not cure. It is about being able to deal with incidents when they occur and taking actions that mitigate loss (or greater loss) during such events. This process calls for the identification of potential incidents that would affect the mission-critical functions and processes of an organization. Assumptions are commonly made about which areas an organization is totally dependent upon, but if the test of mission criticality is applied to these areas, they may be found to be of lesser importance than other areas that had been overlooked. Until the critical areas have been identified, work cannot begin to establish the degree of impact on an organization if such areas are lost or disrupted. Should the level of impact be severe, an assessment must be made regarding the risk of an occurrence that would cause the loss of the critical function or area.

Business continuity planning requires that effective plans be established to ensure an organization can respond to any incident. But the process does not stop at the planning stage. Plans are worthless unless they are rehearsed. The rehearsal of plans is essential. There is not a plan created that will work correctly the first time; rehearsing ensures that disconnections and omissions are fixed before the plan is used in real circumstances. The management of business continuity planning is a continuum; plans must be kept up-to-date as the organization changes. External environments and influences are constantly in a state of flux, so the process, to be valid, must continue throughout the life of the organization. Throughout this book, we will show you how this process works and explain what is required to create an effective plan for your organization. First, however, we need to cover some fundamental concepts to ensure a solid foundation of security understanding before we cover the elements of security necessary to adequately protect business environments.

For those among us who are tasked with managing business, and for the ever-shrinking number of information technology (IT) professionals who are not directly involved in the daily struggles of coping with cybersecurity issues, one might be tempted to ask "What is the big deal about cybersecurity, really?"

- *How does it affect our company infrastructure?*
- *How does it affect users in our organization?*
- *Is it something our management team should worry about?*

These are all legitimate questions. More and more today, IT professionals face an ever-growing and daunting task. Attacks occur **EVERY** single day [2]. The only question to be asked in today's modern computing environment is "Are we prepared to deal with an attack?" This introduction will provide guidance on how to prepare for assaults against organizational infrastructure. It will help network and systems administrators prepare to answer these types of questions and will provide compelling information that can help even the most reluctant manager or administrator come to terms with the changed, threatening computing environment we face today.

Threats to Personal Privacy

Vast data stores in myriad organizations hold personal information about each of us. The accumulation of such large amounts of electronic information, combined with the increased ability of computers to monitor, process, and aggregate this information about people, creates a massive threat to our individual privacy. The reality of today is that all of this information and technology now available can be electronically linked together, allowing unknown entities unabated access to even our most private information. This situation should give us reason to pause and ask ourselves if we have not created a modern information age with an unwanted by product often referred to as "**Big Brother**."

While the magnitude and cost of the threat to our personal privacy is very difficult to determine, it is readily apparent that information technology is becoming powerful enough to warrant fears of the emergence of both government and corporate "Big Brothers." More awareness of the situation is needed at the organizational and personal level. With the increased accessibility of such information, we have created an ever-growing vulnerability that someone, such as a cyberterrorist, is likely to exploit.

The recently legislated "Privacy Acts" that many different countries have enacted in order to try and protect the data assets of their citizens have become an ever-growing part of this modern information age. All companies using computing resources today need to be keenly aware of both these threats and the legal ramifications that ensue when they attempt to monitor, prevent, or provide access to their information resources. One of the largest targets of criminals in this new age of cyberenvironments is fraud and theft, the topic of our next section.

Fraud and Theft

Computer systems can be exploited for the purpose of conducting fraudulent activities and for outright theft. Such criminal acts are accomplished by "automating" traditional methods of fraud and by inventing and using new methods, which are constantly being created by enterprising criminal minds. For example, individuals carrying out such criminal activity may use computers to transfer a company's proprietary customer data to computer systems that reside outside the company premises, or they may try to use or sell this valuable customer data to that company's competitors. Their motives may be for profit; they may be for inflicting damage to the victimized company to compensate for some perceived injustice; or they may just be perpetrating an act of malicious behavior for their entertainment or bragging rights. Computer fraud and theft can be committed by both company insiders and outsiders, but studies have shown that most corporate fraud is committed by company insiders [3].

In addition to the use of technology to commit fraud, computer hardware and software resources may be vulnerable to theft. Actual examples include the theft of unreleased software and storage of customer data in insecure places, such as anonymous FTP accounts, so that it can be accessed and stolen by outsiders. The exposure of data to these threats generates a secondary threat for a company: loss of credibility and possible liability for damages as a result of premature release of information; exposure or loss of information; and so on. Preventative measures that should be taken here are quite simple but are often overlooked. Implementation of efficient access control methodologies, periodic auditing, and firewall usage can, in most cases, prevent fraud from occurring—or at least make it more easily detected.

Internet Fraud

The meteoric rise in fraud perpetrated over the Internet has brought about the classification of nine types of fraud, developed from the data reported to the Internet Fraud Complaint Center (IFCC) [4]. Analysts at the IFCC receive Internet fraud complaints and sort them into one of the nine aforementioned fraud categories:

1.   **Financial Institution Fraud**—A knowing misrepresentation of the truth or concealment of a material fact by a person to induce

a business, organization, or other entity that manages money, credit, or capital to perform a fraudulent activity [5]. Credit/debit card fraud is an example of financial institution fraud that ranks among the most commonly reported offenses to the IFCC. Identity theft also falls into this category; cases classified under this heading tend to be those where the perpetrator possesses the complainant's true name identification (in the form of a Social Security card, driver's license, or birth certificate), but there has not been a credit or debit card fraud committed.

2. **Gaming Fraud**—Risking something of value, especially money, for a chance to win a prize when there is a misrepresentation of the odds or events [6]. Sports tampering and claiming false bets are two examples of gaming fraud.

3. **Communications Fraud**—A fraudulent act or process in which information is exchanged using different forms of media. Thefts of wireless, satellite, or landline services are examples of communications fraud.

4. **Utility Fraud**—A knowing misrepresentation or intention to harm by defrauding a government regulated entity that performs an essential public service, such as the supply of water or electrical services [7].

5. **Insurance Fraud**—A misrepresentation by the provider or the insured in the indemnity against loss. Insurance fraud includes the "padding" or inflating of actual claims, misrepresenting facts on an insurance application, submitting claims for injuries or damage that never occurred, and "staging" accidents [8].

6. **Government Fraud**—A knowing misrepresentation of the truth or concealment of a material fact to induce the government to act to its own detriment [9]. Examples of government fraud include tax evasion, welfare fraud, and counterfeit currency.

7. **Investment Fraud**—Deceptive practices involving the use of capital to create more money, either through income-producing vehicles or through more risk-oriented ventures designed to result in capital gains [10]. Ponzi or pyramid schemes and market manipulation are two types of investment fraud.

8. **Business Fraud**—The knowing misrepresentation of the truth or concealment of a material fact by a business or corporation [11]. Examples of business fraud include bankruptcy fraud and copyright infringement.

9.   **Confidence Fraud**—Reliance on another's discretion and/or a breach in a relationship of trust, resulting in financial loss. A knowing misrepresentation of the truth or concealment of a material fact to induce another to act to his or her detriment [12]. Auction fraud and nondelivery of payment or merchandise are both types of confidence fraud and are the most reported offenses to the IFCC. The **Nigerian Letter Scam** is an offense classified under confidence fraud.

The **Nigerian Letter Scam** [13] has been around since the early 1980s. In this scam, a correspondence outlining an opportunity to receive nonexistent government funds from alleged dignitaries is sent to a "victim," but there is a catch. The scam letter is designed to collect advance fees from the victim. This most often requires payoff money be sent from the victim to the "dignitary" in order to bribe government officials. While other countries may be mentioned, the correspondence typically indicates "The Government of Nigeria" as the nation of origin. This scam is also referred to as "419 Fraud" after the relevant section of the Criminal Code of Nigeria, as well as "Advance Fee Fraud."

Because of this scam, the country of Nigeria ranks second for total complaints reported at the IFCC on businesses by country. The IFCC has a policy of forwarding all Nigerian Letter Scam complaints to the U.S. Secret Service. The scam works as follows:

1.   A letter, e-mail, or fax is sent from an alleged official representing a foreign government or agency.

2.   The letter presents a business proposal to transfer millions of dollars in over-invoiced contract funds into your personal bank account. You are offered a certain percentage of the funds for your help.

3.   The letter encourages you to travel overseas to complete the details.

4.   The letter also asks you to provide blank company letterhead forms, banking account information, and telephone numbers.

5.   Next, you receive various documents with official looking stamps, seals and logos testifying to the authenticity of the proposal.

6.   Finally, they ask for up-front or advance fees for various taxes, processing fees, license fees, registration fees, attorney fees, etc.

Employee Sabotage

Probably the easiest form of employee sabotage known to all system administrators is "accidental" spillage. The act of intentionally spilling coffee or soda on a keyboard for the purpose of making the computer unusable for some time is a criminal offense. Proving the spillage was deliberate however, is next to impossible, without the aid of hidden cameras or other surveillance techniques. Some administrators have even experienced severe cases where servers have been turned off over a weekend resulting in unavailability, data loss, and the incurred but needless cost of hours of troubleshooting by someone. Employees are the people who are most familiar with their employer's computers and applications. They know what actions can cause damage, mischief, or sabotage. The number of incidents of employee sabotage is believed to be much smaller than the instances of theft, but the cost of such incidents can be quite high [14].

As long as people feel unjustly treated, cheated, bored, harassed, endangered, or betrayed at work, sabotage will be used as a method of achieving revenge or a twisted sense of job satisfaction. Later in this book, we will show how implementing methods of strict access control can prevent serious sabotage acts.

Infrastructure Attacks

Devastating results can occur from the loss of supporting infrastructure. This infrastructure loss can include power failures (outages, spikes, and brownouts), loss of communications, water outages and leaks, sewer problems, lack of transportation services, fire, flood, civil unrest, and strikes. A loss of infrastructure often results in system downtime, sometimes in the most unexpected ways. Countermeasures against loss of physical and infrastructure support include the addition of redundant systems and the establishment of recurring backup processes. Because of the damage these types of threats can cause, the Critical Infrastructure Protection Act was enacted.

Malicious Hackers

The term "malicious hacker" refers to someone who breaks into computers without authorization. Malicious hackers can be outsiders or insiders. The hacker threat should be considered in terms of past and potential future damage. Although current losses due to hacker attacks are significantly smaller than losses due to insider theft and sabotage, the hacker problem is widespread and serious. One example of malicious hacker activity is that directed against the public telephone system (which is, by the way, quite common; the targets are usually employee voice mailboxes or special "internal-only" numbers allowing free calls to company insiders). Another common method is for hackers to attempt to gather information about internal systems by using port scanners and sniffers, password attacks, denial-of-service attacks, and various other attempts to break into publicly exposed systems like file transfer protocol (FTP) and World Wide Web (WWW) servers. By implementing efficient firewalls and auditing/alerting mechanisms, external hackers can be thwarted. Internal hackers are extremely difficult to contend with, since they have already been granted access. However, conducting internal audits on a frequent and recurring basis will help organizations to detect these activities.

Malicious Coders

Malicious code refers to viruses, worms, Trojan horses, logic bombs, and other "uninvited" software. Although it is sometimes mistakenly associated only with personal computers, such types of malicious code can attack other platforms. The actual costs that have been attributed to the presence of malicious code most often include the cost of system outages and the cost of staff time for those who are involved in finding the *malware* and repairing the systems. Frequently, these costs are quite significant.

Today, we are subject to a vast number of virus incidents. This fact has generated much discussion on the issues of organizational liability and must be taken into account. Viruses are the most common case of malicious code. In today's modern computing platforms, some form of antivirus software must be included in order to cope with this threat. To do otherwise can be extremely costly. In 1999, a virus named Melissa was released, with devastating results [15]. The Melissa virus caused an estimated $80,000,000.00 in damage and disrupted computer and network operations worldwide.

Melissa was especially damaging, as viruses go, because its author had deliberately created the virus to purposely evade existing antivirus software and to exploit specific weaknesses in corporate and personal e-mail software, as well as server and desktop operating systems software. Melissa infected e-mail and propagated itself in that infected state to 50 other e-mail addresses it obtained from the existing e-mail address book it found on the victim's machine. It immediately began sending out these infectious e-mails from every machine it touched. The Melissa infection spread across the Internet at an exponential rate. Systems were literally brought down from overload as a result of exponential propagation.

Industrial Espionage

A company might be subject to industrial espionage simply because its competitors share some level of sensitive customer information that might be worth millions for interested parties, which range from governments to the press to corporate and private entities. This situation might be encouraging enough for many hackers to tempt fate and attempt to obtain such information. Internal staff might consider the risk minimal and give away such information. There could be active attempts to retrieve information without authorization by hacking, sniffing, and other measures. A case of espionage can have serious consequences for a company, in terms of incurring the cost of lawsuits and resulting damage awards. This situation can also devastate a company's reputation in the marketplace.

Formally defined, industrial espionage is the act of gathering proprietary data from private companies or governments for the purpose of aiding others. Industrial espionage can be perpetrated either by companies seeking to improve their competitive advantage or by governments seeking to aid their domestic industries. Foreign industrial espionage carried out by a government is often referred to as economic espionage. Since information is processed and stored on computer systems, computer security can help protect against such threats; it can do little, however, to reduce the threat of authorized employees selling that information.

Cases of industrial espionage are on the rise, especially after the end of the Cold War, when many intelligence agencies changed their orientation towards industrial targets. A 1992 study sponsored by the American Society for Industrial Security (ASIS) found that proprietary business information theft had increased 260 percent since 1985. The data indicated 30 percent of the reported losses in 1991 and 1992 had foreign involvement. The study also found that 58 percent of thefts were perpetrated by current or former employees. The three most damaging types of stolen information were pricing information, manufacturing process information, and product development and specification information. Other types of information stolen included customer lists, basic research, sales data, personnel data, compensation data, cost data, proposals, and strategic plans.

Within the area of economic espionage, the Central Intelligence Agency has stated that its main objective is obtaining information related to technology, but that information on U.S. government policy deliberations concerning foreign affairs and information on commodities, interest rates, and other economic factors is also a target. The Federal Bureau of Investigation concurs that technology-related information is the main target, but also lists corporate proprietary information, such as negotiating positions and other contracting data, as a target.

Because of the increasing rise in economic and industrial espionage cases from the mid-1980s to the mid-1990s, the U.S. government passed the Economic and Espionage Act of 1996. This law, coded as **18 U.S.C. §1832**, provides:

(a).   Whoever, with intent to convert a trade secret, that is related to or included in a product that is produced for or placed in interstate or foreign commerce, to the economic benefit of anyone other than the owner thereof, and intending or knowing the offense will, injure any owner of that trade secret, knowingly—

  (1). steals, or without authorization appropriates, takes, carries away, or conceals, or by fraud, artifice, or deception obtains such information;

  (2). without authorization copies, duplicates, sketches, draws, photographs, downloads, uploads, alters, destroys, photocopies, replicates, transmits, delivers, sends, mails, communicates, or conveys such information;

  (3). receives, buys, or possesses such information, knowing the same to have been stolen or appropriated, obtained, or converted without authorization;

  (4). attempts to commit any offense described in paragraphs (1) through (3); or

  (5). conspires with one or more other persons to commit any offense described in paragraphs (1) through (3), and one or more of such persons do any act to effect the object of the conspiracy, shall, except as provided in subsection (b), be fined under this title or imprisoned not more than 10 years, or both.

(b).   Any organization that commits any offense described in subsection (a) shall be fined not more than $5,000,000.

In a recent case [16], conviction was upheld against violators of 18 U.S.C. § 1832 in an appeal of Mr. Pin-Yen Yang and his daughter Hwei Chen Yang (Sally) for industrial espionage, among other crimes. Mr. Yang owned the Four Pillars Enterprise Company, Ltd., based in Taiwan. This company specialized in the manufacture of adhesives. Mr. Yang and his daughter conspired to illegally obtain trade secrets from their chief U.S. competitor, Avery Dennison Corporation, by hiring an ex-employee of Avery Dennison, a Dr. Lee. Lee was retained as a consultant by Yang and the group conspired to pass confidential trade secrets from Avery to Four Pillars. When the FBI confronted Lee on the matter, he agreed to be video-taped in a meeting with Mr. Yang and his daughter. During the meeting, enough evidence was gathered to effect a conviction [17].

Measures against industrial espionage consist of the same measures that are taken by companies to counter hackers, with added security obtained by using data encryption technology. Where this is not possible due to government regulations (France, for example), proprietary compression or hashing algorithms can be used, which results in the same effect as encryption but with a higher chance of being broken by a determined adversary. Legal protections exist, of course, but were once very difficult to dissect from the vast amount of legislation in Title 18 of the U.S. Code. Congress amended the many laws dotted throughout Title 18 code into a comprehensive set of laws known as the 1996 National Information Infrastructure Protection Act.

Social Engineering

The weakest link in security will always be people, and the easiest way to break into a system is to engineer your way in through the human interface. Most every hacker group has engaged in some form of social engineering, in combination with other activities, over the years and they have been able to break into many corporations as a result. In this type of attack, the attacker chooses a mark, whom they can scam to gain a password, user ID, or other usable information. Because most administrators and employees of companies are concerned with providing efficiency and helping users, they may be unaware the person they are speaking to is not a legitimate user. And because there are no formal procedures for establishing whether an end-user is legitimate, the attacker often gains a tremendous amount of information in a very short amount of time, often with no way to trace the information leak back to the attacker.

Social engineering begins with the goal of obtaining information about a person or business and can range in activities from Dumpster™-diving to cold-calls or impersonations. As acknowledged in the movies, many hackers and criminals have realized that a wealth of valuable information is often laying in trash bins, waiting to be emptied by a disposal company. Most corporations do not adequately dispose of information, and trash bins often contain information that may identify employees or customers. This information is not secured and is available to anyone willing to dive into the Dumpster™ at night and look for it—hence, the term Dumpster™-diving.

Other information is readily available via deception. Most corporations do not contain security measures that adequately address deception. What happens when the protocol is followed properly, but the person being admitted is not whom they say they are? Many groups utilize members of their group in a fashion that would violate protocols, so as to gather information about what a corporation's admittance policy is. Often the multi-person attack will result in gaining admittance to the company and, ultimately, the information desired. Using the bathroom or going for a drink of water is always a great excuse for exiting from a meeting, often one during which you will not have an escort. Most corporations do not have terminal locking policies, and this is another way an attacker can gain access or load software that could pierce the company's firewall. So long as the person entering the corporation looks the part, and can act according to the role the company has defined for access, it is unlikely that person will be detected.

Remotely, social engineering actually becomes less challenging. There are no visual expectations to meet, and people are very willing to participate with a little coaxing. As is often the case, giving away something free can always be a method for entry. Many social engineering situations involve sending along a piece of software or something of value for free. Embedded within the free software, Trojans, viruses, and worms can go undetected, bypassing system and network security. Since most security that protects the local machine has a hard time differentiating between real and fake software, it is often not risky for the attacker to deliver a keylogger or Trojan to the victim machine. Equally effective, the customer support or employee support personnel can be duped into aiding a needy user with their passwords and with access to information they do not necessarily know about.

Educate Staff and Security Personnel

According to National Institute of Standards and Technology (NIST) Publication SP800-12 [18], the purpose of computer security awareness, training, and education is to enhance security by:

- Improving awareness of the need to protect system resources;
- Developing skills and knowledge so computer users can perform their jobs more securely; and
- Building in-depth knowledge, as needed, to design, implement, or operate security programs for organizations and systems.

Making computer system users aware of their security responsibilities and teaching them correct practices helps users change their behavior. It also supports individual accountability, which is one of the most important ways to improve computer security. Without knowing the necessary security measures (and to how to use them), users cannot be truly accountable for their actions. The importance of this training is emphasized in the Computer Security Act, which requires training for those involved with the management, use, and operation of federal computer systems.

Awareness stimulates and motivates those being trained to care about security and reminds them of important security practices. Explaining what will happen to an organization, its mission, its customers, and its employees when security fails often motivates people to take security more seriously. Awareness can take on different forms for particular audiences. Appropriate awareness for management officials might stress management's pivotal role in establishing organizational attitudes toward security. Appropriate awareness for other groups, such as system programmers or information analysts, should address the need for security as it relates to their job. In today's systems environment, almost everyone in an organization may have access to system resources, and therefore may have the potential to cause harm.

Both dissemination and enforcement of policy are critical issues that are implemented and strengthened through training programs. Employees cannot be expected to follow policies and procedures of which they are unaware. In addition, enforcing penalties may be difficult if users can claim ignorance when they are caught doing something wrong. Training employees may also be necessary to show that a standard of due care has been taken in protecting information. Simply issuing a policy, with no follow-up to implement that policy, may not suffice. Many organizations use acknowledgment statements that employees sign to indicate that they have read and understand computer security requirements.

Awareness is used to reinforce the fact that security supports the mission of the organization by protecting valuable resources. If employees view security as just bothersome rules and procedures, they are more likely to ignore security policies. In addition, they may not make needed suggestions about improving security, nor recognize and report security threats and vulnerabilities. Awareness is also used to remind people of basic security practices, such as logging off a computer system or locking doors. A security awareness program can use many teaching methods, including videotapes, newsletters, posters, bulletin boards, flyers, demonstrations, briefings, short reminder notices at login, talks, or lectures. Awareness is often incorporated into basic security training and can use any method that can change employees' attitudes. Effective security awareness programs need to be designed with the recognition that people tend to practice a tuning-out process (also known as acclimation). For example, after a while, a security poster, no matter how well designed, will be ignored; it will, in effect, simply blend into the environment. For this reason, awareness techniques should be creative and frequently changed.

Security education is more in-depth than security training and is targeted for security professionals and those whose jobs require expertise in security. Security education is normally outside the scope of most organization's awareness and training programs. It is more appropriately a part of employee career development. Security education is obtained through college or graduate classes, or through specialized training programs. Because of this, most computer security programs focus primarily on awareness. An effective Computer Security Awareness and Training (CSAT) program requires proper planning, implementation, maintenance, and periodic evaluation. The following seven steps constitute one approach for developing a CSAT program:

Step 1: Identify Program Scope, Goals, and Objectives

Step 2: Identify Training Staff

Step 3: Identify Target Audiences

Step 4: Motivate Management and Employees

Step 5: Administer the Program

Step 6: Maintain the Program

Step 7: Evaluate the Program

Crafting Corporate Social Engineering Policy

When you begin the process of building a corporate policy for social engineering, there are several important considerations that need to be included in the policy. Ensure that employees are aware of the data they are making available to others and what hackers might do with the knowledge they gain from that data. Train end users in the proper handling of social engineering tactics such as:

- Dumpster-diving
- Phone calls
- E-mail
- IM (Instant Messenging)
- Onsite visits

Teach employees how to prevent intrusion attempts by verifying identification, using secure communications methods, reporting suspicious activity, establishing procedures, and shredding corporate documents. It is important to define a simple, concise set of established procedures for employees to report or respond to when they encounter any of these types of attacks.

It is a good idea to periodically employ external consultants to perform audits and social engineering attempts to test employees and the network security readiness of your organization. Define the regularity of audits conducted by external consultants in a manner that cannot become predictable, such as a rotation of the month in each quarter an audit would occur. For example, if your external audits are conducted semiannually, the first audit of the year may occur in month one of quarter one. The next audit may occur in month three of quarter three. Then, when the next year comes around, you have rotated to another month or even changed to quarters two and four. The point is not which months and quarters the audits are done, but that they are done in an unpredictable fashion that only you and your trusted few will know.

Privacy Standards and Regulations

There has been a lot of activity on the national legislative front over the last couple of years, specifically regarding the protection of information that is unique to the individual. This type of information is regarded as a basic element of our right to privacy and companies are being required to take (sometimes costly and arduous) steps to protect it. Failure to do so can have serious repercussions. Insurance companies, health care providers, financial institutions, service providers, retailers, telemarketing organizations, communications providers, and so on all have a part to play in protecting an individual's right to privacy. The next few sections will highlight some of the more relevant changes made in the last few years.

NAIC Model Act

Beginning in the early 1980s, the National Association of Insurance Companies [19] (NAIC) recognized the importance of protecting the privacy of their customers. With the adoption of the *Insurance Information and Privacy Protection Model Act*, the NAIC established a standard for disclosure of insurance consumers' personal information, including financial and health information. Currently, 13 states have laws based on this 1982 Model Act. The NAIC believes the state laws based on this model act are generally more protective of consumer privacy than the privacy provisions of the Gramm-Leach-Bliley Act (GLBA) discussed in the next section.

In 1998, the NAIC turned its focus specifically to the privacy of personal health information. The *Health Information Privacy Model Act* was developed primarily to give guidance to Congress and the U.S. Department of Health and Human Services, both of which were considering health information privacy protections under the *Health Insurance Portability and Accountability Act* (HIPAA).

In February 2000, the NAIC established the Privacy Issues Working Group in order to give guidance to state insurance regulators in response to the enactment of the GLBA, which required state insurance regulators to promulgate regulations enforcing consumer privacy protection laws. On September 26, 2000, the *Privacy of Consumer Financial and Health Information Model* regulation was adopted by the NAIC.

In 2001, the NAIC reconvened the Privacy Issues Working Group. This group was tasked to increase dialogue among regulators and interested parties who were concerned about privacy standards and regulations, as they deeply affected the conduct of operations for these insurance carriers. One of the principal missions of the Privacy Issues Working Group was to serve as a forum for regulators, industry, and individual consumers. This forum allowed participants to discuss the questions and issues that arose as the states interpreted and began enforcement of their privacy protections. To stay abreast of the states' efforts and to be consistent in their approaches to privacy protection, the Privacy Issues Working Group established a goal to agree on uniform responses to such questions, because many of these issues would be repeated in multiple states. The Privacy Issues Working Group's analysis of particular issues and responses to questions has served as guidance to all NAIC members.

In March 2002, the Privacy Issues Working Group adopted a document entitled ***Informal Procedures for Consideration of Privacy Questions***. These procedures were developed as part of an effort to be responsive to interested party concerns about the drafting and adoption of Question and Answer (Q&A) documents among NAIC members. The informal procedures are a reflection of the evolving efforts of the Privacy Issues Working Group to ensure that members and other interested parties are well informed of the process for consideration of privacy issues.

In early 2002, content found within financial institutions' privacy notices and the degree to which consumers were opting out from disclosure received a great deal of attention. In an effort to make these privacy notices worthwhile for consumers and industry, and to realize the intent of Congress and the regulators who put these protections in place, the NAIC formed a subgroup, the Privacy Notice Subgroup, whose task was to draft a *plain language* model for privacy notices. The Privacy Notice Subgroup began working closely with interested parties to draft samples that make privacy notices more understandable for consumers, while ensuring a high degree of uniformity and compliance with the requirements of the NAIC model privacy regulation for industry. At an annual meeting held in the fall of 2002, the Privacy Notice Subgroup distributed a draft report to the Privacy Issues Working Group and urged recipients to examine the report and submit comments to NAIC staff for inclusion the final report. The draft report outlined specific suggestions to improve privacy notices, including use of simpler sentences, clearer terminology, and easy-to-read formatting. The NAIC has been a vanguard in establishment of privacy protections and will continue to do so for some time.

Gramm-Leach-Bliley Act (GLBA)

The Gramm-Leach-Bliley Act [20] (GLBA) was enacted as Public Law 106-102 on November 12, 1999. This law was intended to enhance competition in the financial services industry by providing a prudential framework for the affiliation of banks, securities firms, insurance companies, and other financial service providers. The GLBA is enforced by several different agencies, depending on the type of financial business involved. Most depository institutions, such as banks and savings and loans, are regulated by either the Office of the Comptroller of Currency (OCC), the Federal Reserve, the Federal Deposit Insurance Corporation (FDIC), or the Office of Thrift Supervision (OTS). These four agencies enacted joint regulations that became effective July 1, 2001 under *12 CFR part 30 et al.* to guide audit and compliance certification processes.

There are also many other nondepository institutions that are regulated by the Federal Trade Commission (FTC), which specifically claims authority over financial institutions *not otherwise subject to the enforcement authority of another regulator,* as outlined in *16 CFR part 313.1 (b)*. The FTC information security requirements were published May 23, 2002 as *16 CFR part 314*, and are available from the FTC. Finally, the Office for Regulatory Audits and Compliance (OFRAC) is an Atlanta-based organization set up to conduct compliance surveys and audits for regulations effecting businesses regulated by GLBA, Department of Transportation (DOT), HIPAA, HHS, CFR 42, 49, 67, the USA PATRIOT ACT and the *Public Health Security and Bioterrorism Preparedness Response Act of 2002 (HR 3448)*. Their services are designed to meet the testing requirements of both GLBA and HIPAA. This is extremely important, as the penalties for not complying with the aforementioned laws are quite severe. Individuals failing to fully comply with the regulations are subject to a $250,000 fine, and any other person (facility or organization) failing to follow the regulations is subject to a fine of $500,000. Prison terms can be up to five years for each violation. As you can see, privacy security has become a very serious issue that mandates business attention at the risk of huge penalty.

HIPAA

The *Health Insurance Portability and Accountability Act* [21] (HIPAA) was enacted in order to accomplish several goals. These goals intended to:

1.   Improve portability and continuity of health insurance coverage in group and individual markets;

2.   Combat waste, fraud, and abuse in health insurance and health care delivery;

3.   Promote the use of medical savings accounts;

4.   Improve access to long-term care services and coverage; and

5.   Simplify the administration of health insurance.

In order to comprehend the total impact of HIPAA, it is important to understand the protections it has created for millions of working Americans and their families. HIPAA includes provisions that may increase an individual's ability to get health coverage for himself and his dependents if he starts a new job. HIPAA can lower an individual's chance of losing existing health care coverage, regardless of whether the individual has that coverage through a job or through individual health insurance. HIPAA can help an individual maintain continuous health coverage for herself and her dependents when she changes jobs. HIPAA also can help an individual buy health insurance coverage on an his or her own if he or she loses coverage under an employer's group health plan and has no other health coverage available. Among its specific protections, HIPAA limits the use of preexisting condition exclusions and prohibits group health plans from discriminating by denying someone coverage or charging extra for coverage based on a covered member's past or present poor health. HIPAA guarantees certain small employers, and certain individuals who lose job-related coverage, the right to purchase health insurance; and it guarantees (in most cases) that employers or individuals who purchase health insurance can renew the coverage regardless of any health conditions of individuals covered under the insurance policy. In short, HIPAA may lower an individual's chance of losing existing coverage, ease an individual's ability to switch health plans, and/or help him or her to buy coverage on his or her own if he or she were to lose coverage under an employer's plan and have no other coverage available.

In setting out to achieve each of the aforementioned six goals, the final bill that was enacted can be summarized into five areas where action was mandated. We will discuss each of these five areas next:

1.   **Standards for electronic health information transactions**. Within 18 months of enactment, the Secretary of Health and Human Services was required to adopt standards from among those already approved by private standards–developing organizations (such as NAIC) for certain electronic health transactions, including claims, enrollment, eligibility, payment, and coordination of benefits. *These standards were required to address the security of electronic health information systems.* This last sentence is of particular concern to security professionals, who must enable organizations to enforce such privacy rules.

2.   **Mandate on providers and health plans, and timetable**. Providers and health plans were *required to use the standards for the*

specified electronic transactions 24 months after they were adopted. Plans and providers were given the option to comply directly or to make use of a health care clearinghouse. Certain health plans, in particular workers' compensation, were not covered.

3.   **Privacy**. The Secretary of Health and Human Services (HHS) was required to recommend privacy standards for health information to Congress 12 months after HIPAA was enacted. There was a provision that stated that if Congress did not enact privacy legislation within three years of enacting HIPAA, the Secretary of HHS should *promulgate privacy regulations for individually identifiable electronic health information.*

4.   **Preemption of State Law**. The HIPAA bill superseded state laws, except where the Secretary of HHS determined the state law was necessary to prevent fraud and abuse, to ensure the appropriate regulation of insurance or health plans, or to address concerns about the use of controlled substances. If the Secretary promulgates privacy regulations, those regulations could not preempt state laws that imposed more stringent requirements. These provisions did not limit a state's ability to require health plan reporting or audits.

5.   **Penalties**. The bill imposed civil money penalties and prison for certain violations. Individuals failing to fully comply with the regulations are subject to a $250,000 fine, and any other person (facility or organization) failing to follow the regulations is subject to a fine of $500,000. Prison terms can be up to five years for *each* violation.

As you can see, items 1, 2, and 3 above have specific provisions for protection of electronic data. **This is the area of HIPAA that is most concerned with cybersecurity**. The preceding sections have been concentrated on standards, laws, and enforcement issues related to security and privacy. In the actual implementation of security measures needed to comply with such regulatory guidance, a security professional relies on adoption of good practices that have been evaluated and adopted as "best practices" across the industry.

Managing Access

Access control is a key element of a good information management (IM) security program. Our intent is to give those requiring general knowledge of access control the necessary background to enhance their reading experience for our chapters that cover IM security risks and best practices. In this section, we will cover the essential elements every security administrator needs to know about access control and password management. Some of the content presented herein has been excerpted from our book *Wireless Operational Security* [22] with the permission of Digital Press, an imprint of Elsevier.

Physical Access

Security managers must be concerned with not only network access, but also physical access to the IT systems. Even the most secure of systems is vulnerable to compromise if anyone can walk in, pick up the computer, and walk out with it. Physical prevention measures must be used in conjunction with information security measures to create a total solution. Many people go to great lengths to secure their network from the outside so that intruders cannot get in, but they are often incredibly lax about ensuring that data system equipment is safe from direct attacks by people physically at the machine.

Physical security is important for securing the data center, the network, and the environment around the equipment. Unless the network is encrypted, anyone with physical access to the office LAN could potentially connect network monitoring tools and tap into a corporation's communications. Even if encryption is used, physical access to corporate servers and gateways may allow an attacker to monitor network traffic or compromise the system in a matter of minutes. If the proper physical countermeasures are not in place to mitigate some of the biggest risks, such as insertion of sniffers or other network monitoring devices, then the installation of a sniffer could result in not just data but all corporate voice and video communications being intercepted. Therefore, it is important to ensure that adequate physical security measures are in place. Barriers, locks, access control systems, and guards are the typically the first line of defense.

Access Control

According to the Information Systems Security Organization (ISSA) [23], "access control is the collection of mechanisms for limiting, controlling, and monitoring system access to certain items of information, or to certain features based on a user's identity and their membership in various pre-defined groups." In this section, we will explore the major building blocks that comprise the field of Access Control as it applies to organizational entities and to the information systems these entities are trying to protect from compromising situations.

Purpose of Access Control

You may be asking yourself, "What are some reasons why we should have access control?" Access control is necessary for several good reasons. Information proprietary to a business may need to be kept confidential, so the **confidentiality** issue that provides a purpose for having access controls. The information that an organization keeps confidential also needs to be protected from tampering or misuse. The organization must ensure the integrity of this data for it to be useful. Having internal **data integrity** also provides a purpose for having access controls. When employees of the organization show up for work, it is important that they have access to the data they need to perform their jobs. The data must be available to the employees for work to continue, or the organization becomes crippled and loses money. It is essential that **data availability** be maintained. Access controls provide yet another purpose in maintaining a reasonable level of assurance the data is available and usable to the organization. Therefore, the answer to the question above is that there are three very good reasons for having access controls: confidentiality, data integrity, and data availability.

Access Control Entities

In any discussion of access control, there are some common elements that need to be understood by all parties. These elements comprise a common body of terminology to ensure that everyone working on security access issues is talking about the same thing. For our purposes, there are four primary elements we will discuss: (1) the Subject, an active user or process that requests access to a resource; (2) the Object, a resource that contains information (*can be interchanged with the word Resource*); (3) the Domain, a set of objects the Subject can access; and (4) Groups, collections of Subjects and Objects that are categorized into groups based on their shared characteristics (e.g., membership in a company department, sharing a common job title, and so on).

Fundamental Concepts of Access Control

There are three concepts basic to implementation of access control in any organization. These concepts are establishment of a security policy, accountability, and assurance. We discuss each of these concepts below.

Establishment of a Security Policy

Security policy for an organization consists of the development and maintenance of a set of directives that publicly state the overall goals of an organization and recommend prescribed actions for various situations that an organization's information systems and personnel may encounter. Policy is fundamental to enabling a continuity of operations. When something happens and the *one person who knows the answer* is on vacation, what is to be done? When policies are in place, administrators know what to do.

Accountability

For any information systems that process sensitive data or maintain privacy information, the organization must ensure that procedures are in place to maintain individual accountability for user actions on that system and also for the users' use of that sensitive data. There have been cases in industry where individuals who were employees of an organization committed criminal acts, such as theft of credit card data, theft of personal information for resale to mailing lists, theft of software or data for resale on eBay, and so forth. The people who committed these criminal acts compromised the integrity of the information system. Such criminal actions cause huge problems for organizations, ranging from embarrassment to legal action. When these criminals have been caught, it has been because there were procedures in place to ensure the accountability of their actions on the data. These procedures could be in the form of log files, audit trails for actions taken within an application, or even keystroke monitoring in some instances.

Assurance

As discussed previously, information systems must be able to guarantee correct and accurate interpretation of security policy. For example, if sensitive data exists on a user's machine, and that machine has been reviewed, inspected, and cleared for processing data of that particular level of sensitivity, when Joe takes the data from that machine and copies it to his laptop to work on when traveling on the airplane, that data has most likely become compromised unless Joe's laptop, too, has been reviewed, inspected, and cleared for processing of that particular level of data sensitivity. If his machine has not been cleared, there is no assurance that the data has NOT been compromised. The policies in place at Joe's organization must be known to Joe in order to be effective, and they must be enforced in order to remain effective.

Access Control Criteria

When implementing security access controls, five common criteria are used to determine whether access is to be granted or denied: location, identity, time, transaction, and role (LITTR). Location refers to the physical or logical place where the user attempts access. Identity refers to the process that is used to uniquely identify an individual or program in a system. Time parameters can be control factors that are used to control resource use (for example, contractors are not allowed access to system resources after 8:00 P.M. Monday through Friday, and not at all on weekends). Transaction criteria are program checks that can be performed to protect information from unauthorized use, such as validating whether or not a database query against Payroll records that is coming from a user identified as belonging to the HR department is valid. Finally, a Role defines which computer-related functions can be performed by a properly identified user with an exclusive set of privileges specific to that role. All of these criteria are implemented in varying degrees across the depth and breadth of a security plan. The policies and procedures used by an organization to make the plan effective determine the interplay among this criteria.

Access Control Models

When an organization begins to implement access control procedures, there are three basic models from which an administrator can choose to implement. These three models are (1) Mandatory, (2) Discretionary, and (3) Nondiscretionary. Each has its particular strengths and weaknesses, and the implementer must decide which model is most appropriate for his or her given environment or situation. It is important to point out that most operating, network, and application systems security software in use today provides administrators with the capability to perform data categorization, discretionary access control, identity-based access control, user-discretionary access control, and non-discretionary access control. This section will provide an overview of each type of access control model. Armed with this information, an implementer of access controls will be able to make better decisions about which model is most appropriate for his or her purposes.

Mandatory Access Control Model

Mandatory access control occurs when both the resource owner and the system grant access based on a resource *security label*. A security label is a designation assigned to a resource [24] (such as a file). According to *The NIST Handbook*:

> Security labels are used for various purposes, including controlling access, specifying protective measures, or indicating additional handling instructions. In many implementations, once this designator has been set, it cannot be changed (except perhaps under carefully controlled conditions that are subject to auditing).
>
> When used for access control, labels are also assigned to user sessions. Users are permitted to initiate sessions with specific labels only. For example, a file bearing the label "Organization Proprietary Information" would not be accessible (readable) except during user sessions with the corresponding label. Moreover, only a restricted set of users would be able to initiate such sessions. The labels of the session and those of the files accessed during the session are used, in turn, to label output from the session. This ensures that information is uniformly protected throughout its life on the system.

Security labels are a very strong form of access control. Because they are costly and difficult to administer, security labels are best suited for information systems that have very strict security requirements (such as that used by government, financial, and R&D organizations that handle classified information or information that, if lost, would severely or critically degrade the financial viability of the organization). Security labels are an excellent means for consistent enforcement of access restrictions; however, their administration and highly inflexible characteristics can be a significant deterrent to their use.

Generally, security labels cannot be changed because they are permanently linked to specific information. For this reason, user-accessible data cannot be disclosed as a result of a user copying information and changing the access rights on a file in an attempt to make that information more accessible than the document owner originally intended. This feature eliminates most types of human errors and malicious software problems that compromise data. The drawback to using security labels is that sometimes the very feature that protects user data also prevents legitimate use of some information. As an example, it is impossible to cut and paste information from documents that have different access levels assigned to their respective labels.

Data Categorization

One method used to ease the burden necessary for administration of security labeling is categorizing data by similar protection requirements (data categorization). As an example, a label could be developed specifically for "Company Proprietary Data." This label would mark information that can be disclosed only to the organization's employees. Another label, "General Release Data," could be used to mark information that is available to anyone.

When considering the implementation of Mandatory Access Controls with security labels, one must decide between using a rule-based approach where access is granted based on resource rules or using an administratively directed approach where access is granted by an administrator who oversees the resources. Using a rule-based approach is most often preferred because members of a group can be granted access simply by validating their membership in that group. Access levels are assigned at a group level so all members of the group share a minimum level of access. All files that are created or edited by any one of the members of that group are equally accessible to any other members, because the security labels that are instituted have all members of the group sharing equal access to the group resources. Trust is extended to the membership as a whole simply because membership in the group without having proper access *would not be allowed*.

However, this approach is less administratively intensive than using the approach where an administrator manually oversees resources, granting or withdrawing access on an individual case-by-case basis. There are some instances where this approach is preferable, however. Consider a scenario where there are only a few members that need access to extremely sensitive information. The owner of this information may choose to manually oversee security label application simply to maintain a personal level of control over the access to highly sensitive materials.

Discretionary Access Control Model

According to a document [25] published in 1987 by the National Computer Security Center, discretionary access control is defined as:

> a means of restricting access to objects based on the identity
> of subjects and/or groups to which they belong. The controls
> are discretionary in the sense that a subject with a certain
> access permission is capable of passing that permission
> (perhaps indirectly) on to any other subject.

Discretionary access controls restrict a user's access to resources on the system. The user may also be restricted to a subset of the possible access types available for those protected resources. Access types are the operations a user is allowed to perform on a particular resource (e.g., read, write, execute). Typically, for each resource, a particular user or group of users has the authority to distribute and revoke access to that resource. Users may grant or rescind access to the resources they control based on "need to know," job-essential, or some other criteria. Discretionary access control mechanisms grant or deny access based entirely on the identities of users and resources. This is known as ***identity-based discretionary access control***.

Knowing the identity of the users is key to discretionary access control. This concept is relatively straightforward in that an *access control matrix* contains the names of users on the rows and the names of resources on the columns. An access control matrix is a two-dimensional matrix with users represented on the matrix rows and resources represented as matrix columns. Each entry in the matrix represents an access type held by that user to that resource. Determining access rights is a simple process of looking up a user in the matrix row and traversing the resource columns to find out what rights are allowed for a given resource.

A variant of this is ***user-directed discretionary access control***. Here, an end user can grant or deny access to particular resources based on restrictions he or she decides, irrespective of corporate policy, management guidance, etc. Once the human factor is injected into this equation, as you might surmise, the level of protection for an organization becomes dependent upon the specific actions of those individuals tasked to protect information. One drawback to the discretionary access control model is that it is both administratively intense and highly dependent on user behavior for success in protecting resources. This has led to the creation of *hybrid access* *control* implementations, which grant or deny access based on both an identity-based model and the use of user-directed controls.

Nondiscretionary Access Control Model

This access control model removes a user's *discretionary ability* and implements mechanisms whereby resource access is granted or denied based on policies and control objectives. There are three common variants of this approach:

1. Role-based, where access is based on user's responsibilities;

2. Task-based, where access is based on user's job duties; and

3. Lattice-based, where access is based on a framework of security labels consisting of a resource label that holds a security classification and a user label that contains security clearance information.

The most common of these approaches is role-based access control (RBAC). The basic concept of RBAC is that users are assigned to roles, permissions are assigned to roles, and users acquire permissions by being members of roles. David Ferraiolo of the National Institute of Standards drafted the *Proposed NIST Standard for Role-Based Access Control* [26], which states:

> Core RBAC includes requirements that user-role and
> permission-role assignment can be many-to-many. Thus the same
> user can be assigned to many roles and a single role can have
> many users. Similarly, for permissions, a single permission
> can be assigned to many roles and a single role can be
> assigned to many permissions. Core RBAC includes requirements
> for user-role review whereby the roles assigned to a specific
> user can be determined as well as users assigned to a specific
> role. A similar requirement for permission-role review is
> imposed as an advanced review function. Core RBAC also
> includes the concept of user sessions, which allows selective
> activation and deactivation of roles.

As an example, Joe is an accountant and serves as the manager of payroll operations at ABC Company. His role in the company as manager of payroll would, in RBAC, allow Joe to see all materials necessary for successful conduct of payroll operations. He is also a member of the whole Accounting Group at ABC Company. In that role, as a member of Accounting, he is given access to all of the general accounting resources that are made available to the accounting group, but he does not have access to specific files that belong to the accounts payable, accounts receivable, or expense processing teams. If the expense processing team decided to make an internal document available to the general accounting group, then Joe would be able to see that document because of his membership in the Accounting Group.

The distinction between role-based and task-based is subtle, but distinctly different. The above scenario was built around Joe's area of responsibility and his membership in a group. In the task-based access control scenario, Joe would only see documents in accounting that were determined by company workflow procedures to be necessary for Joe to successfully manage payroll operations. Based on Joe's current job duties, it is not "job-necessary" for Joe to see what is produced by the expense department, accounts payable, or accounts receivable, *even if* Joe is a member of the Accounting Group. For many, this subtle distinction is more trouble than it is worth when the RBAC model can be more easily implemented with the newer computing platforms of today.

In the lattice-based model, Joe's access is based on a framework of security labels. The documents Joe would need to perform his job would have to have their resource label checked to see what security classification (e.g., *general release* or *company proprietary*) that resource has, and a user label that contains security clearance information would be checked to ensure that Joe is entitled or *cleared* to access that company proprietary level information. In a government scenario, working with classified material, this model is much more prevalent than it is in industry. If you substitute the words **Unclassified, Confidential, Secret**, or **Top Secret** for the words *Company Proprietary* or *General Release,* you will get the idea.

Uses of Access Control

There are seven general uses for access controls. These are shown below:

1.   Corrective, used to remedy acts that have already occurred

2.   Detective, used to investigate an act that has already occurred

3.   Deterrent, used to discourage an act from occurring

4.   Recovery, used to restore a resource to a state of operation prior to when an act has occurred

5. Management, which dictates the policies, procedures, and accountability to control system use

6. Operational, where personnel procedures set by management are used to protect the system

7. Technical, where software and hardware controls are used to automate system protection

Ideally, *management* policies and procedures would dictate *operational* activities that implement *technical* solutions that *deter* unauthorized access and, when that fails, *detect* such access in a manner that allows for rapid *recovery* using *corrective* actions. There, I said it. As simplistic as that sentence sounds, it embodies the very essence of the many uses of access control in an organization. Why make it more complicated?

Access Control Administration Models

Centralized Administration Model

The centralized administration model is based on the designation of a single office location or single individual as the responsible party tasked with setting proper access controls. The advantage to using this approach is that it enforces strict controls and uniformity of access. This is because the ability to make changes to access settings resides with very few individuals in a centralized administration model. When an organization's information processing needs change, personnel who have access to that information can have their access modified, but only through the centralized location. Most of the time, these types of requests require an approval by the appropriate manager before such changes are made. Each user's account can be centrally monitored, and closing all accesses for any user can be easily accomplished if that individual leaves the organization. Because a few centralized resources in an organization manage the process, standard, consistent procedures are fairly easy to enforce. The most obvious drawback to a centralized model approach is the time it takes to make changes when they must be coordinated and approved before being made. Sometimes, when there are many people in an organization, these requests can become backlogged. However, most of the time, the trade-off between having strict enforcement and standardized processes is worth enduring the hassle of going through a little bureaucracy to get something done. An example of a centralized access model would be the use of a RADIUS (Remote Authentication Dial-in User Service) server, which is a centralized server used for a single point of network authentication for all users needing access to the network resources. Another example would be a TACACS (Terminal Access Controller Access Control System) server, which is a centralized database of accounts that are used for granting authorization for data requests against a data store or subsystem (e.g., a company-owned CRM product).

Decentralized Administration Model

In the decentralized administration model, all access is controlled by the specific document or file originator. This allows control to remain with those who are responsible for the information. The belief is that these people are best suited to make a determination of who needs access to a document and what type of access they need. However, there is great opportunity to suffer the consequences of a lack of consistency among document originators over the procedures and criteria for making user access decisions. Also, with the decentralized administration model, it is difficult to get a composite view of all user accesses on the system at any given time. These inconsistencies can create an environment where different application or data owners may inadvertently implement access combinations that create conflicts of interest or jeopardize the organization's best interests. Another disadvantage is that the decentralized administration model needs to be used in conjunction with other procedures to ensure that accesses are properly terminated when an individual leaves the company or is moved to another team within the organization. An example of common use of the decentralized administration model is a domain where all file shares are accessible in read-only mode, but each file share owner would determine whether a user could perform write or execute activities in the file share. In a domain with a few hundred file shares, this lack of uniformity and standardization quickly becomes apparent.

Hybrid Administration Model

The hybrid administration model combines the centralized and decentralized administration models into a single approach. An example would be to use a RADIUS server (centralized login/authentication) for gaining basic access to the network and to distribute resources across the network, so that each domain on the network is controlled by a different administrator. This is a typical corporate model, where the central administration part is responsible for the broadest and most basic of accesses, that of gaining entry to the network, and the decentralized part is where the system owners and their users (the creators of the files) specify the types of access implemented for those files that are under their control. The main disadvantage to a hybrid approach is the haggle over what should and should not be centralized.

Access Control Mechanisms

Many mechanisms have been developed to provide internal and external access controls, and they vary significantly in terms of precision, sophistication, and cost. These methods are not mutually exclusive and are often employed in combination. Managers need to analyze their organization's protection requirements to select the most appropriate, cost-effective logical access controls. Logical access controls are differentiated into internal and external access controls. Internal access controls are a logical means of separating what defined users (or user groups) can or cannot do with system resources.

Internal Access Controls

We will cover four methods of internal access control in this section: Passwords, Encryption, Access Control Lists, and Constrained User Interfaces. Each of these four methods of internal access is discussed next.

Passwords

Passwords are most often associated with user authentication. However, they are also used to protect data and applications on many systems, including PCs. For instance, an accounting application may require a password to access certain financial data or to invoke a restricted application. The use of passwords as a means of access control can result in a proliferation of passwords that can reduce overall security. Password-based access control is often inexpensive because it is already included in a large variety of applications. However, users may find it difficult to remember additional application passwords, which, if written down or poorly chosen, can lead to their compromise. Password-based access controls for PC applications are often easy to circumvent if the user has access to the operating system (and knowledge of what to do).

Encryption

Another mechanism that can be used for logical access control is encryption. Encrypted information can only be decrypted by those possessing the appropriate cryptographic key. This is especially useful if strong physical access controls cannot be provided, such as for laptops, personal digital assistant (PDAs), floppy diskettes, CDs, and other mobile media. Thus, for example, if information is encrypted on a laptop computer, and the laptop is stolen, the information cannot be accessed. While encryption can provide strong access control, it is accompanied by the need for strong key management. Use of encryption may also affect availability. For example, lost or stolen keys or read/write errors may prevent the decryption of the information.

Access Control Lists

Access control lists (ACLs) refer to a matrix of users (often represented as rows in the matrix, which include groups, machines, and processes) who have been given permission to use a particular system resource, and the types of access they have been permitted (usually represented in the matrix as columns). ACLs can vary widely. Also, more advanced ACLs can be used to explicitly deny access to a particular individual or group. With more advanced ACLs, access can be at the discretion of the policymaker (and implemented by the security administrator) or individual user, depending upon how the controls are technically implemented.

Elementary ACLs

The following brief discussion of ACLs is excerpted from the NIST Special Publication 800-12 [27]. Elementary ACLs (e.g., "permission bits") are a widely available means of providing access control on multiuser systems. Elementary ACLs are based on the concept of owner, group, and world permissions. These preset groups are used to define all permissions (typically chosen from read, write, execute, and delete access modes) for all resources in this scheme. It usually consists of a short, predefined list of the access rights each entity has to files or other system resources. (See Figure 1.) The owner is usually the file creator, although in some cases, ownership of resources may be automatically assigned to project administrators, regardless of the identity of the creator. File owners often have all privileges for their resources. In addition to the privileges assigned to the owner, each resource is associated with a named group of users. Users who are members of the group can be granted modes of access distinct from nonmembers, who belong to the rest of the "world" that includes all of the system's users. User groups may be arranged according to departments, projects, or other ways appropriate for the particular organization.

Advanced ACLs

Advanced ACLs provide a form of access control based on a logical registry. They do, however, provide finer precision of control. Advanced ACLs can be very useful in many complex information-sharing situations. They provide a great deal of flexibility in implementing system-specific policy and

Figure 1
Example of elementary ACL for the file "payroll."

Example of Elementary ACL for the file "payroll":

Owner: PAYMANAGER
Access: Read, Write, Execute, Delete

Group: COMPENSATION-OFFICE
Access: Read, Write, Execute, Delete

"World"
Access: None

Example of Advanced ACL for the file "payroll"

PAYMGR:	R,	W,	E,	D
J. Anderson:	R,	W,	E,	-
L. Carnahan:	-,	-,	-,	-
B. Guttman:	R,	W,	E,	-
E. Roback:	R,	W,	E,	-
H. Smith:	,	-,	-,	-
PAY-OFFICE:	R,	-,	-,	-
WORLD:	-,	-,	-,	-

allow for customization to meet the security requirements of functional managers. Their flexibility also makes them more of a challenge to manage. The rules for determining access in the face of apparently conflicting ACL entries are not uniform across all implementations and can be confusing to security administrators. When such systems are introduced, they should be coupled with training to ensure their correct use.

Constrained User Interfaces

Interfaces that restrict a users' access to specific functions by never allowing them to request the use of information, functions, or other specific system resources for which they do not have access are known as constrained user interfaces. They are often used in conjunction with ACLs. There are three major types of constrained user interfaces: menus, database views, and physically constrained user interfaces. Each is discussed below:

1. **Menu-driven systems** are a common constrained user interface, where different users are provided different menus on the same system. Constrained user interfaces can provide a form of access control that closely models how an organization operates. Many systems allow administrators to restrict users' ability to use the operating system or application system directly. Users can only execute commands that are provided by the administrator, typically in the form of a menu. Another means of restricting users is through restricted shells that limit the system commands the user can invoke. The use of menus and shells can often make the system easier to use and can help reduce errors.

2. **Database views** are a mechanism for restricting user access to data contained in a database. It may be necessary to allow a user to access a database, but that user may not need access to all the data in the database (e.g., not all fields of a record nor all records in the database). Views can be used to enforce complex access requirements that are often needed in database situations, such as those based on the content of a field. For example, consider the situation where clerks maintain personnel records in a database. Clerks are assigned a range of clients based upon last name (e.g., A–C, D–G). Instead of granting a user access to all records, the view can grant the user access to the record based upon the first letter of the last name field.

3. **Physically constrained user interfaces** can also limit a user's abilities. A common example is an ATM machine, which provides only a limited number of physical buttons to select options; no alphabetic keyboard is usually present.

External Access Controls

External access controls comprise a variety of methods for managing interactions between a system and external users, systems, and services. External access controls employ many methods, sometimes including a separate physical device placed between the system being protected and a network. Examples include port protection devices, secure gateways, and host-based authentication.

Port Protection Devices

These devices are physically connected to a communications port on a host computer. A port protection device (PPD) authorizes all access to the port to which it is attached. This is done prior to and independently of the computer's access control functions. A PPD can be a separate device in the communications stream, or it may be incorporated into a communications device (e.g., a modem). PPDs typically require a separate authenticator, such as a password, in order to access the communications port.

Secure Gateways/Firewalls

Often called firewalls, secure gateways block and/or filter access between two networks. They are most often employed between a private network and a larger, more public network, such as the Internet. Secure gateways allow network users to connect to external networks while they simultaneously prevent malicious hackers from compromising the internal systems. Some secure gateways allow all traffic to pass through *except* for specific traffic with known or suspected vulnerabilities or security problems, such as remote login services. Other secure gateways are set up to disallow all traffic *except* for specific types, such as e-mail. Some secure gateways can make access-control decisions based on the location of the requester. There are several technical approaches and mechanisms used to support secure gateways.

Types of Secure Gateways

There are various types of secure gateways on the market today. These include packet filtering (or screening) routers, proxy hosts, bastion hosts, dual-homed gateways, and screened-host gateways. Because these secure gateways provide security to an organization by restricting services or traffic that pass through their control mechanisms, they can greatly affect system usage in the organization. This fact reemphasizes the need to establish security policy so that management can decide how the organization will balance their operational needs against the security costs incurred.

Secure gateways benefit an organization by helping to reduce internal system security overhead. This benefit is because they allow an organization to concentrate security efforts on a few machines, instead of on all machines. Secure gateways allow for a centralization of services. They provide a central point for services such as advanced authentication, e-mail, or public dissemination of information, which can reduce system overhead and improve service in an organization.

Host-Based Authentication

The network file system (NFS) is an example of a host-based authentication system. It allows a server to make resources available to specific machines. Host-based authentication grants access based upon the *identity of the host* originating the request rather than authenticating the identity of the user. Many network applications in use today employ host-based authentication mechanisms in order to determine whether or not access is allowed to a given resource. Such host-based authentication schemes are not invulnerable to attack. Under certain circumstances, it is fairly easy for a hacker to masquerade as a legitimate host and fool the system into granting access. Security measures used to protect against the misuse of some host-based authentication systems are often available but require that special steps or additional configuration actions be taken before they can be used. An example would be enabling DES encryption when using Remote Procedure Calls (RPCs).

Techniques Used to Bypass Access Controls

In the realm of security, the use of common terms enables all parties to understand exactly what is meant when discussing security issues. When talking about attacks, there are four terms that are quite common: vulnerability, threat, risk, and exposure. A vulnerability is a flaw or weakness that may allow harm to an information system. A threat is an activity with the potential for causing harm to an information system. Risk is defined as a combination of the chance that threat will occur and the severity of its impact. Exposure is a specific instance of weakness that could cause losses to occur from a threat event.

Hackers use several common methods to bypass access controls and gain unauthorized access to information, principally: brute force, denial of service, social engineering, and spoofing. The brute force method consists of a persistent series of attacks, often trying multiple approaches, in an attempt to break into a computer system. A denial of service (DoS) occurs when someone attempts to overload a system through an online connection in order to force it to shut down. Social engineering occurs when someone employs deception techniques against organizational personnel in order to gain unauthorized access. ***This is the most common method of attack known.*** Finally, spoofing is when a hacker masquerades an ID in order to gain unauthorized access to a system.

Password Management

When granting access to a computer system, such access can be restricted by means of controls based on various kinds of identification and authorization techniques. Identification is a two-step function: first, identify the user, and second, authenticate (validate) the identity of the user. The most basic systems rely on passwords only. These techniques do provide some measure of protection against the casual browsing of information, but they rarely stop a determined criminal. A computer password is much like a key to a computer. Allowing several people to use the same password is like allowing everyone to use the same key. More sophisticated systems today use Smart-Cards and/or biometric evaluation techniques in combination with password usage to increase the difficulty in circumventing password protections. Use of the password methodology is built on the premise that something you know could be compromised by someone getting unauthorized access to the password. A system built on something you "know" (e.g., a password) combined with something you possess (e.g., a SmartCard) is a much stronger system. The combination of knowing and possessing, combined with being (biometrics), provides an even stronger layer of protection. Without having all three elements, even if someone could obtain your password, it is useless without the card and the right biometrics (fingerprint, retinal scan, etc.).

SmartCards

In general, there are two categories of SmartCards. The first is a magnetic strip card and the second is a ChipCard. As its name suggests, the magnetic strip card has a magnetic strip containing some encoded confidential information destined to be used in combination with the cardholder's personal code or password. The ChipCard uses a built-in microchip instead of a magnetic strip. The simplest type of ChipCard contains a memory chip with information, but it has no processing capability. The more effective type of ChipCard contains a microchip with both memory to store some information and a processor to process it; hence, the term SmartCard. Such cards are often used in combination with cryptographic techniques to provide even stronger protection.

Biometric Systems

Biometric systems use specific personal characteristics (biometrics) of an individual (e.g., a fingerprint, a voiceprint, keystroke characteristics, or the pattern of the retina). Biometric systems are still considered an expensive solution for the most part, and as a result of the cost, they are not yet in common use today. However, even these sophisticated techniques are not infallible. The adage that *if someone wants it bad enough, they will find a way to break in and take it* still holds true.

Characteristics of Good Passwords

Passwords should be issued to an individual and kept confidential. They should not be shared with anyone. When a temporary user needs access to a system, it is usually fairly simple to add him or her to the list of authorized users. Once the temporary user has finished his work, his user ID must be deleted from the system. All passwords should be distinctly different from the user ID, and, ideally, they should be alphanumeric and at least six characters in length. Administrators should require that passwords be changed regularly—at least every 30 days. It is possible to warn the user automatically when his password expires. To ensure the user enters a new password, the user should be restricted in his or her ability to enter the system after the expiration date, although they may be allowed a limited number of "grace period" logins.

Passwords must be properly managed. This entails using a password history list that maintains a list of all of the passwords that have been used in the past six to twelve months. New passwords should be checked against the list and not accepted if they have already been used. It is good security practice for administrators to make a list of frequently used forbidden passwords, such as names, product brands, and other words that are easy to guess and therefore not suitable as passwords. This list will be used in the same way as the history list. Only the system manager should be able to change the password history and forbidden lists. In modern computing environments, most operating systems conform to these standards and generate passwords automatically. Passwords should be removed immediately if an employee leaves the organization or gives his or her notice of leaving. Finally, it is important to note that extreme care should be taken with the passwords used by network and systems administrators for remote maintenance. Standard passwords that are often used to get access to different systems, for maintenance purposes, should always be avoided.

Password Cracking

Data gathered from security experts across industry, government, and academia cite weak passwords as one of the most critical Internet security threats. While many administrators recognize the danger of passwords based on common family or pet names, sexual positions, and so on, far fewer administrators recognize that even the most savvy users expose networks to risk due to use of inadequate passwords. Data gathered and reported at one of the largest technology companies in the world [28], where internal security policy required that passwords exceed eight characters, mix cases, and include numbers or symbols, revealed the following startling data:

- L0phtCrack obtained 18% of the user passwords in only 10 minutes
- Within 48 hours, **90% of all the passwords were recovered** using L0phtCrack running on a very modest Pentium II/300 system
- Administrator and most Domain Admin passwords were also cracked

Password cracking refers to the act of attempting penetration of a network, system, or resource with or without using tools to unlock a resource secured with a password. Crack-resistant passwords are achievable and practical, but password auditing is the only sure way to identify user accounts with weak passwords. The L0phtCrack software (now called LC5, described below) offers this capability.

Windows NT L0phtCrack (LC5)

LC5 is the latest version of the password auditing and recovery application, L0phtCrack. LC5 provides two critical capabilities to Windows® network administrators:

1. It helps systems administrators secure Windows-authenticated networks through comprehensive auditing of Windows NT and Windows 2000 user account passwords
2. It recovers Windows user account passwords to streamline migration of users to another authentication system, or to access accounts whose passwords are lost

LC5 supports a wide variety of audit approaches. It can retrieve encrypted passwords from stand-alone Windows NT and 2000 workstations, networked servers, primary domain controllers, or Active Directory, with or without SYSKEY installed. The software is capable of sniffing encrypted passwords from the challenge/response exchanged when one machine authenticates to another over the network. This software allows administrators to match the rigor of their password audit to their particular needs by choosing from three different types of cracking methods: dictionary, hybrid, and brute force analysis. These methods will be discussed in the next section. Finally, using a distributed processing approach, LC5 provides administrators with the capability to perform time-consuming audits by breaking them into parts that can be run simultaneously on multiple machines.

Password Cracking for Self-Defense

Using a tool such as LC5 internally enables an organization's password auditor to get a quantitative comparison of password strength, because LC5 provides a report on the time required to crack each password. A "Hide" feature even allows administrators the option of knowing whether or not a password was cracked without knowing what the password was. Password results can be exported to a tab-delimited file for sorting, formatting, or further manipulation in applications such as Microsoft Excel. LC5 makes password auditing accessible to less-experienced password auditors by using an optional wizard that walks new users through the process of configuring and running their password audit, letting them choose from preconfigured audits. As mentioned previously, when performing the cracking process, three cracking methods (dictionary, hybrid, and brute force analysis) are used. In his Web-based article [29] "Hacking Techniques—Introduction to Password Cracking," Rob Shimonski provides an excellent description of these three methods. They are discussed below:

Dictionary Attack

A simple dictionary attack is by far the fastest way to break into a machine. A dictionary file (a text file full of dictionary words) is loaded into a cracking application (such as L0phtCrack), which is run against user accounts located by the application. Because the majority of passwords are often simplistic, running a dictionary attack is often sufficient to do the job.

Hybrid Attack

Another well-known form of attack is the hybrid attack. A hybrid attack will add numbers or symbols to the filename to successfully crack a password. Many people change their passwords by simply adding a number to the end of their current password. The pattern usually takes this form: first month password is "cat"; second month password is "cat1"; third month password is "cat2"; and so on.

Brute Force Attack

A brute force attack is the most comprehensive form of attack, though it may often take a long time to work depending on the complexity of the password. Some brute force attacks can take a week, depending on the complexity of the password. L0phtcrack can also be used in a brute force attack.

UNIX Crack

Crack is a password-guessing program that is designed to quickly locate insecurities in UNIX password files by scanning the contents of a password file and looking for users who have misguidedly chosen a weak login password. This program checks UNIX operating system user passwords for "guessable" values. It works by encrypting a list of the most likely passwords and checking to see if the result matches any of the system user's encrypted passwords. It is surprisingly effective. The most recent version of Crack is version 5.0. Crack v5.0 is a relatively smart program. It comes preconfigured to expect a variety of crypt() algorithms to be available for cracking in any particular environment. Specifically, it supports "libdes" as shipped, Michael Glad's "UFC" in either of its incarnations (as "ufc" and as GNU's stdlib crypt), and it supports whatever crypt() algorithm is in your standard C library. Crack v5.0 takes an approach where the word guesser sits between two software interfaces:

1.   The Standard Password Format (SPF)

2.   The External Library Crypt Interface Definition (ELCID)

When Crack is invoked, it first translates whatever password file is presented to it into SPF; this is achieved by invoking a utility program called "xxx2spf." The SPF input is then filtered to remove data that has been cracked previously, is sorted, and then passed to the cracker, which starts generating guesses and tries them through the ELCID interface, which contains a certain amount of flexibility to support salt collisions (which are detected by the SPF translator) and parallel or vector computation.

John the Ripper

John the Ripper is a password cracker. Its primary purpose is to detect weak UNIX passwords. It has been tested with many UNIX-based operating systems and has proven to be very effective at cracking passwords. Ports of this software product to DOS and Windows environments also exist. To run John the Ripper, you must supply it with some password files and optionally specify a cracking mode. Cracked passwords will be printed to the terminal and saved in file called */user_homedirectory/john.pot*. John the Ripper is designed to be both powerful and fast. It combines several cracking modes in one program, and is fully configurable for your particular needs. John is available for several different platforms, which enables you to use the same cracker everywhere. Out of the box, John the Ripper supports the following ciphertext formats:

- Standard and double-length DES-based format
- BSDI's extended DES-based format
- MD5-based format (FreeBSD among others)
- OpenBSD's Blowfish-based format

With just one extra command, John the Ripper can crack Andrew File System (AFS) passwords and WinNT LM hashes. Unlike other crackers, John the Ripper does not use a crypt(3)-style routine. Instead, it has its own highly optimized modules for different ciphertext formats and architectures. Some of the algorithms used could not be implemented in a crypt(3)-style routine because they require a more powerful interface (bitslice DES is an example of such an algorithm).

Password Attack Countermeasures

Here are some recommendations for self-defense against password cracking. Perform frequent recurring audits of passwords. It is often a good idea to physically review workstations to see if passwords are placed on notes or hidden under a keyboard, tacked on a bulletin board, etc. You should set up dummy accounts and remove the administrator account. The administrator account is sometimes left as bait to track someone when they are detected attempting to use it. Finally, set local security policy to use strong passwords and change them frequently.

Security Management Practices

Security managers must cope daily with the possibility that electronic information could be lost, corrupted, diverted, or misused. These types of issues represent a real threat to an organization's business performance. Today, companies are more dependent than ever on information technology. Information systems have evolved from merely being an important asset in a business to being the single most essential, mission-critical factor in the performance of a business mission. However, even as corporate dependence on information technology has grown, so too has the vulnerability of this technology and the range of external threats to it.

As a result of such vulnerabilities, considerable effort has been expended by hundreds, if not thousands, of security experts to create the applicable policies that attempt to mitigate the risks these vulnerabilities pose. The U.S. government has moved to keep abreast of such changes, enacting various laws that impose severe penalties for perpetrators of cybercrimes. Furthermore, laws placing specific obligations on corporate entities have also been passed to enable or assist law enforcement in pursuing these cybercriminals. A ***get tough*** attitude towards hackers and cybercriminals has become pervasive since the September 11, 2001 disaster.

No corporate or government entity wants to take chances that expose them to greater risk these days. Security teams must now operate within a highly complex legal and security policy landscape to ensure the resources they are tasked to protect remain safe. Providing security for IT resources is a difficult technical challenge, one that needs to be managed properly and to have support from the top echelons of an organization. IT and network security is also highly dependent on the behavior of human beings. To this end, formal management of both the technology aspects and the human aspects of a security organization are addressed in greater detail in Appendix C of this book.

Chapter Summary

In this introduction to basic security concepts, we discussed in detail threats to personal privacy, fraud and theft, the rise and growth of Internet fraud, and various malicious acts that can be directed against an organization. These acts include employee sabotage, infrastructure attacks, malicious hackers and coders, industrial espionage, and social engineering. We stressed the importance of educating your staff and security personnel and crafting corporate social engineering policy to aid in the prevention of such acts. The subject of audits was discussed. We covered relevant privacy standards and regulations, such as the NAIC model act, the Gramm-Leach-Bliley Act, and HIPAA, to name a few.

The importance of proper controls for physical access was discussed, and we introduced the topic of access control, its purpose, and its fundamental concepts. Establishment of a security policy, accountability, and assurance were explained also. As part of our discussion on access controls, we introduced the various access control models and talked about several internal access controls, such as passwords, encryption, and access control lists. External access controls (port protection devices, secure gateways/firewalls, host-based authentication, etc.) were also discussed. Next we explained various techniques used to bypass access controls and password management. Finally, we explained some basic security management practices that BCP planners should be aware of in order to maximize the effectiveness of their plans in the event they are ever needed. The next chapter introduces you to the BCP planning process in greater detail.

Endnotes

1. Mangal, Vandana. "Business Continuity Planning Is a Challenge for CIOs." *ComputerWorld*, April 7, 2004. http://www.computerworld.com/printthis/2004/ 0,4814,91998,00.html.

2. http://isc.sans.org/trends.html.

3. Computer Security Institute, 2002 CSI/FBI *Computer Crime and Security Survey*. Richard Power, ed., 2002. http://www.gocsi.com.

4. National White Collar Crime Center and Federal Bureau of Investigation, IFCC 2001 Internet Fraud Report, January 1, 2001 to December 31, 2001. Washington, D. C.: National White Collar Crime Center. http://www1.ifccfbi.gov/strategy/statistics.asp

5. *Black's Law Dictionary*, 7th ed., 1999.

6. Ibid.

7. Ibid.

8. *Fraud Examiners Manual*, 3rd ed., vol. 1., 1998.

9. *Black's Law Dictionary*, 7th ed., 1999. *The Merriam Webster Dictionary*, Home and Office ed., 1995.

10. *Barron's Dictionary of Finance and Investment Terms*, 5th ed., 1998.

11. Black's Law Dictionary, 7th ed., 1999.

12. Ibid.

13. National White Collar Crime Center and Federal Bureau of Investigation, IFCC 2001 Internet Fraud Report, January 1, 2001 to December 31, 2001. Washington, D. C.: National

White Collar Crime Center.
http://www1.ifccfbi.gov/strategy/statistics.asp

14.   U.S. Dept. of Justice, Press Release: "Former Computer Network
        Administrator at New Jersey High-Tech Firm Sentenced to 41
        Months for Unleashing $10 Million Computer 'Time Bomb.'"
        February 26, 2002. http://www.usdoj.gov/criminal/cybercrime/
        lloydSent.htm.

15.   U.S. Dept. of Justice, Press Release: "Creator of Melissa Virus
        Sentenced to 20 Months in Federal Prison." May 1, 2001.
        http://www.usdoj.gov/criminal/cybercrime/MelissaSent.htm.

16.   U.S. Dept. of Justice, Electronic Citation: 2002 FED App.
        0062P (6th Cir.), File Name: 02a0062p.06, decided and filed 20
        February 2002.
        http://www.usdoj.gov/criminal/cybercrime/4Pillars_6thCir.htm.

17.   The full text of this rendering can be reviewed at
        http://www.usdoj.gov/criminal/cybercrime/4Pillars_6thCir.htm.

18.   National Institute of Standards and Technology, *Special Publica-
        tion 800-12: An Introduction to Computer Security: The NIST
        Handbook*. October 1995.

19.   http://www.naic.org.

20.   U.S. Public Law 106-102, 106th Cong., November 12, 1999.
        Gramm-Leach-Bliley Act. http://thomas.loc.gov.

21.   Public Law 104-191,aug. 21, 1996 "Health Insurance Portability
        and Accountability Act of 1996," http://www.thomas.loc.gov .

22.   Rittinghouse, John W. and James F. Ransome, *Wireless Opera-
        tional Security*. New York: Digital Press, March 2004.

23.   Information Systems Security Association, Inc., CISSP Review
        Course 2002. Domain 1, "Access Control Systems and Method-
        ology" PowerPoint presentation. August 10, 1999, slide 3.

24.   National Institute of Standards and Technology, *Special Publica-
        tion 800-12: An Introduction to Computer Security: The NIST
        Handbook*. October 1995. Ch. 17, p. 204.

25.   National Computer Security Center, NCSC-TG-003: *A Guide to
        Understanding Discretionary Access Control in Trusted Systems*. Fort
        George G. Meade, MD: National Computer Security Center.
        September 30, 1987.

26.   D. F. Ferraiolo, et al., *Proposed NIST Standard for Role-Based Access Control.* Gaithersburg, MD: National Institute of Standards and Technology, November 2002.

27.   National Institute of Standards and Technology, *Special Publication 800-12: An Introduction to Computer Security: The NIST Handbook.* October 1995.

28.   @stake, Inc. Public Web site.
       http://www.atstake.com/research/lc/index.html.

29.   Shimonski, Rob, "Hacking Techniques—Introduction to Password Cracking." IBM developerWorks, July 2002.
       http://www-106.ibm.com/developerworks/security/
       library/s-crack/

Acknowledgments

from John W. Rittinghouse:

My dear wife, Naree Rittinghouse, is certainly among those I would like to thank for her love and understanding, her encouragement, and most of all, her faith in my work. There are many people, in addition to the authors, who contribute to the great effort required to take an idea from scratch and see it become a finished product. In reality, the author usually depends on quite a few others to help keep things in order. This is something that is very true in the case of getting this book out the door and into your hands. I would like to thank Murray Fish for his tireless efforts reviewing each chapter and providing excellent feedback. Dr. Bill Hancock is another individual who helped contribute to the success of this book. His expertise in the security realm knows no bounds and he worked many late nights reviewing, editing, and validating the work herein to ensure its accuracy and relevancy. Finally, I would like to thank all of the folks at Elsevier/Digital Press for their continued support of my work.

from James F. Ransome:

I would like to take this opportunity to give special thanks to my wife Gail for her continual patience with me as I took time off to complete my third and fourth security book in a rather short period of time. I would also like to thank Paul Kurtz for his support of our book and his significant roles as the special assistant to the President and senior director for critical infrastructure protection, White House Homeland Security Council and as senior director of the Office of Cyberspace Security, and member of the President's Critical Infrastructure Protection Board, White House National Security Council, where he has fought to ensure that our national information infrastructure business continuity and disaster recovery needs are being addressed.

Contingency and Continuity Planning

In the management of risk, a contingency plan is the answer to the question *What do we do if this occurs?* Where a serious risk exists, management may require its staff to create a contingency plan and add the necessary budget for it as a risk allowance, with the proviso that it is only to be used if the risk occurs. Contingency plans provide an outline of decisions and measures to be taken if circumstances should occur in relation to a specific activity. Contingency plans generally relate to a planned event, while business continuity plans relate to services and assets that are already operational (for example, an unexpected power outage prevents your customer service department from functioning for some period of time). In order to ensure that the contingency plan is properly suited to the business task, some key questions to be answered include:

- Is the plan achievable?

- Is there a clearly defined starting point for the plan?

- Does the plan address the situation in a timely, cost-effective, consistent way?

When creating the business contingency plan, we suggest including a plan description as part of the content of the document. This is simply a brief description of the scope of the activity, planning assumptions made and used in the development of the plan, prerequisites for implementation of the plan, and constraints on use of the plan. Information concerning the event (or incident) that is the trigger for implementation of the contingency plan should be very clearly stated. The plan should include a general time-line or some other relevant schedule of activity information. There should be a section describing key outcomes and benefits expected when the plan is executed. Allocated budget information (often allocated by activity) is important and should be included. A table of resource requirements is a critical component of the plan. Since resource allocation may be dependent on contracts, the specific details of all pertinent contracts should be included in the plan. A section discussing the various risks and issues should be a part of the plan. Finally, it is the responsibility of the plan owner to provide details of distribution and storage (showing how people will get a copy of the plan so that they can take the appropriate action).

Business continuity (BC) refers to the ability of a business to maintain continuous operations in the face of disaster [1]. *How does one plan for that? Why plan for a disaster when the chances are so remote?* We live in an age where environmental disasters are almost commonplace. They probably always have been commonplace, but with the instantaneous news reporting we have become accustomed to, it is not uncommon to hear of a typhoon striking the Japanese coast, a forest fire raging out of control in the western section of the United States, extreme flooding in Europe, and earthquakes in Turkey—all in the same week! The devastating tsunami that hit Southeast Asia in late December 2004 is one of the most recent examples of why business continuity planning is so necessary. What is often not mentioned in the news is the havoc that is wreaked on the businesses and organizations that have to cope with the aftermath of such disasters.

1.1   Business Continuity Planning

Business continuity planning and disaster recovery planning are subsets of a more wide-ranging discipline: **business contingency**. Business contingency is the practice of formally preparing for variations in the business environment. These variations can be of any kind, but the primary aim of business contingency planning is to ensure the survival of an organization by preparing for, reacting to, and adjusting to those variations.

Business continuity is a subset of business contingency targeted specifically at measures required to ensure that business processes can be maintained under adverse, sudden changes (crises). **Disaster recovery planning** is a subset of business continuity—it focuses on extreme examples of business interruption (disasters). Another subset to business continuity, known as **continuous availability**, has emerged since organizations have become dependent on technology. This discipline emerged because if an organization's information technology (IT) resources suddenly become unavailable, all supporting business processes of that organization generally cannot continue, and this threatens the survival of an organization.

Disasters can take many forms. We can survive and recover from environmental disasters such as those mentioned above, of course. However, the events of September 11, 2001 also showed us that disasters of an organized and deliberate nature can cause severe disruption to business operations. Disruptions can occur from a loss of utilities and services such as water or gas, from failures in equipment, and from system failures. Each of these types of disasters forces businesses and other organizations to cope with them in order to preserve their unique continuity of operations. Disaster can also occur from compromise of information, creating a serious information security incident. Look what happened to Enron when their sad story of stock manipulation, illegal trading, and shell company money-laundering schemes emerged [2].

1.1.1   Building the Business Continuity Plan

When first initiating the business continuity planning (BCP) project, it is a good idea to form a core team from all segments of the business or organization. As part of the project initiation (kick-off) process, the core team should gather up and review all of the existing BC plans (if available). The core team should understand the benefits of developing a BCP policy statement. This policy statement formalizes their purpose for being! (We will discuss this in further detail later, in Section 1.3.4, *Establish Project Objectives and Deliverables*.) The general process of building a BCP is outlined in six steps below:

Step 1. Project Initiation

- Identify customer and business requirements
- Identify external dependencies (i.e., government, industry, and legal)
- Perform a business risk assessment
- Obtain management support
- Implement project planning and control process

Step 2. Business Impact Analysis

- Define criticality criteria
- Identify vital business processes, applications, data, equipment, etc.
- Determine impact on business processes
- Identify interdependencies
- Define recovery time objectives

Step 3. Recovery Strategies

- Identify process and processing alternatives and offsite data backup alternatives
- Identify communications backup alternatives
- Identify recovery strategy alternatives (replace, outsource, manual, etc.)
- Formulate strategy based on optimum cost-benefit and risk
- Review strategy with recovery teams, management, and customers

Step 4. Plan Development

- Define disaster recovery teams, authority, roles, and responsibilities
- Develop notification and plan activation procedures
- Create emergency response procedures
- Create detailed recovery procedures
- Develop plan distribution and control procedures

Step 5. Plan Validation/Testing

- Develop test plans and objectives
- Conduct simulations
- Perform tests
- Evaluate test results
- Perform plan process improvements based on test results

Step 6. Maintenance and Training

- Develop BCP maintenance process
- Consolidate revision information

- Develop revised BCP, as required
- Create corporate awareness program
- Develop BCP-specific training program

1.1.2   Types of Contingency Plans

In general, universally accepted definitions for IT contingency planning and these related planning areas have not been available. Occasionally, this unavailability has led to confusion regarding the actual scope and purpose of various types of plans. To provide a common basis of understanding regarding contingency planning, this section identifies several other types of plans and describes their purpose and scope relative to contingency planning. Because of the lack of standard definitions for these types of plans, the scope of actual plans developed by organizations may vary somewhat from the descriptions below. However, when these plans are discussed in this book, the following descriptions apply.

1.1.2.1   Business Continuity Plan (BCP)

The BCP focuses on sustaining an organization's business functions during and after a disruption. An example of a business function may be an organization's payroll process or consumer information process. A BCP may be written for a specific business process or may address all key business processes. IT systems are considered in the BCP in terms of their support to the business processes. In some cases, the BCP may not address long-term recovery of processes and return to normal operations, solely covering interim business continuity requirements. A **Disaster Recovery Plan**, **Business Resumption Plan**, and **Occupant Emergency Plan** may be appended to the BCP. Responsibilities and priorities set in the BCP should be coordinated with responsibilities found in the Continuity of Operations Plan (COOP) to eliminate possible conflicts. The National Institute of Standards and Technology (NIST) has an excellent graphic illustrating the interrelationships of these plans [3], shown in Figure 1.1.

1.1.2.2   Business Recovery Plan (BRP)

The BRP (also called a Business Resumption Plan) addresses the restoration of business processes after an emergency has occurred. However, unlike the BCP, the BRP generally lacks procedures to ensure the continued operation of critical business processes during the course of an emergency or disrup-

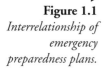

Figure 1.1
Interrelationship of emergency preparedness plans.

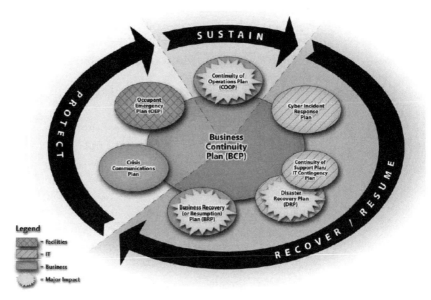

tion. Development of the BRP should be coordinated with the Disaster Recovery Plan (DRP) and BCP. The BRP may be appended to the BCP.

1.1.2.3 Continuity of Operations Plan (COOP)

The COOP focuses on restoring essential functions at an alternate site and performing those functions for an extended period of time before returning to normal operations. A COOP addresses company-wide issues, so it is usually developed and executed independently from the BCP. Because the COOP emphasizes the recovery of an organization's operational capability at an alternate site, the plan often does not include IT operations. However, in today's business environment, it is unlikely that any organization could return to normal operations without including IT operations as a part of the COOP. Additionally, minor disruptions that do not require relocation actions are typically not addressed in the COOP. However, the COOP may include the BCP, BRP, and DRP as appendices.

1.1.2.4 Continuity of Support Plan/IT Contingency Plan

For federal systems, Office of Management and Budget (OMB) Circular A-130, Appendix III, requires the development and maintenance of continuity of support plans for general support systems and contingency plans for major applications. Because an IT contingency plan should be developed for each major application and general support system, multiple contingency plans may be maintained within the organization's BCP. For example, your organization may have separate plans for finance, customer service, and customer contact applications.

1.1.2.5   Crisis Communications Plan (CCP)

Organizations should prepare their internal and external communications procedures prior to a disaster. A Crisis Communications Plan (CCP) is often developed by the organization responsible for public notification, contact, and dissemination. The CCP procedures should be coordinated with all other plans to ensure that only approved statements are released to the public. CCP procedures should be included as an appendix to the BCP. The CCP typically designates specific individuals as the *only* authorities preapproved and empowered to answer questions from the public regarding any disaster response. It may also include procedures for disseminating status reports to the public or to employees. Templates for press releases should be included in the plan.

1.1.2.6   Cyber Incident Response Plan

The Cyber Incident Response Plan establishes procedures to address cyber attacks against an organization's IT system(s). These procedures are designed to enable security personnel to identify, mitigate, and recover from malicious computer incidents, such as unauthorized access to a system or data, denial of service, or unauthorized changes to system hardware, software, or data (e.g., system changes made by *malware* [4], such as a virus, worm, or Trojan horse). This plan should also be included among the appendices of the BCP.

1.1.2.7   Disaster Recovery Plan (DRP)

As suggested by its name, the Disaster Recovery Plan (DRP) applies to major, usually catastrophic, events that deny access to the normal facility for an extended period. Frequently, the DRP refers to an IT-centric plan designed to restore normal operability to the affected system, application, or computer facility at an alternate site after an emergency. The DRP scope may overlap that of an IT contingency plan, but the DRP does not address minor disruptions that would not require relocation actions. Depending on the organization's needs, one or more DRPs may be appended to the BCP.

1.1.2.8   **Occupant Emergency Plan (OEP)**

The OEP provides the response procedures for occupants of a facility in the event of a situation posing a potential threat to the health and safety of personnel, the environment, or property. Such events would include a fire, hurricane, criminal attack, or medical emergency. OEPs are developed at the facility level, specific to the geographic location and structural design of the building. The facility OEP may be appended to the BCP, but is executed separately.

1.1.3   **Preparing Plans**

This book outlines a set of recommended planning and action steps that can be used to help develop your BCP. Remember that any plan you adopt or system you set up should be well rehearsed if it is to be dependable. Establish top-level ownership of business continuity planning within your organization and base your plan on an explicit and up-to-date analysis of the risks your organization faces (i.e., the sorts of major incidents you should plan for). It is important for the core team to determine what credible disruptive events might happen and to understand the impact that such events would have on your organization and its operating environment. Ask yourself, *What would these various disruptive events do to your organization's ability to continue functioning?* Answering this question will help the BCP team identify the critical business functions within your organization that must survive any disruptive event, together with time scales for their recovery. Which of your normal business activities are really essential, and how quickly must you be able to restore them following a disruption? Be clear about your priorities. The core team should build a preliminary BCP project budget and define internal procedures for approving BCP materials. Finally, the team should define a process where their activities can be adequately communicated to all employees of the organization.

1.1.4   **BCP Planning and the Systems Development Life Cycle (SDLC)**

As part of the BCP planning process, many organizations manage the plan much the same as they would manage a system development process. They typically use a process called Systems Development Life Cycle (SDLC), and it is quite appropriate to use this process to manage the BCP. Management should incorporate business continuity considerations into their project plans. Evaluating business continuity needs using the SDLC process facili-

tates the development of a more robust system that will permit easier continuation of business in the event of a disruption. The SDLC refers to the
full scope of activities conducted by system owners who are associated with
a system during its life span. The life cycle begins with project initiation
and ends with system disposal. Although contingency planning is associ-

Figure 1.2
*Five Phases of
SDLC.*

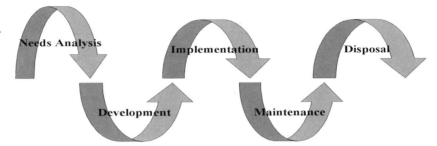

ated with activities occurring in the Operation/Maintenance Phase, contingency measures should be identified and integrated at all phases of the
computer system's life cycle. This approach reduces contingency planning
costs, enhances capabilities, and reduces impacts to system operations when
the contingency plan is implemented. There are five phases (see Figure 1.2)
to the SDLC: Needs Analysis, Development/Acquisition, Implementation,
Operations/Maintenance, and Disposal. We will discuss each phase briefly
in the following sections.

1.1.4.1   Needs Analysis and Initiation Phase

Contingency planning requirements should be considered when a new IT
system is being conceived. In the Initiation Phase, system requirements are
identified and matched to their related operational processes, and initial
contingency requirements may become apparent. Very high system availability requirements may indicate that redundant, real-time mirroring at an
alternate site and fail-over capabilities should be built into the system
design. Similarly, if the system is intended to operate in unusual conditions,
such as in a mobile application or an inaccessible location, the design may
need to include additional features, such as remote diagnostic or self-heal-
ing capabilities. During this phase, the new IT system also should be evaluated against all other existing and planned IT systems to determine its
appropriate recovery priority. This priority will be used for developing the
sequence for recovering multiple IT systems.

1.1.4.2   Development/Acquisition Phase

As initial concepts evolve into system designs, specific contingency solutions may be incorporated. As in the Initiation Phase, contingency measures included in this phase should reflect system and operational requirements. The design should incorporate redundancy and robustness directly into the system architecture to optimize reliability, maintainability, and availability during the Operation/Maintenance Phase. By including them in the initial design, costs are reduced, and problems associated with retrofitting or modifying the system during the Operation/Maintenance Phase are also reduced. If multiple applications are hosted within the new general support system, individual priorities for those applications should be set to assist with selecting the appropriate contingency measures and sequencing for the recovery execution. Contingency measures that should be considered in this phase include: redundant communications paths; lack of single points of failure; enhanced fault tolerance of network components and interfaces; power management systems with appropriately sized backup power sources; load balancing; and data mirroring and replication to ensure a uniformly robust system. If an alternate site is chosen as a contingency measure, requirements for the alternate site should be addressed in this phase.

1.1.4.3   Implementation Phase

Although the system is undergoing initial testing, contingency strategies also should be tested to ensure that technical features and recovery procedures are accurate and effective. Testing the contingency strategies will require developing a test plan. When these contingency measures have been verified, they should be clearly documented in the contingency plan.

1.1.4.4   Operation and Maintenance Phase

When the system is operational, users, administrators, and managers should maintain a training and awareness program that covers the contingency plan procedures. Exercises and tests should be conducted to ensure the procedures continue to be effective. Regular backups should be conducted and stored offsite. The plan should be updated to reflect changes to procedures based on lessons learned. When the IT system undergoes upgrades or any other modifications, such as changes to external interfaces, these modifications should be reflected in the contingency plan. Coordinating and documenting changes in the plan should be performed in a timely manner to maintain an effective plan.

1.1.4.5   Disposal Phase

Contingency considerations should not be neglected because a computer system is retired and another system replaces it. Until the new system is operational and fully tested (including its contingency capabilities), the original system's contingency plan should be ready for implementation. As legacy systems are replaced, they may provide a valuable backup capability if a loss or failure of the new system should occur. In some cases, equipment parts (e.g., hard drives, power supplies, memory chips, or network cards) from hardware that has been replaced by new systems can be used as spare parts for new operational equipment. In addition, legacy systems can be used as test systems for new applications, allowing potentially disruptive system flaws to be identified and corrected on nonoperational systems.

1.2   BCP Standards and Guidelines

Information in this book is consistent with guidance provided in NIST documentation [5] and with other federal mandates affecting contingency, continuity of operations, and disaster recovery planning, including:

- The Computer Security Act of 1987 [6]

- Office of Management and Budget (OMB) Circular A-130, *Management of Federal Information Resources*, Appendix III, November 2000

- Federal Preparedness Circular (FPC) 65, *Federal Executive Branch Continuity of Operations*, July 1999

- Presidential Decision Directive (PDD) 67, *Enduring Constitutional Government and Continuity of Government Operations*, October 1998

- Presidential Decision Directive (PDD) 63, *Critical Infrastructure Protection*, May 1998

- Federal Emergency Management Agency (FEMA) *Federal Response Plan* (FRP), April 1999.

- NIST Special Publication 800-34, *Contingency Planning Guide for Information Technology (IT) Systems*, which provides instructions, recommendations, and considerations for government IT contingency planning.

Additionally, the following international standards are available:

- ISO/International Electrotechnical Commission (IEC) 17799:2000 Information Technology—This code of practice for information security management, an international version of British Standard 7799-1:1999, was published in December 2000. It contains 10 major sections, one of which is Business Continuity Management (Section 11). However, parts of Physical and Environmental Security (7), Asset Classification and Control (5), and Security Policy (3) would also apply.

- ISO/IEC Technical Report (TR) 13335—*Guidelines for the Management of IT Security* (GMITS), 13335-2: Managing and Planning IT Security, contains requirements for procedural security, including business continuity.

- ISO 9002—This quality assurance model applies to organizations that produce, install, and service products. It implies industry standards for IT security and the broader subject of general product security, including continuity planning for IT systems—both as products themselves and as environmental support—and all other aspects of business operations (physical, environmental, personnel) that, if disrupted, would affect product security.

1.2.1   Industry-Specific Standards and Regulations

Regulatory compliance can play a major role in motivating companies to implement thorough business continuity plans. U.S. federal government agencies with essential missions at federal, state, and local levels have always had continuity plans. The Continuity of Operations Planning (COOP) directives produced by the Office of Management and Budget (OMB) and the President of the United States outline the objectives of business continuity planning for all federal departments and agencies. Examples are as follows:

- OMB Circular A-130, Appendix III, "Security of Federal Automated Information Resources" (published in 1993) ensures that appropriate business continuity plans were put in place for all federal general purpose systems and major applications, which include the mission-critical applications identified under the Y2K program.

- Presidential Decision Directive (PDD) 67, issued in October 1998, requires federal agencies to develop Continuity of Operations Plans for Essential Operations.

- Executive Order 12656 [Section 202] requires the head of each federal department and agency to ensure the continuity of essential functions in national security emergencies by providing for safekeeping of essential resources, facilities, and records and establishment of emergency operating capabilities.

- Presidential Decision Directive (PDD) 63, issued in May 1998, calls for a national effort to ensure the security of the United States' critical infrastructures—the physical and cyberbased systems essential to the minimum operations of the economy and government. It sets a goal of a reliable, interconnected, and secure information system infrastructure by the year 2003 and requires the federal government to serve as a model to the rest of the country for how infrastructure protection is to be attained.

1.2.2   Finance Sector Requirements

- **The Gramm-Leach-Bliley Act of 1999**, Section 501(b) Financial Institutions Safeguards, requires that the agencies described in Section 505(a) establish appropriate standards for the financial institutions subject to their jurisdiction relating to administrative, technical, and physical safeguards for the security and confidentiality of customer records and information. The compliance deadline for this legislation was July 1, 2001.

- **The Expedited Funds Availability Act**, enacted by the U.S. Controller of Currency (January 1, 1989), required federally chartered financial institutions to have a demonstrable business continuity plan to ensure prompt availability of funds.

- **SAS70 reports**, in accord with a statement on Auditing Standards Number 70 issued by the Auditing Standards Board of the American Institute of Certified Public Accountants (AICPA) in 1993, review the processing of transactions by service organizations, such as electronic data processing (EDP) centers and banks. SAS70 reports must be performed by certified external auditors, who examine general computer controls, qualified service providers, participant eligibility, and claim system application controls, and review the findings with management.

1.2.3 Health Sector Requirements

- **The Health Insurance Portability and Accountability Act (HIPAA) of 1996**, requiring health care plans, providers, and clearinghouses to adopt standardized electronic claims and payment systems. Noncompliance fines start at $100 for failure to meet a standard, but range up to $250,000 and 10 years of imprisonment for the wrongful use or disclosure of individual health information for commercial advantage, personal gain, and the like. Also, accreditation agencies, such as the Joint Commission on Accreditation of Health Care Organizations (JCAHO), inspect for compliance during their accreditation process.

1.2.4 Telecommunications Sector Requirements

The Telecommunications Act of 1996, Section 256, "Coordination for Interconnection" requires the Federal Communications Commission (FCC) to establish procedures to oversee coordinated network planning by telecommunications carriers and other providers of telecommunications service. It also permits the FCC to participate in the development of public network interconnectivity standards by appropriate industry standards-setting bodies. The act recognizes the need for disaster recovery plans, but also acknowledges the existence of inadequate testing because of the rapid deployment of new technologies.

1.3 BCP Project Organization

There are a number of essential tasks common to the establishment of any significant project. These tasks include assembling the Project Team and appointing a Project Manager and Deputy Project Manager. Outlining the team's scope of responsibilities, determining the correct composition of the team, and getting the project kicked off are all crucial to the success of any BCP project. Once those items are decided, there are other issues that need to be addressed, such as documenting the project milestones, objectives, and deliverables. All of these activities are explained below in further detail.

1.3.1 Scope of Responsibilities

One of the first steps taken by the project sponsor (or by the core team, as the case may be) is to appoint a BCP project manager and a deputy project manager. The project manager and deputy project manager need to have a clear understanding of the tasks that they are required to undertake. They also need to understand their areas of responsibility, project objectives, targets and milestones, deliverables, and performance measurement criteria. The scope of duties should include information on the following:

- Position on project team and the date the position becomes effective
- The person to whom the project manager reports
- Levels of authority for operational issues and financial expenditure
- Level of resources required by the position
- Project structure
- Responsibilities for assessing risk and measuring impact
- Responsibilities for preparing and testing the plan
- Deliverables from the project
- Responsibilities in the event of an emergency occurring
- Duties in respect to training and awareness
- Responsibilities for ongoing BCP maintenances

1.3.2   Team Composition

The project manager and deputy project manager will initially begin the selection process for staffing members of the project team. Remember, the purpose of the core team is to provide overall guidance to the project team, not to do the actual work, since most core team members are mid- to senior-level managers and would not be the ones closest to the day-to-day activities. The project core team members often choose participants in the project team from within their own organizations, so they know best which folks are most capable and up to the task. The BCP Project Team should be carefully selected. Depending on your organizational policies, permission may need to be obtained for the involvement of team members, and each team member should be formally notified of their selection. Each of the main business and operational areas within the organization should be represented on the BCP project team. These representatives from each of the key business areas should have a comprehensive understanding of how their own business area functions, in addition to an overall understanding of the organization as a whole. Each area representative should be able to bring to the BCP project team information on how his or her own area functions, its key business activities or support functions, and its key risk areas.

1.3.3 Project Kick-off Meeting

The BCP project manager should formally notify each member of the BCP project team about his or her selection and explain in the communication information about the project's objectives and the required input from the BCP project team. The notification to the BCP project team about their involvement in the project should establish the date of the initial kick-off meeting for the BCP project team members. Finally, it should include an agenda. Some suggested agenda items are:

- Introduction to BCP by the BCP project manager
- Project organization
- Project initial information requirements
- Consideration of causes of potential disasters or emergencies
- Consideration of key business processes
- Consideration of impact of potential disaster or emergencies
- BCP methodology
- BCP project milestones
- BCP testing
- BCP training
- BCP project team meeting schedule

Once all the members of the project team have been selected, an initial meeting should take place to review the project objectives and deliverables, project milestones should be developed, and the team should establish project-reporting requirements and specify the frequency of such reports. It is a good idea to challenge the BCP project team to consider how different types of disruptive events might affect your organization. For example, a major terrorist incident could have one or more of the following consequences (over and above any commercial impact):

- Damage to your buildings, perhaps making them unavailable for a long period
- Loss of IT systems, records, communications, and other facilities

- Unavailability of staff because of disruptions in transportation

- Loss of staff through death, injury, or unwillingness to travel

- Adverse psychological effects on staff, including stress and demoralization

- Disruption to other organizations or businesses

- Damage to your reputation

- Changes in the business demands placed on your organization

When preparing any plan, challenge the BCP team to estimate what resources are needed to maintain critical business functions following a disruptive event. These resources may include having sufficient people available with the necessary expertise and motivation to lead and manage the organization, ensuring those people have access to key records and IT systems and a reliable means of communication, especially with their staff, during a disruptive event. It is important to plan for an organization to maintain the ability to continue paying staff, to ensure their safety, and to provide them with welfare and accommodations. Simple things like having the ability to procure goods and services cannot be taken for granted. Consider how hard it was just for people to purchase plywood from local hardware stores before the series of hurricanes that slammed into Florida in 2004. Finally, the project team should review all required documents and information available to determine what best suits their purposes for developing a good BCP.

1.3.4 Establish Project Objectives and Deliverables

The objectives and deliverables for the project need to be clearly defined. This will enable the BCP project team to focus their primary efforts on the most important issues and ensure the work undertaken by the BCP project team is relevant. Objectives and deliverables should be approved by the executive management team. The project's objective could be stated as:

> *The development and testing of a plan to enable the organization to recover as quickly and effectively as possible from an unforeseen event that interrupts normal business operations.*

The organization could additionally have a set of subobjectives to cover issues such as specialized research and development activities and to address the need to ensure that employees understand their responsibilities in implementing the plan, that information security policies are adhered to within all planned activities, and that the proposed contingency plans are cost effective. The deliverables should consist of:

- Business Risk and Impact Analysis
- Emergency and Recovery (*sometimes called Resumption*) Procedures
- Checklists for Coping with Disaster Recovery
- Procedures for Managing a Business Recovery Process
- Plans for Testing a Business Recovery Process
- Plans for Training Staff on the Business Recovery Process
- Procedures for Keeping the Plan Current

1.3.5 Set Milestones

It is important to establish realistic and achievable project milestones in order to track progress against a schedule. The following project milestones should be considered, and dates established for these activities:

- Project Approval
- Project Initiation (Kickoff)
- Business Risk and Impact Analysis Plan
- Emergency Preparations Plan
- Initial Emergency Situation Plan
- Plan for Testing the BCP Process
- Plan for Training the Staff in Business Recovery Process
- Approval of the BCP
- BCP Testing Activities
- BCP Training Activities

1.3.6 Establish Reporting Requirements

The BCP Project Manager should prepare a monthly report detailing the activities that have been accomplished in the last month, identifying difficulties encountered and means of overcoming these difficulties. The report should also measure progress against the established milestones and include commentary on the likelihood of meeting these dates. A distribution list should be prepared for the Monthly Progress Report, which would normally include the heads of all business and administrative units. The report should contain an executive summary, which should be distributed to the CEO and/or the executive management team.

1.3.7 Establish Documentation Requirements

You should prepare a list of all necessary documents and information. Where this includes documents containing sensitive information, care must be taken by the BCP project manager to ensure that confidentiality is not compromised. Useful documents and information include the following:

- Organization chart, showing names and positions
- Existing BCP (if available)
- Staff emergency contact information
- List of suppliers and their contact numbers
- List of professional advisers and their emergency contact information
- List of emergency services and their contact numbers
- Facility addresses and maps
- IT systems specification documents
- Communications system specification documents
- Copies of all pertinent maintenance agreements or service-level agreements
- Existing evacuation procedures and fire regulations
- Health and safety procedures
- Operations and administrative procedures
- Personnel administrative procedures
- Copies of floor plans

- Asset inventories

- Inventories of key/strategic information assets

- IT asset inventories

- Offsite storage procedures

- Relevant industry regulations and guidelines

- Insurance policy information

1.4   Chapter Summary

This chapter has covered the basics steps necessary for preparing to develop business contingency and continuity plans. We have introduced you to the process of building the Business Continuity Plan. Part of the purpose of this chapter was to introduce you to the various types of contingency plans, which include the following:

- Business Continuity Plan (BCP)

- Business Recovery Plan (BRP)

- Continuity of Operations Plan (COOP)

- Continuity of Support Plan/IT Contingency Plan

- Crisis Communications Plan (CCP)

- Cyber Incident Response Plan

- Disaster Recovery Plan (DRP)

- Occupant Emergency Plan (OEP)

We discussed steps that you should take in preparing these various plans, and how you should try to adhere to established BCP standards and guidelines. It is important to understand and adhere to industry-specific standards and regulations, and whether your business is in the finance, health, or telecommunications sector, you should be aware of those sector-specific requirements and account for them in any planning process.

BCP project organization was also covered in this chapter. We talked about the importance of defining the scope of responsibilities for the team, and how the project leader should ensure proper team composition to maximize the participation of key individuals across an organization. The project should begin with a kick-off meeting where the team can establish project objectives and define the required deliverables. It is important to set key milestones and define a timeline for accomplishment of those milestones. Establishing reporting requirements and documentation requirements is recommended at this kick-off meeting.

Adhering to the aforementioned will create a solid foundation from which to work and help you better protect your enterprise. The ideas and methods presented herein should provide you with all of the fundamental concepts necessary to develop a BCP and implement it into your work environment. In the next chapter, we will discuss risk—what it is, how to determine risk, and how to assess its impact on your organization. It is just the next step you must take in implementing all of the necessary measures to protect your company.

1.5 Endnotes

1.   Texas Department of Information Resources, *Business Continuity Planning Guidelines*.

2.   The reader is encouraged to visit http://news.findlaw.com/legalnews/lit/enron/ for more information on the downfall of Enron.

3.   National Institute of Standards and Technology, *Special Publication 800-34: Contingency Planning Guide for Information Technology Systems*. June 2002. Section 2.2, p. 11.

4.   Malicious software is often referred to as *malware*.

5.   National Institute of Standards and Technology, Special Publication 800-12: *An Introduction to Computer Security: The NIST Handbook*. October 1995. Chapter 11, Preparing for Contingencies and Disasters.

6.   U.S. Public Law 100-235. 100th Cong., 40 U.S. Code 759, 101 Stat. 1724-1730, January 8, 1988. *The Computer Security Act of 1987*.

2

Assessing Risk

Risk has been defined as "the possibility of incurring loss as a result of inadequate or failed preparation to respond to a perceived or potential threat." A threat is the potential for a particular *threat-source* [1] to successfully exercise a vulnerability. A threat-source is defined as any circumstance or event with the potential to cause harm to a system. Common threat-sources can be natural, human, or environmental, and can include the following:

- **Natural threats**: floods, earthquakes, tornadoes, landslides, avalanches, electrical storms, and other such events

- **Human threats**: events that are either enabled by or caused by human beings, such as unintentional acts (inadvertent data entry) or deliberate actions (network based attacks, malicious software upload, unauthorized access to confidential information)

- **Environmenttal threats**: long-term power failure, pollution, chemicals, liquid leakage

2.1 Determining Threats

A threat-source does not present a risk when there is no vulnerability that can be exploited. In assessing threat-sources, it is important to consider all potential threat-sources that could cause harm to a system or its processing environment. Although the threat statement for a system located in the desert may not include natural flood because of the low likelihood of such an event occurring, environmental threats such as a bursting pipe can

Figure 2.1
*Vulnerability
Analysis Chart.*

Vulnerability Analysis Chart

TYPE OF EMERGENCY	Probability	Human Impact	Property Impact	Business Impact	Internal Resources	External Resources	Total
	High 5 ◄──► Low 1	High Impact 5 ◄────► 1 Low Impact			Weak Resources 5 ◄──► 1 Strong Resources		

The lower the score the better

quickly flood a computer room and cause damage to an organization's assets and resources. Humans can see threat-sources through intentional acts, such as deliberate attacks by malicious persons or disgruntled employees, or unintentional acts, such as negligence and errors. A deliberate attack can be either:

- A malicious attempt to gain unauthorized access to an IT system (e.g., via password guessing) in order to compromise system and data integrity, availability, or confidentiality; or

- A benign, but nonetheless purposeful, attempt to circumvent system security. One example of the latter type of deliberate attack could be a programmer writing a Trojan horse program to bypass system security in order to *get the job done.*

The objectives of a Threat Risk Assessment (TRA) are to identify sensitive system assets; to identify how these assets can be compromised by threat agents; to assess the level of risk the threat agent poses to an asset; and to recommend how to proceed in the life cycle. The TRA occurs at various stages of the system development life cycle. In the TRA analysis, vulnerabilities and existing safeguards are identified and examined to determine the ways an asset can be compromised by a threat agent. The level of risk to the asset is a measure of the likelihood of the compromise and the consequences of the compromise, where the consequences are a function of the asset's sensitivity.

An assessment of the adequacy of existing or proposed safeguards that protect system assets forms part of the TRA process. Where the assessment of safeguards indicates that certain vulnerabilities are not appropriately offset, appropriate additional safeguards are recommended in order to reduce the risk to an acceptable level. Conversely, if safeguards are no longer appropriate, their removal is recommended. If additional safeguards cannot reduce the risk to an acceptable level for an acceptable cost, the risk may be avoided or transferred by moving the location of the system or removing the asset that is at risk.

The TRA process provides the system manager with an appreciation of the security status of the system. The TRA recommendations will suggest either possible changes to the system design or acceptance of the risk. Each option will have an associated cost: that is, risk, time, money, people, and equipment. Management must choose the most appropriate option, based on the likelihood of the undesirable or intolerable consequences of a threat scenario occurring.

A **vulnerability** is defined as a flaw or weakness in system security procedures, design, implementation, or internal controls that, if exercised (accidentally triggered or intentionally exploited), would result in a security breach or a violation of the system's security policy. In determining the likelihood of a threat, one must consider threat-sources, potential vulnerabilities, and existing controls. The analysis of the vulnerabilities associated with the system environment is intended to develop a list of system vulnerabilities (flaws or weaknesses) that could be exploited by the potential threat-sources. Such threats may include people, processes, systems, or external events. To determine the likelihood of a potential adverse event, threats must be analyzed in conjunction with the potential vulnerabilities and the controls already put in place for the organization. An example vulnerability analysis chart (see Figure 2.1) is useful in performing this exercise.

The threat statement, or the list of potential threat-sources, should be tailored to the individual organization and its processing environment (e.g., end-user computing habits). In general, information on natural threats (e.g., floods, earthquakes, storms) should be readily available. Known threats have been identified by many government and private sector organizations. Intrusion detection tools also are becoming more prevalent, and government and industry organizations continually collect data on security events, thereby improving the ability to realistically assess threats.

Impact refers to the magnitude of harm that could be caused by a threat actually taking place. The level of impact is governed by the potential mission impacts and in turn produces a relative value for the assets and resources affected. If it is determined that risks are to be reduced, security requirements can be defined in terms of the security functionality required to reduce the risk. It should be possible for the functionality requirement to be satisfied by more than one safeguard or set of safeguards. Technical and/ or nontechnical safeguards must be selected to meet the functional security requirements and to adequately mitigate the identified risks. Nontechnical safeguards include the establishment of the administrative security structure; personnel and physical security measures; and the establishment and documentation of security procedures and practices. The cost of safeguards, in terms of expense, system performance, user acceptance, schedules and other potential impacts, must be balanced against the resulting reduction of risk. To support this type of cost-benefit analysis, safeguards must be specified in parallel with design of the system.

Once the system security requirements have been identified and safeguards have been selected, the IT system can be constructed and implemented. Security acceptance procedures ensure that the risk of operating the system as it has been implemented is acceptable. These procedures are usually referred to as risk certification and accreditation procedures.

2.1.1   Risk Certification

Risk certification is a comprehensive assessment of the technical and nontechnical security features of an IT system that establishes the extent to which the system satisfies the specified security requirements. It should include:

1.   Validation that security safeguards meet security requirements and security policy

2.   Testing of security safeguards

3.   Evaluation of technical security measures in terms of functionality and assurance

4.   Verification of physical, personnel, and procedural safeguards

5.   Comparison of the system residual risk with the target risk

Certification results in a set of reports that support the accreditation decision. If the certification documentation is complete and all requirements are adequately met, the process moves to the accreditation step.

2.1.2 Accreditation

At this point in the process, the system design is reviewed for completeness and compliance to requirements. If the design is not complete, or if the certification documentation indicates that not all requirements are adequately met by the design, the risk management process returns to the preparation step in order to adjust the system design. Accreditation represents approval to operate a system. Accreditation is the formal declaration by the responsible manager that the system is approved under specified controls and operating procedures. It signifies official acceptance of residual risk by responsible organizational management.

2.2 Risk Management

Risk management encompasses three processes: risk assessment, risk mitigation, and risk evaluation. The risk assessment process includes identification and evaluation of risks and risk impacts, and recommendation of risk-reducing measures. Risk mitigation refers to prioritizing, implementing, and maintaining the appropriate risk-reducing measures recommended from the risk assessment process. Generally, a risk evaluation is performed by a risk manager (see below) who is responsible for determining whether the remaining risk is at an acceptable level or whether additional security controls should be implemented to further reduce or eliminate the residual risk before authorizing (or accrediting) the mitigation measure for operational use.

Risk management is a process that allows managers to balance operational and economic costs of protective measures and achieve gains in mission capability by protecting the resources that support their organizational mission(s). This process is not unique to the IT environment. It pervades decision making in all areas of our daily lives. Take the case of home security, for example. Many people decide to have home security systems installed and pay a monthly fee to a service provider to have these systems monitored for the better protection of their property. Presumably, the homeowners have weighed the cost of system installation and monitoring against the value of their household goods and their family's safety, a fundamental "mission" need.

2.3   The Risk Manager

A risk manager is someone assigned to deal with overall compliance with state, federal, and corporate requirements. Coordination between risk management, information resource recovery, and business recovery planning activities is highly recommended. The organization's risk manager may be placed as part of the other support functions in the organization chart. The risk manager, including information resource management, has the bulk of recovery responsibilities following an interruption to the overall operations of the organization.

2.4   Risk Assessment

A key part of the BCP process is the assessment of the potential risks to the business that could result from disasters or emergency situations. It is necessary to consider all the possible incidents and the impact each may have on the organization's ability to continue to deliver its normal business services. This risk assessment section of the BCP should examine the possibility of serious situations disrupting the business operations and the potential impact of such events.

2.4.1   Basics Elements of the Risk Assessment Process

Risk assessments, whether they pertain to information security or other types of risk, are means of providing decision makers with the information needed to understand factors that can negatively influence operations and outcomes, so that they can make informed judgments concerning the extent of actions needed to reduce risk. For example, bank officials have conducted risk assessments to manage the risk of default associated with their loan portfolios, and nuclear power plant engineers have conducted such assessments to manage risks to public health and safety. As reliance on computer systems and electronic data has grown, information security risk has joined the array of risks that governments and businesses must manage. Regardless of the types of risk being considered, all risk assessments generally include the following elements:

- Identifying threats that could harm and, thus, adversely affect critical operations and assets. Threats include such things as intruders, criminals, disgruntled employees, terrorists, and natural disasters.

- Estimating the likelihood that such threats will materialize, based on historical information and judgment of knowledgeable individuals.

- Identifying and ranking the value, sensitivity, and criticality of the operations and assets that could be affected should a threat materialize, in order to determine which operations and assets are the most important. This is sometimes referred to as "asset characterization" and will be described later in this chapter.

- Estimating, for the most critical and sensitive assets and operations, the potential losses or damage that could occur if a threat materializes, including recovery costs.

- Identifying cost-effective actions to mitigate or reduce the risk. These actions can include implementing new organizational policies and procedures, as well as technical or physical controls.

- Documenting the results and developing an action plan.

2.4.2 Risk Assessment Models

There are various models and methods for assessing risk, and the extent of an analysis and the resources expended can vary depending on the scope of the assessment and the availability of reliable data on risk factors. In addition, the availability of data can affect the extent to which risk assessment results can be reliably quantified. A quantitative approach generally estimates the cost of risk and risk-reduction techniques based on three things:

1. The likelihood that a damaging event will occur

2. The costs of potential losses

3. The costs of mitigating actions that could be taken

The major advantage of a quantitative impact analysis is that it provides a measurement of the impacts' magnitude, which can be used in the cost-benefit analysis of recommended controls. The disadvantage is that, depending on the numerical ranges used to express the measurement, the meaning of the quantitative impact analysis may be unclear, requiring the result to be interpreted in a qualitative manner. Additional factors often must be considered to determine the magnitude of impact. These may include, but are not limited to:

- An estimation of the frequency of the threat-source's exercise of the vulnerability over a specified time period (e.g., one year)

- An approximate cost for each occurrence of the threat-source's exercise of the exercise of the vulnerability over a specified time period (e.g., one year).

- A weighted factor based on a subjective analysis of the relative impact of a specific threat's exercising a specific vulnerability

When reliable data on likelihood and costs are not available, a qualitative approach can be taken by defining risk in more subjective and general terms, such as high, medium, and low. In this regard, qualitative assessments depend more on the expertise, experience, and judgment of those conducting the assessments. It is also possible to use a combination of quantitative and qualitative methods. The main advantage of the qualitative impact analysis is that it prioritizes the risks and identifies areas for immediate improvement in addressing the vulnerabilities. The disadvantage of the qualitative analysis is that it does not provide specific quantifiable measurements of the magnitude of the impacts, therefore making a cost-benefit analysis of any recommended controls difficult.

Reliably assessing information security risks can be more difficult than assessing other types of risks, because the data on the likelihood and costs associated with information security risk factors are often more limited, and because risk factors are constantly changing. This lack of reliable and current data often precludes precise determinations of which information security risks are the most significant and comparisons of which controls are the most cost-effective. Because of these limitations, it is important that organizations identify and employ methods that efficiently achieve the benefits of risk assessment while avoiding costly attempts to develop seemingly precise results that are of questionable reliability. In the following sections, we will discuss Emergency Incident Assessment, the Business Risk Assessment, and IT/Communications Assessments.

2.5   Emergency Incident Assessment

The true value of an Emergency Incident Assessment is only seen after an incident occurs. However, that fact should not deter one from creating an Emergency Incident Assessment for each major type of incident mentioned in Figure 2.2.

- Environmental Disasters
- Organized and/or Deliberate Disruption
- Loss of Utilities and Services
- Equipment or System Failure
- Serious Information Security Incidents
- Other Emergency Situations

Each of these broad categories of incident should have an Incident Assessment Plan associated with it. For example, what happens if the north end of the campus floods, or if the north end floods and the west side of the campus suffers from being hit by a tornado? What is the impact of the damage to operations? We will briefly discuss each of the aforementioned categories.

2.5.1 Environmental Disasters

There are many types of environmental disasters that can occur, such as tornado, hurricane, blizzards, drought, fire, flood, etc. You will need to examine each potential environmental disaster or emergency situation. The focus should be on the level of business disruption that is likely to result from each particular situation. Potential emergencies include business disruption caused by one or more of the following environmental disasters listed in Figure 2.3. We will discuss each briefly in the following paragraphs.

- Tornados
- Hurricanes
- Floods
- Severe Winter Storms
- Drought
- Earthquakes
- Electrical Storms
- Fire

2.5.1.1 Tornado

Tornadoes are tight columns of circling air creating a funnel shape that extends to the ground. They are incredibly violent local storms with whirling winds that can reach 300 miles per hour. Spawned from powerful thunderstorms, tornadoes occur with little or no warning. They can uproot trees and buildings and turn harmless objects into deadly missiles in a matter of seconds. Damage paths can be in excess of one mile wide and fifty miles long. Tornadoes can occur anywhere, but in the United States they occur more frequently in the midwest, southeast, and southwest. Tornadoes can often travel in excess of 50 miles per hour. They can cause significant structural damage, severe injuries, and death.

When planning for tornadoes, it is important to know what local warning systems are in place. Ask your local emergency management office about the community's tornado warning system. It is a good idea to purchase a National Oceanic & Atmospheric Administration (NOAA) weather radio with a warning alarm tone and battery backup. In the event the weather looks inclement, you can listen for tornado watches and warnings. Remember, a **Tornado Watch** means that tornadoes are likely to occur, so you should be ready to take shelter and stay tuned to radio and television stations for additional information. A **Tornado Warning** means that a tornado has been sighted in the area or is indicated by radar, so you should take shelter immediately.

Your plan should establish procedures to inform personnel when tornado warnings are posted. Consider the need for spotters to be responsible for looking out for approaching storms. Work with a structural engineer or architect to designate shelter areas in your facility and ask your local emergency management office or National Weather Service office for additional guidance. When planning for a tornado emergency, you should consider the amount of space you will need in your shelter. Normal, healthy adults require about six square feet of space each, but nursing home and hospital patients require more. The best protection in a tornado is usually an underground area. If an underground area is not available, consider designating small interior rooms on the lowest floor of your building (preferably one without windows) or hallways on the lowest floor that are well away from doors and windows. Rooms constructed with reinforced concrete, brick, or block, with a heavy concrete floor or roof system overhead and no windows provide good shelter. If that is not possible, you can designate protected areas away from doors and windows. You should take note of the fact that auditoriums, cafeterias, and gymnasiums that are covered with a flat, wide-span roof are not considered safe and should not be used as shelters in a tornado emergency. It is a good idea to make plans for evacuating personnel away from lightweight modular offices or mobile home–size buildings. These structures offer no protection from tornadoes. Conduct tornado drills to verify that the plan is effective and known to all employees. Once in the shelter, personnel should protect their heads with their arms and crouch down for protection.

2.5.1.2 **Hurricane**

Hurricanes are severe tropical cyclones with sustained winds of 74 miles per hour or greater, swirling around a calm eye, or center. Hurricane winds can reach 160 miles per hour and extend inland for hundreds of miles. Hurricanes bring torrential rains and a storm surge of ocean water that crashes into land as the storm approaches. Hurricanes also spawn tornadoes. Hurricanes can cause flooding, massive structural damage to homes and business premises, associated power failures, and even injury and death. The National Weather Service issues hurricane advisories as soon as a hurricane appears to be a threat. The hurricane season lasts from June through November. In addition to the recommendations for tornados, we recommend you establish facility shutdown, warning and evacuation procedures, and make plans for assisting employees who may need transportation. It is necessary to make plans for communicating with employees' families before and after a hurricane. The use of an NOAA weather radio with a warning alarm tone and battery backup is highly recommended. Listen for hurricane watches and warnings. A **Hurricane Watch** means that a hurricane is possible within 24 to 36 hours. Stay tuned for additional advisories and tune to local radio and television stations for additional information. An evacuation may become necessary. A **Hurricane Warning** means that a hurricane will make landfall within 24 hours, so take precautions at once. If advised, evacuate immediately.

When preparing for a hurricane, it is a good idea to survey your facility and make plans to protect outside equipment and structures. You should have plans in place to protect windows. Permanent storm shutters offer the best protection. Covering windows with 5/8" marine plywood is a second option. Consider the need for backup systems, such as portable pumps to remove flood water; alternate power sources such as generators or gasoline-powered pumps to provide temporary power; and battery-powered emergency lighting. Make preparations to move records, computers, and other items within your facility or to another location to enable alternate site operations and provide a continuous service capability, if your business requires that.

2.5.1.3 **Flood**

Floods result from thunderstorms, tropical storms, snow thaws, or heavy and prolonged rainfall, which can cause rivers to overflow their banks and flood the surrounding areas. Floods are the most common and widespread of all natural disasters. Most communities in the United States can experience some degree of flooding after spring rains, heavy thunderstorms, or winter snow thaws. Most floods develop slowly over a period of days. Flash floods, however, are like moving walls of water that develop in a matter of minutes. Flash floods can be caused by intense storms or by dam failure. Floods can seriously affect buildings and equipment, causing power failures and loss of facilities, and can even result in injury or death.

Landslides are often caused through a change in the composition of the earth's surface. This change can often result from flooding, where flowing water can create cavernous open areas beneath structures. Subsidence or landslides can cause structural damage and can also disrupt transport services and affect traveling conditions. The heavy rains that occurred in California in late February 2005 are a prime example of the devastation a landslide can cause.

When making preparations for floods, it is a good idea to ask your local emergency management office whether your facility is located in a flood plain. Learn the history of flooding in your area and learn the elevation of your facility in relation to steams, rivers, and dams. Review the community's emergency flood plan and the community's evacuation routes. Know where to find higher ground in case of a flood. Establish warning and evacuation procedures for the facility and make plans for assisting employees who may need transportation. Inspect areas in your facility subject to flooding. Identify records and equipment that can be moved to a higher location and make plans to move records and equipment in case of flood. Use a NOAA weather radio with a warning alarm tone and battery backup to listen for flood watches and warnings. A **Flood Watch** means that flooding is possible, so you should be prepared to evacuate. Tune to local radio and television stations for additional information. A **Flood Warning** means that flooding is already occurring or will occur soon, so you must take precautions at once. Be prepared to go to higher ground. If advised to evacuate, evacuate immediately.

Other recommendations for preparing for a flood disaster include asking your insurance carrier for information about flood insurance. Regular property and casualty insurance does not cover flooding. It is a good idea to consider the feasibility of flood-proofing your facility. Permanent floodproofing measures are taken before a flood occurs and require no human intervention when floodwaters rise. These measures include:

- Filling windows, doors or other openings with water-resistant materials, such as concrete blocks or bricks (this approach assumes the structure is strong enough to withstand floodwaters)

- Installing check valves to prevent water from entering where utility and sewer lines enter the facility

- Reinforcing walls to resist water pressure

- Sealing walls to prevent or reduce seepage

- Building watertight walls around equipment or work areas within the facility that are particularly susceptible to flood damage

- Constructing flood walls or levees outside the facility to keep floodwaters away

- Elevating the facility on walls, columns or compacted fill (this approach is most applicable to new construction, though many types of buildings can be elevated)

Contingent floodproofing measures are also taken before a flood, but require some additional action when flooding occurs. These measures include installing watertight barriers called flood shields to prevent the passage of water through doors, windows, ventilation shafts or other openings, installing permanent watertight doors, constructing movable flood walls, and installing permanent pumps to remove flood waters.

Emergency floodproofing measures are generally less expensive than those listed above, but they require substantial advance warning and do not satisfy the minimum requirements for watertight flood proofing [as set forth by the National Flood Insurance Program (NFIP)]. Emergency floodproofing measures include building walls with sandbags; constructing a double row of walls with boards and posts to create a "crib," then filling the crib with soil; and constructing a single wall by stacking small beams or planks on top of each other. Just as with other environmental disasters we have discussed, it is a good idea to think about the necessity of having backup systems, such as portable pumps to remove flood water; alternate power sources such as generators or gasoline-powered pumps; and battery-powered emergency lighting.

2.5.1.4 Severe Winter Storms

Severe winter storms bring heavy snow, ice, strong winds, and freezing rain. Snowstorm conditions can include blizzards, strong winds, and subzero temperatures. Freezing conditions can occur in winter periods, and the effects can be devastating. Where temperatures fall below zero, they can create conditions that significantly disrupt businesses, and even cause death or injury. Businesses and homes can be seriously affected through burst pipes, inadequate heating facilities, disruption to transportation, and malfunctioning equipment. Work performed outside in the open environment will obviously be seriously affected. Winter storms can prevent employees and customers from reaching the facility, leading to a temporary shutdown until roads are cleared and public transportation is restored. Heavy snow and ice can also cause structural damage and power outages. Snow and ice can impact power and communications. It is possible for buildings to collapse under the weight of snow, and injuries or even death could occur through freezing temperatures and icy conditions.

When preparing for winter storms, listen to a NOAA weather radio as well as the local radio and television stations for weather information. A **Winter Storm Watch** is issued when severe winter weather is possible. A **Winter Storm Warning** means that severe winter weather is expected. A **Blizzard Warning** means that severe winter weather, with sustained winds of at least 35 miles per hour, is expected. A **Traveler's Advisory** is issued when severe winter conditions may make driving difficult or dangerous. You must establish procedures for facility shutdown and early release of employees. Additionally, you must plan to store food, water, blankets, battery-powered radios with extra batteries, and other emergency supplies for employees who become stranded at the facility. It is often necessary to provide a backup power source for critical operations and to arrange for snow and ice removal from parking lots, walkways, loading docks, etc.

2.5.1.5 Drought

Drought is a normal part of virtually every climate on the planet, even rainy ones. It is the most complex of all natural hazards, and it affects more people than any other hazard. Analysis shows that it can be as expensive as floods and hurricanes. Droughts are caused through lack of rainfall, and can have a devastating effect on human life, animal life, and plant life. These conditions are often seasonal and some regions of the world are more prone to these extreme conditions. Severe droughts can cause considerable human loss and suffering. There can also be significant effects on businesses that depend on the availability of water for their products or processes. In the last few decades, interest in planning for drought has increased at all levels. In 1980, only three states (New York, South Dakota, and Colorado) had drought plans. Today, 38 states either have some type of plan or are in the process of developing a plan [2]. The impacts of drought are greater than the impacts of any other natural hazard. They are estimated to be between $6 billion and $8 billion annually in the United States and occur primarily in agriculture, transportation, recreation and tourism, forestry, and energy sectors. Social and environmental impacts are also significant, although it is difficult to put a precise cost on these impacts. The tremendous cost (economic, social, and environmental) associated with drought impacts is one of the reasons for this interest. The actual process of planning for drought is not static. It has been evolving since the early 1980s, through trial and error. That process can be confusing, and the prospect of drought planning can be daunting.

Society's vulnerability to drought is affected by (among other things) population growth and shifts, urbanization, demographic characteristics, technology, water use trends, government policy, social behavior, and environmental awareness. These factors are continually changing, and society's vulnerability to drought may rise or fall in response to these changes. For example, increasing and shifting populations put increasing pressure on water and other natural resources—more people need more water.

Although drought is a natural hazard, society can reduce its vulnerability and therefore lessen the risks associated with drought episodes. The impacts of drought, like those of other natural hazards, can be reduced through mitigation and preparedness (risk management). Planning ahead to mitigate drought gives decision makers the chance to relieve the most suffering at the least expense. Reacting to drought in "crisis mode" decreases self-reliance and increases dependence on government and donors.

Planning for drought is essential, but it may not come easily. There are many constraints to planning, including politicians, policy makers, and the general public, who may lack an understanding of drought. In areas where drought occurs infrequently, governments may ignore drought planning, give it low priority, or simply have inadequate financial resources to deal with it. Most countries lack a unified philosophy for managing natural resources, including water, and policies such as disaster relief and outdated water allocation practices may actually deter good long-term natural resource management. One of the major impediments to drought planning is its cost. Officials may find it difficult to justify the costs of a plan, which are immediate and fixed, against the unknown costs of some future drought. Studies have shown that crisis-oriented drought response efforts have been largely ineffective, poorly coordinated, untimely, and inefficient in terms of the resources allocated [3]. An investment in drought-preparedness programs is a sound economic decision. Moreover, drought-planning efforts can use existing political and institutional structures, and plans can (and should) be incorporated into general natural disaster or water management plans, thus reducing the cost of planning effort.

2.5.1.6   Earthquake

Earthquakes are caused by a shifting of the rock plates beneath the earth's surface, resulting in violent shaking and movement of the earth's upper surface. Earthquakes occur most frequently west of the Rocky Mountains, although historically the most violent earthquakes have occurred in the central United States. Earthquakes occur suddenly and without warning. Significant damage to structures can occur, including total collapse of buildings, bridges, or other elevated structures. Earthquakes can also bring landslides, damage to dams, and aftershocks; the resulting damage can hinder rescue efforts. They can disrupt gas, electric, and telephone services, and trigger landslides, avalanches, flash floods, fires, and huge ocean waves called tsunamis. A recent example of this is the tsunami that struck in December 2004 in Southeast Asia, killing hundreds of thousands of people and destroying an almost incalculable amount of property. Aftershocks can occur for weeks following an earthquake. In many buildings, the greatest danger to people in an earthquake is when equipment and nonstructural elements, such as ceilings, partitions, windows, and lighting fixtures, shake loose. Severe earthquakes can destroy power and communication lines and disrupt gas, water, and sewerage services. In addition to being trapped in a collapsing building, the possibility of falling glass or other objects is of particular danger to human life.

We recommend following some well-established guidelines for preparing for earthquakes. Assess your facility's vulnerability to earthquakes, and ask local government agencies for seismic information for your area. Have your facility inspected by a structural engineer and take steps to develop and prioritize strengthening measures. Such measures may include:

1.   Adding steel bracing to frames

2.   Adding sheer walls to frames

3.   Strengthening columns and building foundations

4.   Replacing nonreinforced brick filler walls

Follow safety codes when constructing a facility or making major renovations. Inspect nonstructural systems, such as air conditioning, communications, and pollution control systems, and assess the potential for damage. Prioritize measures to prevent damages and carefully inspect your facility for any item that could fall, spill, break, or move during an earthquake. For all those items you identify during this inspection, take steps to reduce these hazards by moving large and heavy objects to lower shelves or to the floor. Hang heavy items away from where people work. Secure shelves, filing cabinets, tall furniture, desktop equipment, computers, printers, copiers, and light fixtures. Fixed equipment and heavy machinery should be secured to the floor. Larger equipment can be placed on casters and attached to tethers that, in turn, are attached to the wall. It is often necessary to add bracing to suspended ceilings and install safety glass to provide additional protection. Secure large utility and process pipes so they do not shake around during the earthquake. It is a good idea to keep copies of design drawings of the facility to be used in assessing the facility's safety after an earthquake. Processes for handling and storing hazardous materials should be reviewed, and you should have incompatible chemicals stored separately. Ask your insurance carrier about earthquake insurance and mitigation techniques and establish procedures to determine whether an evacuation is necessary after an earthquake. When establishing these procedures, designate areas in the facility away from exterior walls and windows where occupants should gather after an earthquake if an evacuation is not necessary, and conduct earthquake drills. Provide personnel with safety information that, at a minimum, should include the following:

> *If an earthquake occurs, if you are indoors, stay there. Take cover under a sturdy piece of furniture or counter, or brace yourself against an inside wall. Protect your head and neck. If you are outdoors, move into the open, away from buildings, streetlights, and utility wires. After an earthquake, stay away from windows, skylights, and items that could fall. Do not use the elevators. Use stairways to leave the building if it is determined that a building evacuation is necessary.*

2.5.1.7 Electrical Storms

The action of rising and descending air within a thunderstorm separates positive and negative charges. Water and ice particles also affect the distribution of electrical charge. Lightning results from the buildup and discharge of electrical energy between positively and negatively charged areas. Most lightning occurs within the cloud or between the cloud and ground.

The average flash of lightning could turn on a 100-watt light bulb for more than three months; the air near a lightning strike is hotter than the surface of the sun! The rapid heating and cooling of air near the lightning channel causes a shock wave that results in thunder.

The impact of lightning strikes can be significant. Lightning can cause disruption to power and can also cause fires. Many fires in the western United States and Alaska are started by lightning. In the past 10 years, more than 15,000 fires have been started by lightning. Lightning may also damage electrical equipment, including computer systems. Structural damage is also possible through falling trees or other objects. FEMA, the Federal Emergency Management Agency, recommends ways to recognize approaching thunderstorms and lightning to keep yourself and your employees safe. Here is a list of precautionary safety measures to communicate to your employees if they are indoors or outside during a storm:

- If you are indoors, stay there until the storm passes.
- Do not use the telephone during an electrical storm. Telephone lines conduct electricity.
- Do not work in or around water, as it is a conductor.
- Stay away from trees, fences, power lines, and utility poles.
- If you are outside and able to move to a low area, do so quickly.
- If you are outside and surrounded by trees, move to the shortest tree you can see.
- Stay away from metal objects, and make yourself as small as possible by crouching or lying down.

Most lightning deaths and injuries occur when people are caught outdoors, and most happen in the summer. Your chances of being struck by lightning are estimated to be 1 in 600,000, but those chances can be reduced if you follow the basic safety rules presented above.

2.5.1.8 Fire

Fire is the most common of all the hazards. Every year, fires cause thousands of deaths and injuries and billions of dollars in property damage. Fires are often devastating and can be started through a wide range of events, which may be accidental or environmental. The impact on the business will vary depending on the severity of the fire and the speed within which it can be brought under control. A fire can cause human injury or death, as well as damage to records, equipment, and the fabric or structure of premises. When developing your plan, we recommend that you meet with the local fire department to talk about the community's fire response capabilities. Talk about your business operations and try to identify processes and materials that could cause or fuel a fire, or contaminate the environment in a fire. Ask the fire department to inspect your facility for fire hazards, and ask them about local fire codes and regulations. Ask your insurance carrier to recommend fire prevention and protection measures. Your carrier may also offer training. You should also distribute fire safety information to employees. Specifically, this information should explain how to prevent fires in the workplace, how to contain a fire, how to evacuate the facility, and where to report a fire. Instruct your personnel to use the stairs—not elevators—in a fire. Instruct them to crawl on their hands and knees when escaping a hot or smoke-filled area.

Most companies conduct evacuation drills and post maps of evacuation routes in prominent places. We recommend that you keep evacuation routes (including stairways and doorways) clear of debris. You should assign fire wardens for each area to monitor shutdown and evacuation procedures. Establish procedures for the safe handling and storage of flammable liquids and gases to prevent the accumulation of combustible materials. Provide for the safe disposal of smoking materials and place fire extinguishers in appropriate locations. Establish a preventive maintenance schedule to keep safety equipment operating safely and train your employees in use of fire extinguishers. Consider installing a sprinkler system, fire hoses, and fire-resistant walls and doors. Ensure that key personnel are familiar with all fire safety systems and identify and mark all utility shut-off valves so that electrical power, gas, or water can be shut off quickly by fire wardens or responding personnel. Determine the level of response your facility will take if a fire occurs. The basic response options are as follows:

- Immediately evacuate all personnel on alarm.
- Train all personnel in fire extinguisher use. Personnel in the immediate area of a fire should attempt to control it. If they cannot, the fire alarm is sounded and all personnel evacuate.
- Train only designated personnel in fire extinguisher use.

- Train a fire team to fight incipient-stage fires that can be controlled without protective equipment or breathing apparatus. (Beyond this level of fire, the team evacuates.)

- Train and equip a fire team to fight structural fires using protective equipment and breathing apparatus.

2.5.2 Organized or Deliberate Destruction

You will need to examine each potential disaster or emergency situation caused through activities that can be described as "organized disruption." The focus should be on the level of business disruption likely from each situation. Potential emergencies include business disruption caused by one or more of the following organized disruptive events:

- Terrorism

- Sabotage

- War

- Theft

- Arson

- Labor Disputes/Industrial Action

We will discuss each of the aforementioned disruptive events in the following sections.

2.5.2.1 Act of Terrorism

Acts of terrorism include explosions, bomb threats, hostage taking, sabotage, and organized violence. Whether this is perpetrated through a recognized terrorist organization or a violent protest group, the effect on individuals and business is the same. Such acts create uncertainty and fear and serve to destabilize the general environment. The increasing prevalence of terrorism resulted in the creation of the Department of Homeland Security (DHS) after the September 11, 2001 attacks. This is one of the most significant transformations in the U.S. federal government in decades. The DHS's first priority is to protect the nation against terrorist attacks. Within the DHS, the Directorate of Emergency Preparedness and Response (EP&R) is focused on ensuring that our nation is prepared for catastrophes, including both natural disasters and terrorist assaults. Central to this mission is the protection of people and critical infrastructure of the built environment.

On November 26, 2002, President Bush signed into law The Terrorism Risk Insurance Act of 2002, or H.R. 3210 [4]. The primary objective of the Terrorism Risk Insurance Act of 2002 is mainly to ensure the availability of commercial property and casualty insurance coverage for losses resulting from acts of terrorism. The purpose of this title is to establish a temporary federal program that provides for a transparent system of shared public and private compensation for insured losses resulting from acts of terrorism, in order to:

1. Protect consumers by addressing market disruptions and ensure the continued widespread availability and affordability of property and casualty insurance for terrorism risk

2. Allow for a transitional period for the private markets to stabilize, resume pricing of such insurance, and build capacity to absorb any future losses, while preserving state insurance regulation and consumer protections

Section 102(1) defines an *act of terrorism* for purposes of the Act. Section 102(1)(A) states:

> The term "act of terrorism" means any act that is certified by the Secretary of the Treasury, in concurrence with the Secretary of State and the Attorney General of the United States, to be an act of terrorism or to be a violent act or any act that is dangerous to human life, property, or infrastructure and to have resulted in damage within the United States, or outside of the United States in the case of an U.S.-registered air carrier or vessel, or within the premises of a United States mission and to have been committed by an individual or individuals acting on behalf of any foreign person or foreign interest, as part of an effort to coerce the civilian population of the United States or to influence the policy or affect the conduct of the United States Government by coercion.

Section 102(1)(B) further states, "No act shall be certified by the Secretary as an act of terrorism if the act is committed as part of the course of a war declared by the Congress, except that this clause shall not apply with respect to any coverage for workers' compensation or property and casualty insurance losses resulting from the act, in the aggregate, that do not exceed $5,000,000." Section 102(1)(C) and (D) specify the determinations are final and not subject to judicial review, and the Secretary of the Treasury cannot delegate the determination to anyone.

In response to the continued acts of terrorism we have faced in the United States over the past decade, Congress recently passed **S. 2845**, the Intelligence Reform and Terrorism Prevention Act of 2004. It was passed in the House of Representatives on December 7, 2004 and passed in the Senate the next day. Significant items of this act are that it established a Director of National Intelligence, and it created the National Counter-terrorism Center, the National Counter-proliferation Center, and the National Intelligence Center. It established a Joint Intelligence Community Council and made provisions for the improvement of education for the intelligence community. The bill also addressed privacy and civil liberties issues and made some rather dramatic changes to the Federal Bureau of Investigation in terms of its mission, scope, and operations.

The Mitigation Division of FEMA is developing a series of manuals for the design community that seek to reduce the physical damage to structural and nonstructural components of buildings and related infrastructure that might be anticipated in a terrorist assault. The first four publications in the Multi-Hazard Risk Management Series are available for download from the FEMA Web site [5]. Three of the manuals in this series contain guidance specifically geared to designing, constructing, and engineering high-occupancy structures, such as commercial buildings and schools, while the fourth one relates to insurance, finance, and building regulations. The FEMA manual related to terrorist attack mitigation strategies [6] presents incremental approaches that can be implemented over time to decrease the vulnerability of buildings to terrorist threats. It describes a threat assessment methodology and presents a building vulnerability assessment checklist to support the assessment process. The publication also discusses architectural and engineering design considerations; standoff distances; explosive blasts; and chemical, biological, and radiological (CBR) information. The reader is encouraged to consult the FEMA Web site for more information [7].

2.5.2.2   Act of Sabotage

An act of sabotage is a deliberate disruption of an organization's activities with an attempt to discredit or financially damage the organization. Business will often be seriously affected by a successful act of sabotage. The effect of an act of sabotage is most often seen immediately after the act has taken place. Such acts can affect the normal operations of a business and destabilize workforce morale. Water and food supplies have been sabotaged throughout history. While acts of sabotage have most often occurred during military campaigns, a new trend has evolved over the past 50 years. In situations not associated with open warfare, sabotage has been used to terrorize and intimidate people. Terrorists may have a variety of motives, from settling grudges to creating political destabilization. They have learned that it is not necessary to inflict mass casualties to cause widespread panic and disruption, with particularly devastating economic effect. Quite often, these acts will have catastrophic consequences for public health and public confidence. While deliberate contamination of all food supplies in a given area is unlikely, a preexisting food shortage could be considerably worsened by such contamination. All populations are vulnerable to such attacks. Governments as well as commercial and other organizations in the private sector should be aware of the need to prevent and respond to deliberate contamination.

While threats aimed at extorting money, particularly from organizations in the commercial sector, are usually not considered terrorism, they are far more common than is generally believed. Their economic and social impacts can be the same as those of acts that are clearly terrorist in nature. Security and safety precautions should be evaluated to make sure emergency personnel or support teams can respond to threats of sabotage. Providers of water supplies, manufacturers, and other private sector organizations must be involved in the development and implementation of safety assurance plans designed to prevent, detect, and respond to deliberate contamination. Such plans must include consumer education and active means of communicating with the press and the public. An improved climate of vigilance will reduce vulnerability to both deliberate and accidental contamination. The threat of terrorism should not be allowed to cause panic.

Since drinking water, food, and medicines are all consumed by humans, they probably provide the easiest way to deliver lethal or debilitating amounts of toxic chemicals or biological agents in an act of sabotage. Drinking water systems and water systems used for the manufacture and distribution of food and other consumer products present many opportunities for a saboteur to cause deliberate contamination. Although globalization and the complex production and delivery systems for many foods and medicines have increased vulnerability, this diversity of sources also reduces the likelihood that all supplies of food and medicines will be contaminated. For water supplies, it is the lack of alternative sources in most areas that creates a more serious problem and increases the potential for panic and hysteria.

Widespread human illnesses have been associated both with a variety of food and waterborne microorganisms. Large-scale disruption of food supplies caused by diseases of farm animals has also occurred. Such outbreaks, such as the recent bird influenza outbreaks in Thailand and other parts of Southeast Asia, have strained or overwhelmed public services, and given rise to intense media coverage. There have been scores of deaths from people consuming infected poultry. The solution of destroying tens of millions of chickens has had severe adverse economic, social, and political impact on the local economy in those countries affected by the "bird flu" outbreaks. The entire situation created a huge loss of public confidence.

Whenever terrorists are successful in spreading contamination or otherwise disrupting services, the same devastating effects are likely to occur. Any prevention or preparedness plan designed to prevent the sabotage of drinking water, food and other consumer products, such as cosmetics and medicines, should be based on three factors: prevention, detection, and response.

There is no way of preventing all contamination, whether accidental or the result of the deliberate introduction of chemical, biological, and radioactive agents. A determined terrorist with access to the required resources can penetrate virtually any system. However, the risk of human exposure can be reduced by increasing security and the ability to detect contamination or disruption. Early detection of contamination or attempts to contaminate would prevent or significantly reduce the magnitude of any resulting disease outbreak. While systems that rapidly and effectively detect and respond to disease outbreaks resulting from contamination and other causes are essential, those available are often not rapid enough to prevent all human exposure.

Given the large number of potential threat agents, it is impossible to monitor all of them all of the time. However, adopting sensible precautions is an effective approach to safeguarding public health, whether in areas with complex modern production and distribution systems for water and food or in those where drinking water is obtained from a catchment and most food is locally produced, stored, and consumed. Proactive risk analysis can reduce vulnerability in the same way as for accidental contamination. Available resources should be allocated based on threat and vulnerability assessments, and should be appropriate to the nature and likelihood of the threats, whether accidental or deliberate.

An internal attack on the IT systems through the use of malicious code can also be considered to be an act of sabotage. One type of sabotage involves access to the computer or system by unauthorized persons. For the most part, preventative measures are the same as those described above. In particular, you should be aware of the fact that anyone who can access the systems can execute commands that could be detrimental to operations.

Another type of sabotage that is much harder to prevent is sabotage from internal sources. Examples include disgruntled employees, and accidental sabotage resulting from the inadvertent introduction of destructive software (Trojan horses, viruses) into the system. Sabotage by users with otherwise legitimate access to a system can be minimized by enforcing limitations on user capabilities and file access. System logging facilities can be used to establish accountability for all users. Such accountability cannot prevent sabotage, but it can aid in identifying the culprit. Even users at the highest levels can be made accountable by such techniques as maintaining a log of everyone who accesses or modifies the system configuration. Prevention of accidental sabotage from destructive software can be minimized or prevented by employee education, enforcement of strict rules against using unauthorized software, and well-publicized penalties for those who get caught breaking those rules. Establishment of accountability can aid the process of identifying culprits in such incidents.

2.5.2.3 Act of War

An act of war is the commencement of hostilities between two countries. This could take the form of air strikes, ground strikes, invasion, or blockades. Business could be immediately affected where they are either located near the outbreak of hostilities or where they are dependent upon imports or exports for survival. Many businesses do not survive a prolonged outbreak of war. After the September 11, 2001 attacks, U.S. Senator Kay Bailey-Hutchinson stated, "We must act decisively when an act of war has been perpetrated on innocent people of our country. The only way we can respond to the kind of attack made on our people and our way of life is to say we will fight, not just today or next month or two months from now, but to proclaim that we are in this for the long haul. We are going to rid the world of the despots who prey on innocent, freedom-loving citizens." To back up her statements, she introduced legislation to expand the Sky Marshal program. This bill, **S. 1421**, provided three important measures to keep American skies safe. First, it provided for the random deployment of sky marshals on domestic commercial flights and on international flights on American carriers into or out of the United States. Secondly, it provided for background and fitness checks for, and appropriate training, supervision, and equipment of, the sky marshals. Finally, it required commercial air carriers to provide seating for a sky marshal on any selected air passenger flight without regard to the availability of seats on the flight. The Sky Marshal Program is funded by requiring the public to pay an added fee to airline tickets of $1.00 per domestic flight segment. The airline industry suffered greatly because of the September 11, 2001 incidents. Our country treated those incidents as an act of war; although the attacks were perpetrated by terrorists, they were, in fact, conducting war against the American way of life.

Our nation reacted so strongly to this act of war that the following list of bills and joint resolutions [8] were signed into law in response:

- **HR2882**: Public Safety Officer Benefits Bill

- **HR2883**: Intelligence Authorization Act for Fiscal Year 2002

- **HR2884**: Victims of Terrorism Relief Act of 2001

- **HR2888**: 2001 Emergency Supplemental Appropriations Act for Recovery from and Response to Terrorist Attacks on the United States

- **HR2926**: Air Transportation Safety and System Stabilization Act

- **HR3162**: Uniting and Strengthening America by Providing Appropriate Tools Required to Intercept and Obstruct Terrorism (USA PATRIOT ACT) Act of 2001

- **HR3275**: Terrorist Bombings Convention Implementation Act of 2001

- **HR3448**: Bioterrorism Response Act of 2001

- **HR3525**: Enhanced Border Security and Visa Entry Reform Act of 2002

- **HR3986**: To extend the period of availability of unemployment assistance under the Robert T. Stafford Disaster Relief and Emergency Assistance Act in the case of victims of the terrorist attacks of September 11, 2001.

- **H.J.Res. 71**: Designating September 11 as Patriot Day

- **S1372**: Export-Import Bank Reauthorization Act of 2002

- **S1424**: A bill to amend the Immigration and Nationality Act to provide permanent authority for the admission of "S" visa nonimmigrants.

- **S1438**: National Defense Authorization Act for Fiscal Year 2002

- **S1447**: Aviation and Transportation Security Act

- **S1465**: A bill to authorize the President to exercise waivers of foreign assistance restrictions with respect to Pakistan through September 30, 2003, and for other purposes.

- **S1573**: Afghan Women and Children Relief Act of 2001

- **S1793**: Higher Education Relief Opportunities for Students Act of 2001

- **S2431**: Mychal Judge Police and Fire Chaplains Public Safety Officers' Benefit Act of 2002

- **S.J.Res. 22**: A joint resolution expressing the sense of the Senate and House of Representatives regarding the terrorist attacks launched against the United States on September 11, 2001.

- **S.J.Res. 23**: Authorization for Use of Military Force

2.5.2.4 Theft

This hazard could range from the theft of goods or equipment to the theft of money or other valuables. In addition to possibly causing financial damage to the organization, theft can cause suspicion and uncertainty within the workforce when it is believed that one or more of the workers could have been involved. To prevent theft, you should establish a coordinated safety and loss control program to reduce liability exposure, safeguard assets, and reduce costs associated with liability and property losses. We recommend you develop and maintain centralized loss history information to identify and analyze risk. This material should be kept confidential and reported only to appropriate management personnel. You should also develop methods of statistically monitoring effectiveness in controlling loss and routinely review loss control programs to suggest improvements. It is important to identify and recognize successful safety policies and procedures and provide loss control assistance to organizational departments as needed.

The business community is suffering an ever-increasing number of internal thefts. Some businesses actually are forced to close as a result of internal theft. The most commonly described varieties of theft are shrinkage, embezzlement, and fraud. Shrinkage is taking, consuming, removing, or converting someone else's property for personal use. This can be as simple as the unauthorized consumption of food in a restaurant or the removal of products, cash, or equipment from businesses. It also includes intellectual properties, such as patented processes, copyright-protected computer programs, or private client information. Embezzlement is taking or using money or property without the proper right or authority to do so, or intentionally making errors in bookkeeping practices to allocate funds for one's own use. Fraud is the commission of an act of deceit for personal financial gain.

Most employees would never take cash from their employer's or another establishment's cash register or shoplift. An asset of your business, however, might be seen as a job benefit or something so insignificant that it will never be missed. The sad fact is that dishonest employees account for two-thirds of the theft that businesses experience. Employee theft ranges from pilfering pens and pencils to grand larceny of equipment or finished goods. Items are slipped into pockets, pocketbooks, or briefcases with little or no forethought. Or someone might plan ahead, hide when the business closes, then carry out the theft in solitude. In any case, the action constitutes theft. Stealing is stealing. It is a cost of doing business that steals from the available and potential funds that cover other expenses, including the wages and salaries of all employees and the profit of the company.

Computer-assisted fraud pits the clever geek against the big, bad computer-run company. Computer-assisted fraud is a crime. It is no different than embezzlement, and in some ways it is a more serious threat to the assets of the company and to the privacy of its workers, suppliers, and customers. There are several categories of high-tech crime you should consider when considering this hazard.

- **Computer Component Theft:** Chief methods of component theft include burglary and robbery at manufacturing sites, storage facilities, and retail stores. Other methods include cargo theft, employee theft, and fraud. Most component theft is committed by highly organized gangs that move equipment rapidly throughout the country by selling stolen goods up to a dozen times before shipping them out of the country to "*grey*" markets overseas.

- **Telecommunications Fraud:** Theft of long-distance telephone service, called toll fraud, is accomplished by various means such as hacking into company PBX telephone systems or by using a more low-tech scheme, such as looking over the shoulder of callers using public phones to steal access numbers and PINs. Cloning is also used to perpetrate fraud. This is a process of programming a cellular phone to match the electronic serial number and mobile ID number of a legitimate phone. The cloned phone can incur charges on the legitimate account until the legitimate owner or the telecommunications provider detects the fraudulent use. Unfortunately, detection generally occurs when the statement is sent out, well after the damage has been done.

- **Subscription Fraud:** This is usually seen after identity theft has occurred. The stolen information is used to pose as someone else and set up credit-based accounts that may be used for as long as 90 days before detection.

- **Theft of Proprietary Information:** Stolen information still is the fastest way to develop new products. This often occurs as a result of a computer intrusion, when hackers break into a computer system to commit fraud, destroy or alter records, or simply to create havoc. Hacking is such a complex and sophisticated act that only specially trained investigators understand what is happening, and their evidence collection and investigation methods are much different than for traditional crimes.

- **Counterfeiting:** Scanners, color printers and other photographic types of equipment have become so affordable that criminals can create excellent copies of checks, false identifications, and currency.

- **Software Piracy:** Although the federal copyright acts and laws offer protection against copyright infringement, piracy continues to grow at alarming rates. In North America, one of every four major software applications is pirated.

Most of the keys to preventing computer crime are similar to other safeguards against embezzlement. Document procedures in writing for systems development, maintenance, and security. Test the procedures and update the documentation regularly. Secure data processing facilities by using locks, security guards, badges, access cards, electronic controls, access codes, and passwords. Secure remote terminals, personal computers, and communications lines, especially those connected to networks. Communicate clear company policies to all employees for data access, security standards, security codes, and security violations. Periodically revise security codes and immediately delete codes of terminated employees. Limit who has access to system files and documentation, and track access with user logs. Control and monitor access to confidential data. Incorporate features in systems to identify repeated attempts to gain access. Logout users after periods of inactivity. Regularly back up software and data files so that data can be recovered when lost, damaged, contaminated, or altered, intentionally or unintentionally. Correct rejected transactions on a timely basis to limit the exposure to transactions circumventing normal processes and controls. Assign someone who is not involved in routine data processing to reconcile critical master file transactions with documentation, so that all file changes are authorized. Where possible, segregate the tasks of developing systems from the jobs that involve using the systems. Control access to specific accounts by restricting them to certain individuals. Systems people should not be involved in addressing customer or supplier account discrepancies. Segregate the identification of errors and reconciliation of batch control totals from systems applications. Apply the same sort of careful planning, organizing, staffing, and controlling skills to your data processing operation that you would to any other area. Realize that access to computers is no different than access to the financial books and files about your business. If you suspect or detect computer-assisted fraud, act quickly. Contact the authorities immediately. Rely on experts, and follow the same precautions you would for handling embezzlement or theft.

Some preventative measures you can take to reduce the incident of theft are to screen and select new employees carefully by using reference checks, credit checks, psychological tests, polygraph tests (where allowed by law), and personal character examinations. Detect dishonest new employees by watching them closely. Adopt a standard of excellence in conduct and performance. Encourage your employees to be the best and to take pride in their jobs. People who feel pride in their work accept responsibility for their performance. Employees who see their managers adhering to high ethical standards are likely to follow their example. Treat employees fairly and with dignity. Set reasonable work rules and apply guidelines consistently.

For retail operations, assign a supervisor to inspect and verify the receipt of returned merchandise either as a means of double-checking refunds or before authorizing refunds made by the salesperson or cashier. Require the completion of receiving reports as soon as items are received, then conduct a second check of materials to verify quantities logged in by employees who handle receiving. Make sure that supervised shipping personnel, not unsupervised drivers, help load trucks. Implement internal controls in retail operations. With the advent of bar-coded inventory controls and programmable cash registers, it is possible to maintain a perpetual inventory. Spot-check inventory records at random to detect and discourage shortages. Conduct unannounced inspections of work areas, warehouses, storerooms, and loading docks at frequent and random intervals. Also, a method some owners and managers find effective is to commit deliberate errors to gauge the effectiveness of internal controls; they then monitor the error, discover when and where it is caught, and evaluate how employees handle it. Another often overlooked area to consider is trash disposal. Supervise trash pickups and occasionally check trash collection sites and trucks. Collusion between dishonest employees and haulers is not uncommon. Also, don't accumulate trash or have it picked up near where valuable materials are stored.

Physical security measures you can take include the use of key controls, time locks, alarms, and security guards to discourage dishonest employees. For maximum protection, limit the number of active doors. Motion detectors, electronic eyes, and central station alarms can be effective in preventing "breakouts." This type of theft occurs when someone, often an employee, conceals himself in your establishment until after hours, removes property, then closes the door behind him, leaving no evidence of intrusion.

2.5.2.5 Arson

Arson is the deliberate setting of a fire to damage the organization's premises and contents. As arson can cause both loss of premises and loss of goods and other assets, this can be highly disruptive to the organization. More than 4,000 Americans die each year in fires, and more than 25,000 are injured. Arson is the second leading cause of residential fire deaths in the country. Two million fires are reported each year in the United States, including as many as 573,000 arson fires! Arson is a serious crime. It injures and kills people, destroys property, and destabilizes neighborhoods. In the case of arson, every second counts. Make sure everyone in your organization knows two ways to escape from the workplace. Escape first, then notify the fire department using the 911 system or the local emergency number in your area. Ask law enforcement and fire authorities to identify buildings at risk for arson. Preventative measures you can take to prevent arson include the following:

- Monitor run-down and vacant buildings and report suspicious activity.

- Keep boxes, trash, wood, and other combustibles away from buildings.

- Install a smoke alarm system on every level of your building and test it every month.

- Instruct employees to never open doors that are hot to the touch.

- Practice exit drills to reinforce training.

2.5.2.6　Labor Disputes / Industrial Action

This threat is usually organized by a union that employee groups belong to and is often seen by them as a tool to settle wage disputes or benefits issues. It can follow an unresolved dispute between the workers and the management of a company. A withdrawal of labor (called a strike) is often accompanied by picketing across the entrance of the company's premises to try to discourage anyone from entering. This sort of action is highly disruptive to the business and normally results in a shutdown until the dispute is resolved.

Each scenario described above needs to be developed and examined in detail and an analysis prepared of the consequences of each potential threat. Each scenario should also be assessed for possibility of occurrence (probability rating) and for its possible impact (impact rating). When performing an assessment, it is often helpful to create a matrix to help manage the type of disaster with the level of damage. An example of such a matrix is shown below in Figure 2.4:

Figure 2.4
Organized or deliberate destruction probability and impact assessment worksheet.

Probability of Event Occurrence		Impact Rating for Event Occurrence	
Ranking	Likelihood	Ranking	Severity
1	very high probability	1	unrecoverable damage
2	high probability	2	devastating
3	medium probability	3	major repairs
4	low probability	4	some repairs needed
5	very low probability	5	minor cosmetic

2.5.3　Loss of Utilities or Service

You will need to examine each potential disaster or emergency situation. The focus here should be on the level of business disruption likely from each loss of utilities or public services. Potential emergencies include business disruption caused by the loss of one or more of the following utilities or services.

2.5.3.1   **Electrical Power Failure**

All organizations depend on electrical power to continue normal operations. Without power, the organization's computers, lights, telephones, and other communication media will not be operational, and the impact on normal business operations can be devastating. All organizations should be prepared for a possible electrical power failure, as the impact can be so severe. Data can be lost, customers can be lost, and there can be a serious impact on revenue. Preplanning is essential, as a regional power outage can cause a shortage of backup electrical generators. Consideration should be given to installing UPS systems to avoid brownouts.

2.5.3.2   **Loss of Gas Supply**

The loss of gas supply can be extremely serious where the business relies on gas to fuel its production processes or to provide heating within its premises. A loss of gas supply can result in the whole production process shutting down. The impact on the organization will also be particularly acute where the loss of gas-fired heating could render the premises unusable during periods of low external temperatures.

2.5.3.3   **Loss of Water Supply**

The loss of the water supply is likely to close down a business premises until the supply is restored. Where the water is used in the production process, this is particularly serious. The loss of water supply is also a health and safety issue, as minimum sanitary needs cannot be met. This is often caused through a fault in a water supply route or as a result of a particularly severe drought.

2.5.3.4   **Petroleum and Oil Shortage**

For most countries in the world, a petroleum shortage can occur at any time. This has a serious impact on businesses, as rationing is likely to be imposed immediately, affecting transportation and the normal operations of diesel- or petrol-fueled machinery. For example, this type of shortage can be caused by a sudden reduction in production output imposed by one of the OPEC members. It could also be caused through the short-term failure of a refinery, thereby affecting output of particular grades of fuel.

2.5.3.5 Communications Services Breakdown

Most businesses are fully dependent upon their telecommunications services to operate their normal business processes and to enable their networks to function. A disruption to the telecommunications services can result in a business losing revenue and customers. The use of cell-based telephones can help to alleviate this, but the main reliance is likely to be on land-based lines.

2.5.3.6 Loss of Drainage/Waste Removal

The loss of drainage or waste removal is likely to cause a serious sanitation and health issue for most businesses. This is likely to have an impact on the business through the possible loss of its workforce during the period where drainage services are not available. This, in turn, will have an immediate impact on revenue. A large number of businesses also rely on waste removal for their production processes, and this will be impacted also.

Each scenario needs to be developed and examined in detail, and an analysis that details the consequences of each potential threat should be prepared. Each scenario should also be assessed for possibility of occurrence (probability rating) and possible impact (impact rating). When performing an assessment, it is often helpful to create a matrix to help manage the type of disaster with the level of damage. An example of such a matrix is shown in Figure 2.5.

Figure 2.5
Loss of utility or service probability and impact assessment worksheet.

Probability of Event Occurrence		Impact Rating for Event Occurrence	
Ranking	Likelihood	Ranking	Severity
1	very high probability	1	unrecoverable damage
2	high probability	2	devastating
3	medium probability	3	major repairs
4	low probability	4	some repairs needed
5	very low probability	5	minor cosmetic

2.5.4 Equipment or System Failure

Such emergencies include any interruption or loss of a utility service, power source, life support system, information system, or any other equipment needed to keep the business in operation. It is necessary to identify all critical operations, including utilities (e.g., electric power, gas, water, hydraulics, compressed air, municipal and internal sewer systems, and wastewater treatment services). The following are suggestions for planning for technological emergencies:

1. Determine the impact of service disruption.

2. Ensure that key safety and maintenance personnel are thoroughly familiar with all building systems.

3. Establish procedures for restoring systems. Determine need for backup systems.

4. Establish preventive maintenance schedules for all systems and equipment.

The focus should be on the level of business disruption potentially likely from each equipment or system failure. Potential emergencies include business disruption caused by one or more of the following equipment or system incidents.

2.5.4.1 Internal Power Failure

An internal power failure is an interruption to the electrical power services caused through an *internal* equipment or cabling failure. This type of fault will need to be repaired by a qualified electrician, and delays will inevitably have an impact on the business process. Where particularly serious faults have occurred, such as damage to main cables, the repairs could take some time and could have a severe effect on the business.

2.5.4.2 Air Conditioning Failure

An air conditioning (AC) failure could have serious consequences if the AC unit is protecting particularly sensitive equipment, such as a main computer processing unit, and the rise in temperature could cause the equipment to fail and be damaged. It can also affect the workforce, as conditions in buildings can become extremely uncomfortable with a significant rise in temperatures. Portable AC equipment may possibly be used as backup.

2.5.4.3 Production Line Failure

Mechanical or electronic failure on an organization's production line can have serious financial consequences. This is a particularly critical problem where the equipment needs to be replaced and is not easily repairable. The workforce may need to be laid off until the problem is rectified, and sales and customers may be lost. Particularly vulnerable are the fully automated processes being used in the automotive and other industries.

2.5.4.4   **Cooling Plant Failure**

Businesses that rely on cooling equipment for their production processes are particularly severely affected when the cooling plant fails. Dairy product processing and ice cream manufacturing are just two examples of a huge frozen and refrigerated food industry that is fully dependent upon cooling plants. Good backup arrangements are essential to avoid serious loss or damage to foodstuffs and deliveries.

2.5.4.5   **Equipment Failure (Excluding IT Hardware)**

All businesses rely on a whole range of different types of equipment in order to run their business processes. In many cases, it is possible to move to alternative processes to enable the business processes to continue, but this requires considerable planning and preparation. Consider mapping out security and alarm systems; elevators; lighting; life support systems; heating, ventilation, and air conditioning systems; and electrical distribution systems. Identify manufacturing equipment, pollution control equipment, communication systems, both data and voice computer networks, and transportation systems including air, highway, railroad, and waterway.

Figure 2.6
Equipment or system failure probability and impact assessment worksheet.

Probability of Event Occurrence		Impact Rating for Event Occurrence	
Ranking	**Likelihood**	**Ranking**	**Severity**
1	very high probability	1	unrecoverable damage
2	high probability	2	devastating
3	medium probability	3	major repairs
4	low probability	4	some repairs needed
5	very low probability	5	minor cosmetic

Each scenario needs to be developed and examined in detail, and an analysis prepared of the consequences of each potential threat. Each scenario should also be assessed for possibility of occurrence (probability rating) and possible impact (impact rating). When performing an assessment, it is often helpful to create a matrix to help manage the type of disaster with the level of damage. An example of such a matrix is shown in Figure 2.6.

2.5.5   Information Security Incidents

You will need to examine each potential disaster or emergency situation. The focus in this section should be on the level of business disruption likely from each serious information security incident. The adverse impact of a security event can be described in terms of loss or degradation of any, or a combination of any, of the following three security goals: integrity, availability, and confidentiality. The following list provides a brief description of each security goal and the consequence (or impact) of its not being met:

- **Loss of Integrity**—System and data integrity refers to the requirement that information be protected from improper modification. Integrity is lost if unauthorized changes are made to the data or IT system by either intentional or accidental acts. If the loss of system or data integrity is not corrected, continued use of the contaminated system or corrupted data could result in inaccuracy, fraud, or erroneous decisions. Also, violation of integrity may be the first step in a successful attack against system availability or confidentiality. For all these reasons, loss of integrity reduces the assurance of an IT system.

- **Loss of Availability**—If a mission-critical IT system is unavailable to its end users, the organization's mission may be affected. Loss of system functionality and operational effectiveness, for example, may result in loss of productive time, thus impeding the end users' performance of their functions in supporting the organization's mission.

- **Loss of Confidentiality**—System and data confidentiality refers to the protection of information from unauthorized disclosure. The impact of unauthorized disclosure of confidential information can range from the jeopardizing of national security to the disclosure of Privacy Act data. Unauthorized, unanticipated, or unintentional disclosure could result in loss of public confidence, embarrassment, or legal action against the organization.

Some tangible impacts can be measured quantitatively in lost revenue, the cost of repairing the system, or the level of effort required to correct problems caused by a successful threat action. Other impacts (e.g., loss of public confidence, loss of credibility, damage to an organization's interest) cannot be measured in specific units but can be qualified or described in terms of high, medium, and low impacts.

Because of the generic nature of this discussion, this book describes only the qualitative categories: high, medium, and low impact. High impact is when exercise of the vulnerability may result in the costly loss of major tangible assets or resources; or may significantly violate, harm, or impede an organization's mission, reputation, or interest; or may result in human death or serious injury. Medium impact is when exercise of the vulnerability may result in the loss of tangible assets or resources; or may violate, harm, or impede an organization's mission, reputation, or interest; or may result in human injury. Finally, low impact is when exercise of the vulnerability may result in the loss of some tangible assets or resources or may noticeably affect an organization's mission, reputation, or interest. In the following sections, we list some potential emergencies that you should evaluate for business disruption as a serious information security incident.

2.5.5.1   Cybercrime

Cybercrime is a major area of information security risk. It includes attacks by hackers, denial-of-service attacks, virus attacks, hoax virus warnings, and premeditated internal attacks. All cybercrime attacks can have an immediate and devastating effect on the organization's normal business processes. The average cost of an information security incident has been estimated at US$30,000, and more than 60% of organizations are reported to experience one or more incidents every year.

2.5.5.2   Loss of Records or Data

The loss of records or data can be particularly disruptive where poor backup and recovery procedures result in the need to reinput and recompile the records. This is normally a slow process and is particularly labor intensive, which can result in an increase in costs through additional working hours and a great deal of embarrassment when information is unexpectedly not available.

2.5.5.3   Disclosure of Sensitive Information

This is a serious information security incident, which can result in severe embarrassment, financial loss, and even litigation where damage has been caused to someone's reputation or financial standing. Further types of serious disclosure involve secret patent information, plans and strategic directions, secret recipes or ingredients, information disclosed to legal representatives, and so on. Deliberate, unauthorized disclosure of sensitive information is also referred to as espionage.

2.5.5.4   IT System Failure

With the almost total level of dependence on IT systems within the vast majority of businesses, a failure to these systems can be particularly devastating. The types of threats to computer systems are many and varied, including hardware failure, damage to cables, water leaks and fires, air conditioning system failures, network failures, application system failures, telecommunications equipment failures, and so on. Each of the above scenarios needs to be developed and examined in detail and an analysis prepared of the consequences of each potential scenario. Each scenario should also be assessed for possibility of occurrence (probability rating) and possible impact (impact rating) using the worksheet provided in Figure 2.7.

Figure 2.7
Information security incident probability and impact assessment worksheet.

Probability of Event Occurrence		Impact Rating for Event Occurrence	
Ranking	Likelihood	Ranking	Severity
1	very high probability	1	unrecoverable damage
2	high probability	2	devastating
3	medium probability	3	major repairs
4	low probability	4	some repairs needed
5	very low probability	5	minor cosmetic

2.5.6   Other Emergency Situations

You will need to examine each potential disaster or emergency situation. The focus should be on the level of business disruption likely from other emergency situations not already covered above. Potential emergencies include business disruption caused by one or more of the following incidents.

2.5.6.1   Contamination and Environmental Hazards

Contamination and environmental hazards include polluted air, polluted water, chemicals, radiation, asbestos, smoke, dampness and mildew, toxic waste, and oil pollution. Many of these conditions can disrupt business processes directly and, in addition, cause sickness among employees. This can result in prosecution or litigation if more permanent damage to employees' health occurs. Hazardous materials are substances that are either flammable or combustible, explosive, toxic, noxious, corrosive, oxidizable, an irritant, or radioactive. A hazardous material spill or release can pose a risk to life, health or property. An incident can result in the evacuation of a few people, a section of a facility, or an entire neighborhood. There are a number of federal laws that regulate hazardous materials, including:

- The Superfund Amendments and Re-authorization Act of 1986 (SARA)
- The Resource Conservation and Recovery Act of 1976 (RCRA)
- The Hazardous Materials Transportation Act (HMTA)
- The Occupational Safety and Health Act (OSHA)
- The Toxic Substances Control Act (TSCA)
- The Clean Air Act

Title III of SARA regulates the packaging, labeling, handling, storage, and transportation of hazardous materials. The law requires facilities to furnish information about the quantities and health effects of materials used at the facility, and to promptly notify local and state officials whenever a significant release of hazardous materials occurs.

In addition to onsite hazards, you should be aware of the potential for an offsite incident affecting your operations. You should also be aware of hazardous materials used in facility processes and in the construction of the physical plant. Detailed definitions, as well as lists of hazardous materials, can be obtained from the Environmental Protection Agency (EPA) and the Occupational Safety and Health Administration (OSHA).

2.5.6.2 Epidemic

An epidemic can occur when a contagious illness affects a large number of persons within a country or region. This can have a particularly devastating short-term impact on business through a large number of persons being absent from work at the same time. Certain illnesses can have a longer-term effect on the business, when long-term illness or death results. An example of this extreme situation is occurring in certain third world countries, where the AIDS virus is considered to be of epidemic proportions.

2.5.6.3   Workplace Violence

Acts of violence in the workplace can affect morale, encourage absenteeism, create fear and uncertainty, and increase the employee turnover rate. This can have a significant effect on productivity and could also result in claims for workers compensation, harassment claims, and a need for increased security measures. Statistically, this type of incident is especially prevalent at organizations that have recently merged or are being resized or restructured, where there are regular threats of industrial action, or where permanent employees have been replaced with temporary employees.

2.5.6.4   Public Transportation Disruption

Disruption to public transportation has a major effect on businesses through the inability of employees to get to their normal place of work. This disruption can be caused through major accidents, industrial action, equipment failure, bad weather conditions, and major preventative repairs. Difficult traveling conditions increase absenteeism, as well as lower morale and productivity.

2.5.6.5   Neighborhood Hazard

A neighborhood hazard is defined as a disruptive event in the close vicinity that directly or indirectly affects your own premises and employees. An example would be the seepage of hazardous waste from a neighboring factory, or the escape of toxic gases from a local chemical plant. Health and safety regulations require the organization take suitable action to protect its employees. This may have severe disruptive implications for the business, particularly when it can take some time to clear the hazard.

2.5.7   Nonemergency Factors

Several nonemergency factors can have a negative impact on your ability to resume business operations after an emergency or disaster. We have highlighted a few of the most important factors in the following paragraphs. It is important that these areas be addressed as part of the BCP so that none of these becomes a disaster unto itself. It will be much more cost-effective and efficient, and less distractive to your limited resources, to plan ahead for these potential issues than to try an address them on the fly during an emergency and during recovery.

2.5.7.1   Health and Safety Regulations

For organizations that do not properly and fully observe all the necessary health and safety regulations, a complaint or an inspection can result in the operation being completely closed down until the situation is corrected. This could result in substantial delays on major projects with significant financial implications. Organizations should ensure that they meet the necessary regulations and requirements at all times.

2.5.7.2   Employee Morale

A large number of internal or external factors can have a direct impact on the level of employee morale. This can often arise where there is a combination of poor management, uncertainty, and difficult working conditions. Productivity will be affected and employee turnover is likely to rise.

2.5.7.3   Mergers and Acquisitions

Mergers and acquisitions can be extremely destabilizing on the employees of both businesses involved. Employees may be uncertain about how they will be affected, or even whether they are about to lose their jobs. Unless the merger/acquisition is managed well, the effect on the staff could be considerable, with a dramatic lowering of morale and productivity.

2.5.7.4   Negative Publicity

Unfavorable press comments can result in a lowering of employee morale or a loss of customers. Any company can suffer from negative publicity, and an internal crisis is best resolved from within, prior to the media feeding of the uncertainties and disputes. Reports may also be inaccurate, particularly where reliable information is not available, and therefore, well-worded press statements may be issued to counter adverse reports. Information can be leaked to the press from disgruntled employees and industry competitors.

2.5.7.5   Legal Problems

Legal problems are both time-consuming and expensive. Organizations can experience a wide range of legal issues, including sexual harassment, contract disputes, copyright disputes, health and safety regulations, and discrimination. It is important that organizations are fully aware of their legal duties and of the rights of their employees.

2.6   Business Risk Assessment

A key part of the BCP process is the assessment of the potential risks to the business that could result from potential disasters or emergency situations. This section will examine the possibility of serious situations disrupting the business operations and the potential impact of such events. Risk assessment is the exercise of identifying and analyzing the potential vulnerabilities and threats. It is necessary to consider all the types of possible incidents and the impact each may have on the organization's ability to deliver its normal business services. The sources of risks could be community-wide hazardous events, accidents, or sabotage, causing extreme material disaster, security threats, network and communication failures, or disastrous application errors. Each of these areas should be examined in the light of the business and the exact possible source located.

2.6.1   Asset Characterization

For each source identified, the magnitude of the risk and the probability of its occurrence must be evaluated to judge the extent of risk exposure. Risk exposure is the easiest way to know how much attention needs to be paid to a source of risk. Planning is done for both prevention and control. Accidents and sabotage can be prevented using measures of physical security and personnel practices. Vulnerability assessment and reviews of existing security measures can expose areas where access control, software and data security, or backups are required. Application errors can be prevented by effective reviews and testing during the software releases. Whenever you conduct the risk assessment, you must first collect system-related information, which is usually classified as follows:

- Hardware, software, and system interfaces (e.g., internal/external connectivity)
- Data and information
- Persons who support and use the asset
- Mission (e.g., the processes performed)
- Criticality (e.g., the value or importance to an organization)
- Sensitivity

Additional information could include functional requirements of an asset, key users, security policies governing the asset (organizational policies, federal requirements, laws, industry practices), security architectures, network topology, information storage protection safeguards, technical controls (e.g., built-in or add-on security products that support identification and authentication; discretionary or mandatory access control; audit; residual information protection; and encryption methods), management controls (e.g., rules of behavior, security planning), and operational controls (e.g., personnel security, backup, contingency, and resumption and recovery operations; system maintenance; offsite storage; user account establishment and deletion procedures; and controls for segregation of user functions, such as privileged user access versus standard user access). It is important to include physical security environments in this process (e.g., facility security, data center policies) and environmental security environments (e.g., controls for humidity, water, power, pollution, temperature, and chemicals).

For an asset that is in the initiation or design phase, information can be derived from the design or requirements documents. For an IT system under development, it is necessary to define key security rules and attributes planned for the future IT system. System design documents and the system security plan can provide useful information about the security of an IT system that is in development. For an operational IT system, data is collected about the IT system in its production environment, including data on system configuration, connectivity, and documented and undocumented procedures and practices. Therefore, the system description can be based on the security provided by the underlying infrastructure or on future security plans for the IT system.

2.6.2 Risk Benefit (Likelihood) Analysis Statement

The end result of the risk assessment should be a risk-benefit analysis (or likelihood) statement giving the exact threats and the estimated exposure, together with the contingency and mitigation actions required, and also the benefits arising out of covering the risk. This statement should also delineate any assumptions or constraints that exist. To derive an overall likelihood rating that indicates the probability that a potential vulnerability may be exercised within the construct of the associated threat environment, the following governing factors must be considered:

- Threat-source motivation and capability
- Nature of the vulnerability
- Existence and effectiveness of current controls

The likelihood that a potential vulnerability could be exercised by a given threat-source can be described as high, medium, or low. Often, this exercise will show the complete physical disaster has a remote probability of occurring and application crashes, or security break-ins are very frequent. However, only having a procedure for handling catastrophic disasters without a plan for application failure, or vice versa, is not advisable. The solution is to prepare a BCP for the worst-case scenario, i.e., complete destruction of the site providing the services. Any other outage can then be easily tackled using a subset of the main plan.

Each scenario needs to be developed and examined in detail and an analysis prepared of the consequences of each potential threat. Each scenario should also be assessed for its possibility of occurrence (likelihood) and the possible impact (severity) it would have on an organization. In a perfect world scenario, each potential disaster an organization could face would have multiple impact assessment scenarios performed. Each scenario would cover all levels of probability of occurrence against each level of severity. While this is not practical in most circumstances, it is always useful for developing disaster scenarios for emergency procedure training within an organization.

When performing an assessment, it is often helpful to create a matrix to help manage the type of disaster with the level of damage. An example of such a matrix is shown in Figure 2.8.

Figure 2.8
Incident probability and impact assessment worksheet.

Probability of Event Occurrence		Impact Rating for Event Occurrence	
Ranking	Likelihood	Ranking	Severity
1	very high probability	1	unrecoverable damage
2	high probability	2	devastating
3	medium probability	3	major repairs
4	low probability	4	some repairs needed
5	very low probability	5	minor cosmetic

Each scenario should be covered in the organizational planning process. Each disaster or situation needs to be developed and examined in detail, and an analysis should be prepared for the consequences of each combination of potential threat that could occur.

2.6.3 Risk Level Matrix

Any determination of risk is derived by multiplying the ratings assigned for threat likelihood (e.g., probability) and threat impact. A risk level matrix presented by NIST [9] (see Figure 2.9) shows how the overall risk ratings might be determined based on inputs from the threat likelihood and threat impact categories. The matrix shown below is a 3×3 matrix of threat likelihood (high, medium, and low) and threat impact (high, medium, and low).

Figure 2.9
Risk level matrix.

Threat Likelihood	IMPACT RATING		
	LOW (10)	MEDIUM (50)	HIGH (100)
HIGH (1.0)	10 * 1.0 = 10	50 * 1.0 = 50	100 * 1.0 = 100
MEDIUM (.5)	10 * 0.5 = 5	50 * 0.5 = 25	100 * 0.5 = 50
LOW (.1)	10 * 0.1 = 1	50 * 0.1 = 5	100 * 0.1 = 10

(NOTE: Risk Scale: High (>50 to 100); Medium (>10 to 50); Low (1 to 10))

The determination of these risk levels or ratings can be subjective. The rationale for this justification can be explained in terms of the probability assigned for each threat likelihood level and a value assigned for each impact level. For example, the probability assigned for each threat likelihood level is 1.0 for High, 0.5 for Medium, 0.1 for Low in the figure above. The value assigned for each impact level is 100 for High, 50 for Medium, and 10 for Low. These values could be adjusted higher or lower, depending on the organization's requirements. Depending on the specific requirements and the granularity of risk assessment desired, some sites may use a 4×4 or a 5×5 matrix. The latter can include a Very Low /Very High threat likelihood and a Very Low/Very High threat impact to generate a Very Low/Very High risk level. A Very High risk level may require possible system shutdown or stopping of all IT system integration and testing efforts. The sample matrix in the figure above shows how the overall risk levels of High, Medium, and Low are derived.

2.6.4 Risk Assessment Report

A risk assessment report helps senior management—the mission owners—make decisions on policy, procedural, budget, and system operational and management changes. Unlike an audit or investigation report, which looks for wrongdoing, a risk assessment report should not be presented in an accusatory manner but as a systematic and analytical approach to assessing risk, so that senior management will understand the risks and allocate resources to reduce and correct potential losses. For this reason, some people prefer to address the threat/vulnerability pairs as observations instead of findings in the risk assessment report. A suggested report format is shown in Appendix A.

2.7   Business Impact Analysis (BIA)

A business impact analysis is a process of identifying the critical business functions and the losses and effects if these functions are not available. It involves talking to the key people operating the business functions in order to assess the impact an event would have on business operations. The purpose of the BIA is to correlate specific system components with the critical services that they provide and, based on that information, to characterize the consequences of a disruption to the system components. The BIA process must begin with executive sponsorship of the effort and the support and involvement of senior management, because a good BIA will involve an unprecedented study of the organization. The BIA is a collective undertaking with those whose continuity is sought and those who are major contributors to the various business processes and are intimately involved in the assessment of their value. The results of a BIA will rank, order, and position each business and support function in an order for recovery based on organizational knowledge. Results from the BIA should be appropriately incorporated into the analysis and strategy development efforts for the organization's COOP, BCP, and BRP.

Effective analysis is essential in plan development, strategy selection, and reduction of recovery costs. Impact analysis involves the owner/business function/program manager's input to understand precisely what the agency risks losing, should there be a disruption or disaster. While overall responsibility lies with the business functional unit leader, information needed for recovery comes from all levels of management. The IS organization alone cannot provide that information. The effort needs to be a "meeting of the minds" that results in identifying, qualifying, and quantifying the terms "critical" and "intolerable impacts." Only the owner can identify, quantify, and qualify these impacts. Impact analysis ensures the intolerable impacts are the main consideration in defining the direction, scope, and appropriate recovery strategies for plan development. Simply put, the shorter the time in which the impacts become intolerable, the hotter the strategy (most resources in place, ready to use). Conversely, if the impacts are tolerable for two weeks or more, then a colder strategy (resources identified, but not in place) is indicated.

One of the lesser-known advantages of performing a BIA is the awareness level of many of the organization's employees rises significantly as BIA interview questions and "what if" scenarios are discussed. This can have the advantage of speeding the progress of the project and helps to gather consensus and support from areas of the organization, which otherwise would not have understood the importance of enterprise-wide recovery plan development, testing, and maintenance.

Impact analysis is often confused with risk assessment. Risk assessment is associated with determining the potential losses of a threat versus the cost of the protective measure against the value of the asset. It is related to determining how much to spend on prevention and protection. Although risk assessments are a very important step in the analysis, all of the information needed for recovery planning does not result from this one step.

Interview people from all the functional and support areas who know the business processes and can respond to a structured questionnaire quantitatively. Interviewees should range from those who feel the organization "cannot survive without me" to those who "hold the organization together with their bare hands." BIA conveys the needs of the organization and what the impacts would be if critical functions were not recovered in a timely fashion. BIA results are the foundation and cornerstone of the plan and strategies selected to use in the event of a disaster.

2.7.1   Identification of Key Business Processes

The BIA should include a list of the key business areas of the organization. This list should be in order of importance to the business. Areas that should be considered include:

- Accounting and Reporting
- Customer Service Handling
- E-mail and Ecommerce Processes
- Finance and Treasury
- Human Resources
- Information Technology
- Maintenance and Support
- Marketing and Public Relations
- Production Processes

- Quality Control Mechanisms
- Research and Development Activities
- Sales and Sales Administration
- Strategic Business Planning Activities

Each item identified above should include a brief description of the business process, its main dependencies on IT (or other) systems, what communications are involved, key personnel, and other relevant information that may be helpful in a recovery process.

2.7.2 Establishing Requirements for Business Recovery

In the event of a disaster, it is advisable to have the immediate answers to several crucial questions. Examples of the types of questions critical to business continuity are:

- What resources and records would be required to continue the business function?
- What are the bare minimum resource requirements to maintain operations?
- Which of the resources would come from external sources?
- What other business functions it would be dependent upon, and to what extent?
- What other business functions would depend on it, and to what extent?
- Upon which external business/suppliers/vendors would it be dependent, and to what extent?
- Which Service Level Agreements (SLAs) and measures for continuity would these external entities follow?
- What would the backup needs be?
- What time and effort is required to recreate current data from the backups?
- What precautions need to be taken for recovering without a test environment?

2.7.3   BIA Questionnaire Development

In preparing the BIA questionnaire, all of the metrics used should be decided on and followed consistently throughout the questionnaire. Even if automated tools are used, it is recommended that some of interviews be conducted face-to-face, with the understanding that there will be iterations and opportunities to fine-tune the responses. In order to obtain greater consistency in responses and ease of comparison, describe precisely the business function being interviewed, use consistent critical timing elements and orders of magnitude for specifying quantity, or provide selections from which to choose. Remember, the BIA questionnaire determines impacts to an organization as if it were experiencing an actual interruption.

2.7.3.1   Information Provided by the BIA Questionnaire

In order to determine initial discovery and response to an event, your questionnaire should have a series of questions that begin with the phrase "**When would the disruption . . .**" Some key questions for consideration include the following items shown in Figure 2.10:

Figure 2.10

Questions to ask in the BIA Questionnaire regarding initial discovery and response to an event..

"When would the disruption...	Response
...first become noticeable by the average person?"	
...result in a large number of complaints or severe criticism?"	*(List positive actions to reduce complaints and criticism.)*
...substantially increase, decrease?"	*(State the time period(s) and the cause.)*
...be countered by positive action to reduce complaints?"	*(Explain the actions needed.)*

Answers to the questions above will allow you to develop specific focus on matters that unfold as the disaster is discovered and reported, as well as how people in the vicinity are likely to respond to it. If a disruptive event occurs, there should be specific activities that are prepared for with planned responses to the various stages of the event as it unfolds. The next set of questions address dealing with the *impact of the event* as opposed to discovery and dispatch of a response.

BIA questions beginning with ***When would the disruption impact . . .*** are generally directed at understanding how the event will affect the organization. Figure 2.11 shows you some questions for consideration:

Of course, there is no limit to the number of questions that can be asked on the questionnaire, but our recommendation is to keep it as short as possible and focus on specific areas of interest that address the aforementioned areas.

There may be extenuating circumstances that your organization must consider and include in such a survey; always take those into consideration when developing the questions. For example, if your organization is spread across a large campus and an event occurs specific to a single building, what would be different in the questionnaire if the event were to affect multiple buildings, or all of the campus?

Figure 2.11
BIA questions used to determine impact of an event.

"When would the disruption impact...	Response
...current revenue generation or control?"	*(What is the source and amount?)*
...future revenue generation or control?"	*(What is the source and amount?)*
...infrastructure support (power, water, sanitation, telecommunications) responsibilities?"	*(State how this could occur.)*
...any number of employees?"	*(How many?)*
...employee safety or health?"	*(State how this could occur.)*
...environmental conditions?"	*(State how this could occur.)*
...statutory and legal obligations?"	*(Is there a legal mandate to perform under any circumstances?)*
...exposures to legal liabilities if a function was not performed?"	*(State how this could occur.)*
...contractual obligations or financial penalty?"	*(State how this could occur.)*
...public access to information?"	*(State how this could occur.)*
...public image of your organization?"	*(State how this could occur.)*

2.7.4 BIA Report Format

The structured questionnaire allows data collection in a format that enables direct comparison of results. Patterns will emerge that define the impacts in the loss categories. The most critical functions will group accordingly. The report should provide prompt and specific feedback of the impacts, with time frames, to the interviewees and executive management in meaningful, recovery-related statements. The BIA process and feedback increases heightened awareness of the need for continuity that supports its effective implementation and allows for adjustments over or under estimated responses.

2.7.5 Fine-Tuning Priorities

Information collected from the BIA provides a subset of functions that are critical. To fine-tune the priorities of these functions, a business process study is required. The basis of this analysis is collected early in the questionnaire under internal functional areas. This analysis looks at where work flows begin and end and gets down to the level of business processes and how each functional area of an organization is connected. Suppose business function X is considered the most critical, based on the business impact analysis. However, business function X depends on inputs from business function Y before work can begin. Therefore, the process performed by business function Y must be recovered before business function X can begin work.

2.7.6 Determining Resource Dependencies

The purpose of this part of the questionnaire is to document the resources that the essential work conducted by a particular function depends on. It is recommended to identify resource dependencies for at least each critical and essential business function. The goal is to determine the very minimum of resources required to perform only the most critical or essential processes and tasks. During recovery, resources (e.g., phones, faxes, PCs, printers, and so on) should be shared among all of the critical and essential business functions to a greater degree than in normal business. When all the dependencies are known, tabulate them together according to the resource and the time period in which they are needed to result in the minimum resource requirements—the basis of strategy selection. For each critical business function interviewed, ask the questions found in the figures on the following pages for each specific resource. Add the details based on the function's specific requirements.

The questions found in the BIA allow plan developers to determine how much value the use of equipment and key staff is in performing critical or essential work. Depending on the type of business, the use of telephones, fax machines, computers, printers, etc. may or may not have a significant impact. If you are in the business of running a call center, for example, and find yourself in a situation where you are without telephones, chances are pretty good that your business is at a dead stop until the phone service is restored.

Figure 2.12
Is critical or essential work dependent on key job functions?

JOB FUNCTION	SKILLS	TASK	QUANTITY	TIME
What supplies are required?				
Service dependency (major, medium, minor):				
List actions to reduce impacts:				
Other remarks:				

The questions found in Figure 2.12 are primarily used to determine if there are key jobs that must be staffed in any emergency. The ability of the organization to recover is impacted negatively if these positions are not adequately staffed and provisioned. The question about supplies is extremely important, because if someone does try to perform a key task and needs some special or unique hardware to accomplish that task, it must be made available and accessible. The plan should account for primary and backup situations for personnel and equipment where possible.

Figure 2.13
Is critical or essential work dependent on the telephone?

JOB FUNCTION	TELEPHONE SPECIFICATIONS*	VOLUME	QUANTITY	TIME
What supplies are required?				
Service dependency (major, medium, minor):				
List actions to reduce impacts:				
* Voice, data, incoming, outgoing, voice mail, call distribution, voice response, conference, multi-track voice, recorder, video, speaker phone; peak times of day, week, year.				

Figure 2.14
Is critical or essential work dependent on the fax?

JOB FUNCTION	FAX SPECIFICATIONS*	VOLUME	QUANTITY	TIME
What supplies are required?				
Service dependency (major, medium, minor):				
List actions to reduce impacts:				
* Incoming, outgoing, advanced capabilities, peak times of day, week, year.				

Communication is a critical aspect of a BCP, and part of your planning should address communications with emergency personnel, employees, directors, regulators, vendors and suppliers, customers, and the media. Alternate communication channels should be considered, such as cellular telephones, pagers, satellite telephones, and Internet-based communications, such as e-mail or instant messaging. For example, if you are in the business of running a call center, for example, and find yourself in a situation where you are without telephones, chances are pretty good that your business is at a dead stop until the phone service is restored. Figures 2.13 and 2.14 should be replicated for each of the groups (emergency personnel, employees, directors, regulators, vendors and suppliers, customers, and the media). Since voice and data infrastructures are typically a shared resource across the different business areas of an organization, the dependency and criticality of these resources should not be underestimated. The telecommunications infrastructure contains single points of failure that represent vulnerabilities and risks for organizations. Elements of risk that reside within the public telecommunications network infrastructure are outside the control of a single organization. Financial organizations must be proactive in establishing robust processes to ensure telecommunication

Figure 2.15
Is critical or essential work dependent on a personal computer (PC)?

JOB FUNCTION	PC SPECIFICATIONS*	QUANTITY	TIME
What supplies are required?			
Service dependency (major, medium, minor):			
List actions to reduce impacts:			
* Manufacturer, model, type of work performed, software/hardware requirements, PC connectivity.			

JOB FUNCTION	SERVER/MID-RANGE SYSTEM SPECIFICATIONS*	QUANTITY	TIME
What supplies are required?			
Service dependency (major, medium, minor):			
List actions to reduce impacts:			
* Manufacturer, model, type of work performed, software/hardware requirements, PC connectivity.			

resiliency and diversity. Organizations need to develop risk management practices to identify and eliminate single points of failure across their network infrastructures.

Personal computers are not often subject to contingency planning. However, they should be, because desktop users may be directed to take backups to the alternate site. If this is not practical, consider using a networked disk. Users can be given instructions pertaining to the folders in the networked disk and detailing which required data should be saved. The networked disk is backed up periodically and can be taken to an offsite storage location. The restoration process will benefit from knowing the system and application configurations of the desktops. We recommend that documentation on each desktop be maintained. (See Figure 2.15.) Wherever possible, systems should be set up with identical configurations so that they can be quickly restored them in an emergency. Another consideration is that personal computers that contain highly sensitive data most likely will have power-on passwords, or even be encrypted. The particulars for managing passwords and encryption information should be maintained by the IT department and available to recovery teams in an emergency.

JOB FUNCTION	MAINFRAME SYSTEM SPECIFICATIONS*	QUANTITY	TIME
What supplies are required?			
Service dependency (major, medium, minor):			
List actions to reduce impacts:			
* Manufacturer, model, type of work performed, software/hardware requirements, PC connectivity.			

JOB FUNCTION	PRINTER SPECIFICATIONS*	QUANTITY	TIME
What supplies are required?			
Service dependency (major, medium, minor):			
List actions to reduce impacts:			
* Manufacturer, model, type of work performed, software/hardware requirements, PC connectivity.			

The loss of servers can be devastating, as they host all the applications and support several users. This is the most important area to focus on while performing contingency planning. Adequate documentation of the system and applications hosted must be kept to enable ease of recovery.

Midrange and mainframe systems are essential for conducting business and connecting critical elements such as business areas, vendors, customers, and service providers. New technologies allow greater geographic separation between people, system resources, and primary and alternate processing locations. Network technologies are key to enabling distributed processing environments, but they require an increased reliance on telecommunications networks for both voice and data communications. Given their critical nature and importance, it is necessary to design high levels of redundancy and resiliency into their infrastructures. (See Figure 2.17.)

JOB FUNCTION	EQUIPMENT SPECIFICATIONS*	QUANTITY	TIME
What supplies are required?			
Service dependency (major, medium, minor):			
List actions to reduce impacts:			
* Calculators, copiers, typewriters, transcribers, audio recorder/Dictaphone, audio/visual, etc.			

Comprehensive inventories will assist with the business recovery efforts and ensure all components are considered during plan development. (See Figures 2.18 and 2.19.) Planning should include identifying critical business unit data that may reside on workstations and may not adhere to backup schedules. Organizations should exercise caution when identifying such noncritical assets.

Figure 2.20
Is critical or essential work dependent on a LAN/WAN?

JOB FUNCTION	LAN/WAN SPECIFICATIONS*	QUANTITY	TIME
What supplies are required?			
Service dependency (major, medium, minor):			
List actions to reduce impacts:			
* Manufacturer, model, type of work performed, software/hardware requirements, PC connectivity.			

When addressing LAN/WAN issues (Figure 2.20), don't forget about virtual private networks (VPNs), which are often used for recovery. A VPN runs securely over public networks. It allows user access to a corporate network. Once login to the corporate network occurs, it is like using the corporate Intranet from the Internet. The tunnel is established for the VPN connection via a request to the destination server from the Internet user. The destination server first authenticates the user and, if authentication is successful, allows the connection to proceed. Security is created through the use of encryption and the Internet tunneling protocol used to establish the connection. In the event of disaster, VPNs will allow recovery teams to work on the recovery server even before the alternate site is up and operational.

The criticality of external or third-party systems used by an organization (see Figure 2.22) is often underestimated. These systems share the same recovery strategies as internal systems. Recovery after a disaster often requires people with extensive skills in networking, environmental conditioning, and systems support. Be aware that external parties are notoriously slow in restoring data. Reliance on third-party providers, key suppliers, or

Figure 2.21
Is critical or essential work dependent on any internal work group?

WORK GROUP	DESCRIPTION/LOCATION*	TYPE OF WORK	VOLUME	TIME NEEDED
What supplies are required?				
Service dependency (major, medium, minor):				
Operational dependency (major, medium, minor):				
System dependency (major, medium, minor):				
List actions to reduce impacts:				
* Number peak times of day, week, year.				

Figure 2.22
Is critical or essential work dependent on any external computer systems?

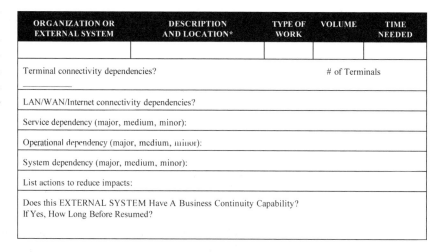

ORGANIZATION OR EXTERNAL SYSTEM	DESCRIPTION AND LOCATION*	TYPE OF WORK	VOLUME	TIME NEEDED
Terminal connectivity dependencies?			# of Terminals	
LAN/WAN/Internet connectivity dependencies?				
Service dependency (major, medium, minor):				
Operational dependency (major, medium, minor):				
System dependency (major, medium, minor):				
List actions to reduce impacts:				
Does this EXTERNAL SYSTEM Have A Business Continuity Capability? If Yes, How Long Before Resumed?				

business partners may expose your organization to points of failure that could prevent resumption of operations in a timely manner.

The risks in outsourcing include threats to the security, availability, and integrity of systems and resources, to the confidentiality of information, and to regulatory compliance.

In addition, when a third party performs services, risk levels can be increased. Review and understand service providers' BCPs and ensure critical services can be restored within acceptable time frames based upon the needs of your business. The service contract you enter into with third-party providers should address their responsibility for maintenance and testing of disaster recovery and contingency plans. They should provide testing and audit results to help you determine the adequacy of their plans and the effectiveness of the testing process. The BCP should also address how it will

Figure 2.23
Is critical or essential work dependent on any vital records?

JOB FUNCTION	VITAL RECORD NAME AND DESCRIPTION/LOCATION	NORMAL RECOVERY SOURCE	NORMAL RECOVERY MEDIA	TIME NEEDED
What supplies are required?				
Service dependency (major, medium, minor):				
List actions to reduce impacts:				
*Paper, microfilm, fiche, PC/LAN, PC, mid-range, mainframe, optical, Rolodexes, directories, etc.				

exchange information with service providers in the event that your organization must operate from an alternative location.

2.7.7 Organizing and Tabulating the Results

The results of the resource dependencies may be formatted by listing all the resources that are needed down one column. Across the top of the table, have columns for the time periods in which recovery must begin. Fill in the matrix, matching the quantity of the resources needed with the time period in which they are needed. Complete a matrix for each function, and total all resource needs in a similar matrix. A sample is provided in Figure 2.24:

Figure 2.24
Resource requirements matrix.

Business Function A Resource Needs	Day 1	Day 2-5	Day 6-14
Personnel	5	9	15
Telephones	2	3	5
Printers	1	2	2
Personal Computers	5	9	15
LAN/WAN Connections	5	9	15
Other (specify)			

Review all the resource requirements and look for opportunities to share resources and reduce the overall amount. Combine all resource needs and the time they are needed into a consolidated master matrix for strategy selection, and document what is needed and when it is needed. An example is shown in Figure 2.25.

Figure 2.25
Consolidated resource requirements matrix.

Business Function A Resource Needs	Day 1	Day 2-5	Day 6-14
Personnel	5	9	15
Telephones	2	3	5
Printers	1	2	2
Personal Computers	5	9	15
LAN/WAN Connections	5	9	15
Other (specify)			

2.7.8   Determining Impact on Operations

It is important to understand how vital the function is to the overall business strategy. This requires you to determine how long the function could be inoperative without any impact or losses. You must also determine how the rest of the business would be affected by this function's outage—*the operational impact.* Part of this process would be to understand what the revenue lost due to its outage would be—*the financial impact*—and whether its outage would result in violation of Service Level Agreements (SLAs), regulatory requirements, any contractual liabilities, or penalties, or whether it would create legal issues—*the regulatory and legal impact.* For many businesses, it is crucial to determine whether the function's outage would affect relationships with customers—*loss of customer confidence*—or whether it would affect the market rates—*decline in market rates.* Sometimes, a disaster can ruin a company. Knowing the impact of catastrophic events helps you to determine whether it would affect the industry ranking—*loss of competitive edge*—or whether it could result in losing future sales—*loss of opportunities.*

Figure 2.26
Recovery cost balancing.

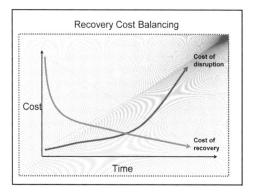

To identify disruption impacts and allowable outage times, we should analyze the critical resources identified previously and determine the impact(s) on IT operations, should a given resource be disrupted or damaged. The analysis should evaluate the impact of the outage in two ways: over time and across resources. The effects of the outage may be tracked over time. This will enable the BCP team to identify the maximum allowable time that a resource may be denied before it prevents or inhibits the performance of an essential function. The effects of the outage may be tracked across related resources and dependent systems, identifying any cascading effects that may occur as a disrupted system affects other processes that rely on it. The BCP team should determine the optimum point to recover the system by balancing the cost of being down against the cost of resources required for restoring the system. This can be depicted using a simple chart, such as the example in Figure 2.26. The point where the two lines meet defines how long the organization can afford to allow the system to be disrupted. Knowing all of the aforementioned data will help your organization to discover what the maximum acceptable (or permissible) outage period would be during and after a disruptive event.

2.7.9 Prioritization and Classification of Business Functions

It is necessary to classify business functions based on their criticality. They can be broken down into critical functions, essential functions, necessary functions, and desirable functions. At this point, you may be asking, "What constitutes a critical function?" Critical functions are those functions that, if interrupted or unavailable for some period of time, can completely jeopardize the business and cause heavy damages. Essential functions are those whose loss would seriously affect the organization's ability to function for any sustained period of time. Necessary functions are those that would not be required for the organization to continue functioning, but their absence would limit the business effectiveness to a great extent. Finally, desirable functions would be those that are beneficial to the organization, but their absence would not affect the capability of the organization.

This impact analysis helps to rank the business functions and come up with an order in which they should be restored; in other words, it defines recovery priorities. The BIA helps define the recovery objectives. In the course of this study, it might be possible to discover that when resuming operations after a disaster, it is enough to recover to a limited capacity, i.e., recover to the extent of handling 40% of the usual workload within 24 hours. It will also be possible to define in detail the resource requirements for making a business function operational after disaster or interruption. This will include infrastructure, manpower, documents, records, machines, phones, fax machines, whatever is needed—with complete specifications.

Having adequate details is important, since in the event of disasters there is bound to be some amount of panic, and it may not be possible to come down to such details. The team and managers actually involved in the day-to-day operations of the business functions would be the best people to talk to during the impact analysis, as they would certainly know the details of the functions. Moreover, they can perform a brainstorming exercise on how an outage of their function would affect revenue objectives, market position, and customer expectations, or how they could restore normal operations, or what resources they would require to operate in normal mode.

Interdependence between various functions (internal and external) is crucial information obtained as part of the analysis. While consolidating the information gathered from the questionnaires/discussions and ranking the functions to derive the recovery priority, one must not overlook functions that are considered low priority on their own but, however, have some critical functions depending on them. By virtue of this dependence, they also become important.

2.7.10 Establish Time Frames for Service Interruption Measurement

It is often necessary to establish standard time frames for measuring periods of outage when normal business services could become interrupted. Based on each business's unique recovery needs, organizations can come up with standard recovery time frames for the business function classifications cited previously. For example, for critical functions, recovery should occur in less than one day and, using the time frame/outage interval chart shown in Figure 2.27, those recovery procedures could be instituted for each phase of recovery, using the various time frames. For Time Frame A, actions that must be taken within the first three hours of an outage would be identified and checklists would be made for that phase of recovery. Once those actions were completed, then actions needed in the next time frame would begin. The process would continue until critical functions were restored. For essential functions, perhaps recovery would be necessary with a two- to three-day time frame. Necessary functions would be required to be recovered in four to seven days, and desirable functions would be reinstated within fourteen days. For each key business process, an assessment is made of the financial and operational impact of outages. These time frames are applied to each critical function or key process to assist in quantifying the level of severity of the outage. Of course, the chart should be adjusted to satisfy the needs of each business entity. These are only examples.

2.7.11 Determine Financial and Operational Impact

Cost considerations must not be overlooked. Keep in mind that revenue losses and opportunity losses will be directly proportional to the time taken for recovery. Following an interruption, losses become intolerable within a specific period. This is the recovery window. Selection of the correct strate-

Figure 2.27
Time frame/outage interval chart.

Time Frame	Outage Interval
A	0 - 3 hours
B	4 - 12 hours
C	13 - 24 hours
D	more than 1 day

gies should be based on the recovery window resulting from the impact analysis process. Therefore, if intolerable impacts would occur in one week or less, a hotter recovery strategy is indicated. A hot strategy is one that requires most of the recovery resources to be already in place and ready to use. If intolerable impacts would occur after longer periods, a colder recovery strategy is indicated. A cold strategy is one in which recovery resources are put in place following an interruption. Even with a cold strategy, it is critical that the recovery resources be identified, listed, prearranged, and preplanned as to how/where they will be acquired and how/when they will be delivered, installed, and used. Usually, a combination of recovery strategies should be planned.

The cost of a recovery strategy will be inversely proportional to the time permitted for recovery. The cost of the possible recovery strategy must be compared with the actual loss due to the outage before accepting the strategy. If the solution proposed costs much more than the projected losses, it will not be possible to justify the investment to the management. When presenting the findings of the business impact analysis, express the results in business terms. Quantifying the impact, possibly in terms of money, will catch the attention of the management. Stating the impact in terms of time will help in proposing concrete recovery goals. Stating the requirements in technical terms will help in planning the recovery strategies. Ultimately, the BIA must justify the continuity plan and aid selection of the best possible recovery strategy within the budget. As an example, if an interruption of electrical power, isolated to one power panel, caused the e-mail server in an organization to become unavailable, a loss of e-mail for three hours would have a quantification factor calculated using Time Frame A. Now, let's suppose there are 1,000 employees working during the time of the outage. We will assume the outage occurred during the morning hours, when e-mail is most often read by employees. If we are to assume that at 8:00 am approximately 50% of the employees were in the office checking e-mail, at 9:00 am that number increased to 75%, and at 10:00 am 90% of employees were checking e-mail, the loss of productivity could be quantified as shown in Figure 2.28:

Figure 2.28
*Example of the
impact of e-mail
downtime.*

Assume an average burdened salary of $80,000 per employee per annum. This calculates to an average labor cost of $41.66 ($80,000/1920 hrs) per hour.

08:00 - 09:00 we find 1,000 * .50 = 500 employees @ 41.66 =$20,833 loss
09:00 - 10:00 we find 1,000 * .75 = 750 employees @ 41.66 =$31,245 loss
10:00 - 11:00 we find 1,000 * .90 = 900 employees @ 41.66 =$37,494 loss

Therefore, for the three hours mail was down, the loss in productivity was potentially $89,572. The effect is cumulative. Now, the only question remaining is what factor email plays in the overall productivity of organizational personnel. If email is critical to getting work done, that factor may be 1.0, if it is important, but not critical, it may be assigned a value of .8 for example. In our example, lets assign an importance factor of .5 and that yields a loss of $44,786 for the three-hour outage.

In the example above, if e-mail were down for 12 hours, then the impact could be much more severe. Most risk officers use the worst-case scenario for each time frame, so a B-frame outage would be four times more costly, or $179,144.00 to the organization.

It is quite easy to see that such outages provide considerable risk to business. Being able to quantify such risks by category allows an organization to plan for contingency and take actions that prevent such outages. For the example shown above, it is certainly much cheaper to fix the electrical problem in the power panel than it is to endure another three-hour outage.

2.8   Information Security, IT and Communications

IT contingency planning represents a broad scope of activities designed to sustain and recover critical IT services following an emergency. IT contingency planning fits into a much broader emergency preparedness environment that includes organizational and business process continuity and recovery planning. Ultimately, an organization would use a suite of plans to properly prepare response, recovery, and continuity activities for disruptions affecting the organization's IT systems, business processes, and the facility. Because there is an inherent relationship between an IT system and the business process it supports, there should be coordination between each

Figure 2.29
*Critical IT system
vendor contact list.*

Support System	Product	Version	Vendor Contact	Platform	Key User Contact
Accounting: AR/AP	Oracle	8i	Joe Knowsit	Solaris	Nancy Aviduser
Accounting: FA	Oracle	8i	Jim Alsoknowsit	Solaris	Bill Keepsitstraight

plan during development and updates to ensure that recovery strategies and supporting resources neither negate each other nor duplicate efforts.

Data and the electronic and manual systems through which they are processed have evolved into critical facets of the corporate structure. Data in these systems is relied on heavily:

- To perform routine corporate business;

- To supply staff and external organizations with related information;

- To comply with legal and contractual requirements; and

- As a basis for management decision-making.

Additionally, although increased automation of corporate administrative operations and research projects provides substantial efficiencies, it also exposes the operations/research to severe disruption if the electronic data systems are not available on a continuous basis. Data processing and business applications are no longer restricted to mainframe computer environments. The use of distributed platforms (including midrange computers, client/server technology, and local and wide area networks) for mission-critical functions not only expands the scope of business continuity planning but also makes it more important. This increased importance arises from the fact that nonoperational areas are finding themselves responsible for systems that are critical or that highly impact the functioning and reputation of the corporation.

The level of most organizations' dependency on IT and communications systems has steadily increased through the last decade. IT and communication systems are now seen as mission-critical operations. Organizations provide customer service and support, and the nature of these customer services often necessitates maintaining a 24/7 operation. For these reasons, it is essential that businesses be able to keep their IT networks and communications systems operational at all times. This section examines some of the issues that should be considered when assessing the level of risk associated with IT services and communications. To effectively determine the specific risks to an IT system during service interruption, a risk assessment of the IT system environment is required. A thorough risk assessment should identify the system vulnerabilities, threats, and current controls and attempt to determine the risk based on the threats' likelihood and impact. These risks should then be assessed and a risk level assigned (e.g., high, medium, or low). Because risks can vary over time and new risks may replace old ones as a system evolves, the risk management process must by ongoing and dynamic. The person responsible for IT contingency planning must be aware of risks to the system and recognize whether the current contingency plan is able to address residual risks completely and effectively. Ongoing contingency plan maintenance and testing, in addition to periodic reviews, is recommended.

2.8.1 The OCTAVE Methodology

The Operationally Critical Threat, Asset, and Vulnerability Evaluation (OCTAVE®), is an approach for managing information security risks. OCTAVE is a risk-based strategic assessment and planning technique for security. OCTAVE is self-directed, meaning that people from an organization assume responsibility for setting the organization's security strategy. The technique leverages people's knowledge of their organization's security-related practices and processes to capture the current state of security practice within the organization. Risks to the most critical assets are used to prioritize areas of improvement and set the security strategy for the organization.

The OCTAVE approach is driven by two of the aspects: operational risk and security practices. Technology is examined only in relation to security practices, enabling an organization to refine the view of its current security practices. By using the OCTAVE approach, an organization makes information-protection decisions based on risks to the confidentiality, integrity, and availability of critical information-related assets. All aspects of risk (assets, threats, vulnerabilities, and organizational impact) are factored into decision-making, enabling an organization to match a practice-based protection strategy to its security risks.

2.8.2 Specify IT/Communications Systems and Dependencies

IT systems are vulnerable to a variety of disruptions, ranging from mild (e.g., short-term power outage, disk drive failure) to severe (e.g., equipment destruction, fire). Many vulnerabilities can be minimized or eliminated through technical, management, or operational solutions as part of the organization's risk management effort; however, it is virtually impossible to completely eliminate all risks. Contingency planning is designed to mitigate the risk of system and service unavailability by focusing on effective and efficient recovery solutions. As defined in NIST Special Publication 800-18 [10], an IT system is identified by defining boundaries around a set of processes, communications, storage, and related resources (an architecture). All components of an IT system need not be physically connected. For example, they could be any combination of the following:

- Stand-alone personal computers (PCs) in an office
- PCs placed in employees' homes under defined telecommuting program rules
- Portable PCs provided to employees who require mobile computing capability for their jobs
- Systems with multiple identical configurations installed in locations with the same environmental and physical controls

Every organization should develop a detailed specification of the main IT business critical systems and their corresponding network configurations. For larger organizations with highly complex IT infrastructures, documentation of these systems may constitute an entirely separate document than the BCP and should be referenced in the BCP as such. Accuracy and currency of information is of crucial importance. Also, it is important that these specification documents are updated each time the IT systems are modified. This places additional burden on systems administrators, so prudent BCP planners often work with IT to establish processes that combine these document updates with other internal reporting processes (for example, job ticket closure, etc.).

2.8.3   Identify Key IT, Communications, and Data Systems

In creating a BCP, it is necessary to list all critical IT processes and information processing systems. This will help identify which business processes will be affected when there is an interruption to services. It will also help in an organization's efforts in developing a backup and recovery strategy. Most often, a table such as the one shown in Figure 2.29 is all that is required. Its format is one that is recommended for most organizations.

2.8.4   Key IT Personnel and Emergency Contact Information

In the event of an emergency, whom do you call? The purpose of this contact list is for contingency. If something does happen to any of the IT systems, your organization should know the name and numbers of the best person to get the system operational. A list of systems and contact information is all that is necessary to satisfy this requirement. A sample is shown in Figure 2.30.

Figure 2.30
Key IT support personnel contact list.

Support System	Key IT Contact	Normal Hours	After Hours
Oracle 8i	Fred Gotfingered	123.456.7890	123.444.0090
Peachtree Accounting	Jim Kancount	123.456.7891	123.444.0800

2.8.5 Key IT Suppliers and Maintenance Engineers

A list of key IT and communications suppliers and contracted maintenance engineers should be prepared and maintained, together with emergency contact information. It is important for the organization to understand the supplier's response times and service level availability. Most likely, the supplier will have various response times, but the costs for shorter response times will normally be higher. You should obtain quotations for the desired level of service and then conduct a simple cost-benefit analysis to justify costs based on projections of the lost revenue from a disruption to service levels. A sample is shown in Figure 2.31.

Figure 2.31
Key IT supplier/ maintenance list.

Support System	Vendor Contact	Response Time	SLA Notes	Emergency Contact Number to call
Oracle 8i	Fred Solditume	< 1 hour	Vendor must respond within 1 hour otherwise no charge is incurred	Primary: 123.444.0090 Alternate: 123/444/0091

2.8.6 Review Existing IT Recovery Procedures

A summary of the existing IT backup and recovery procedures should be documented within the BCP. It must be ensured that the offsite facility has the necessary infrastructure, equipment, hardware, software, and communication facilities. It is necessary to test whether the site is capable of handling full operations. The operational data must then be uploaded at this secondary site, and the emergency site gradually dismantled. This information should cover both hardware and software systems, in addition to data back-up and recovery processes. Information should also be included on any offsite data storage arrangements. An example for a small organization may be stated as follows:

```
A twice-daily backup of all data is made to a CD and
stored in the safe. Weekly, one master CD containing a
copy of all weekly backup data is stored at offsite
location Alpha. The on-duty system administrator
reviews system logs daily to ensure all back-up
processes have executed successfully. The data recovery
process is tested biweekly to ensure recovery
procedures are valid. One copy of all original system
programs is stored onsite in the IT library, and another
copy is stored offsite at location Alpha. A backup copy
of all system programs is made on a monthly basis to
ensure relevant software patches will be included in
any future recovery process. The monthly backup copy is
tested on a bimonthly basis to ensure the recovery
process is valid. ACME, Inc. has a HW maintenance
agreement with XYZ Inc., who is contractually required
to respond to outage requests within two hours of any
call. The aforementioned agreement includes tiered
escalation procedures when the fault has not been fixed
within four hours and further escalation when not fixed
in six hours.
```

An important consideration, whether you find existing procedures or not, is whether the critical operations can be resumed at the normal business site or at an alternate site. In situations when access to the primary site is denied or the site is damaged beyond use, the operations could move to an alternate site. Alternate sites can be of the following kinds:

- **Cold site**—A cold site is a facility that is environmentally conditioned, but devoid of any equipment. It is ready for all the equipment to move in; i.e., it has telephone points, power supply, and a UPS facility, among others. It takes a little time to make this site operational. Using a cold site implies that the business entity has contracts with the providers of all the necessary equipment. These contracts are specifically for a business resumption scenario and therefore will have clauses on the time within which the setup will be completed.

- **Hot site**—A hot site is an alternate facility that has workspace for the personnel, is fully equipped with all resources and stand-by computer facilities needed to recover, and can support critical business functions after a disaster. It is a fully equipped site where the BCP team moves in to start work without further delay.

- **Warm site**—A warm site is a partially equipped hot site, where the data is not too old.

- **Mobile site**—A mobile site is a portable site with a smaller configuration. It can be positioned near the primary site, thus saving travel for the key staff.

- **Mirrored site**—A mirrored site is identical in all aspects to the primary site, right down to the information availability. It is equivalent to having a redundant site in normal times, and is naturally the most expensive option.

At the alternate site (or primary site, if still usable), the work environment is restored. Communication, networks, and workstations are set up. Contact with the external world can now be resumed. An organization might choose to function in manual mode until the critical IT services can resume. If the recovery alternative (described in a later section) permits, the critical functions can also be resumed in the automated mode very quickly.

At the site of recovery (either primary or alternative), the operating system is restored on the standby system. Necessary applications are restored in the order of their criticality. When the applications to serve the critical functions are restored, data restoration from backup tapes or media obtained from the offsite storage can be initiated. Data must also be synchronized, i.e., be rebuilt accurately to a predetermined point of time before the interruption. The point to which the restoration is done depends on the requirements of the critical services. Business data comes from different sources, each of which must be reconstructed to reach the desired state of data integrity. The synchronized data must be reviewed and validated. This is mandatory, because under such disastrous circumstances, it is possible that there is no test environment available and that applications will resume directly in the production environment. It is therefore necessary to have a clear method, strategy, or checklist to perform this validation exercise.

Once the data has reached a reliable state, transactions that have been accumulating since the disaster can be processed, and all the critical functions can then resume. Gradually, other services of the business can also begin functioning. Some of the steps described above are not required for certain recovery strategies. The mechanism of the recovery strategy itself is the reason for it. A description of the technical alternatives is covered along, with the recovery goals, in subsequent sections.

2.9   Chapter Summary

This chapter has attempted to help you learn about assessing the risk impact for potential emergencies. In assessing risk, we began by learning how to determine threats. A process called risk certification and accreditation was presented. We talked about the process of risk management, the role of the risk manager, and the process of risk assessments. The basics elements of the risk assessment process were discussed, along with a discussion of the various risk assessment models one may choose to use. The Emergency Incident Assessment (EIA) process was presented, and therein we explained the various types of environmental disasters one should plan for, such as tornado, hurricane, flood, severe winter storms, drought, earthquake, electrical storms, and fire. Organized or deliberate acts of destruction were another consideration we presented for the EIA. Such actions included acts of terrorism, act of sabotage, act of war, theft, arson, and labor disputes. Common items that also must be a part of your assessment include the loss of utilities or service, such as electrical power failure, loss of gas supply, loss of water supply, petroleum and oil shortage, communications services breakdown, and the loss of drainage/waste removal capabilities. We discussed facilities issues, such as system failures, internal power failures, air conditioning failures, production line failures, cooling plant failures, and equipment failures.

We presented many types of information security incidents that must also be factored into the assessment process. We talked about cybercrime, loss of records or data, disclosure of sensitive information, and coping with IT system failures. Other emergency situations we presented related to contamination and environmental hazards, epidemics, workplace violence, public transportation disruption, and neighborhood hazards. Non-emergency factors, such as health and safety regulations, employee morale, mergers and acquisitions, negative publicity, and legal problems must also be considered as part of the incident assessment process.

Next, we moved from the EIA to cover business risk assessment, which consists of a multistaged process of performing asset characterization and developing a risk/benefit (likelihood) analysis statement and risk level matrix. We discussed the risk assessment report and how it should be formatted for your organization. In order to gather necessary information for the assessment, it is necessary to perform a BIA, which requires you to begin by identifying key business processes and establishing requirements for business recovery. This information is usually gathered by creating a BIA questionnaire.

The information provided by the BIA questionnaire will allow you to gain better understanding of the impact of a given threat on your operation. We discussed the recommended BIA analysis report format and how to use the data gathered in the report to fine-tune your business priorities. Determining resource dependencies is a critical step in the process of developing an impact analysis. Once your data has been gathered, it is necessary to organize and tabulate the results in order to begin determining any impact on operations. The report must be based on a prioritization and classification of business functions in order to tell the user what is most important to cope with in an emergency. To do this, it is necessary to establish time frames for service interruption measurement and determine what the financial and operational impact may be on your organization.

The last part of this chapter covered the information security, IT and communications, considerations. We presented an overview of the OCTAVE® methodology and outlined some preventive and recovery measures for information security managers to use in your organization. We also talked about theft prevention for proprietary/intellectual property. Part of the process of determining impact on operations for IT systems requires you to specify IT/communications systems and dependencies, identify key IT, communications, and data systems, identify your key IT personnel and have emergency contact information readily available. This is also needed for key IT suppliers and maintenance engineers. It is also a good idea to periodically review your IT recovery procedures and ensure they are current with any changes that may have occurred in the organization. In this chapter, we have suggested some steps that will help you to determine the impact resulting from a disaster. The next chapter will go into greater detail on how to mitigate the effects of such events.

2.10 **Endnotes**

1. National Institute of Standards and Technology, *Special Publication 800-34: Contingency Planning Guide for Information Technology Systems.* June 2002.

2. National Drought Mitigation Center, University of Nebraska at Lincoln. Information retrieved from http://www.drought.unl.edu/plan/plan.htm on March 5, 2005.

3. IBid.

4. U.S. House of Representatives, H. R. 3210, 107th Cong., 1 November 2001. *Terrorism Risk Insurance Act of 2002.* http://thomas.loc.gov/cgi-bin/bdquery/ z?d107:HR03210:@@@L&summ2=m&.

5. http://www.fema.gov/library/prepandprev.shtm#terrorprev

6. Federal Emergency Management Agency, *FEMA 426: Reference Manual to Mitigate Potential Terrorist Attacks Against Buildings.* Washington, DC: U.S. Federal Emergency Management Agency, December 2003.

7. http://www.fema.gov/fima/rmsp.shtm#426.

8. URL reference is http://thomas.loc.gov/home/terrorleg.htm.

9. National Institute of Standards and Technology, *Special Publication 800-30: Risk Management Guide.* June 2001.

10. National Institute of Standards and Technology, *Special Publication 800-18: Guide for Developing Security Plans and Information Technology Systems.* December 1998.

3

Mitigation Strategies

All organizations should prepare for emergency situations. Part of this preparation process is a review of what is already in place, what needs to be put in place, who needs to be contacted when something happens, what they should do when contacted, and so on. Many organizations have a wide range of existing procedures for dealing with various types of unusual situations. These procedures may have been developed in response to a legal or regulatory requirement. This section will review what are considered the most pertinent procedures for mitigating a disaster situation. It is by no means an exhaustive list. The BCP should contain a brief summary of each of these procedures, including the issues that are relevant in the event of handling an emergency disaster situation. Risk mitigation is a systematic methodology used by senior management to reduce mission risk and can be achieved through any of the following risk mitigation options:

- **Risk Assumption.** This is accepting the potential risk and either continuing to operating the IT system or implementing controls to lower the risk to an acceptable level. Even if your procedures are aligned to your risk assumptions, if your plans are based on the previously available amount of required resources, it is more than likely that these requirements have increased. For example, renewal may not be an option for contracts at alternative sites that are effective for only a two-month period. After September 11, 2001, many businesses that recovered operations at commercial "hot sites" found their subscribed resources were insufficient for their actual needs.

- **Risk Avoidance.** This is the making an informed decision to not become involved in or otherwise avoid a risk situation by eliminating the risk cause and/or consequence. For example, you could forgo certain functions of the system, or shut down the system when risks are suspected or known.

- **Risk Limitation.** This is the selective application of appropriate techniques and management principles to reduce the likelihood of an occurrence, its consequences, or both, limiting the risk by implementing controls that minimize the adverse impact of a threat's exercising a vulnerability. For example, use supporting, preventive, detective controls as part of a business continuity plan or emergency response plans.

- **Risk Planning.** This is the management of risk through the development of a risk mitigation plan that prioritizes, implements, and maintains controls. Uncertainty in life is a certainty. Our lives are in a constant state of flux, family relations change, government constantly enacts new and often conflicting laws, and our financial situation is in a constant state of change. Notwithstanding the constant state of change we live in, we all plan for the future. In planning for the unexpected, five criteria are generally considered:

1.   Determine what unexpected events might occur. Many events are reasonably foreseeable, such as the death of a loved one, divorce, changes in the economy, financial reversal, and so forth.

2.   Determine what "unexpected" events are likely to occur. For example, if you are a stockbroker, syndicator, real estate developer, investment banker, physician, accountant, or attorney, there is a substantial likelihood that you will be named in a lawsuit. More than half of all marriages end in divorce (the other half end in death of one of the parties).

3.   Analyze the impact that unexpected events could have on your tentative plans. For example, a savings and loan, into which you put all of you money, may go broke; you can determine the effect on your plans and make contingencies (e.g., don't put more money in one financial institution than can be federally insured).

4.   In advance, plan alternatives in case an unexpected event occurs. This is also referred to as "don't put all your eggs in one basket."

5.   As part of the planning process, implement appropriate techniques or devices to deal with the unexpected.

Set forth below are some of the practical considerations that go into planning for the unexpected.

Each business person should consider implementing various actions and plans in order to be prepared to address the unforeseen, including: providing built-in adjustments to deal with economic fluctuations, especially in long-term contracts; making certain contracts conditional; negotiating for appropriate representations, warranties, conditions, and guarantees when entering into a deal; and providing for rescission rights, savings clauses, cancellation rights, and so forth.

When entering into contracts on behalf of corporate, partnership, or limited liability entities of which you own a major part, never give your personal guarantee, and insist on a clause in the agreement that limits the other party's damages to the assets of the corporation or partnership and that prevents the other party from piercing or ignoring the corporate/partnership veil. Planning for the unexpected requires long-range vision and is a never-ending process. You should review your personal and financial situation constantly to determine what the next "unexpected" event might be, and then begin planning for that event.

- **Acknowledgment and Research.** This is the acknowledgment, through research, that a vulnerability exists and the process of researching appropriate controls. This should be considered a temporary strategy, reserved for use during the implementation phase of the security rule, the implementation of a new information system, or when a completely new threat becomes known.

- **Risk Transference.** This is the shifting of responsibility or burden for loss to another party through legislation, contract, insurance, or other means to compensate for the loss. Risk transference can be done via contracts, hold-harmless agreements, being named as an Additional Insured, using subrogation waiver endorsements, and, of course, through the insurance process. Insurance must be measured on the basis of a cost, exposure, and benefit analysis. There are times when risk cannot be eliminated, reduced, or transferred. In such situations, it is of great value simply to know the nature and scope of that risk, and to plan methods to deal with it. Risk transference will generally be used in combination with other strategies. For example, risk transfer can also refer to shifting a physical risk, or part thereof, elsewhere.

3.1   Preventative Measures for Information Security Managers

The preventive measures for information security (or InfoSec) managers to implement as a part of the continuity planning are very important. They can be organized in terms of Virtual Private Networks (VPNs) and remote access, firewalls, encryption, intrusion detection and prevention systems, antivirus, anti-spyware, and anti-spam software, all of which will be discussed in the following paragraphs.

3.1.1   VPNs and Remote Access

Virtual private networks (VPNs) are "tunnels" between two endpoints that allow data to be securely transmitted between the nodes and, in many cases, an extension of a private network. A private network is one where all data paths are hidden from everyone except a limited group of people, generally the customers or employees of a company. In theory, the simplest way to create such a private network would be to isolate it entirely from the Internet. However, for a business with remote location needs, this is clearly not a practical solution. While it is technically possible to create a private network using frame relay, ATM, or some other leased-line solution, that solution could easily become cost-prohibitive. Also, that solution may not even provide the required degree of security needed for the organization's remote access users.

When using leased lines to establish a private network, another consideration to factor into the mix is what happens when (not if) the line goes down. This outage situation would cause all connected nodes in the private network to go "COMM OUT" until the leased line came back up. Clearly, this is not a practical solution either. What if we wanted to share resources on the private network with customers? That would not be possible over a physically separated or isolated network. A remote dial-up server may solve the problem, but then we would have to question the very concept of "virtual" in our virtual private network.

In today's environment, a VPN makes use of existing infrastructure, public or private. This may encompass the use of both LANs and WANs. The transfer of data over a public network is accomplished by using what is referred to as tunneling technology (further explained below) to encrypt data for secured transmission. The preferred definition of a VPN, as used in this text, is "a dedicated private network, based on use of existing public network infrastructure, incorporating both data encryption and tunneling technologies to provide secure data transport."

There are several good reasons why organizations choose to use VPNs. Data security is undoubtedly a prime consideration, but we must also understand the risks and corresponding trade-offs involved when using remote access technologies. For example, if a company can provide remote access to its employees, it is an assumed benefit that they will be able to access the network and be productive regardless of where they happen to be physically located when they connect to the VPN. The risk to providing such remote access is that if the data they are attempting to transmit or access is not secured in some fashion, it could become compromised through a variety of means. This may or may not be a devastating issue to that particular company, but each organization must make such determinations as a matter of deciding the level of risk they are willing to take for providing a remote access capability.

Most companies today choose to use a technology that fully supports data protection. This generally means that in order to gain access to the company network, a remote access user must first authenticate to the remote host server. Additionally, once an authenticated connection is established, the client and host machines jointly establish a shared secure channel (often referred to as establishing a tunnel) in which to communicate. The advantage of using this secure channel for communication is that all subsequent data packets transmitted and received are encrypted to minimize risk of data compromise.

The current VPN growth that has emerged in the industry in the last couple of years is mostly centered on IP-based networks, such as the Internet. One of the major problems of VPN technologies is that there are a wide variety of implementation styles and methods, which cause a lot of confusion when trying to develop a strategy for their use in a company. Currently, the following VPN implementations are in use:

- Router-to-router VPN-on-demand "tunnel" connections between sites
- Router-to-router VPN-on-demand multiprotocol "tunnel" connections between sites over an IP network
- Router-to-router VPN-on-demand encrypted session connections between sites

- Firewall-to-firewall VPN-on-demand "tunnel" connections between sites

- Client-to-firewall IP tunnel VPN facilities

- Client-to-server IP tunnel VPN facilities

- Client and server firewall implementation with full VPN capabilities

- Dedicated VPN box

- Nonsecure VPNs

A bewildering array of VPN choices and solutions is available to the customer, depending upon need and fiscal resources. With these implementations, however, the VPN must interoperate with existing protocol suites in the network environments that are used in companies. Nearly all companies use more than one protocol suite to transport network information. While many routers offer site-to-site VPN capability, many times the capability is limited to IP-only traffic or, if non-IP, it must be a routable protocol with a routing layer, and that layer must be implemented on the router itself. In sites where nonroutable protocols are used, bridging must be used, and it is not implemented as a VPN connection in most bridge/router combinations.

Tunneling is a technique that leverages an internetworked infrastructure (such as the Internet or a corporate WAN) to transfer data from one network over another network. The tunneling process consists of payload encapsulation, transmission, decoding of packet data, and routing to end point. The data (referred to as a payload) to be transmitted can be sent in packets that are built using another protocol. The data is wrapped with a header that provides routing information. Instead of sending a packet produced by the originator in its original form, a tunneling protocol encapsulates the packet with a new packet header (thus, wrapping the old header in the new header). The additional header provides routing information so the encapsulated payload can traverse the intermediate internetwork. The encapsulated packets are then routed between established tunnel endpoints over the internetwork.

The logical path the encapsulated packets travel through the internetwork is referred to as a tunnel. Once the encapsulated frames reach their destination on the internetwork, the packet is decoded into its original form and forwarded to its final destination. Tunneling technology has been around for some time. Current tunneling technologies include PPTP, L2TP, and IPSec.

Tunnels can be created in one of two ways: voluntary or compulsory. With voluntary tunnels, a user or client computer can issue a VPN request to configure and create a tunnel. In this case, the user's computer is a tunnel endpoint and acts as the tunnel client. For compulsory tunnels, a VPN-capable dial-up access server configures and automatically creates a tunnel. With a compulsory tunnel, the user's computer is not a tunnel endpoint. The dial-up access server, which sits between the user's computer and the tunnel server, is considered the tunnel endpoint and acts as the tunnel client.

When a VPN connection is created, several security features come into play. These features include authorization, authentication, encryption, and filtering. Any organization considering implementing a VPN must take each of these features into account during their planning process.

By logging in to corporate networks from less-protected home machines, employees make the entire corporate network more vulnerable to malicious hackers who attempt to propagate viruses and code through corporate VPNs. If use of remote access is to be selectively allowed, it needs to be restricted to secured desktops and only authorized users. The use of remote access by authorized corporate users from home desktops to a corporate network must be managed and controlled separately from the internal corporate network.

3.1.2   Firewalls

A firewall is a system designed to prevent unauthorized access to or from a private network. Firewalls can be implemented in both hardware and software, or a combination of both. Firewalls are frequently used to prevent unauthorized Internet users from accessing private networks connected to the Internet, especially intranets. All messages entering or leaving the intranet pass through the firewall, which examines each message and blocks those that do not meet the specified security criteria. There are several types of firewall techniques, and in practice, many firewalls use two or more of these techniques in concert:

- **Packet filter:** Looks at each packet entering or leaving the network and accepts or rejects it based on user-defined rules. Packet filtering is fairly effective and transparent to users, but it is difficult to configure. In addition, it is susceptible to IP spoofing.

- **Application gateway:** Applies security mechanisms to specific applications, such as FTP and telnet servers. This is very effective, but can impose performance degradation.

- **Circuit-level gateway:** Applies security mechanisms when a TCP or UDP connection is established. Once the connection has been made, packets can flow between the hosts without further checking.

- **Proxy server:** Intercepts all messages entering and leaving the network. The proxy server effectively hides the true network addresses.

3.1.3 Encryption

Although a firewall is considered a first line of defense in protecting private information, data can also be encrypted for greater security. Encryption is the translation of data into a secret code, and is the most effective way to achieve data security. To read an encrypted file, you must have access to a secret key or password that enables you to decrypt it. Unencrypted data is called plain text; encrypted data is referred to as cipher text. For cryptographic solutions, the longer the encryption keys are, the stronger they are. The strength of the crypto solution is measured in bit length. The bit length of the algorithm determines the amount of effort that is required to crack the system using a "brute force" attack, where computers are combined to calculate all the possible key permutations. Two basic cryptographic systems exist today: symmetric and asymmetric. Symmetric cryptography is commonly used to exchange large packets of data between two parties who know each other and use the same private key to access the data. Asymmetric systems are far more complex and require a pair of mathematically related keys. One key is a public version, the other a private version. This method is commonly used for transmitting more sensitive data. It is also used during the authentication process.

Many different encryption schemes are available today in the United States. Data Encryption Standard (DES) is more than 20 years old and has been thoroughly tested. It is considered a venerable benchmark encryption scheme. It uses a highly complex symmetric algorithm, but, even with that, it is considered less secure than more recent systems. Triple DES uses multiple passes of the original version to increase the key length and strengthen its level of security. While it is theoretically possible, an unbreakable algorithm has not been developed to date.

3.1.4 **Intrusion Detection and Prevention Systems**

Unauthorized traffic can be identified by network intrusion detection systems. Intrusion detection signatures can detect worms, blended threats, and hacking attempts on corporate systems and client machines. Network intrusion detection systems are used to detect malformed or suspicious packets as they travel through the network. Intrusion detection systems (IDSs) gather and analyze information from various areas within a computer or a network to identify possible security breaches, which include both intrusions (attacks from outside the organization) and misuse (attacks from within the organization). IDSs also utilize scanning to conduct a vulnerability assessment of the security of a computer system or network. The functionality of IDS includes:

- Monitoring and analyzing both user and system activities

- Analyzing system configurations and vulnerabilities

- Assessing system and file integrity

- Ability to recognize patterns typical of attacks

- Analysis of abnormal activity patterns

- Tracking user policy violations

Intrusion prevention systems (IPSs) are a preemptive approach to network security used to identify potential threats and respond to them swiftly. IPS is similar to IDS in that they both monitor network traffic. However, because an exploit may be carried out very quickly after the attacker gains access, IPSs also have the ability to take immediate action, based on a set of rules established by the network administrator.

3.1.5 **Antivirus, Anti-Spyware, and Anti-Spam Software**

Antivirus software is a class of computer program that attempts to identify, thwart, and eliminate computer viruses and other malware on your network, servers, or clients. It typically examines (scans) files for known viruses matching definitions in a virus dictionary and identifies suspicious behavior from any computer program that might indicate infection.

Anti-spyware is a program designed to detect and defeat spyware and adware. It scans your hard disk for spy programs and defeats them. Like antivirus programs, anti-spy programs need to be updated to scan for new spyware applications and, more importantly, to scan for changes in existing spyware applications. Spyware is software that covertly gathers user information through the user's Internet connection without his or her knowledge, usually for advertising purposes. Spyware applications are typically bundled as a hidden component of freeware or shareware programs that can be downloaded from the Internet; however, it should be noted that the majority of shareware and freeware applications do not come with spyware. Once installed, the spyware monitors user activity on the Internet and transmits that information in the background to someone else. Spyware can also gather information about e-mail addresses and even passwords and credit card numbers. Because spyware exists as independent executable programs, it has the ability to monitor keystrokes; scan files on the hard drive; snoop other applications, such as chat programs or word processors; install other spyware programs; read cookies; change the default home page on the Web browser; and consistently relay information back to the spyware author, who will either use the information for advertising/marketing purposes or sell it to another party. Spyware also steals from the user by using the computer's memory resources and by eating bandwidth as it sends information back to the spyware's home base via the user's Internet connection. Because spyware uses memory and system resources, the applications running in the background can lead to system crashes or general system instability.

Adware is considered a legitimate alternative offered to consumers who do not wish to pay for software. Programs, games, or utilities can be designed and distributed as freeware. Sometimes freeware blocks features and functions of the software until you pay to register it. Today, we have a growing number of software developers who offer their goods as "sponsored" freeware until you pay to register. Generally most or all features of the freeware are enabled, but you will view sponsored advertisements while the software is being used. The advertisements usually run in a small section of the software interface or as a box on your desktop. When you stop running the software, the ads should disappear. This allows consumers to try the software before they buy, and they always have the option of disabling the ads by purchasing a registration key. Some freeware applications that contain adware do track your surfing habits in order to serve ads related to you. When the adware becomes intrusive like this, it is categorized as spyware or spam, and it should be avoided for privacy and security reasons.

3.1.6 Theft Prevention for Proprietary/Intellectual Property

A tornado hits one section of your building. CDs, none of which were secured in locked safes, are strewn across the campus lawn and surrounding neighborhoods. Some of the CDs are from corporate HQ and contain HR files; others are from your R&D lab and contain the latest engineering drawings for your soon-to-be-released competitive product. Good Samaritans are everywhere on scene helping you sort through the debris. Are you sure all those helpers are good folks? Perhaps some of the helpers are employees from your competitor across the highway, helping themselves to your data so later they can sit in the parking lot and glean information from your facilities using that "lost" data to gain entry/access to your corporate information. Or maybe they are identity theft professionals, who targeted your company information shortly after hearing of your company's misfortune. Sound unreal? It is a nightmare *spy versus spy* scenario that is all too real to an information security manager.

3.2 Information Security Preventative Controls

Preventive controls should be documented in the contingency plan, and the personnel associated with the system should be trained on how and when to use the controls. These controls should be maintained in good condition to ensure their effectiveness in an emergency. In some cases, the outage impacts identified in the BIA can be mitigated or eliminated through preventive measures that deter, detect, and/or reduce impacts to the system. Where they are feasible and cost-effective, preventive methods are preferable to actions that may be necessary to recover the system after a disruption. There are a number of information security considerations and risks associated with BCP in regards to backing up data, restoring data, and archiving data. Some of the key areas of concerns result from restarting or revering your system, backing up data on portable computers, managing backup and recovery procedures, and archiving information.

3.2.1 Restarting or Recovering Your System

Restarting or recovering your system constitutes the facilities and techniques used to ensure that your computer processing restarts successfully after a voluntary or enforced close down. The unavailability of both your systems and data following an interruption to normal processing can have a negative impact on business operations and efficiency. You should ensure that your backup procedures enable an efficient restore to the most recent backup state, such as the end of the previous business day, for each of your key systems. It is also imperative that you safeguard the backup tapes or disks for such systems. Typically, this is done through an offsite storage facility. In many cases, critical business data are replicated or stored in a different region to ensure continuation or resumption of business in the case of a catastrophic disaster. You should also perform a restore on a periodic basis to ensure that these procedures continue to support a timely recovery, and modify your procedures if the results indicate it is necessary. Eliminate procedures that are too general, requiring *ad hoc* decisions that could cause problems, and ensure that the procedures consider the specific environment involved.

The corruption or loss of data following an interruption to normal processing can disrupt operations and delay business processing. You should always create backup files periodically throughout general working hours to enable a rapid recovery to an earlier version, if needed. It is also important to ensure that recovery from transaction processing systems disruptions is fully tested to verify that transactions cannot be lost.

3.2.2   Backing up Data on Portable Computers

Data of significant value held on a laptop computer may be lost, due to an internal system failure. It is important that data held on portable computing devices be backed up as a means to protect against loss. All computer systems, including portable computers and their associated data files, must have agreed backup and restore procedures for the data files. It is important to require and enforce the user of a portable computer to be personally responsible for backing up stored data and synchronizing it with the central system.

3.2.3   Managing Backup and Recovery Procedures

End-of-day backup files are critical in maintaining the ability to restore either the whole system or selected data files to a specified end-of-day position. The procedures used to initiate such a recovery must be clearly documented and tested, because the information security implications of an inappropriate or incorrect file restore are significant. If the restore procedures have not been tested, a partial or invalid restore can corrupt the entire system, which may partly or significantly have a negative effect on (and possibly terminate) business operations. Inadequate or nonexistent backup procedures may compromise an organization's business processes due to data being lost, unavailable, or compromised. Also, malicious modification of the daily backup sequence can result in a failure to safeguard all required data.

3.2.4 Offsite Storage of Backup Media and System Documentation

Offsite media storage is the only way to protect tangible data assets from disaster. By storing copies of important data at an offsite location, you minimize the fallout from unforeseen events at your primary data storage site. If your original data is compromised in any way, your file backup can be retrieved from the offsite tape storage facility. You will be up and running again within 24 hours. Many offsite media storage facilities offer at least two media storage options. One option is simple storage in a climate-controlled room. A second option is to store tape media in a fireproof safe. A fireproof safe is more expensive, but for truly critical data, it is the only way to go. Most offsite media storage companies use media pouches, which hold data as it is transported to and from the storage facility. A company inserts its tape media into the pouch and has it taken to (or picked up by) the storage facility. When the company fills a second pouch, that second pouch is sent to the storage facility, where it replaces the first pouch. The first pouch is then sent back to the company to be filled with new media. Any number of pouches can be used in a rotation system. Also, there is virtually no limit to how long each package can be saved. Some companies only store their most recent backups. Other companies store backups for five, ten or even thirty years! While storing for longer periods of time obviously costs more money, the peace of mind gained by knowing that all of your data is safe is well worth the cost.

3.2.5 Archiving Information

Archived information is information that is not required on a day-to-day basis but must be retained for a certain period and retrieved periodically but infrequently. Organizations reduce the overhead on storage and processing resources by removing this data from their day-to-day processing. However, weaknesses in the processes or methodology for long-term storage of data, such as the data being retained in a proprietary format that is no longer supported by your present systems, can result in a failure to restore the required data when it is needed.

3.2.6 **Archiving Electronic Files**

There are a couple of significant issues to consider when archiving electronic data files. Legacy documents may not be able to be located or retrieved due to inappropriate deletion or premature archiving. This can be as a result of an unsuitable or unenforced retention policy. Also, confidential data can be lost or stolen while stored offsite, and due diligence must be performed when choosing the vendor and method by which the data will be stored offsite.

3.2.7 **Recovery and Restoring of Data Files**

As discussed previously, saving data on a backup tape or disk should be a core element of your information security program. There are, however, a few security issues that should be addressed when managing the security of the backup process. It is possible for unauthorized parties that use similar backup software to access and restore your backup data. If the restored data are not on the designated backup tape or disk, this can result in confusion and potential loss when the data are restored. It is possible for data to be lost or overwritten if the restoration from the backup media is incorrect. There is also a procedural handling issue if the data are found to be corrupt after being located and restored.

BCP/DRP planning is meant to prepare for all plausible scenarios for the location of your company's facilities. If there is a credible risk of natural disaster, terrorist activity, effects of war, and so on in your area, then your proprietary/intellectual property and other sensitive or mission-critical data should be protected accordingly. In this case, if unsecured digital data are left on desks or other nonsecure areas in areas or times of high risk, then the data should be encrypted. Better yet, unattended sensitive media in high-risk areas should be stored in locked safes, when at all possible.

3.3 **Other Preventative Controls**

A wide variety of preventive controls are available, depending on your organization's unique type and configuration. Some common measures applicable to most organizations are listed below:

- Appropriately sized uninterruptible power supply (UPS) systems provide short-term backup power to all system components (including environmental and safety controls), and should be required for 24/7 operations. UPS systems provide continuous battery uptime for IT and communications equipment through relatively short power outages, and provide ride-through support for transfer to backup generators for long-term outages. UPS systems range from the most basic single-phase units installed in communication closets to sophisticated, scalable, redundant, three-phase, installations in large Internet data centers.

- Gasoline- or diesel-powered generators to provide long-term backup power. Effective power distribution is key to a highly available data center. Conditioning can be in the form of isolation and K-rated transformers (to address harmonic loads), surge suppression, and other protection features. Various techniques are used to provide redundant power feeds to create highly available systems for dual and single cord loads. Methods employed include stationary static switches, power distribution units (PDUs), transient voltage surge suppressors (TVSSs), automatic transfer switches (ATSs), rack-based transfer switches, and more. The nature of today's 24/7 business environments requires a continuous and reliable power supply. An emergency backup generator can provide you with a secondary power source when the primary power is interrupted. Backup generators can be fully automatic systems that monitor the incoming electricity and provide an extended secondary power source on loss of primary power. Backup generator power systems should be designed for your specific needs, considering the voltages and kilowatt requirements. Your backup generator system can be customized with larger fuel tanks for longer run times, bypass options on ATSs for easy maintenance, and sound attenuation enclosures for environmentally sensitive areas.

- Air-conditioning systems with adequate excess capacity to permit failure of certain components, such as a compressor, are required. IT environment equipment requires rigid environmental conditions for reliable operation. Precision air conditioning systems and rack-based air handling systems are specifically designed for the concentrated vertical heat loads of today's data centers. Data center/computer room air conditioners provide efficient heat removal, humidity control, greater airflow, better air filtration, greater flexibility and expandability, and numerous alarm and redundancy options. You should not jeopardize your data center by installing comfort cooling air conditioners. You must calculate the proper tonnage, top discharge, bottom discharge, ceiling-hung, floor-mounted, water-cooled, air-cooled or glycol-cooled system that fits your application. Today's high-density loads provide a unique situation in which the ability to provide increased power for a given load is curtailed only by the data center environment's ability to remove the heat from that load. In this case, specialized rack-based air distribution and heat removal strategies for power-dense enclosures and low static pressure access floor environments are used. Rack-based air distribution units work with an existing precision air conditioning system to deliver cool air to the equipment contained in a rack enclosure. These systems connect into the raised floor and pull supply air directly into the enclosure, thereby preventing the conditioned air from mixing with warmer room air before reaching the equipment. The rack air distribution unit helps to eliminate temperature differences between the top and bottom of the enclosure. It also prevents hot exhaust air from circulating to the inlet of the enclosure. It is generally recommended that a rack air distribution unit for rack enclosures with loads greater than 1.5 kW should be able to provide airflow for loads up to 3.0 kW. Additionally, it is recommended for raised floor environments, where underfloor air distribution is inadequate for adjacent IT loads. An access floor is actually a floor raised above a floor. Its purpose is to create a controlled area for wire management and air distribution. In today's computer room environment, many pieces of electrical equipment are being used. Each requires various power cords and data connectivity. You should segment the space within the access floor to create zones where cords, cables and mechanical piping can be routed, while still maintaining the necessary clearance to provide adequate air flow through perforated tiles and/or vents placed throughout the access floor. An access floor is typically constructed of 24" square and 1 7/16" thick panels of various materials that provide different weight-loading characteristics. The floor panels can be rearranged at any time to suit your data center needs.

- Fire suppression and control systems are used in data centers, Network Operations Center (NOCs), server farms, and computer rooms. Once installed, an automatic computer room fire suppression system is on guard 24 hours a day to protect your computer data and equipment. Fire protection and detection is an absolute necessity for your business's survival. In the event of a fire, heat and smoke can at best only damage delicate electronic equipment and at worst take out the building. A fire protection strategy has two parts: an FM-200 system that protects the data center equipment, and a "wet" or "preaction" sprinkler system that is used to save the building. You should always evaluate code and insurance requirements to determine the best technique for a given project. In a typical system, the extinguishing agent is stored in cylinders or spheres. It is delivered to distribution nozzles through a system piping network. Critical to the functioning of the system is the fire detection and control network. Typically, smoke detectors sense the presence of fire in the protected facility. The detection and control panel then sounds an alarm, shuts down air handlers, disconnects power from the protected equipment, and then releases the extinguishing agent into the protected area. FM-200 is a fire suppression agent that is quick, clean, and effective. It is people- and planet-safe, given that it has a zero ozone-depleting potential. FM-200 can be dispensed into a room within 10 seconds or less and leaves no particulates or oily residue behind.

In the late 1980s, Halon fire extinguishers were exceedingly popular for large corporate computer rooms. Halon is a chemical that works by "asphyxiating" the fire's chemical reaction. Unlike water, Halon does not conduct electricity and leaves no residue, so it will not damage expensive computer systems. Unfortunately, Halon may also asphyxiate humans in the area. For this reason, all automatic Halon systems have loud alarms that sound before the Halon is discharged. After Halon is released into the environment, it slowly diffuses into the stratosphere, where it acts as a potent greenhouse gas and contributes to the destruction of the ozone layer. Halon is therefore being phased out and replaced with systems that are based on carbon dioxide (CO_2), which still asphyxiates fires (and possibly humans), but which does not cause as much environmental degradation.

Individual fire extinguishers are also important. You can increase the chances that your computer will survive a fire by making sure that there is good fire-extinguishing equipment nearby. Make sure that you have a handheld fire extinguisher by the doorway of your computer room. Train your computer operators in the proper use of the fire extinguisher. Repeat the training at least once a year. One good way to do this is to have your employees practice with extinguishers that need to be recharged (usually once every year or two). Check the recharge state of each extinguisher every month. Extinguishers with gauges will show if they need recharging. All extinguishers should be recharged and examined by a professional on a periodic basis (sometimes those gauges stick in the "full" position!).

If you have a Halon or CO_2 system, make sure everyone who enters the computer room knows what to do when the alarm sounds.

Post warning signs in appropriate places. If you have an automatic fire-alarm system, make sure you can override it in the event of a false alarm. Ensure that there is telephone access for the operators and users who may discover a fire or a false alarm.

- Good smoke detectors and fire extinguishers are crucial. Gas (such as FM200) and water systems are commonly used for fire suppression. Smoke detectors and temperature sensors should be located throughout the data center so conditions can be monitored and controlled in zones. Make sure the fire suppression system can be started and stopped manually. Computers are notoriously bad at surviving fires. If the flames don't cause your system's case and circuit boards to ignite, the heat might melt your hard drive and all the solder holding the electronic components in place. Your computer might even survive the fire, only to be destroyed by the water used to fight the flames.

- Water sensors in the computer room ceiling and floor can help protect valuable equipment. Plastic tarps may be unrolled over IT equipment to protect it from water damage. Many modern computers will not be damaged by automatic sprinkler systems, provided the computer's power is turned off before the water starts to flow (although disks, tapes, and printouts out in the open may suffer). Consequently, you should have your computer's power automatically cut if the water sprinkler triggers. Be sure the computer has completely dried out before the power is restored. If your water has a very high mineral content, you may find it necessary to have the computer's circuit boards professionally cleaned before attempting to power up. Remember, getting sensitive electronics wet is never a good idea.

- A subfloor cabling and water detection system helps detect moisture below the floor. Moisture can damage subfloor wiring or equipment and cause costly downtime. A subfloor water detection system can provide immediate warning. Alarms can be provided via various audible, visual, in-band and out-of-band methods.

- Heat-resistant and waterproof containers are needed for backup media and vital nonelectronic records. If the backup media goes bad, your data is lost forever. A fireproof media or record cabinet should be used when storing backup media onsite. A media and record cabinet should also provide protection from heat, dust and humidity.

- Emergency master system shutdown switches help protect equipment. Although emergency shutdown switches are critical to BCP, because they cut power instantly when required in an emergency, it should be remembered the machines haven't been shut down properly, and it will most likely take more than an hour to get everything back online.

3.4   Summary of Existing Emergency Procedures

Emergency summaries include things such as emergency evacuation procedures, fire regulations and procedures, health and safety procedures, approved procedures for dealing with hazardous materials, and ways to respond to suspected gas leaks, electrical hazards, or radiation. Many organizations have a wide range of existing procedures for dealing with various types of unusual situations. These procedures may have been developed in response to a legal or regulatory requirement.

The BCP should contain a brief summary of each of these procedures, including the issues that are relevant in the event of handling an emergency disaster situation. These include emergency evacuation procedures, fire regulations and procedures, and health and safety procedures, together with approved procedures for dealing with hazardous materials, suspected gas leaks, electrical hazards, or radiation. The summary should note the location of the detailed procedures, and consideration should be given to including these detailed procedures as an appendix to the BCP, if considered appropriate. Information should also be included on the frequency of testing and the number of trained staff capable of carrying out the procedures.

3.5   Key Personnel for Handling Emergency Procedures

This section of the BCP should include information on all of the key personnel responsible for handling emergency procedures. Your employees are your most important and valuable asset. These people should be familiar with the implementation of emergency procedures and they should be properly trained. A list of key contacts will allow those at the scene of the emergency to call the properly trained persons to respond. In any emergency, in addition to its systems recoveries, the organization relies on its employees to recover normal business operations in the minimum amount of time. You will also rely on your main suppliers of critical goods and services to continue to support recovery of your business operations through to normal operating mode. A well-organized and structured approach will avoid the unexpected crisis deteriorating into chaos. This section of the

BCP will contain information on who should be contacted in the event of an emergency, and how to contact keys suppliers, key staff, and other employees. It should, at a minimum, contain documentation, such as the following:

- Functional Organization Chart
- Appointment Letters for Key Personnel
- Key Personnel and Emergency Contact Information
- Key Suppliers and Vendors, and Emergency Contact Information
- Manpower Recovery Strategies
- Disaster Recovery Team Constitution Instructions
- Business Recovery Team Mobilization Instructions

3.5.1 Functional Organization Chart

The BCP should contain information on the functional structure of the organization. The functional organization chart should include the names of all key managers and staff. This information is needed to identify responsibilities and dependencies, which will be useful in the early stages of the emergency. It is important to periodically update this chart, as organizational change is a fact of life we all must contend with—people enter and leave the company, and they move around; and their positions within the organization can frequently change. Updated organization charts are a necessity in an emergency, and it is critical to keep them current.

3.5.2 Appointment Letters for Key Personnel

In addition to the BCP project team, each functional area within your organization should appoint a BCP project coordinator and a deputy coordinator. These folks are responsible for working with the BCP project team members and providing input to the BCP process. They will coordinate their own functional unit's preparation of detailed backup and recovery procedures and manage the BCP testing and training activities. It is likely that the BCP project coordinator and deputy BCP project coordinator for each unit will be considered for nomination to the business recovery team. This section of the BCP will list each functional area and also the name, position, and contact number of the nominated project coordinator and deputy for each area.

For a project of this significance and complexity to be successful, a well-qualified project manager should be appointed. The project manager should possess good leadership qualities, a good understanding of business processes and business management, solid experience with IT and information security management, and strong project management capabilities. If the organization has an information security officer, that person may be an ideal candidate for the role. A deputy project manager should also be appointed. The deputy would be able to take over, as necessary, in the absence of the project manager. He or she could also provide support and perform some of the necessary duties, tasks, and functions. The management of day-to-day functions related to creating business continuity plans and procedures and disaster recovery operations should be the responsibility of the BCP project team. This would also include responsibility for interfacing with senior management and auditors, while also implementing and supporting the following services:

- **Risk Management**—Identify and categorize outage exposures that could cause a business interruption, then obtain insurance and vendor agreements to safeguard against a disaster event. Ensure business and regulatory requirements are known and adhered to, and ensure implemented recovery procedures and contracts are cost-justifiable.

- **Contingency Planning**—Identify potential business interruptions, develop safeguards against these interruptions, and implement recovery procedures in the event of a business interruption.

- **Disaster Recovery**—Safeguard data processing operations by identifying potential problem areas and single points of failure that may result in interruptions. Develop and implement data sensitivity, library management, backup and recovery, and disaster recovery plans and procedures.

- **Business Recovery**—Develop safeguards and business recovery plans and procedures governing the remote business offices and operations associated with the organization. Ensure that corporate asset protection procedures cover critical business resources located at business offices.

3.5.3 Key Personnel and Emergency Contact Information

When an emergency occurs, it is critical to have access to all key personnel for the functional areas and systems affected by the crisis. This information should be made available to BCP recovery teams and it should be kept up-to-date. This section of the BCP should contain a list of key personnel, positions, functional areas, and procedures for systems they are responsible for maintaining. This section normally includes the business, home, and emergency contact information for key staff members.

3.5.4 Key Suppliers and Vendors, and Emergency Contact Information

This section of the BCP should include a list of key suppliers, the critical goods and/or services they are supplying, their normal contact information, and their emergency contact information. Consideration should also be given to a further list of suppliers who would be able to provide critical goods and services in the event of failure to deliver from one of your identified key suppliers. Do not forget to include suppliers of services needed only in an emergency, and also include the organizations that provide maintenance support services for equipment and systems.

Depending upon the nature of the disaster, it is quite possible that your organization's key suppliers and vendors of critical goods or services could also be affected. This can affect backup and recovery arrangements if your organization is dependent upon a third-party vendor or supplier for such services. Ensure that your key suppliers have an effective BCP for dealing with such emergencies. Request information from them to verify that they have this contingency accounted for in their BCP.

3.5.5 Manpower Recovery Strategies

A key component in any BCP is the development of a manpower recovery strategy. It is critical for a plan to account for both the needs of the business and the needs of the staff and their families (where affected). This aspect of plan development must be handled with sensitivity. An up-to-date staff list must be available, and should include normal and emergency contact details for all employees. At the initial stage of a disaster recovery process, there should be a procedure to account for all members of the organization and ensure their safety. If the disaster happens outside of normal working hours the BCP team should be contacted to inform them of the event and to issue instructions to each member on how to keep in touch with events during the recovery process. Options here may include prerecorded messages left on a special telephone number. For disasters that affect a whole city or area, family circumstances may dictate the need for employees to deal with home problems before being available to deal with work-related issues. It may be necessary to consider line-of-succession plans for key staff, in case any key individual is unavailable. It is also necessary to identify key personnel needed to manage or participate in the actual recovery operation.

3.5.6 Establishing the Disaster Recovery Team

It is necessary to establish a disaster recovery team to handle the initial emergency situation. The disaster recovery team should be made up of a group of specialists who have previously been nominated as being able to assist in dealing with the initial emergency. These will not necessarily be the same persons who are members of the business recovery team. During the initial emergency, the following personnel may need to be involved, depending upon the circumstances:

- Key members of senior management
- Personnel manager
- Premises of facilities manager
- Fire and safety officer
- Premises maintenance staff
- IT technicians
- Communication technicians
- Security staff
- Information security officer

The disaster recovery team (DRT) is responsible for working with the emergency services to clear the initial emergency crisis situation so that the business recovery team can start their activities. The DRT itself will only be able to start its own recovery activities once the emergency services have given permission for these duties to commence. During the initial emergency, the DRT will normally be available to provide assistance to emergency services, as appropriate. The configuration of the DRT will depend upon the type and severity level of the emergency.

Members of the DRT should be on-call and should ensure their contact details are known to emergency services. All members of the DRT should maintain an up-to-date copy of the BCP in a secure location offsite. Each member of the DRT should also be issued special equipment such as flashlights, hard hats, gloves, overalls, hand-held dictaphones, walkie-talkies, and mobile phones to use in such emergencies.

3.5.7   Business Recovery Team Mobilization Instructions

We recommend that you establish a dedicated business recovery team (BRT) consisting of specialists and operations staff tasked with implementing recovery procedures when a serious emergency happens. The BRT should be led by a senior member of the organization's management. In the event of a serious emergency, the BRT leader is responsible for taking charge of the process and ensuring the organization returns to normal operations as early as possible. The BRT will consist of senior representatives from the main business and support units and is supported by nominated task forces for each recovery process, as appropriate. Each member of the BRT should keep an up-to-date copy of the BCP in a secure offsite location and should be fully familiar with its contents.

3.5.8   Constituting a Recovery Team

Recovery teams should be developed specific to the contingency planning needs of each business functional area. Team development depends on the size and complexity of the tasks that need to be accomplished for planning and recovery. The following functional areas need to be considered when building teams to deal with the immediate tasks at hand:

- Administration
- Business Function Recovery
- Command Center
- Damage Assessment
- Emergency Management
- Emergency Purchasing
- Equipment Installation
- Executive Management
- Facilities Preparation

- Finance
- Information Services
- Legal
- Physical Security
- Public Relations

A sample recovery checklist (originally published by the Texas Department of Information Resources) [1] can be found in Appendix B. The following sections will describe each of these areas in further detail and provide reasons why it is important that each be a part of your plan.

- **Administration**—This team reports to the command center to support the emergency management team and the business recovery coordinators and provides administrative support services, including travel and lodging, petty cash disbursement, notifications to customers, and preparation of all reports for the recovery operation. Risk administration is a supporting tool for organizations that run a large number of complex projects. Typically, these organizations have a project management office or some other monitoring structure. Risk administration provides a workspace and tools for the ongoing evaluation of projects in a secure, restricted area. Risk administrators can evaluate overall project risk and log specific risks that could be critical. Risks include concerns with the project manager, customer, or political issues that could affect the project. This information can be summarized to give an organization's management key information. Key benefits include evaluation of project, allowing key management to have visibility to risk information, and providing capabilities to perform project reviews.

- **Business Function Recovery**—This team responds to and manages any serious interruption to specific business function operations; it develops recovery strategies and procedures based on a BIA. Once the business recovery team (BRT) is mobilized, the first task is to assess the extent of the damage and its impact on the business process. This activity must be focused on the business impact, as opposed to damage assessment carried out by the DRT, which is mainly focused on the impact on people and the physical infrastructure. The BRT reviews the effect of the disaster by examining each area of the business that has been affected and assessing the impact on the various key business processes. This section of the BCP should contain a list of the areas of the business affected by the disaster and the actual business processes affected. Cross-dependencies between affected processes and other processes should be listed. For each affected business process, there should be a preliminary estimate of the recovery time involved with restoring normal operations. A damage assessment form for use by the BRT should be included in the BCP.

- **Command Center**—The command center team activates the facility to be used for assembling the emergency management team, help desk team, administration team, and the business recovery coordinators when a disaster has occurred. They are also responsible for the initial distribution of supplies, forms, and offsite boxes stored at the warehouse. This team is made up of warehouse and facilities personnel. Command post operations personnel should be familiar with incident command systems; the ways that a corporate Emergency Operations Center (EOC) can interface with appropriate public sector agencies; information flow techniques; command post design and layout; documentation and accountability; and communications, including effective briefing skills.

- **Damage Assessment**—This recovery team assesses the damage of the disabled facility and its contents, conducting both preliminary (immediately after an event) and comprehensive assessments. Activities are coordinated with the business recovery coordinator, IS recovery coordinator, emergency management, and facility preparation team. Members of this team usually include building engineers, data services and risk management personnel, and any related vendors or technical experts. Hazardous materials (hazmat) teams are allowed in facilities first when hazardous materials are involved. Damage assessment teams must wait until access has been granted to the damaged facility. During the damage assessment phase, the management team will identify specifically who and what has been affected by the disaster. The team leaders will evaluate the event and determine what recovery teams are required to respond to the situation. The decision to activate the disaster recovery plan for the affected areas may be made at this point or after notification and review with the executive team. If, after the assessment, it is determined that activation of the recovery plan is required, notification to the executive team is made.

- **Emergency Management**—The emergency management team provides overall management to all recovery teams; authorizes the disaster declaration; manages business recovery functions for all operating business units; provides guidance for all restoration activities; makes agency funding and expenditure arrangements; and provides public relations information. These individuals report directly to the command center and are responsible for overseeing the recovery and restoration process being executed by the emergency response teams. They are responsible for communicating the recovery status to the executive management team and making the necessary management decisions to support the recovery efforts. The emergency management team leader has overall responsibility for the recovery team and communications with the executive management team. The objectives and the functions of the emergency management team are to make a preliminary assessment of the damage and notify senior management on current status, impact to business, and plan of action. They will declare the situation as a disaster if necessary and initiate the plan during the emergency situation. Next, they will need to organize and control the Command Center as a central point of control of the recovery efforts. They must also organize and provide administrative support to the recovery effort and administer and direct the problem management function.

- **Emergency Purchasing**—This team coordinates the replacement (purchase and/or lease) of all damaged equipment at the disabled facility as well as the purchase of equipment required for alternate operations. They also coordinate the delivery and installation of such equipment at the alternate facility. This team handles the procurement for all information resources, general office needs, and facilities requirements. The team may also request a suspension of purchasing rules and regulations to facilitate recovery. The recovery process relies heavily upon vendors to quickly provide replacements for resources that cannot be salvaged. This team will rely upon emergency procurement procedures documented in this plan and approved by the purchasing office to quickly place orders for equipment, supplies, software, and any other needs.

- **Equipment Installation**—This team controls the installation of all terminals, PCs, and printers at the alternate site. Personnel for this team are primarily from PC/LAN and telecommunications support areas. This team interfaces with all business units and works directly with the emergency purchasing and facilities preparation teams. This team will also assist in contracting with outside parties for work to be done during the recovery process. Team members should be liberal in their estimate of the time required to repair or replace a damaged resource. Take into consideration cases where one repair cannot begin until another step is completed. Estimates of repair time should include ordering, shipping, installation, and testing time.

- **Executive Management**—The fundamental responsibility for business continuity planning and disaster recovery (BCP/DR) lies with the corporate executives. Vendors, contractors, and staff all play important roles to ensure continuity of operations, but it is essential that BCP/DR be regarded as a central business process. Critical business processes, along with underlying systems, environments, facilities, people, and processes must have availability requirements and business value well defined by executive management. A clearly articulated and managed vision will help to overcome coordination, technology, or vendor bias and cost justification challenges. The organization's executive management communicates support of the business recovery process by issuing a formal policy statement; periodically reviewing the recovery assumptions, potential loss assumptions, strategic considerations, and definitions of resumption priorities. Executive management ensures that adequate resources are devoted to the project by approving recovery strategies, possible alternatives, funding, and ongoing maintenance.

- **Facilities Preparation**—The facilities preparation team coordinates and directs all activities necessary to restore company facilities, build new facilities, and/or lease a replacement building. The team reviews business unit requests for office space; provides alternate site facilities to continue critical business functions; and participates in damage assessment of the affected facility. This team conducts a complete inventory of the components of each of the computer and network systems and their associated software, all of which must be restored after a disaster. The inevitable changes that occur in the systems over time require the plan be periodically updated to reflect the most current configuration. Where possible, agreements are made with vendors to supply replacements on an emergency basis. To avoid problems and delays in the recovery, every attempt should be made to replicate the current system configuration. However, there will likely be cases where components are not available or the delivery time frame is unacceptably long. The recovery management team will have the expertise and resources to work through these problems as they are recognized. Although some changes to the procedures documented in the plan may be required, using different models of equipment or equipment from a different vendor may be suitable to expediting the recovery process.

The preparation of the designated cold site for the recovery of primary computing and network facilities after a disaster has occurred is another function of this team for large organizations. This same team may also include the appropriate personnel to survey the disaster scene and estimate the amount of time required to put the facility (in this case, the building and utilities) back into working order. A decision is then made whether to use the cold site, a location some distance away from the scene of the disaster where computing and networking capabilities can be temporarily restored until the primary site is ready. Work begins almost immediately at repairing or rebuilding the primary site. The repair and rebuilding process may take months, the details of which are beyond the scope of this book. The following hot site approach is probably the most expensive option for being prepared for a disaster, and is typically most appropriate for very large organizations: a separate computer facility, possibly even located in a different area, can be built, complete with computers and other facilities ready to cut in on a moment's notice in the event the primary facility goes offline. The two facilities must be joined by high-speed communications lines so that users at the primary site can continue to access the computers from their offices.

- **Finance**—The finance group oversees proper authorization and support of expenses during emergency procurement. This group identifies how finance issues are handled during the recovery, such as procedures for ordering equipment or supplies, expense reports, identification of the cost center for recovery expenses, and so forth. BCP planning must address the establishment of a cost center to be used for all travel, lodging, meals, equipment, cash advances or any other type of expense related to the recovery effort. The cost center is only effective in a declared disaster. It is imperative that this cost center be used so that all expenses can be tracked for insurance purposes. Equipment purchases will require the generation of requests for items like PCs, fax machines, modems, office supplies, PC software, and so forth. Purchases may be made directly by recovery team members using a corporate credit card or through a direct billing arrangement with the vendors. Existing vendor relationships should be used wherever feasible to facilitate billing and payment for services. For expense reports, we recommend using the normal procedures for submitting expense reports during the recovery effort. All disaster-related expenses should reference the designated disaster-related cost center. Every effort should be made to reimburse employees for out-of-pocket expenses as expeditiously as possible. The organization may also need to provide cash advances to employees after a disaster.

- **Information Services**—The IS team maps the recovery of the information resources (mainframe computer and associated services, telecommunications and connectivity, LANs, WANs, and PCs) for business function recovery at an alternate site. The organization may have a central computing center and/or distributed systems, which would dictate the size, complexity, and areas of responsibility of the teams. The basic responsibilities include the following:

  - *Applications*—restores and supports application systems at the recovery center and defines data files retention periods for offsite storage.
  - *Database Administration*—restores all critical databases and evaluates their integrity; closely coordinates file synchronization and balancing conditions with the applications team prior to resuming production processing.
  - *Data Security*—maintains data security of the electronic records and files throughout the recovery operations. Data security entails system access via passwords. The team is functional throughout the entire recovery effort.
  - *IS Recovery Coordinator*—coordinates all activities of the recovery teams for the agency's central computing center and works closely with the business recovery coordinator and the other teams; depending on the size of the organization, this function may also be the business recovery coordinator.
  - *Help Desk*—processes all end-user inquiries and requests concerning the recovered computer systems during the recovery effort.
  - *Mainframe Distribution*—controls all printed output, including output created by outside vendors. This team interfaces with all business recovery teams and the operations team.
  - *Network*—restores both voice and data critical circuits and maintains a backup telecommunications network. The team interfaces closely with business recovery, systems software, operations, and facility preparation teams.
  - *Operations*—supports restoration of the mainframe utilities, critical applications and databases, and input/output (I/O) controls; also schedules all production applications. Most team members are staff from central computer operations.

- *Offsite Storage*—retrieves all required electronic media from the offsite storage location and transports it to the recovery center. Reestablishes or maintains an alternate offsite storage location for rotation of electronic vital records throughout the recovery effort.

- *System Software*—restores the operating system and all subsystems at the alternate recovery center. The team also prepares the operating system configuration to be used in the alternate site and restored primary home site.

- **Legal**—The legal team ensures that legal issues or procedures related to potential agency liabilities are addressed in the plan. Despite the widespread reporting of disasters and their effects, many companies, corporate directors, and officers remain apathetic toward implementing a disaster recovery plan. Companies are generally unwilling to commit the finances and resources to implement a plan unless forced to do so. However, implementing a disaster recovery plan is a strategic, moral, and legal obligation to one's company. If the billions of dollars spent on technology annually to maintain a competitive edge are an indication of how reliant our society is on technology, then failing to implement a disaster recovery plan is an indication of corporate negligence. Standards of care and due diligence are required of all corporations, public or private. Not having a disaster recovery plan violates that fiduciary standard of care. The legal issues involved in corporate contingency planning are some of the most misunderstood and confusing aspects of the entire process of creating a disaster recovery plan. Disaster recovery planners are not expected to be lawyers; however, they are encumbered with the responsibility of understanding the minutiae and vagueness of existing regulatory guidelines and the legal consequences of their company's failure to implement an effective disaster recovery plan. Although no specific laws state categorically that you must have a disaster recovery plan, there is a body of legal precedents that can be used to hold companies and individuals responsible to those who are affected by a company's inability to cope and/or recover from a disaster (see Chapter 8).

- **Physical Security**—This recovery team provides physical security for all personnel, the buildings, and all alternate sites. When dealing with security in today's technological world, physical security is often overlooked. Good physical security is critical. There is little point in securing your networks and IT systems if a member of the public can walk off the street into your data center, or if vandals attack and damage critical equipment, causing a lengthy outage. The most advanced firewalls and network perimeters are worthless if your critical information assets are physically carried out the door. A critical and often overlooked aspect of information security is the physical security of your data center and facilities. Physical security is assessed from the physical location of critical information assets to the outside world. Assessments can be made of existing sites or sites under consideration for purchase/lease, and the physical security team can assist at the design stage of new construction.

- **Public Relations**—The public relations team provides accurate, essential, and timely information to employees, employees' families, the media, and customers about what has happened and how the recovery plan is working. This team ensures that the appropriate spokesperson addresses environmental, health, and safety issues. This part of the plan recognizes and acknowledges the importance of providing the general public and the media with pertinent information as rapidly as possible in case of an emergency/disaster. Major events create significant media interest that will bring reporters, photographers, and camera crews to an incident. External sources are interested in major operations, devastation, and high-impact and human-interest events. A public relations function should provide for the effective collection, monitoring, management, and dissemination of accurate, useful, and timely information to media outlets during emergencies/disasters. This functionality is used for both routine and emergency conditions to effectively respond to media inquiries and public interests. In the case of an emergency, the public relations function will maintain contact with the media before, during, and after an event. It is important to keep the media informed of general progress of associated events. Efforts should be made to report positive information regarding emergency responses to reassure the public that the situation is being dealt with, using appropriate resources. Information and education efforts will rely on the cooperation of commercial media organizations, including both electronic news-gathering and print sources.

3.5.8.1   Team Leaders

A team leader from each business unit is assigned to be responsible for coordinating all team planning, testing, and recovery activities. Ideally, team leaders are members of first-line management or project leaders with strong leadership and organization skills; they should be detail-oriented and have a basic knowledge of the business unit's functions. They are responsible for all liaison activities between the agency's recovery coordina-tors and other team leaders.

3.5.8.2 Team Members

The skills and abilities of the combined team members must cover a wide range of responsibilities, many of which are dictated by the business func-tion(s). Ideally, team members are supervisors who can effectively invoke a business unit's recovery process in the event of a disaster. Team members are responsible for researching their respective parts of the plan and for meeting deadlines. It is recommended that one team member serve as a scribe to cre-ate the plan documentation. If the plan is executed, the scribe maintains a log of recovery activities and expenses. Also, one team member should be responsible for maintaining any offsite storage.

3.6 External Emergency Services

Your DRP and BCP will rely principally on key members of management and staff, who will provide the technical and management skills necessary to achieve a smooth business recovery process. These handpicked, key members of management or staff are responsible for the implementation of the BCP in the event of an emergency. However, in the case of most disasters, your employees and staff will need to rely on the help of outside agencies for fire, police, and medical assistance. The September 11, 2001 attack on the World Trade Center in New York City tested the contin-gency plans of American businesses and NYC emergency services to an unanticipated degree.

Companies that had business continuity plans and contracts in place with vendors of recovery services were able to continue business at alternate sites with minimum downtime and minimum loss of data, and the alternate facilities provided by the vendors were not overcrowded even in this largest of disasters. Unfortunately, the massive loss of life and its dramatic impact on coworkers, business processes, and communities was not anticipated.

After the events of September 11, 2001, organizations throughout the world started to return to business as usual. They undertook the very neces-sary review and revision of their business continuity plans and contracts. In the aftermath of events like natural disasters, terrorism, and equipment breakdown, businesses have recognized more than ever the need for an organization to be prepared. Companies are striving to meet the demand for continuous service. With the growth of ecommerce and other factors driving system availability expectations toward a 24×7×365 standard, the average organization's requirement for recovery time from a major system outage now ranges between two and twenty-four hours. This requirement is pushed by the expectations an organization faces on all sides:

- Customers expect supplies and services to continue—or to resume rapidly—in all situations.

- Shareholders expect management control to remain operational through any crisis.

- Employees expect both their lives and livelihoods to be protected.

- Suppliers expect their revenue streams to continue.

- Regulatory agencies expect their requirements to be met, regardless of circumstances.

- Insurance companies expect due care to be exercised.

Business survival necessitates planning for every type of business disruption, including the following:

- Natural disasters

- Hardware and communications failures

- Internal or external sabotage or acts of terrorism

- The failures of supply chain and sales affiliates

While such disruptions cannot be predicted, they can wreak havoc upon the business, with results ranging from insured losses of replaceable tangibles, to uninsurable capital losses, to customer dissatisfaction and possible desertion, to complete insolvency. Some business disruptions, such as a hurricane, may give advance warning. Others, such as terrorism, flash floods, fire, and so forth, can strike without notice. In nearly every event, it is necessary to have contact information for all external services readily available to the recovery team members and posted throughout the organization so the people who survive such catastrophes can easily find the information they need. Remember, in many instances, people left on the ground after a disaster are in shock and may not be thinking clearly. An emergency contact list, such as the one shown in Figure 3.1, is essential.

Figure 3.1
*Emergency 911
contact list.*

Emergency Service	First Contact	Report	Second Contact
Police	911	Location of incident by Bldg, Floor, Section	123.123.1234 - Corporate Crime Prevention Office (24 hour number)
Fire	911	Location of incident by Bldg, Floor, Section	123.123.1232 - Corporate Fire Safety Office (24 hour number)
Utility outage	Water, Gas or Energy Services Water: 123.333.4444 Gas: 123.333.5555 Power: 123.333.6666	Type and kind of outage, location of incident by Bldg, Floor, and Section	123.123.1233 - Bldg Maintenance Office (24 hour number)

3.7   Premises Issues

This section of the BCP should include contingency plans for designating who is given responsibility and authority for building repair decisions, what backup power arrangements have been made, and so forth. In a situation where building repairs need to be made, there should be a list of contractors for each type of building process that may be necessary. For example, for damage to walls and roof, you may need to contact masonry and roofing contractors. Appendix C of this book is a physical facility questionnaire that is useful in developing mitigation strategies for this section of the plan. In the event that the emergency situation affects the organization's premises, it is necessary to have information at hand regarding the authority levels (and responsibility) of individuals involved in the emergency recovery procedures, which would enable them to effect repairs immediately. If the premises are leasehold, the information on the responsibilities of the organization to make emergency repairs will normally be contained in the lease documentation. If the premises are freehold, then the organization will not normally have to seek approval from outside parties before making emergency repairs. The team charged with restoring the premises to normal working conditions will need to understand their levels of authority for commissioning works from outside contractors. Very often, in an actual emergency situation, it is difficult to obtain approvals urgently. For this reason, the BCP should contain information on the authority levels available and how further approvals may be obtained in the event of such emergencies occurring.

3.8   Chapter Summary

In this chapter, we took a look at various mitigation strategies that you can employ in your organization. We started by discussing preventative measures that information security managers can take to protect the assets they are responsible for managing, such as VPNs and remote access devices, firewalls, use of encryption, intrusion detection and prevention systems, and so on. We discussed the need to install and maintain antivirus, anti-spyware, and anti-spam software. Preventing the theft of corporate proprietary information and intellectual property information has become an issue that information security managers must contend with on a more and more frequent basis.

We also discussed several important security-related preventative controls that can be implemented in your organization. These include restarting or recovering a system, backing up data, and developing and managing backup and recovery procedures. The importance of having offsite storage of backup media and system documentation was emphasized. This also includes the process of archiving information and electronic files, in the event restoration is ever necessary. The process of recovering and restoring data files is also something that information security managers must ensure is outlined in policy and enforced. Next, we took a look at other types of preventative controls besides those specific to IT, such as fire suppression systems, cooling systems, and so on.

We discussed how you should review existing emergency procedures and update the contact and instructional data related to them. We talked about the need for identifying and training key personnel for handling emergency procedures, constituting a recovery team, appointing team leaders and team members, and identifying all external emergency service organizations and coordinating with them as much as possible. Finally, we discussed various premises issues that should be taken into consideration when planning risk mitigation activities. In the next chapter, we will delve into the preparation phase of preparing for emergencies.

3.9   **Endnotes**

1.   Texas Department of Information Resources. Business Continuity Planning Guidelines. December 2004.

4

Preparing for a Possible Emergency

4.1 Backup and Recovery Procedures

Part of the emergency preparation process should take into consideration backup and preventive strategies for each functional area of the business or organization. The ultimate cost of implementing such backup and recovery procedures will depend on the speed with which systems or business processes need to be restored. The organization should have BCP documentation for each of the strategies shown in Figure 4.1.

4.1.1 Alternate Business Process Handling

The organization's key business processes should have been listed in this plan. For each key process, it is necessary to determine the type of backup process that would be appropriate. For example, for a business process that consists of an active ecommerce site, it may be considered appropriate to run a full mirrored backup site that can be switched to as soon as the main site is unable to function. For an automated administra-

Plan
Assess Risk
Mitigate
Prepare
Disaster Recovery
Business Recovery
Test, Audit, and Train
Maintain

Figure 4.1
Various recovery strategies available to an organization.

- IT Systems Backup and Recovery
- Premises and Essential Equipment Backup and Recovery
- Customer Service Backup and Recovery
- Administration and Operations Backup and Recovery
- Information and Documentation Backup and Recovery
- Insurance Coverage(s) and Claims Process Documentation

tive process, it may be considered adequate to back up the business process with a manual process supported by stand-alone PCs. Very often, cost is a major factor in the speed of recovery, and a mirrored backup site would normally be significantly more expensive to set up and maintain than a manual process. Within the BCP, the key processes and the recommended strategic approach for each should be listed. There are a number of strategic options to be investigated when considering IT systems' backup and recovery processes. Impractical as it may be, **Relocate and Restore** is a strategy that involves the identification of a suitable location, hardware, and peripherals, and reinstalling the systems and backed-up software and data after an emergency has occurred. This strategy is considered inadequate for today's business needs. **No strategy** is the cheapest strategy, of course. This approach also carries the highest risk and will involve no offsite backup of system or data. This option usually ends up with the organization going out of business.

For any practical business approach, the two most important factors to be considered are the criticality of the IT systems to the business processes (the speed of recovery needed), and the amount of money available for IT backup and recovery strategies. Although major disruptions with long-term effects may be rare, they should be accounted for in the contingency plan. Thus, the plan must include a strategy to recover and perform system operations at an alternate facility for an extended period. In general, three types of alternate sites are available:

1.   Dedicated site owned or operated by the organization

2.   Reciprocal agreement or memorandum of agreement with an internal or external entity

3.   Commercially leased facility

Regardless of the type of alternate site chosen, the facility must be able to support system operations as defined in the contingency plan. The three alternate site types may be categorized in terms of their operational readiness. Based on this factor, sites may be identified as mirrored sites, (switchable) hot sites, warm sites, mobile sites, and cold sites. Each is briefly described below.

4.1.1.1 Fully Mirrored Recovery Site

This strategy entails the maintenance of a fully mirrored duplicate site that would enable instantaneous switching between the live site and the backup site. This is normally the most expensive option. Mirrored sites are fully redundant facilities with full, real-time information mirroring. Mirrored sites are identical to the primary site in all technical respects. These sites provide the highest degree of availability, because the data are processed and stored at the primary and alternate site simultaneously. These sites typically are designed, built, operated, and maintained by the organization.

4.1.1.2 Switchable Hot Site

This strategy involves the establishment of a commercial arrangement with a vendor who will guarantee to maintain an identical site with communications to enable you to switch your IT operations to his site within an agreed-upon time period, usually less than one to two hours. Hot sites are office spaces appropriately sized to support system requirements and configured with the necessary system hardware, supporting infrastructure, and support personnel. Hot sites are typically staffed 24 hours a day, 7 days a week. Hot site personnel begin to prepare for the system's arrival as soon as they are notified that the contingency plan has been activated.

4.1.1.3 Warm Site

Warm sites are partially equipped office spaces that contain some or all of the system hardware, software, telecommunications, and power sources. The warm site is maintained in an operational status ready to receive the relocated system. The site may need to be prepared before receiving the system and recovery personnel. In many cases, a warm site may serve as a normal operational facility for another system or function, and in the event of contingency plan activation, the normal activities are displaced temporarily to accommodate the disrupted system.

4.1.1.4 Mobile Site

Mobile sites are self-contained, transportable shells custom-fitted with specific telecommunications and IT equipment necessary to meet system requirements. These are available for lease through commercial vendors. The facility often is contained in a tractor-trailer and may be driven to and set up at the desired alternate location. In most cases, to be a viable recovery solution, mobile sites should be designed in advance with the vendor, and an SLA should be signed between the two parties. This is necessary because the time required to configure the mobile site can be extensive, and without prior coordination, the time to deliver the mobile site may exceed the system's allowable outage time.

4.1.1.5 Cold Site

This strategy involves the setting up of an emergency site once the crisis has occurred. The company has a standby arrangement with a vendor to deliver the minimum configuration urgently. This option usually enables the organization becoming operational within two to three days.

4.2 IT Systems Recovery

Recovery strategies provide a means of restoring IT operations quickly and effectively following a service disruption. The strategies should address disruption impacts and allowable outage times identified in the BIA. Several alternatives should be considered when developing the strategy, including cost, allowable outage time, security, and integration with larger, organization-level contingency plans. The selected recovery strategy should address the potential impacts identified in the BIA and should be integrated into the system architecture during the design and implementation phases of the system life cycle. The strategy should include a combination of methods that complement one another to provide recovery capability over the full spectrum of incidents. A wide variety of recovery approaches may be considered; the appropriate choice depends on the incident, the type of system, and its operational requirements.

4.2.1 High Availability/Fault Tolerance

There are several approaches to building fault-tolerant and high-availability systems; however, there are certain characteristics common to any system built with less than perfect components (which, of course, do not exist). Namely, in order to manage a failure, there must be an alternative component that continues to function in the presence of the failure. Thus, redundancy is a fundamental prerequisite for a system that either recovers from or masks failures. Redundancy can be provided in two very different ways, called passive redundancy and active redundancy, each with very different consequences. Failures in systems can be managed in two different ways, each providing a different level of availability and very different restoration processes. The first is to recover from failures, as in passively redundant systems, and the second is to mask failures so they are invisible to the user, as in actively redundant systems.

Availability is the assurance of sufficient bandwidth and timely access to resources. High availability means the availability of a system has been secured to offer very reliable assurance that the system will be online, active, and able to respond to requests in a timely manner, and that there will be sufficient bandwidth to accomplish requested tasks in the time required.

High availability is a form of fault tolerance, or, rather, a benefit of providing reliable fault tolerance. Fault tolerance is the ability of a network, system, or computer to withstand a certain level of failures, faults, or problems and continue to provide reliable service. Fault tolerance is also a means of avoiding single points of failure. A single point of failure is any system, software or device that is mission critical to the entire environment: if that one element fails, then the entire environment fails. Your environment should be designed with redundancy so that there are no single points of failures. A redundant design such as this is considered fault tolerant.

4.2.2 Backup and Recovery Processes

One of the most important aspects of planning for the majority of organizations is in choosing an appropriate strategy for the backup and recovery of the company's IT based systems. In this section of the plan, key business processes are matched to their supporting IT system, and an appropriate speed of recovery strategy is chosen. This may require some research to determine relevant costs of each strategy. It may be necessary to prepare a Request for Proposal (RFP) for vendors to assist you in implementing the preferred strategic approach. Consideration should also be given to the impact severe damage to both premises and communication systems would have, as it could also have a significant impact on the organization's IT services and systems.

4.2.3 Storage Solutions

It is considered good business practice to store backed-up data offsite. Commercial data storage facilities are specially designed to archive media and protect data from threatening elements. If using offsite storage, data is backed up at the organization's facility and then labeled, packed, and transported to the storage facility. If the data is required for recovery or testing purposes, the organization contacts the storage facility requesting specific data to be transported to the organization or to an alternate facility. Commercial storage facilities often offer media transportation and response and recovery services. Conventional backup is the method used for backing up your organization's various servers and shipping the tapes off to a safe offsite or alternate location.

RAID (redundant arrays of inexpensive disks) is an extremely effective solution for implementing redundancy on your systems. In 1987, David A. Patterson et al. of the University of California at Berkeley published a paper [1] that described various types of disk arrays, referred to by the acronym RAID. The basic idea was to combine multiple small, inexpensive disk drives into an array of drives to yield performance exceeding that of a single large expensive drive, or SLED. Additionally, this array of drives appears to the computer as a single logical storage unit or drive. Disk arrays can be made fault tolerant by redundantly storing information in various ways. The Berkeley paper defined five types of array architectures, RAID-1 through RAID-5, each providing disk fault tolerance and each offering different trade-offs in features and performance. In recent years, the original five levels of RAID have been extended to include RAID-6, RAID-10, RAID-50, and RAID-0+1. RAID solutions of an appropriate level can be chosen based on an organization's specific needs. In addition to these nine redundant array architectures, it has become popular to refer to a non-redundant array of disk drives as a RAID-0 array. The illustration in Figure 4.2 shows several of the more common RAID configurations used by businesses today.

The strategy for RAID employs two or more drives in combination for fault tolerance and performance. RAID drives are used frequently on servers, but are rarely necessary for personal computers. **Data striping** is a concept that is fundamental to RAID. It is a method of concatenating multiple drives into one logical storage unit. Striping involves partitioning each drive's storage space into stripes that may be as small as one sector (512 bytes) or as large as several megabytes. These stripes are then interleaved in a round-robin fashion so that the combined space is composed alternately of stripes from each drive. In effect, the storage space of the drives is shuffled like a deck of cards.

The original RAID was described as having five levels, with each successive level offering increased protection over the previous level. RAID-0 is not redundant, so it does not fit the RAID model *per se*. In RAID-0, the data is split across multiple drives, resulting in higher data throughput. Since no redundant information is stored, performance is very good, but the failure of any disk in the array results in data loss.

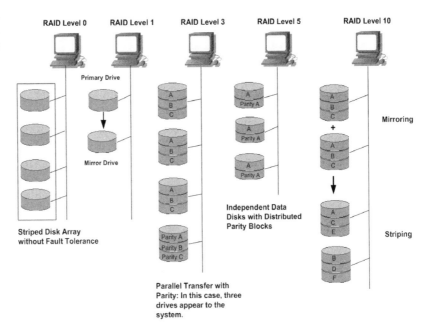

Figure 4.2
Common RAID Configurations.

RAID-1 provides redundancy by writing data to two or more drives. The performance of a RAID-1 array tends to be faster on read operations and slower on write operations compared to a single drive, but if either drive fails, no data is lost. This is a good entry-level solution to provide for a redundant system, since only two drives are required. Since one drive is used to store a duplicate of the data, the cost per megabyte is high. This process is commonly referred to as ***mirroring***. Mirroring is a synchronous process whereby the changes are applied on the replicated server in synchronization with the primary server. This is the best method to use when the requirement is for *zero data loss.* A drawback of mirroring is that it can cause performance degradation and requires adequate bandwidth. Ideally, it should not be used over long distances, when transaction volumes are high, when the bandwidth available is too little, or when the network latencies are high.

RAID-2 is intended for use with drives that do not have built-in error detection. All SCSI (small computer system interface) drives support built-in error detection, so this level is of little use when using SCSI drives. Each bit of data is written to a drive using a process of error correction known as a Hamming Error Correction Code (ECC). On a read operation, the ECC verifies correct data or corrects single-disk errors as the need arises. This *on-the-fly* data error correction process allows for an extremely high data transfer rate. Entry-level cost for this solution tends to be very high. With this solution, the transaction rate is equal to that of a single disk (with spindle synchronization). To our knowledge, there are no commercial implementations for this solution.

RAID-3 stripes data at a byte level across several drives, with parity stored on one drive. Byte-level striping requires hardware support for efficient use. In this process, the data block is subdivided (i.e., *striped*) and written on the data disks. Stripe parity is achieved on writes where parity data is recorded on the parity disk and checked on subsequent reads. RAID-3 requires a minimum of three drives to implement and provides a very high read/write data transfer rate. With this solution, disk failure has an insignificant impact on throughput. The low ratio of ECC (parity) disks to data disks means high efficiency, but it is also a pricey solution.

RAID-4 stripes data at a block level across several drives, with parity stored on one drive. The parity information allows recovery from the failure of any single drive. The performance of a RAID-4 array is very good for reads, but writes require that parity data be updated each time. This slows small random writes in particular, though large writes or sequential writes are fairly fast. Because only one drive in the array stores redundant data, the cost per megabyte of a RAID-4 array can be fairly low.

RAID-5 is similar to RAID-4, but distributes parity among the drives. This can speed small writes in multiprocessing systems, since the parity disk does not become a bottleneck. Because parity data must be skipped on each drive during reads, however, the performance for reads tends to be considerably lower than a RAID-4 array. The cost per megabyte is about the same as for RAID-4. RAID-5 provides striping with parity: three or more drives are used in unison, and one drive's worth of space is consumed with parity information. The parity information is stored across all drives. If any one drive of a RAID-5 volume fails, the parity information is used to rebuild the contents of the lost drive on the fly. A new drive can replace the failed drive, and the RAID-5 system will rebuild the contents of the lost drive onto the replacement drive.

RAID-6 is essentially an extension of RAID-5 that allows for additional fault tolerance by using a second independent distributed parity scheme (known as two-dimensional parity). With this approach, data is striped on a block level across a set of drives, just like in RAID-5, and a second set of parity is calculated and written across all the drives. RAID-6 provides extremely high data fault tolerance and can sustain multiple simultaneous drive failures. It is considered the perfect solution for mission-critical applications.

RAID-10 is implemented as a striped array whose segments are comprised of RAID-1 arrays. RAID-10 has the same fault tolerance as RAID-1 and also has the same overhead for fault tolerance as does mirroring alone. Very high I/O rates are achieved by striping RAID-1 segments, and under certain circumstances, a RAID-10 array can sustain multiple simultaneous drive failures. For this reason, it is considered an excellent solution for sites that would have otherwise gone with RAID-1 but need additional performance. A significant drawback to using RAID-10 is that it can be very expensive. Also, all drives must move in parallel to properly track, which lowers sustained performance. It provides very limited scalability at a very high inherent cost.

RAID-50 is implemented as a striped (RAID-0) array whose segments are RAID-3 arrays. For this reason, some might argue that it should be called RAID-0+3. RAID-50 has the same fault tolerance as RAID-3 as well as the same fault tolerance overhead. It provides high data transfer rates via its RAID-3 configuration, and high I/O rates for small requests are achieved from its RAID-0 striping scheme. This solution may be good for sites that would normally choose a RAID-3 configuration but want additional performance.

RAID-0+1 is implemented as a mirrored array whose segments are RAID-0 arrays. It has the same fault tolerance as RAID-5 and incurs the same overhead for fault tolerance as does mirroring alone. High I/O rates are achieved from this configuration, due to multiple stripe segments. This is considered an excellent solution for sites that need high performance and are not overly concerned with achieving maximum reliability.

There are basically two possible approaches that can be taken to implement RAID, hardware or software. For the hardware RAID approach, the system manages the RAID subsystem independently from the host and presents to the host only a single disk per RAID array. In this manner, the host doesn't have to be aware of the RAID subsystems(s). Software-based arrays occupy host system memory, consume CPU cycles, and are operating system–dependent. By contending with other applications that are running concurrently and simultaneously vying for host CPU cycles and memory, use of software-based arrays will tend to degrade overall server performance. Also, unlike hardware-based arrays, the performance of a software-based array is directly dependent on server CPU performance and load. Each of the various operating systems requires unique drivers for this type of RAID solution, which makes it very error-prone and not very compatible.

Remote journaling is a method used to enable data recovery in which every write and update operation is written to another device that may or may not be the same as the primary device. Often, journaling involves not only the process of collecting the writes on a drive and writing them to the secondary device, but also transmitting them to a drive physically situated at a remote site. Journaling is usually needed for synchronization of servers that require transactional data integrity (such as database servers or an Exchange™ server). Journaling enables the replication of files that are always kept open by an application by recording all of the operations performed on those open files in a journal. The journal is transferred to secondary devices in real-time or in batches, and the operations that were recorded in the journal are retrieved and executed on the replicated file. This ensures that all write operations that are performed on the secondary devices occur in exactly the same order they were carried out on the original file. Therefore, data integrity is preserved at all times. Journaling enables recovery to the point of the last transmission, because it uses metadata to associate the write operation with the location in primary storage where the data belongs.

Normally, journaling accompanies another replication strategy as part of an overall approach for complete recovery for business data. Journals are especially good for protecting an organization from intrusions and from data corruption, enabling a restore operation to go back to a point in time just before the corruption occurred. Unlike mirroring, however, the secondary copy is a sequential history of write events. All write operations are queued to the secondary device, which is called the journal device. The journaling device can be either a disk or tape device. Journaling can be done in real time by simultaneously transmitting the writes (synchronous approach), or it can be achieved by extracting the writes and periodically transmitting them (asynchronous approach). However, if the journal copy was not created as a mirrored copy, journaling is not a substitute for a physical device failure. Journaling can reconstruct a full volume only if the journal was initially created as a mirrored copy of the primary volume. This method of securing data at a remote location over a communications link means that should a disaster ever happen at a local site, recovery can be achieved very quickly.

Disk replication is the process of writing the data onto both the primary server and the replicated server. It protects from disk failures and provides an up-to-date copy of the data. If the replicated server is placed at the hot site, only logs of uncommitted work need to be run for complete recovery. Data is exchanged between the primary and the replicated server at periodic intervals. When the replicated server fails to receive a signal, it in turn signals a possible problem in the primary server. This alert can cause either a manual planned switch to the replicated server, or it can be set up for an automatic switchover to occur. There are two options here: mirroring and shadowing.

Shadowing is an asynchronous process. Changes are collected in the form of logs, which are periodically applied on the replicated server. Data replication solutions may be used at the database, file system, operating system, or application level, based on the needs. When choosing replication as a solution, one needs to remember that replication has to be planned for each server that matters, and that any corruption or loss at the primary server is also replicated at the replication server.

Server clustering is considered a preferred solution for high availability. Its purpose is to use a secondary server to provide access to applications and data when the primary server fails. If it is a local cluster, then the two servers exchange a "heartbeat" periodically to indicate their status.

Clusters can be symmetric or asymmetric. In asymmetric clusters, the secondary server remains inactive under normal circumstances. Both the primary and secondary servers have access data and applications using shared, or mirrored, storage, as shown in Figure 4.3. Server clustering is a technology that connects several duplicate systems together so they act cooperatively. If one system cluster fails, the other systems take over its workload. From a user's perspective, the cluster is a single entity with a single resource access name.

Figure 4.3
An illustration of server clustering.

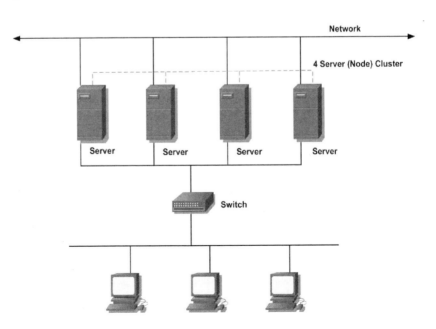

Server clustering is essential in today's business environment, in order to provide the high availability and scalability of services that are required to support 24/7 operations. This requirement encompasses network operating systems, application services, and LAN/WAN network resilience. Clustering improves the reliability of Internet-based systems because it eliminates many of the single points of failure that are possible in a single server system. For example, with clustering you could have two or more Web servers supporting your Internet site. If one of the servers fails, your throughput might be impacted to some degree, but the site would still be available on the second server. In this example, the secondary server becomes active, its access to the storage and network is activated, and it takes over the functions of the primary server.

In symmetric clusters, the two servers are always active, each one running its set of applications. In the event of the failure of one server, the other takes over the functions of the failed server as well. It could also be that both servers run the same applications. In normal times, they serve as a cluster for load balancing, and in the event of disaster, each can take the entire load. It is also possible that the primary and secondary servers do not share the storage. This is done when the two servers are running independent applications; the backup server is provided access to the other server's storage as soon as it goes down. Another option is to mirror each server's storage onto the other server's storage. In the event of disaster, the backup server can access the mirror. In addition to being a high-availability solution, symmetric clusters provide the possibility of load balancing, but this solution is an expensive alternative; cost-benefit analysis is suggested before you implement it.

Electronic vaulting is a process that transmits data electronically and automatically creates the backup offsite. Automation implies that no transportation of backups needs to be done, as data reaches offsite faster, and backups can be performed more frequently without the need for manual supervision. When used with remote journaling, it can drastically reduce the outage time. Electronic vaulting requires adequate bandwidth. If the transmission costs are a hurdle, then the vault can be at a more local secure site. It would help greatly to have the alternate site fairly near the hot site, as it reduces the time taken to transport the backup to the hot site at the time of disaster. If the vault is not at the hot site, then the organization can arrange to periodically ship the backups to the hot site. Not only will this improve the availability, it will also safeguard against a situation when a calamity affects transport to the hot site.

Standby operating systems require having the operating system loaded and ready in a disk that can be attached to the machine at the alternate site. This method, when used with other techniques, can save the time and effort required getting the operating system ready in the backup server after a disaster.

Storage virtualization provides a single logical view of all the storage devices, irrespective of the actual configuration or physical location. It minimizes the differences between the underlying systems and simplifies the administration of storage. In the conventional scenario, it is not always possible to match the storage needs with the application type; e.g., file servers consume space faster than mail servers. Also, any major increase in storage usage requires an entire hardware upgrade. In storage visualization, since the logical and physical views of the storage are separated, it is possible to easily upgrade, replace, or add more storage without affecting server availability. It causes true sharing of data, as it allows heterogeneous servers to connect to the storage. It also offers the benefits of serverless backup and recovery. Virtualization complements network-attached storage (NAS) and storage area networks (SANs).

Network-attached storage (NAS) is another option. The storage device has a built-in network interface that can be plugged into the network to provide access to data. It supports all the file service protocols to share files across systems, and is easy to install and maintain. Enterprise systems' storage of this form are proprietary, therefore every time an upgrade is needed, it is necessary to go back to the manufacturer; this also requires you to be tied to a specific vendor. Data transfer and backups need to use the network.

A **storage area network (SAN)** is a dedicated, high-speed network based on the fiber channel, switches, and hubs that connect many heterogeneous servers to storage devices. In effect, the storage devices are removed from their servers and made available to many servers across a network. In addition, SAN increases the manageability of storage and allows easy addition of storage or servers. It further removes the vendor dependence. The largest chunk of LAN traffic has been observed to pertain to backup, mirroring, "heartbeat," and disaster recovery–related activities. With SAN, all these housekeeping activities are done off the LAN, and happen over the SAN fiber. This frees the server power and the network for applications.

The many-to-many server-to-storage connectivity makes it easier to plan for continuity. If a server goes down, its applications can easily be taken over by its backup server, since connecting to the storage is not a problem.

4.2.4 **Network Solutions**

Hot network nodes are an operational network at the alternate facility. This network can be regularly monitored for function. After a disaster, hot network nodes will save setup and testing time for the networks. This method is often used along with VPNs, which are used for WAN recovery. A VPN runs over public networks and allows access to a corporate network. Once an entry into the corporate network is accomplished, using a VPN is like using the company's intranet via the Internet. The tunnel request to the destination server from the Internet first authenticates the user. In addition to this, encryption and the Internet tunneling protocol serve as security measures. In the event of disaster, VPN would enable the recovery team to work on the recovery server even before they reach the alternate site.

4.2.5 **Desktop Computers**

A desktop computer or portable system (e.g., laptop or handheld device) typically consists of a central processing unit (CPU), memory, disk storage, and various input and output devices. A PC is designed for use by one person at a time. Desktop computers are stationary PCs that fit conveniently on top of an office desk or table. They are not well suited to move or travel. Most desktops are networked to allow for communications with other networked devices, applications, and the Internet. Portable systems, such as laptops (also called notebook computers) or handheld computers, are PCs that can be carried for convenience and travel purposes. Portable systems can be compact computers that can have processing, memory, and disk storage comparable to desktop computers, or they can have limited processing memory and disk storage, such as a handheld computer. Portable systems can connect with other networked devices, applications, and the Internet through various mechanisms, such as dialup lines. They are not often subject to contingency planning. Contingency considerations for desktop and portable systems should emphasize data availability, confidentiality, and integrity. To address these requirements, the systems manager should consider each of the following practices:

■ **Store backups offsite**—Backup media should be stored offsite in a secure, environmentally controlled facility. If users back up data on a stand-alone system rather than saving data to the network, a means should be provided for storing the media at an alternate site. A copy of the contingency plan, software licenses, vendor SLAs and contracts, and other important documents should be stored with the backup media. The BIA conducted by the Contingency Planning Coordinator should help to ascertain how often to send backups off-site.

- **Encourage individuals to back up data**—If the PC backup process is not automated from the network, users should be encouraged to back up data on a regular basis. This task can be conducted through employee security training and awareness.

- **Provide guidance on saving data on personal computers**—Instructing users to save data to a particular folder eases the IT department's desktop support requirements. If a machine must be rebuilt, the technician will know which folders to copy and preserve while the system is being reloaded.

- **Standardize hardware, software, and peripherals**—System recovery is faster if hardware, software, and peripherals are standardized throughout the organization. If standard configurations are not possible throughout the organization, then configurations should be standardized by department or by machine type or model if possible. Additionally, critical hardware components that would need to be recovered immediately in the event of a disaster should be compatible with off-the-shelf computer components. This compatibility will avoid delays in ordering custom-built equipment from a vendor.

- **Document system configurations and vendor information**—Well-documented system configurations ease recovery. Similarly, vendor names and emergency contact information should be listed in the contingency plan so that replacement equipment may be purchased quickly.

- **Coordinate with security policies and system security controls**—Desktop and portable computer contingency solutions described below should be coordinated with security policies and system security controls. Therefore, in choosing the appropriate technical contingency solution(s), similar security controls and security-related activities (e.g., risk assessment, vulnerability scanning) in the production systems should be implemented in the contingency solution(s) to ensure that, during a system disruption or emergency, executing the technical contingency solution(s) does not compromise or disclose sensitive data.

■ **Use results from the BIA**—Impacts and priorities of associated major applications and general support systems discovered through the BIA should be reviewed to determine related requirements.

4.2.6 Software and Licenses

Software and licenses must be backed up and stored at an offsite storage location. Software backup for all hardware platforms consists of three basic areas: operating system software, application software, and utility software. All software and related documentation should have adequate off-premises storage. Even when using a standard software package from one vendor, the software can vary from one location to another. Differences may include parameter settings and modifications, security profiles, reporting options, account information, or other options chosen by the institution during or subsequent to system implementation. Therefore, comprehensive backup of all critical software is essential. The operating system software should be backed up with at least two copies of the current version. One copy should be stored in the tape and disk library for immediate availability in the event the original is impaired; the other copy should be stored in a secure, off-premises location. Duplicate copies should be tested periodically and recreated whenever there is a change to the operating system. Application software, which includes both source (if the institution has that in its possession) and object versions of all application programs, should be maintained in the same manner as the operating system software. Backup copies of the programs should be updated as program changes are made. Given the increased reliance on the distributed processing environment, the importance of adequate backup resources and procedures for LANs and WANs is important. Management should ensure that all appropriate programs and information are backed up. Depending on the size of the institution and the nature of anticipated risks and exposures, the time spent backing up data is minimal compared with the time and effort that would be necessary for restoration. Files that can be backed up within a short period of time may require days, weeks, or months to recreate from hard copy records, assuming hard copy records are available. Comprehensive and clear procedures are necessary to recover critical networks and systems. Procedures should, at a minimum, include:

1. Frequency of update and retention cycles for backup software and data

2. Periodic review of software and hardware for compatibility with backup resources

3. Periodic testing of backup procedures for effectiveness in restoring normal operations

4. Guidelines for the labeling, listing, transportation, and storage of media

5. Maintenance of data file listings, their contents, and locations

6. Hardware, software, and network configuration documentation

7. Controls to minimize the risks involved in the transfer of backup data, whether by electronic link or through the physical transportation of disks and tapes to and from the storage site

8. Controls to ensure data integrity, client confidentiality, and the physical security of hard copy output, media, and hardware

4.2.7 LAN

Restoration of the LAN requires documentation of the network configuration and all the devices used. Preventive measures, in the form of network security controls and identification of single points-of-failure, need to be taken. A possible contingency strategy can be remote access using VPNs. VPNs provide a secure, centrally-managed remote access over a broad range of browser-based and browserless applications. Hot network nodes can also provide real-time switchover. For these solutions, data bandwidth will need to be scaled appropriately.

4.2.8 Servers

A server is a computer that runs software to provide access to a resource or part of the network and network resources, such as disk storage, printers, and network applications. A server can be any type of computer running a network operating system. A server may be a standard PC, or it can be a large computer containing multiple disk drives and a vast amount of memory that will allow the computer to process hundreds of requests at once. Servers support file sharing and storage, data processing, central application hosting (such as e-mail or a central database), printing, access control, user authentication, remote access connectivity, and other shared network services. Local users log into the server through networked PCs to access resources the server provides. The loss of servers can be devastating, as they host all the applications and support multiple users. Because servers can support or host numerous critical applications, server loss could cause significant problems to business processes.

4.2.9   Web Sites

Web sites are often the entry point for hackers, so necessary security controls must be implemented. Documentation of the Web site and its configuration, along with the application code, would speed recovery. During recovery, it is possible to recover the Web site from an alternate site with an IP address different from the usual. Care should be taken to anticipate this during the initial design and development of the site. Clustering across two servers is also a popular option that offers dual benefits: load balancing at normal times, and fail-over during disaster.

4.2.10   Premises and Essential Equipment Backup and Recovery

Many unexpected events can affect premises and essential equipment that are naturally vital to continuation of normal business activities. These include fire, flood, earthquake, terrorist activity, and so forth. The organization should therefore develop a plan of how to continue to provide business services to its customers in the event of a disaster that affects either its premises or its essential equipment. Strategies to be considered include having access to an empty facility that can be used immediately. This is not normally a viable option to most businesses, due to the high costs of maintaining such a facility. If the organization has more than one location, it could consider moving essential services, personnel, and equipment into areas where less-critical services are currently located. Other alternatives would include having a standby arrangement with an office services provider or an arrangement with a real estate broker. Whichever strategy is considered to be appropriate, keep in mind that only proper planning will ensure that such arrangements work.

4.2.11   Customer Service Backup and Recovery

It is critical for organizations to be able to continue to provide an adequate level of service to their customers throughout an emergency. This is an especially important area, which should be given a high level of priority. A customer lost is normally a customer lost forever, and your customers have the right to expect you to plan for unexpected emergencies. The main customer service activities should be listed in this section of the plan, and should be ordered in priority sequence. For each essential customer service activity, the outline strategy to be followed in the event of an unexpected emergency is to be stated. The impact of serious disruption to each of these essential customer services should also be stated. Each strategy should be stated in a manner that can be easily understood and implemented. The aspect of customer relations management must be considered so that in the event of an emergency, affected customers may be immediately notified and informed of the potential impact on the supplies of products and services.

4.2.12 Administration and Operations Backup and Recovery

Administration and operations activities should be organized into essential and less-essential activities, within the context of a short-term emergency. For emergencies of longer durations, it is likely that more of these activities are regarded as essential. An example of an activity that might move from less essential to essential is the accounting operation. In many businesses, it may not be necessary for accounting operations to be kept up-to-date for a few days, but after three or four days, accounting operations may well become critical to restore invoicing, credit control, and expense control to a more manageable position. This section of the plan should contain a list of the key administration and operational processes, with an indication of the criticality of the process within the disruption period. You should identify the potential disruption to each of these processes, and also the potential impact. Identify alternative methods of handling each of these activities, together with an estimate of the costs of each option. It is likely that manual backup procedures were developed for administration and operations functions, as these are usually relatively easy to implement when the IT systems are not available. These can often be supported by business or office software providing spreadsheet, database, and word-processing capability.

4.2.13 Key Business Information and Documentation Backup and Recovery

Recovery and backup strategies need to be determined for critical information and documentation. Many business processes today are totally dependent upon the availability of digitized information in order to function. It is necessary to identify these dependencies and develop workable strategies for continuing a satisfactory measure of business operations, even though the disruption may make access to all such information extremely difficult or, in some cases, impossible. This section of the plan will contain a list of the main information, data, and documentation used by the organization in carrying out its normal business processes. It should identify potential disruptions to the availability of this information and their resultant impact on continuing a satisfactory level of business operations. Consider carefully here the cross-relationship between information and data and the availability of the information system where such data or information may be held or processed. Assess the adequacy of existing backup arrangements and alternative methods for accessing such data or information.

4.2.14   Insurance Coverages and Claims Process

Insurance coverage is another consideration the BCP should account for. In cases of disaster, knowing the name of the insurance agent, how to contact that person, and when to contact the insurance agency are all very important. The BCP should have guidelines established for such purposes and, often, it is helpful to have a checklist of conditions to help emergency response teams decide if and when they should contact the insurance agency.

4.3   Key BCP Personnel and Supplies

Employees are an organization's most important and valuable asset. In any emergency, in addition to its systems recoveries, the organization will rely on its employees to recover normal business operations in the least amount of time possible. Likewise, the organization will also rely on its main suppliers of critical goods and services to continue to support recovery of business operations. The plan you establish as a part of your organization's BCP will rely on key members of management and staff to provide the technical and management skills needed to achieve a smooth business recovery process. These key members of management and staff are responsible for the implementation of the BCP in the event of an emergency. A well-organized and structured approach will avoid the unexpected crisis deteriorating into chaos. To facilitate these efforts, the plan should include a functional organization chart. The BCP project coordinator and deputy for each functional area should be listed. A table of key personnel and emergency contact information is vital. Listing the key suppliers and vendors and their emergency contact information will speed up the resupply process. There should be a manpower recovery strategy to reestablish processes after a disaster. The plan should establish who is on the disaster recovery team and, likewise, it should establish who is part of the business recovery team.

4.4   Key Documents and Procedures

In every business or organization, there are certain documents and records vital to the business operation. These types of documents should be identified and kept in a list. Duplicates should be made of these documents, and they should be moved to an offsite storage location. In preparation for disaster, the organization should set aside a supply of emergency stationery and office supplies. When disasters strike, media-handling procedures should be established to deal with news crews covering the event. When these situations occur, it is necessary to establish emergency authorization procedures to allow people the ability to begin the recovery process without having to wait on someone to make a decision. Finally, a special budget should be prepared for backup and recovery phase operations.

4.5 Chapter Summary

This chapter has covered the basics of preparing for a possible emergency. We discussed backup and recovery procedures and alternate business process handling. Part of this discussion delved into the strategies for implementing a fully mirrored recovery site, a switchable hot site, a warm site, a mobile site, or a cold site. For IT systems recovery processes, we covered the details of backup and recovery processes, storage solutions, network solutions, desktop computers, software and licenses, LANs, servers, and Web sites. Next, we discussed the issues regarding premises and essential equipment backup and recovery, customer service backup and recovery, administration and operations backup and recovery, key business information and documentation backup and recovery, and the importance of reviewing insurance coverages and knowing the carrier claims process. Key BCP personnel and supplies were covered, as well as understanding why it was important to plan for the management and availability of your organization's key documents and procedures in a crisis situation. In the next chapter, we will review the disaster recovery phase and the steps you can take during the disaster to help your company.

4.6 Endnotes

1. Patterson, D., G. Gibson, and R. Katz, *A Case for Redundant Arrays of Inexpensive Disks (RAID)*. Berkeley: University of California at Berkeley, 1987.

5

Disaster Recovery Phase

As discussed earlier in the book, the terrorist attacks of September 11, 2001 raised concerns among Americans about the safety of their cities, communities, and workplaces, as well as about the ability to respond quickly and effectively in the wake of a disaster. Although these events were unprecedented, sooner or later every institution will face some type of unforeseen event that could have a severe impact on its operations, assets, or employees. To survive a catastrophe, preparedness is crucial. Effective disaster response management calls for risk analysis, disaster response planning, crisis management communications, and business recovery strategies. Disaster Recovery Plan (DRPs) are now mandated by law. The Occupational Safety and Health Administration (OSHA) requires facilities with more than ten employees to have a written emergency plan. Top management support and the involvement of every employee are imperative factors to having a successful plan.

There is no hard and fast definition of what constitutes a disaster. Sometimes a disaster develops quickly, hitting full-force with little or no warning. Other times, a disaster looms on the horizon for a long period of time until it becomes large enough to become a threat. When disasters occur, emergency response significantly affects the extent of damages and injuries sustained. Disasters do happen, and often they include injuries to people, fires, explosions, chemical spills, toxic gas releases, and vandalism. Anticipating disasters and planning our response can greatly lessen the extent of injuries and limit equipment, material, and property damage. A critical part of handling any serious emergency situation is in the management of the disaster recovery phase.

By definition, the disaster recovery phase is likely to involve, to a significant degree, external emergency services. The priority during this phase is the safety and well-being of human life, the handling of the emergency itself, the removal of the threat of further injury or damage, and the reestablishment of external services such as power, communications, water, and so on. A major task during this phase is also the completion of damage assessment forms. In addition to the emergency services, the disaster recovery phase may involve different personnel, depending upon the type of emergency, and a disaster recovery team (DRT) should be nominated according to the requirements of each specific crisis.

5.1   Disaster Recovery Legal Issues

Standards of care and due diligence are required of all businesses. Not having an appropriate disaster recovery plan (DRP), which includes a reliable backup/restore system, violates that fiduciary standard of care. Although no specific law states that a business must have a DRP, there is a body of legal precedent that has been used to hold companies and even individuals responsible for the recovery of data after a disaster [1]. Legal precedent as a result of the case of *FJS Electronics v. Fidelity Bank* has set the standard of due care and diligence that corporations must now uphold. In that case, Fidelity Bank had a data disaster that ended up costing FJS Electronics. FJS took Fidelity to court and won. In another case, *Parr v. Security Nat. Bank* [2], the decision rendered cited the actions of Fidelity in the *FJS v. Fidelity* case:

> *Fidelity made a choice when it elected to employ a technique which searched for stopped checks by amount alone. It evidently found benefits to this technique which outweighed the risk that an item might be inaccurately described in a stop order. This is precisely the type of inevitable loss which was contemplated by the code drafters and addressed by the comment above. The focus of § 4-403 is the service which may be expected by the customer, and a customer may expect a check to be stopped after the bank is given reasonable notice. A bank's decision to reduce operating costs by using a system which increases the risk that checks as to which there is an outstanding stop payment order will be paid invites liability when such items are paid.*

The entire basis of law relating to the development of disaster recovery plans is based on civil statutes and an interpretation of applicability to disaster recovery planning. Liability statutes like the Foreign Corrupt Practices Act (FCPA) have been interpreted is such a way that we now hold corporate managers personally liable for protecting corporate assets. The FCPA requires corporations to "… make and keep books, records, and accounts, which, in reasonable detail, accurately and fairly reflect the transactions and dispositions of the assets …" The section of this Act that keeps it at the forefront of disaster recovery liability is the "Standard of Care" wording, whereby management can be judged on their mismanagement of corporate assets. The FCPA is unique in that it holds corporate managers personally liable for protecting corporate assets. Failure to comply with the FCPA exposes individuals and companies to the following:

- Personal fines up to $10,000

- Corporate fines up to $1,000,000

- Prison terms up to five years

The Federal Financial Institutions Examinations Council (FFIEC) [3] has issued various circulars regarding the need for financial institutions to implement disaster recovery plans. In 1989, a joint-agency Circular was issued on behalf of the following member agencies:

- Board of Governors of the Federal Reserve System (FRB)

- Federal Deposit Insurance Corporation (FDIC)

- National Credit Union Administration (NCUA)

- Office of the Comptroller of the Currency (OCC)

- Office of Thrift Supervision (OTS)

The Circular stated: "The loss or extended interruption of business operations, including central computing processing, end-user computing, local area networking, and nationwide telecommunications poses substantial risk of financial loss and could lead to failure of an institution. As a result, contingency planning now requires an institution-wide emphasis . . ." FFIEC guidelines relating to contingency planning are actually contained within ten technology related Supervisory Policy Statements. These policies are revised every two years and can be acquired through any of the agencies listed above.

Other examples include the Federal Computer Security Act, which covers instances of computer fraud, abuse, and the misappropriation of computerized assets. The IRS Records Retention Requirements is an example of a Vital Records Management Statute. All of these various statutes are based on the precept of Standard of Care, which is described [4] as ". . . directors and officers owe a duty to the corporation to be vigilant and to exercise ordinary or reasonable care and diligence and the utmost good faith and fidelity to conserve the corporate property; and, if a loss or depletion of assets results from their willful or negligent failure to perform their duties, or to a willful or fraudulent abuse of their trust, they are liable, provided such losses were the natural and necessary consequences of omission on their part . . ."

Courts will assess liability by determining the probability of loss, multiplied by the magnitude of the harm, balanced against the cost of prevention. Should your company ever end up in court, the burden of proof would be on your company to prove that all reasonable measures had been taken to mitigate the harm caused by the disaster. There are clearly enough legal precedents for the courts to draw on in determining whether a "Standard of Care" was maintained or whether "Due Diligence" was exercised in mitigating the effects of the disaster on your company's critical business operations. As a result of these statutes, information technology professionals are now held to a standard of reasonable care, and can breach that standard simply by not diligently pursuing the development of a disaster recovery plan.

5.2   **Planning for Handling the Emergency**

The first stage of handling an emergency involves an assessment of the situation. The assessment must determine whether the disaster recovery team (DRT) is required to be involved. This section explains how the process of identification of the emergency situation should occur, when it is necessary to call in the DRT, and how to determine the scale of the emergency.

If a disaster recovery plan does not already exist, it will be necessary to initiate the preparation of the first version of such a plan. In order to initiate a planning project, the Board and/or top-level management would normally receive a proposal. Projects as important as DRP development should be approved at the highest level to ensure the required level of commitment, resources, and management attention are applied to the process. The proposal should present the reasons for undertaking the project, and could include some or all of the following:

- Increased dependency by the business over recent years on computerized production and sales delivery mechanisms, thereby creating increased risk of loss of normal services

- Increased dependency by the business over recent years on computerized information systems

- Increased recognition of the impact that a serious incident could have on the business

- Necessity of establishing a formal process to be followed when a disaster occurs

- Intention of reducing costs and losses arising from serious incidents

- Increased likelihood of inadequate IT and information security safeguards

- Necessity of developing effective backup and recovery strategies to mitigate the impact of disruptive events

- Avoidance of business failure from disruptive incidents

5.2.1 Planning and Insurance Considerations

Consider making contractual arrangements with vendors for such post-emergency services as records preservation, equipment repair, earthmoving or engineering. Meet with your insurance carriers to discuss your property and business resumptions policies. Most companies discover that they are not properly insured only after they have suffered a loss. The lack of appropriate insurance can be financially devastating. Discuss the following topics with your insurance advisor to determine your individual needs:

- How will my property be valued?

- Does my policy cover the cost of required upgrades to code?

- How much insurance am I required to carry to avoid becoming a co-insurer?

- What perils or causes of loss does my policy cover?

- What are my deductibles?

- What does my policy require me to do in the event of a loss?

- What types of records and documentation will my insurance company want to see? Are records in a safe place where they can be obtained after an emergency?

- To what extent am I covered for loss due to interruption of power? Is coverage provided for both on- and off-premises power interruption?

- Am I covered for lost income in the event of business interruption because of a loss? Do I have enough coverage? For how long is coverage provided? How long is my coverage for lost income if my business is closed by order of a civil authority?

- To what extent am I covered for reduced income due to customers not all immediately coming back once the business reopens?

- How will my emergency management program affect my rates?

Determine critical operations and make plans for bringing those systems back online. The process may entail:

- Repairing or replacing equipment

- Relocating operations to an alternate location

- Contracting operations on a temporary basis

Take photographs or videotape the facility to document company assets. Update these records regularly.

5.2.2   Identification of Potential Disaster Status

One of the first tasks is to determine whether an actual or pending crisis is likely to become sufficiently serious to require the evacuation of staff. All organizations should have tested procedures for handling the evacuation processes and also for maximizing the safety of the employees. If a serious emergency situation has already occurred, causing injury, loss of life, or damage to premises or equipment, then the DRT should be mobilized immediately. A primary task to complete during the initial stages of a disaster is to determine whether a situation is likely to require the evacuation of organizational staff. All organizations should have procedures for handling the evacuation process. These procedures should be tested periodically in order to ensure the safety of the company's employees. If an emergency situation has already occurred and has caused injury, loss of life, or damage to the premises or the equipment therein, the DRT should be activated immediately. Some criteria for determining whether a potential disaster situation exists could include the following:

- Is there an actual or potential threat to human safety?
- Is there an actual or potential serious threat to buildings or equipment?
- Is there likely to be a need to involve the emergency services?

If the answers to any of the above are positive, the DRT should also be notified.

A major part of the disaster recovery planning process is the assessment of the potential risks to the organization, which could themselves result in the disasters or emergency situations. It is necessary to consider all the possible incident types, as well as the impact each may have on the organization's ability to continue to deliver its normal business services. This work can be complex and demanding. To assist in this area, therefore, there are a number of tools available. The most widely known of these is Consolidated Omnibus Budget Reconciliation Act (COBRA), which employs a method aligned to various international standards.

5.2.3 Involvement of Emergency Services

The involvement of emergency services is almost certain if the answer to any of the questions above is *yes,* and the BCP should emphasize priority in bringing them into the situation as soon as it is determined that any of the criteria have been met. Lives may be at stake. Additionally, part of the recovery process will include making an assessment of the potential business impact the emergency caused. This may require the initiation of specific project management activities to ensure that the management of the disaster recovery phase will be properly structured and controlled. The recovery process is likely to require a significant level of coordination using many resources, including public emergency services. During the handling of the disaster recovery process, all events should be planned and recorded. To facilitate recording events as they unfold, a Disaster Event Log is recommended. A sample format is shown in Figure 5.1.

Figure 5.1
A sample format
for a Disaster Event
Log.

Date/Time of Event	Description of Event	Location of Event	Response Actions Taken	Notification of
12/31/2005 14:27	Fire in paint room	East corridor paint room	called 911	Safety Team x 4567
12/31/2005 14:33	Fire Team Response	East corridor	directed to paint room	Disaster Recovery Team

It is likely that public emergency services will be involved in many disaster recovery situations where there is danger to human life or serious damage to property and assets. The emergency services will initially deal with the actual emergency event such as an accidental spillage of toxic material, a fire, or a flood. The emergency services will concentrate their efforts on rescuing any persons trapped within buildings or vehicles and also on minimizing the impact of the emergency event on premises and assets, wherever possible. The protection of human life and the treatment of any wounded persons will be afforded the highest priority. The emergency services will need to liaise with responsible individuals from the organization who can provide information that they may require.

The emergency services have specialists who can provide advice on how to prepare for the outcome of such situations and how to minimize the likelihood of their occurrence. Once the emergency situation is brought under control, the emergency services will hand over the situation to the responsible officials representing the organization. This will normally be the DRT. In certain circumstances, other specialist emergency services may be required. These emergency services could include bomb disposal specialists, hazardous waste clearing, or terrorist negotiation specialists. The BCP should contain contact numbers of specialists within the emergency services who can provide advice in minimizing certain types of incidents. Also, you should include the names of the persons who should provide on-the-ground assistance to the emergency services teams.

5.2.4 State and Federal Involvement

The emergency management structure of each state typically sets up a structure that has four levels of intervention (local, county, state, and federal). The basic concept of this plan is that the lowest level of government shall have initial responsibility for disaster response and relief, attempting to mitigate the situation with the resources available at that level. Requests for assistance from the next higher level of government will be made when the magnitude of the disaster either exceeds the resources of the local level of government, or the resources needed are not available at the local level.

Each county government or township typically operates an emergency management agency for the purpose of coordinating disaster relief efforts in that county or township. Upon exhaustion of resources at the county level, requests for state assistance will be made to the appropriate emergency management organization, and an element of that organization will be sent to evaluate the damage and the assistance needed through the state. The governor may declare a state of emergency and direct state resources into the affected area. The State Emergency Operations Center (SEOC) will be activated at this time and will provide a direct liaison to the County EOC regarding the coordination of state resources operating and/or responding into the affected area. When local and state resources are determined to be inadequate to respond to the disaster, the governor will request assistance through the Federal Emergency Management Agency (FEMA). The requests will be based on state and local damage reports and expenditure reports for disaster-related activities. When the President of the United States declares an emergency or a major disaster, federal assistance is then authorized to assist state governments. Each state designates an agency responsible for coordinating assistance received through federal programs.

5.2.5   Assessing the Business Impact of an Emergency

Assessments need to be made at various stages during the recovery process as to the potential scale of the emergency from a business perspective. During the disaster recovery process, these will include a preliminary damage assessment. The initial assessments will normally be carried out by the DRT, who may call on other specialists to help with this process as appropriate. The assessments will be based on the particular circumstances by applying a five-point scale similar to the one shown in Figure 5.2.

As discussed previously, the BIA is an essential component of an organization's business continuance plan; it includes an exploratory component to reveal any vulnerabilities and a planning component to develop strategies for minimizing risk. The result of analysis is a BIA report, which describes the potential risks specific to the organization studied. One of the basic assumptions behind BIA is that every component of the organization is reliant upon the continued functioning of every other component, but that some are more crucial than others and require a greater allocation of funds in the wake of a disaster. For example, a business might be able to continue more or less normally if the cafeteria had to close, but would come to a complete halt if the information system crashed.

As part of a disaster recovery plan, BIA is likely to identify costs linked to failures, such as loss of cash flow, replacement of equipment, salaries paid to catch up with a backlog of work, loss of profits, and so on. A BIA report quantifies the importance of business components and suggests appropriate fund allocation for measures to protect them. The possibilities of failures are likely to be assessed in terms of their impacts on safety, finances, marketing, legal compliance, and quality assurance. Where possible, the impact is expressed monetarily for purposes of comparison. For example, a business may spend three times as much on marketing in the wake of a disaster to rebuild customer confidence.

Figure 5.2
*A chart to help
determine the
severity of a
disruptive event.*

SEVERITY	POTENTIAL LONGER TERM IMPACT FROM DISRUPTIVE EVENTS
1	Is likely to seriously affect normal business operations for over four weeks
2	Is likely to seriously affect normal business operations for over one week
3	Is likely to seriously affect normal business operations for less than one week
4	Is likely to seriously affect normal business operations for less than two days
5	Is likely to seriously affect normal business operations for less than one day

5.2.6 Secure Recovery

Secure recovery ensures that mission-critical, sensitive, or secured servers can be restored after a disaster with minimal loss or security violations. Secure recovery ensures that affected systems reboot into a secured state and that all resources open and active at the time of the fault, failure, or security violation are restored from backup, and their proper security labels are reapplied.

5.2.7 Alternate Sites

Secure recovery can also be expanded to an entire organization under a disaster recovery plan. An organization-wide secure recovery procedure involves the use of an alternate site: a secondary location where the business can move to and continue performing mission-critical business operations. As we previously discussed in Chapter 2, there are three basic levels of alternative sites: hot, warm, and cold. Although a hot site is the most desired form of alternate site, it is the most expensive. A cold site is the least costly, but it makes recovery nearly impossible. When you return from the alternate site, the disaster could be repeated. The primary site is the new environment, because the original network and computer systems were damaged beyond their capability to support the business; significant changes, repairs, and replacements have occurred to restore the environment. The restored primary site must be stress-tested before the mission-critical operations of the business are transferred back to it. To prevent problems, the least critical functions should be moved back to the primary site first. Then, after the site shows resiliency, you can move more critical functions as the network proves its ability to support the organization once again.

5.3   **Disaster Recovery Team Management Actions**

Recovery operations begin after the contingency plan has been activated, damage assessment has been completed (if possible), personnel have been notified, and appropriate teams have been mobilized. Recovery phase activities focus on contingency measures to execute temporary IT processing capabilities, repair damage to the original system, and restore operational capabilities at the original or new facility. Depending on the recovery strategies defined in the plan, these functions could include temporary manual processing, recovery and operation on an alternate system, or relocation and recovery at an alternate site. Teams with recovery responsibilities should understand and be able to perform these recovery strategies well enough that if the paper plan is unavailable during the initial stages of the event, they can still perform the necessary activities.

It is necessary for the management of the disaster recovery phase to be properly structured and controlled. Where practical, this phase should be organized in accordance with best project management practices. The recovery process is likely to require a significant level of coordination, utilizing diverse resources including public emergency services. During the handling of the disaster recovery process, all events should be planned and recorded. The planning part of the process is dealt with here. The recording process is dealt with in the Event Log. This section of the BCP should establish a suggested format to be used for planning the recovery process. Information should include:

- Activity number
- Activity name
- Activity description
- Activity commencement

- Activity completion
- Activity resources

The plan should also include a critical path for the recovery process. The plan will need to be updated regularly during the disaster recovery process, and this is an important part of the DRT leader's duties. A critical path, in its simplest form, is the shortest time in which a particular group of tasks may be accomplished. Each task on the critical path must be completed on schedule if the entire project or group of tasks is to be finished on schedule.

5.4   Notification and Reporting in Disaster Recovery Phase

Maintaining good levels of communication is one of the most important elements of the disaster recovery phase. It is important that any information released is both accurate and timely. It is necessary to keep various groups informed, including the DRT, the business recovery team, the senior and middle management, families of affected employees, media, and other key members of staff. In the event of any emergency, the organization's DRT should be notified as soon as possible. This notification should also be made to upper management and key employees. In certain situations, it is warranted to establish a team to handle notification of employees' families or next-of-kin (in worst-case scenarios). A specific person should be designated to handle media during the disaster recovery phase, and another person should be assigned the task of maintaining an event log during the disaster recovery phase. Finally, when the danger has passed, a Disaster Recovery Phase Report must be completed.

5.4.1   Mobilizing the Disaster Recovery Team

One of the tasks during the early stages of the emergency is to notify the DRT that an emergency has occurred. This notification would normally be in a preagreed format. Normally, the notification will request that the members of the DRT assemble at the site of the problem and will include sufficient information to enable the request to be communicated effectively. The BCP team leader or deputy should initially be alerted, and that person will be responsible for notifying the rest of the DRT, who are required to attend the site of the emergency. A succession of alternates should be provided in case the leader or deputy is unavailable or incapacitated. This section of the BCP should contain a list of persons to contact, including contact information, time and date of contact, who made the contact, messages left with, instructions issued, response, and subsequent time of arrival on site.

5.4.2   Notification to Management and Key Employees

During the disaster recovery phase, the management and key employees should be kept informed of key developments affecting the overall business process and, in particular, the impact on their own areas of responsibility. If, for example, the emergency affects the main buildings in which the business is conducted, and the emergency has occurred outside normal business hours, it may be necessary to instruct the employees to remain at home until further instructions can be issued. Key employees and certain members of management may, on the other hand, be needed to attend the emergency site or the Command Center at an early stage in the process to consider how to minimize the impact of the emergency on their areas of responsibility. The BCP team leader, deputy, or nominated alternate is responsible for undertaking this notification activity. This section of the BCP should contain a list of management and key employees who should be contacted in an emergency situation. It should contain each person's name, normal and emergency contact information, and a brief description regarding the area of responsibility.

5.4.3   Handling Notification of Personnel Families

If the emergency event has resulted in a situation that would cause concern to an employee's immediate family, such as the hospitalization of injured persons, it will be necessary to notify immediate family members urgently. This type of communication needs to be handled with sensitivity and care, so as not to increase the level of distress to the persons being notified. This type of work would normally be handled by a trained manager or a member of senior management. The need to deal sensitively with employee situations is one of the reasons why it may be beneficial to include executive management from the HR department of your organization in the disaster recovery team. This section of the BCP will contain the names and emergency contact details of the persons nominated to undertake this particular type of notification. In the event of serious injury or even death of an employee, it would be beneficial if the person notifying had access to counseling service contact numbers, in order to be able to offer this type of support and advice.

5.4.4 Handling Media during the Disaster Recovery Phase

Media contact during the disaster recovery phase has to be handled very carefully. All information released to the public at this time has to be accurate, and speculation should be reduced to the minimum. Media interviews and press release statements should be handled by persons who have been specifically authorized to undertake such duties. Other persons who have not been authorized to speak to the media should be strongly discouraged from doing so. Prepare a policy or strategy in advance of an emergency situation to be followed by the person authorized to release information to the media. This section of the BCP should contain information on the policy to be followed and the name and emergency contact numbers of the persons authorized to speak to the media.

5.4.5 Maintaining an Event Log during Disaster Recovery Phase

It is important that all key events during the disaster recovery phase be recorded. An event log should be maintained by the leader of the disaster recovery team. This event log should be started at the commencement of the emergency, and a copy of the log should be passed on to the business recovery team once the initial dangers have been controlled. The format of the event log was discussed previously but, at a minimum, it should include the date, time, title of the event, a brief description of the event, and outcomes. It should also include follow up action needed, as appropriate.

5.5 Disaster Recovery Phase Report

On completion of the initial disaster recovery phase, the DRT leader should prepare a report on the activities undertaken. The report should contain information on the emergency, who was notified and when, the actions taken by members of the DRT, and the outcomes arising from those actions. The report will also contain an assessment of the impact to normal business operations. This report is also known as an "After-Actions Report" and should answer the following questions:

- *What have you learned while managing this disaster?*
- *How can it help in future disaster response operations?*

The process of writing the After-Actions Report really begins when the disaster is declared. Documents are generated, incidents occur, problems are solved, and lessons are learned. All become part of the After-Actions Report. These elements must be recorded and maintained as they happen.

5.6   Chapter Summary

This chapter has explained the disaster recovery phase. We started by discussing various disaster recovery legal issues and by providing statutory examples. Next, we explained the necessity for organizations to plan methods of handling the emergency and the insurance considerations. These considerations start with the identification of potential disaster status and the involvement of emergency services, both state and FEMA. We talked about the importance of assessing the business impact of an emergency and managing a secure recovery at the recovery site or at one or more alternate sites.

Disaster recovery team management actions and the process of notification and reporting during the disaster recovery phase were also covered in this chapter. Actions discussed included mobilizing the disaster recovery team, notifying management and key employees, handling the notification of employees' families, handling media during the disaster recovery phase, and maintaining an event log during the disaster recovery phase.

After recovery, the importance of creating a disaster recovery phase report was stressed. FEMA and state interactions, including interaction with state and local emergency services, were also covered. Finally, we explained the various other recovery issues that organizations must contend with, such as the process of internal and external communication to everyone dealing with the organization. Once the disaster recovery phase has concluded, organizations must contend with business recovery, the topic of our next chapter.

5.7   Endnotes

1.   Schreider, Tari. White Paper: "The Legal Issues of Disaster Recovery Planning." *Disaster Recovery World IV*, vol. 9, no. 2 (1996): 233–235.

2.   *Parr v. Security Nat. Bank*, 1984 OK CIV APP 16 680 P.2d 648, Case Number: 59733. Decided: 03/13/1984. Retrieved from

http://caselaw.lp.findlaw.com/scripts/getcase.pl?court=ok&vol=/
appeals/1984/&invol=9764 on March 11, 2005.

3.   Federal Financial Institutions Examination Council, *Information Technology Examination Handbook*, vols. 1–8 . Washington, DC: FFIEC, August 2004. http://www.fdic.gov/regulations/information/information/FFIEC.html.

4.   *Corpus Juris Secundum*, vol. 19, section 491.

6

Business Recovery Phase

Once personnel safety is no longer threatened, the fires are out, and imminent danger has past, the organization must begin the process of managing the business recovery phase. A team should be established specific to business recovery activities and mobilized as soon as danger has subsided. Part of this team's responsibility will be to assess the extent of damage and determine the overall impact the disaster has had on the business. Their mission will include creation of a recovery plan. The team will implement the recovery plan and make sure it stays on track. During these times, when there is great uncertainty, it is also very important to keep everyone informed about progress. As soon as possible, the recovery team should begin handing business operations back to regular management. After their task is completed, the business recovery team should prepare a business recovery phase report and submit it to the BC team leader.

6.1 Business Recovery Planning Process

We have said that BCP (business continuity planning) is the process of identifying critical data systems and business functions, analyzing the risks of disruption to the data systems and business functions, determining the probability of a disruption occurring, and then developing business recovery plans (BRPs) to enable those systems and functions to be resumed in the event of a disruption. The goal of an effective BRP and process is to facilitate and expedite the recovery of business after a disruption of critical or impacting data systems and operations has occurred. Disruptions may be minor, or may include instances where normal functions and services cannot be performed and may not be performed for an extended period of time. Business continuity planning minimizes the impact of disruption while maximizing resources available to resume normal operations. The principle objectives are to:

- Minimize disruptions of service to the business and any external entity relying on business data systems and the information stored in them.

- Provide a road map of predetermined actions that will reduce decision-making during recovery operations. Good planning will reduce the number and magnitude of decisions that must be made during the period when exposure to error is at a peak.

- Ensure the timely recovery of critical and impacting systems, and enable the recovery of normal business/service at the earliest possible time in the most cost-effective manner.

- Limit the impact of the disruption on the business mission and reputation, and limit any financial losses.

6.1.1   Mobilizing a Business Recovery Team

Immediately following an emergency that seriously affects one or more of the organization's normal business processes, the business recovery team (BRT) is to be notified. If there is need of a disaster recovery phase, then initially the BRT is likely to be put on standby. If there is no disaster recovery phase, or the disaster recovery phase is nearing completion, the BRT will be asked to assemble at the Emergency Command Center set up to control and manage both the emergency and the recovery process. This section of the BCP contains a procedure for mobilizing the BRT and an appropriate standard wording for notification. It may also contain the process for alerting the members of the BRT, moving them from "standby status" to "mobilization status." It may be considered appropriate to include a suitable three-stage alert status procedure:

Yellow:	Place DRT on standby alert
Orange:	Place DRT on alert
Red:	Mobilize DRT

6.1.2 Assessing Extent of Damage and Business Impact

Once the BRT is mobilized, the first task is the assessment of the extent of the damage and its impact on the business process. This activity must be focused on the business impact, as opposed to the damage assessment carried out by the DRT, which is mainly focused on the impact on people and the physical infrastructure. The effects of the disaster will be reviewed by examining each area of the business that has been affected and then assessing the impact of the disaster on the various key business processes. This section of the BCP should contain a list of the areas of the business affected by the disaster and the actual business processes affected. Cross-dependencies of affected processes to other processes should be listed. For each affected business process, there should be a preliminary estimate of the recovery time needed to restore normal operations. A damage assessment form for use by the BRT is included in the BCP.

6.1.3 Preparing Specific Recovery Plans

Following the business impact assessment phase, a recovery plan needs to be prepared. As this will be prepared once the disruptive event has occurred, it is likely to initially be an outline plan only, as the most important requirement will be to mobilize the resources toward recovery as fast as possible. Nevertheless, in order to be effective, the process must be carefully planned and structured, and the business recovery team leader must be adept at planning, organization, and decision making under extreme conditions. The recovery plan will identify those areas that need to be addressed immediately and will establish a prioritized sequence for the recovery process to proceed.

Once critical and impacting business applications have been identified and ranked, the team will develop BRPs for these applications. Copies of the BRPs must be accessible from any offsite location. Key personnel should know the exact location of the BRPs and be familiar with how to access this information. BRPs should be maintained electronically in relational database software, when possible. BRPs for critical and impacting systems should contain a clarification of what constitutes a disruption (what level/extent of disruption) in response to which the specific BRP needs to be implemented. The BRP should state the maximum acceptable downtimes that can be incurred (i.e., how long the unit/business can function before the data system must be available). Business functions and/or services that must be restored within two to four hours require significantly different recovery actions than those which can be delayed a number of hours, days, or weeks.

It is important to decide who determines whether the incident is classified as a business disruption, what level of disruption has occurred, and to what degree the plan needs to be implemented. When a disruption occurs, the level and extent of the disruption must be immediately determined, and appropriate steps must be taken to safeguard lives and prevent further destruction or escalation of the problem. The BRP should also detail which staff are to be involved in the business recovery effort and at what disruption level they are involved. Specify the recovery team member responsibilities and the way that nonavailability of certain key team members will be addressed. You should provide step-by-step, definitive procedures for each team member. Plans for cross-training on duties should also be formulated. Preplanned processes and trained personnel will significantly reduce the cost and time necessary to achieve full recovery and resume normal business operations. It is critical to have current contact names, phone lists, and initiation procedures that are updated quarterly or as needed. An emergency call list for key personnel should be developed. Additionally, similar procedures should be developed for all other administrative functions that may be affected, such as human resources, safety, public relations, data center personnel, and so on. The plan should detail the location of a BRP coordination site and set criteria to determine whether it is needed or not.

Preplanning what should be communicated will help on-scene personnel determine what information about the disruption can be made public and how this information will be disseminated. The incident scene must be isolated as soon as the emergency is discovered. Although no one should place him- or herself in danger, the discoverer should attempt to secure the scene and control access. When possible, and if danger risks do not exist, the basic security measures include:

1. Closing file cabinets or desk drawers

2. Closing doors or windows

3. Putting containment materials, such as absorbent pads, in the path of leaking materials

4. Establishing temporary barriers with furniture after people have safely evacuated

Only trained personnel should be allowed to perform advanced security measures. Access to the facility, the EOC, and the incident scene should be limited to persons directly involved in the response. The physical security of your building and contents should receive immediate consideration in post-disaster situations, and the actions necessary to secure entry points to unstable buildings, as well as the reduction of the likelihood of unauthorized people gaining entry, must be determined. Some of these actions may include the restoration of burglar alarm systems and the possible use of security guards to provide additional protection and reduce the chance of further loss to your business property. Temporary repairs, such as boarding up windows or doors and covering holes in the roof, may be necessary to protect your property from further damage.

Once personnel safety is secured, the next step is to conduct an inspection of your property. This inspection is performed to assess damage, and you should compile a complete description of damages, including damage to your building, equipment, and inventory. If circumstances require immediate disposal of any property, it is advisable that photographs or other documentation be retained in order to identify all items destroyed. Itemized damaged property should be set aside in the best possible order for examination. The condition of the ventilation, drainage, and other sanitation systems within the building must also be considered.

The local EOC and your business's property/casualty insurer should be contacted to register a claim for relief. Review the policy with an insurer representative and discuss the loss and business interruption coverage for loss of income, as well as reimbursement for expenses such as temporary office space and equipment. You should also obtain guidance about how to avoid malpractice liability if the firm will miss client deadlines. Communicate with everyone important to the business, such as firm members and employees, to inform them of the status of the situation and to establish communication procedures, such as telephone trees and an emergency information hotline until office space is acquired and everyone can get under one roof again. Also, contact vendors to let them know where the temporary location is. If necessary, you should also stay in touch with the payroll service, contact banks for replacement checks, and advise the post office and other delivery services to stop shipments to the damaged location and reroute services to the temporary site.

Another critical step is to reinstate your telephone service and arrange for an answering service with an appropriate message until a new system is in place. Also, arrange temporary service with the local telephone company at the interim location for phones, fax, modem, and Internet use, have phone calls forwarded to the new number, and, if appropriate, get cellular phones. You must also obtain workspace, furnishings, equipment, and office supplies for staff. Identify alternative work locations, call local realtors to find office space, arrange for temporary space by sharing with other organizations, or rent a hotel suite. To equip the employees, it may be necessary to rent, borrow, or purchase desks, chairs, lamps, filing cabinets, and bookshelves. For your staff to begin operations again, most likely you will have to obtain computers and operating systems, which may include computers, computer networks, printers, fax machines, copiers, word processors, and calculators. Another solution is to have staff members use personal laptops and home computers for the business, if this is permissible during the recovery period. An often-overlooked item in recovery is office supplies. We recommend you contact the local supply vendors to obtain whatever supplies are necessary, and, if necessary, contact a printer to print stationery and business cards and a forms vendor to obtain billing and other forms. Contact equipment vendors to discuss existing leases, contracts, and performance obligations under the terms of the lease or contract. Get vendors to assist with the recovery of computer hardware and peripherals, if necessary.

6.1.4 Assess Damaged Property and Documents

Assign a high priority to damaged documents; documents or records of critical importance should be separated from the records that can wait. The most critical documents should be organized in a way that protects them from further damage as they wait to be restored. The physical status of the documents should be identified with colored tape or markers. For example, red can be used to identify documents that are of greatest importance and must be recovered first; green can be used for documents that are not damaged and can be used immediately; and black for documents that are beyond hope and cannot be recovered.

Damage assessment begins as soon as the workplace is accessible. If documents are waterlogged, you can freeze them and have a commercial restorer salvage them. Freezing will preserve paper documents for up to six years. If backup records are available, the originals aren't necessary. If water damage has occurred, the following supplies are recommended to handle water-damaged documents:

- Pumps if necessary
- Mops, buckets, sponges, and rubber gloves

- Fans and dehumidifiers

- Irons, plastic clips, and clothesline or nylon fish line to dry a small number of records

- Freezer or waxed paper

- New boxes, file pockets, folders, plastic milk containers, plastic garbage cans or pails, and, in some cases, sawhorses, plywood, and plastic sheeting to wrap wet records for removal

- Refrigerated facilities or trucks when available

Specific techniques to recover water-damaged documents include separating sheets of paper for drying by hanging them on a clothesline, or interleaving them with absorbent paper. Individual sheets can be dried by ironing them on low heat. You can use clear mylar to protect damaged documents, photocopy them, and then discard the original and use the photocopy. New file folders, pockets, or boxes should be created to organize the documents as you restore them. Wet documents should be packed for freeze-drying in cut-off plastic milk containers; stand the documents upright and pack the containers two-thirds full. There are other options available for treating water-damaged materials, such as air-drying, freezing, vacuum freeze-drying, and vacuum-drying. Each choice has advantages and issues, and the choice of treatment will depend on the extent and type of damage incurred and the personnel, expertise, funding, and facilities available.

Air-drying requires a great deal of space and is labor-intensive, but it is inexpensive and can be done by anybody easily. Additionally, it can be done onsite so the materials can be watched while they dry, which adds confidence in the security of the material. The ideal environment for air-drying is a cool, dry, stable environment, to inhibit the growth of mold. Unless extreme care is taken, coated stock material, such as that in magazines, should not be air-dried because the pages will likely be permanently stuck together. Wet materials can be stabilized by freezing, which will buy you time until you have decided a course of action. Further deterioration from water will be inhibited when the materials are in a frozen state. Smoke odor can also be minimized, but not eliminated, through freezing. Blast freezing services are available commercially and can minimize the damage from ice crystals by rapid-freezing the materials. Wet materials will freeze and begin to dry at temperatures below 15° F. If the outside temperature is below 15° and freezer space is not available, you can cover the materials in plastic in a secure area outside to buy time, but materials still must be dried afterwards.

The most successful, albeit expensive, salvage method for paper is vacuum freeze-drying. In this process, frozen materials are placed in a sublimation chamber that operates under a high vacuum and applied heat. This process sublimates the ice, which turns it directly into water vapor without becoming liquid. The vapor goes to the sides of the chamber where it forms as ice. Vacuum-drying pulls the moisture out of wet materials by means of a vacuum. When frozen materials are vacuum-dried, most of the water will pass through the liquid state before vaporizing, which may cause water-soluble inks and dyes to bleed.

If fire was involved, make sure all file cabinets or other containers are cold to the touch before opening them. Flash fires may occur upon opening a warm cabinet. Fire-damaged documents should be handled as little as possible. However, if they must be handled, the following techniques should be used to recover fire-damaged documents: look at charred records that are not wet to see if they are completely destroyed or just have burned edges, and if the record is legible and recoverable, photocopy it.

Vendors provide a variety of salvage services, ranging from handling the total effort (trained personnel, equipment, transportation, and so forth) to drying a few books shipped to them. Some also salvage film and electronic media. Check the Internet for details.

An inventory of all critical resources necessary to resume processing includes, but is not limited to:

a.   Software (systems and applications)

b.   Communication requirements (e.g., front-end processors, lines, modems)

c.   An alternate facility, whose physical site requirements include air conditioning, power, a raised floor, cabling, communications, total square footage, personnel and office space needs, and so on

d.   Hardware and peripherals (e.g., PCs, printers)

e.   Data files (note format: .doc, .html, .pdf, and so on)

f.   Forms/documents

g.   Vendor support

h.   Staff

i. Security, which should include any modifications to physical, data, and networks needed to allow the recovery team members to implement the BRP

j. Office equipment (e.g., telephones, copiers, typewriters, fax machines)

k. Storage for supplies, forms, and other items

l. Funding and acquisitions; this includes the funding needed to implement the recovery plan and the source of that funding, and should also include a provision for incidental costs so that small needs do not hamper the recovery effort

m. Transportation logistics (e.g., trucking, packing services) for personnel, supplies, input/output delivery between critical system users and the recovery site, and delivery between the recovery site and the backup facility

It is very important to document all losses. Destruction of items should be documented for legal and insurance purposes. A disposal certificate is used to indicate what is beyond recovery and why, and to describe what was destroyed, how it was destroyed, how it was pertinent to a client (if it was). The certificate should be signed and dated.

One primary task to accomplish as quickly as possible is to reestablish and begin using data backup schedules and offsite storage procedures. Keep current schedules and backups for all critical/impacting systems at offsite storage locations. Special backup and restore procedures should enable loading only the most critical items. Use contracted or agreed-upon alternate facilities/operating sites, if appropriate. These may be hot, warm, or cold sites, depending on the degree of disruption and the need.

Communication Systems

Copies of any reciprocal agreements or contracts should be kept at an offsite location. Information regarding the type and level of hardware and software vendor support required, available, and contracted should be a part of the recovery plan. This should include any necessary purchases or leases needed in the event of a disruption (e.g., office, communications, and/or computer equipment), estimated costs of specific support, payment arrangements, and vendor response times. Information of this nature can be obtained through meetings, requests for information, acquisition terms and conditions, joint vendor meetings, and so forth as part of the business continuity planning efforts. The offsite location of data (whether paper, tapes, cassettes, disks, etc.), duplicate copies of documentation (BRP, system/ application manuals, contracts, procedure manuals, etc.), supplies, and forms must also be documented. This section should also include hardware and software (system and application) restore procedures.

A schedule for BRP testing should be developed and maintained. BRPs should be tested at least annually using various testing approaches (e.g., structured walk-through; checklists; simulations; parallel testing; and full-interruption testing). Tests should be carefully planned to minimize disruption to normal operations and should address partial and full disruptions of various types. Each test scenario should be carefully developed so that all facets of the BRP are fully tested. Planning and conducting test exercises should be the joint responsibility of the data center, application administrators, and the user(s). Some areas to test include, but are not limited to:

- Data backup

- Documentation backup

- Facilities backup

- Recovery team training

- Critical applications (first singly, then in groups); response times during different processing periods and shifts should also be tested

- Alternate processing procedures

Develop additional procedures for documenting formal plan tests and test results, following up these tests, and implementing corrective actions/ recommendations arising from these tests. After each test exercise, results should be thoroughly reviewed for flaws, omissions, and overlaps in the business recovery procedures. Test results should be made available to the risk manager and business audit.

Activities will, wherever possible, be carried out simultaneously, but the critical path must be identified to ensure that those activities directly on the critical path receive the highest priority. The recovery plan will list the activities that need to be carried out in priority sequence, and which persons or teams are responsible for completing those tasks. Where suppliers and vendors are required to supply goods or services as part of the recovery process, then these activities will be involved also. The recovery plan will activate the recovery process and will activate the various people or task forces involved.

The BRT are to be fully briefed on the extent of the recovery operation and the activities they are expected to carry out. The impact of each of their tasks on the critical path must also be communicated.

At its very core, a business continuity plan ensures that if a company's main office is damaged or destroyed, its information is retrievable. This essentially allows businesses to continue their operation at another location, if necessary. While the concept is simple, the creation of a business continuity plan can be complex, becoming more complicated as the scope of the enterprise increases.

6.1.5   Backup Recovery Site

The business recovery team should stand-up a data center or work area that provides your organization with the relevant work area for recovery, including telecommunications and IT interfaces and environmentally controlled space capable of providing relatively immediate backup data processing support to maintain the organization's mission-critical activities. Cost is typically a major factor in the speed of recovery, and a mirrored backup site is normally significantly more expensive to set up and maintain than a manual process. In the cases where speed of recovery is more important than cost, corporations should use a hot, warm, or cool site. In general, the hot site is the most sophisticated—and expensive—type of data replication routine. Data is replicated on two separate servers—one in the operational location and one housed at a different physical site. Transactions are updated on both systems simultaneously.

6.1.5.1   Designate Recovery Site

Appropriate personnel should conduct a survey of the disaster scene to estimate the amount of time required to put the facility back into working order. A decision is then made whether to use a predetermined alternate location, such as a cold, warm, or hot site, some distance away from the scene of the disaster, where computing and networking capabilities can be temporarily restored until the primary site is ready. The repairing or rebuilding of the primary site should begin almost immediately after the recovery process starts.

6.1.5.2   Purchase New Equipment

Vendors are relied upon to quickly provide replacements for the resources that cannot be salvaged. Emergency procurement procedures should be documented in the plan and approved by the appropriately designated parties to quickly place orders for equipment, supplies, software, and any other needs.

6.1.5.3   Begin Reassembly at Recovery Site

Both salvaged and new components are reassembled at the recovery site according to the instructions contained in this plan. Since all plans of this type are subject to the inherent changes that occur in the computer industry, it may become necessary for recovery personnel to deviate from the plan, especially if the plan has not been keep up-to-date. If vendors cannot provide a certain piece of equipment on a timely basis, it may be necessary for the recovery personnel to make last-minute substitutions. After the equipment reassembly phase is complete, the work turns to concentrate on the data recovery procedures.

6.1.5.4   Restore Data from Backups

Data recovery may rely entirely on the use of backups stored in locations offsite from the primary facility. Backups can take the form of magnetic tape, CD-ROMs, disk drives, and other storage media. Early data recovery efforts focus on restoring the operating system(s) for each computer system, and then the first line recovery of application and user data from the backup tapes is done. Individual application owners may need to be involved at this point, so teams are assigned for each major application area to ensure that data is restored properly.

6.1.5.5   Restore Applications Data

The recovery plans for users and departmental application owners must merge with the completion of the technology recovery plan. Since some time may have elapsed between the time the offsite backups were made and the time of the disaster, application owners must have means of restoring each running application database to the point of the disaster. They must also take all new data collected since that point and input it into the application databases. When this process is complete, the computer systems can be reopened for business. Some applications may be available only to a limited few key personnel, while others may be available to anyone who can access the computer systems.

6.1.5.6 Move Back to Restored Permanent Facility

If the recovery process has taken place at an alternative site, physical restoration of the primary facility should have begun. When the primary facility is ready for reoccupancy, the systems assembled at the alternate site are to be moved back to their permanent home.

6.1.6 Monitoring Progress

It is necessary for the BRT leader to closely monitor progress of the individual recovery tasks during this phase. Difficulties experienced by one group of persons could have a significant effect on other dependent tasks. It is also important to ensure that each task is properly resourced and the efforts required to restore normal business operations have not been underestimated. This section of the BCP should contain information needed for regular progress monitoring. The tasks to be achieved should be listed together with estimate of when you expect each task to be completed. It should also contain information on resources and related information, including:

- Milestones
- Dependencies
- Critical path
- Progress reporting frequency

Where progress is not maintained at an adequate level, it is necessary to have escalation procedures in place so that top management are kept fully informed of the implications of delay.

6.1.7 Keeping Everyone Informed

During the business recovery phase it is extremely important that all affected persons and organizations are kept properly and fully informed. This could include the following groups:

- Board of Directors
- Management and staff
- Customers

- Appropriate authorities or industry regulatory bodies
- Insurance broker/loss adjustors
- Suppliers and vendors
- Contracted staff
- Joint venture partners

A particularly important area to be considered is in notifying customers about the impact on deliveries of products or services. At an early stage in the business recovery process, a list of customers who may be affected by the outage or damage should be compiled. An estimate should be made of the delays to goods, deliveries, or services, and each customer should be notified accordingly. Whenever possible, efforts should be made to identify alternative methods of supplying the goods and services where the delays are likely to be critical, particularly to important clients. Affected customers should be apprised of the progress of recovery, as appropriate.

A further area requiring special attention is the media. Depending upon the prominence of the organization and the scale of the emergency, the level of interest from the media will vary. Only persons authorized to release information to the media should be permitted to do so. The information given to all parties must be accurate and timely. Estimates of the timing of normal working operations should be announced with care. This section of the BCP should list the groups of persons or organizations who could be affected by disruption to normal business operations. It should also contain the names, positions and contact numbers of the persons nominated to coordinate the communication to each group.

6.1.8 Handing Business Operations Back to Regular Management

Once normal business operations have been restored, it may be necessary to hand the responsibility for specific operations back to the regular management process. This process should be formalized to ensure that all parties understand the change in overall responsibility. It is likely that during the recovery process, overall responsibility may have been assigned to the business recovery process leader. Inevitably, the regular management should be fully involved throughout, but in order for the recovery process to be fully effective, overall responsibility during the recovery period should probably be with the BRP team. On the other hand, some organizations may prefer that regular management remain overall responsible for a particular business process throughout the BRP. Where this approach is preferred, it is recommended the chief executive officer (or another member of top management) undertake the leadership role for this period. This section of the BCP contains a proposed handover form to be completed and signed by the BRT leader and the regular manager responsible for each process. A separate form is to be used for each business process.

6.1.9 Preparing Business Recovery Phase Report

Upon completion of the business recovery phase, the BRT leader should prepare a report on the activities undertaken. The report should contain information on the disruptive event, who was notified and when, action taken by members of the BRT, and the outcomes arising from those actions. The report should also contain an assessment of the impact on normal business operations. The report should be distributed to senior management as appropriate. This section of the BCP should contain a suggested format for such a report.

6.2 Planning Business Recovery Activities

The efficiency and effectiveness of the procedures in the BCP have a direct bearing on the organization's ability to survive an emergency. While there is no plan that can account for all possible contingencies, most plans can account for a majority of possibilities. These possibilities should include, at a minimum, the areas shown in Figure 6.1.

Figure 6.1
Common areas of consideration for BCP purposes.

- Human resources
- Corporate proprietary information and documentation
- IT systems (hardware and software)
- Office supplies
- Operations and administration (support services)
- Power and other utilities
- Premises, fixtures and furniture (facilities recovery management)
- Production equipment
- Trading, sales and customer service
- Warehouse and stock

6.2.1   Communication Systems

If communications equipment has been damaged during the emergency, it will need to be repaired or replaced. This category of procedures excludes the production equipment and IT equipment, which have dedicated procedures for those restoring specialized services. It includes all other equipment owned or used by the organization. The linked procedure is given as a guideline that must be carefully reviewed and amended by the organization to ensure that it fully meets the organization's own requirements. In many cases, the services or support of outside specialists may be required to carry out the activity. Amend the predefined items within the plan template, as appropriate.

6.2.2   Human Resources

During a particularly serious incident, it is necessary to take special care of the employees, as they may have been subjected to unusual and distressing circumstances. The recovery teams may also need to remain near the recovery site for long periods, and may require temporary accommodation. This category of the procedures covers the Human Resources Management (HRM) considerations following a particularly disruptive incident. Amend the predefined items within the plan template, as appropriate.

6.2.3   Corporate Proprietary Information and Documentation

Information and documentation is the lifeblood of most organizations. It is therefore important to ascertain whether any damage has occurred to this data. If the damage to computerized or other information is widespread, it is recommended to concentrate initially on essential and vital records. As a matter of good practice, wherever possible, vital records should be duplicated and stored in an offsite location so permanent loss will not be a realistic problem. Amend the predefined items within the plan template, as appropriate.

6.2.4   IT Systems (Hardware and Software)

If IT systems equipment has been damaged during the emergency, it will need to be repaired or replaced. This section of the BCP excludes production equipment and telecommunications equipment, both of which are specialized services with dedicated procedures for restoration. It does, however, include all other equipment owned or used by the organization. The linked procedure is given as a guideline that must be carefully reviewed and amended by the organization to ensure that it fully meets the organization's own requirements. In some cases, the services of outside specialists may be required to carry out the activity. Amend the predefined items within the plan template, as appropriate.

6.2.5 Office Supplies

In certain types of emergencies, it is likely that stationery and office supplies could be destroyed or rendered unusable. The status of these items should be ascertained as early as possible so that urgent replacements may be obtained. Consideration may be given to keeping a certain level of stock at an offsite location for use in these circumstances. The BRT should be prepared to arrange for urgent delivery of replacements from the vendor. Amend the predefined items within the plan template, as appropriate.

6.2.6 Operations and Administration (Support Services)

This area of the business requires special consideration following a disruption to the normal business processes. There is likely to be an immediate and noticeable effect on customers or trading partners. It is therefore necessary to make an assessment as to when service will be restored, and the impact of any period of service outage. It is important that affected customers and trading partners are made fully aware of both the circumstances and the efforts being expended to restore normal operations. Amend the predefined items within the plan template, as appropriate.

6.2.7 Power and Other Utilities

The continuity of power, telecommunications, and water utilities is a critical element in the planning process for your organization. Large or regulated business and services (banks, insurance companies, brokerages, Internet communications services) must depend on these infrastructures, which, in turn, support thousands or even hundreds of thousands of users. When organizations of such magnitude are involved in a disaster, the involvement of the federal government is inevitable. For example, the U.S. Federal Communications Commission (FCC) oversees coordinated network service continuity planning by telecommunications carriers and other providers of telecommunications service. The U.S. Environmental

Protection Agency (EPA) enforces many environmental regulations, including its provisions for business continuity, to ensure the availability of safe power and water supplies and services despite disruption scenarios. State Departments of Environmental Services and Public Utilities Commissions (in some states called Public Services Commissions) oversee enforcement of state public utilities code legislation, ensuring reliability (continuity) of business and service. In other countries, national and regional governmental agencies enforce similar legislation, requiring plans for the continuity of critical infrastructure services after disruptive emergencies. As these entities' operations' continuity needs have expanded into total business continuity, so have their plans and the software infrastructure supporting the plans.

Power and other utilities are an essential service, because a building or infrastructure is disabled without them. This not only includes water, gas, and electricity, but also standby power systems, environmental control systems, and communication networks. Even if you use RAID, the data in random access memory (RAM) and even cache memory is lost when the power source is lost, and a loss of power at the wrong time can be devastating. An appropriately sized uninterruptible power supply (UPS) and, of course, a data backup are the best ways to protect against a power failure. A critical part of the recovery process is the restoration of electric power, other public utilities, or services such as water and gas. This will normally require the involvement of the utility suppliers, maintenance engineers, outside technical specialists, and in-house premises maintenance staff. In many cases, the services of outside specialists will be required to complete the activity. Amend the predefined items within the plan template, as appropriate.

6.2.8   Premises, Fixtures, and Furniture (Facilities Recovery Management)

The procedure to recover premises, fixtures, and furniture can be collectively referred to as facilities recovery management. The extent of this activity is hard to predefine, as it will be affected greatly by the actual scale of the emergency. The linked procedure is given as a guideline that must be reviewed by the organization undertaking the preparation of the BCP, to ensure it fits with the organization's own requirements. In many cases, the services of outside specialists may be required to carry out the activity. Amend the predefined items within the plan template, as appropriate.

The BCP plan should include a complete inventory of the components of each of the computer and network systems and their software that must be restored after a disaster. This list must be periodically updated to reflect the most current configuration, because the systems will inevitably change over time. Every attempt should be made to replicate the current system configuration, so as to avoid problems and delays in recovery. Although some changes to the procedures documented in the plan may be required, using different models of equipment, or equipment from a different vendor, may be suitable to expedite the recovery process. Where possible, agreements will be made with vendors to supply replacements on an emergency basis.

6.2.9   Production Equipment

If production equipment has been damaged during the emergency it will need to be repaired or replaced. This section of the BCP excludes the IT equipment and telecommunications equipment, both of which are specialized service with dedicated procedures for restoration. If equipment has been damaged during the emergency, it will need to be repaired or replaced.

6.2.10   Nonproduction Equipment

This section covers all other equipment owned or used by the organization, including such items as photocopiers, calculators, refrigerators, kitchen equipment, water coolers, and so forth. Each piece of equipment that serves a business purpose should be considered, no matter how trivial. Working through the aftermath of a disaster is hard enough. Trying to do so without the proper equipment makes the situation much more difficult than it should be.

6.2.11   Trading, Sales, and Customer Service

This area of the business requires special consideration following disruption to the normal business processes. There is likely to be an immediate and noticeable effect on customers or trading partners. It is necessary, therefore, for an assessment to be made as to when service will be restored and the impact of any period of service outage. It is important that affected customers and trading partners are made fully aware of the circumstances and the efforts being expended to restore normal operations. Amend the predefined items within the plan template, as appropriate.

6.2.12 Warehouse and Stock

If the organization's warehouse facilities or stock have been damaged during the emergency, it is necessary to assess the extent of the damage and prepare a claim from the insurance company. It will also be necessary to inform customers who may be relying on delivery of that stock in the near future. The damaged items will need to be repaired or replaced. In some cases, it may be necessary to use the services of outside specialists to carry out the activity. Amend the predefined items within the plan template, as appropriate.

6.3 Chapter Summary

In this chapter, we talked about what measures are needed to accomplish a business recovery effort. Although the term "Disaster Recovery" has become a popular industry buzzword, the majority of discussion on this topic concentrates on IT operations recovery. In reality, business recovery must take precedence over IT systems recovery, since the business is responsible for continuity of operations and, therefore, service to the customer. Businesses can experience all kinds of interruptions, ranging from catastrophic natural disasters to acts of terrorism to technical glitches, so organizations need business continuity and recovery resources, plans, and above all management. Business recovery planning provides for the recovery of mission-critical business processes at an alternative site. Just as a disaster is an event that makes the continuation of normal functions impossible, a disaster recovery plan consists of the precautions taken so the effects of a disaster will be minimized and the organization will be able to either maintain or quickly resume mission-critical functions.

The business recovery planning process was outlined in detail. From mobilizing a business recovery team and assessing the extent of damage and the business impact a disaster may have on your business, we discussed various methods of recovering your business functions. We also discussed the importance of using a backup recovery site. This backup strategy starts with the designation of a recovery site, the purchase of any necessary equipment that would be used to build the site, the reassembly of that equipment at the recovery site, and the operations needed to actually restore data from backups. The process of restoring applications data, as well as proprietary data, was explained. Once the emergency has passed and you are able to move back to your restored permanent facility, it is important to have someone monitor overall progress and keep everyone informed. Usually, once the business functions have been restored, a process of handing business operations back to regular management takes place. The BRT should be tasked with preparing a business recovery phase report to address what or how things could have been improved in the event they are ever reconstituted for another emergency.

When planning business recovery activities, we stressed covering all areas of the business, including your communication systems; human resources; corporate proprietary information and documentation; IT systems; office supplies; operations and administration (support services); power and other utilities; premises, fixtures, and furniture (facilities recovery management); all of your production equipment and nonproduction equipment; and whatever is needed to preserve your organization's ability to conduct trading, sales, and customer service activities. Finally, don't forget about warehouse and stock matters. There are dozens of details you must account for that are unique to your organization. This chapter has attempted to bring to the forefront the areas most important to getting normal operations restored. In the next chapter, we will discuss how to test, audit, and train to ensure continuity of your business.

7

Testing, Auditing, and Training

Some of the information in this section was abstracted from the Federal Financial Institutions Examination Council (FFIEC) IT Examination Handbook. According to the FFIEC Web site, the Council is a formal interagency body empowered to prescribe uniform principles, standards, and report forms for the federal examination of financial institutions by the Board of Governors of the Federal Reserve System (FRB), the Federal Deposit Insurance Corporation (FDIC), the National Credit Union Administration (NCUA), the Office of the Comptroller of the Currency (OCC), and the Office of Thrift Supervision (OTS), and to make recommendations to promote uniformity in the supervision of financial institutions. While our purpose here is not to focus specifically on the security controls of financial institutions, it is worthwhile to understand their examination process, because the rigor applied to IT and security controls in financial institutions is generally much greater than that of everyday corporate settings—the privacy of individual data and protection of money, let alone the legal issues surrounding the protection of privacy, are strong motivators for protecting data.

Information security is the process by which an organization protects and secures systems, media, and facilities that process and maintain information vital to its operations. The security of systems and information is essential to the privacy of organizational and corporate customer information. Security professionals must maintain effective security programs adequate for their organization's operational complexity. These security programs must have strong board- and senior management-level support, integration of security responsibilities and controls throughout the organi-

Plan

Assess Risk

Mitigate

Prepare

Disaster Recovery

Business Recovery

Test, Audit, and Train

Maintain

zation's business processes, and clear accountability for carrying out security responsibilities. This chapter provides guidance to security professionals and organizations on determining the level of security risks to the organization and evaluating the adequacy of the organization's risk management.

Organizations often inaccurately perceive information security as the state or condition of controls at a single point in time. Security is an ongoing process, in which the condition of security controls is just one indicator of overall security posture. Other indicators include the ability of the institution to continually assess its posture and react appropriately in the face of rapidly changing threats, technologies, and business conditions. This requires an organization to continuously integrate processes, people, and technology to mitigate risk in accordance with risk assessment and acceptable risk tolerance levels. Organizations protect their information by instituting a security process that identifies risks, forms a strategy to manage the risks, implements the strategy, tests the implementation, and monitors the environment to control the risks.

7.1　Testing the Business Recovery Process

In order to ensure the effectiveness of any plan put in place for contingency operations, it must be tested. Like everything else related to BCP, the testing process itself requires planning. Once testing begins, test scenarios should test each part of the business recovery process and the accuracy of employee and vendor emergency contact numbers. When completed, it is important to assess test results and determine whether the test was adequate to meet business needs and prevent injury or loss of life.

7.1.1　Develop Objectives and Scope of Tests

The first step in planning a testing process is to define the objectives and the scope of the testing. The test plan must determine the conditions and environment for conducting the test to try and simulate real-world conditions as much as possible. The BCP should contain a description of the objectives and scope of the testing phase. This will enable the tests to be structured and organized in a manner that the results can be measured, and the plan fine-tuned, as appropriate. The objectives for the tests could be as follows:

To undertake a thorough and rigorous testing of the business recovery process, including the simulation of a disruptive event, which pro-

duces results that can be measured and evaluated together with feedback, thus enabling enhancement and streamlining of the BCP.

The scope of the tests could be along the following lines:

The tests are to be carried out in a comprehensive and exhaustive manner so that all aspects of the plan may be tested. The tests should be contributed to, in a significant manner, by all business and support units within the organization. The tests will include recovery of all aspects of the Business Recovery Activities section of the BCP, including IT systems recovery.

7.1.2   Setting the Test Environment

One of the greatest challenges in testing the business recovery process is creating realistic conditions for carrying out the tests. For example, if the tests are carried out following a simulated fire affecting the main organization's premises, then all involved in the testing process have to be working within the limitations the team would expect to experience following an actual fire. These scenarios need to be carefully thought out to create an effective set of conditions that simulate an actual disruptive event. It is important also that these tests do not disrupt the normal business process in any way; therefore, they may need to be conducted outside normal business hours, if feasible. This section of the BCP should contain a list of the conditions to be expected with each potential disruptive emergency. The following are suggestions that could be incorporated into a test. These suggestions need to be further developed by the organization preparing the BCP to ensure that they fit with the organization's own situation and predicted circumstances in a potential disruptive emergency. At a minimum, you should prepare for the following types of scenarios:

- Environmental disasters
- Organized and/or deliberate disruption
- Loss of utilities and services
- Equipment or system failure
- Serious information security incidents
- Other emergency situations

7.1.3   Prepare Test Data

The next step is to prepare test cases that will be used. Each test case should simulate a single scenario, but multiple test cases can be conducted simultaneously to make a test more realistic. For example, a tornado strikes a building, causing fires in one area and flooding in another. Additionally, personnel injury and rescue scenarios can be tested in this example.

7.1.4   Identify Who Is to Conduct the Tests

It is important to identify who is to conduct the tests and who is to control and monitor the testing process. The test preparation team should construct feedback questionnaires to be used during various phases of testing. Of course, diverting personnel from their day-to-day activities to perform such testing costs the organization money, so the test team should prepare a budget for testing.

7.1.5   Identify Who Is to Control and Monitor the Tests

To ensure consistency when measuring the results, the tests should be independently monitored. This task would normally be carried out by a nominated member of the business recovery team or a member of the business continuity planning team. This section of the BCP will contain the names of the persons nominated to monitor the testing process throughout the organization. It will also contain a list of the duties to be undertaken by the monitoring staff.

7.1.6   Prepare Feedback Questionnaires

It is vital to receive feedback from the persons managing and participating in each of the tests. This feedback will hopefully identify weaknesses within the business recovery process so they can be eliminated. Completion of feedback forms should be mandatory for all persons participating in the testing process. This section of the BCP should contain a template for a feedback questionnaire.

7.1.7   Prepare Budget for Testing Phase

Each phase of the BCP process that incurs a cost requires the preparation and approval of a budget. The "Preparing for a Possible Emergency" phase of the BCP process will involve the identification and implementation of strategies for backup and recovery of data files or a part of a business process. It is inevitable that these backup and recovery processes will involve additional costs. Critical parts of the business process, such as the IT systems, may require particularly expensive backup strategies to be implemented. Where the costs are significant they should be approved separately, with specific detailed budgets for the establishment costs and the ongoing maintenance costs. This section of the BCP will contain a list of the testing phase activities and a cost for each. It should be noted whenever part of the cost is already incorporated within the organization's overall budgeting process.

7.1.8 Training Core Testing Team for Each Business Unit

For the testing process to proceed smoothly, it is necessary for the core testing team to be trained in the emergency procedures. This is probably best handled in a workshop environment and should be presented by the persons responsible for developing the emergency procedures. Before conducting a test event, it is imperative to conduct training for the core testing team. This testing team should be representative of each business unit. This section of the BCP should contain a list of the core testing team for each of the business units who will be responsible for coordinating and undertaking the business recovery testing process. It is important that clear instructions regarding the simulated conditions be given to the core testing team, and that the team knows that the instructions must be observed.

7.2   Security Testing

Organizations should gain assurance of the adequacy of their risk mitigation strategy and implementation by:

- Basing their testing plan, test selection, and test frequency on the risk posed by potentially non-functioning controls

- Establishing controls to mitigate the risks posed to systems from testing

- Using test results to evaluate whether security objectives are met

Information security is an integrated process that reduces information security risks to acceptable levels. The entire process, including testing, is driven by an assessment of risks. The greater the risk, the greater the need for the assurance and validation provided by effective information security testing. In general, risk increases with system accessibility and the sensitivity of data and processes. For example, a high-risk system is one that is remotely accessible and allows direct access to funds, fund-transfer mechanisms, or sensitive customer data. Information-only Web sites that are not connected to any internal organization system or transaction-capable service are lower-risk systems. Information systems that exhibit high risks should be subject to more frequent and rigorous testing than low-risk systems. Because tests only measure the security posture at one point in time, frequent testing provides increased assurance that the processes in place to maintain security over time are functioning.

7.2.1   Testing Concepts and Application

A wide range of test options for security controls exists today. Some options address only discrete controls, such as password strength. Others address only technical configuration, or may consist of reviews against standards. Some tests are overt studies to locate vulnerabilities. Other tests can be designed to mimic the actions of attackers. In many situations, management may decide to perform a range of tests to give a complete picture of the effectiveness of the organization's security processes. Management is responsible for selecting and designing tests so the test results, in total, support conclusions about whether the security control objectives are being met.

7.2.2   Testing Risks to Data Integrity, Confidentiality, and Availability

Management is responsible for carefully controlling information security tests to limit the risks to data integrity, confidentiality, and system availability. Because testing may uncover nonpublic customer information, appropriate safeguards to protect the information must be in place. Contracts with third parties to provide testing services should require that the third parties implement appropriate measures to meet the objectives of section 501(b) of the GLBA. Management also is responsible for ensuring that the employees and contract personnel who perform the tests or have access to the test results have passed appropriate background checks, and that contract personnel are appropriately bonded. Because certain tests may pose more risk to system availability than other tests, management is responsible for considering whether to require the personnel performing those tests to maintain logs of their testing actions. Those logs can be helpful if the systems react in an unexpected manner.

7.2.3 Confidentiality of Test Plans and Data

Since knowledge of test planning and results may facilitate a security breach, organizations should carefully limit the distribution of their testing information. Management is responsible for clearly identifying the individuals responsible for protecting the data and for providing guidance for that protection, while making the results available in a useable form to those who are responsible for following up on the tests. Management also should consider requiring contractors to sign nondisclosure agreements and to return to the organization all information they obtained in their testing.

7.2.4 Measurement and Interpretation of Test Results

Organizations should design tests to produce results that are logical and objective. Results that are reduced to metrics are potentially more precise and less subject to confusion, as well as being more readily tracked over time. The interpretation and significance of test results are most useful when tied to threat scenarios.

7.2.5 Traceability

Test results that indicate an unacceptable risk in an organization's security should be traceable to actions subsequently taken to reduce the risk to an acceptable level. Audit trails are an example of traceable actions.

7.2.6 Thoroughness

Organizations should perform tests sufficient to provide a high degree of assurance that their security plan, strategy and implementation are effective in meeting the security objectives. Organizations should design their test program to draw conclusions about the operation of all critical controls. The scope of testing should encompass all systems in the organization's production environment and contingency plans and those systems within the organization that provide access to the production environment.

7.2.7 Frequency

Test frequency should be based on the risk that critical controls are no longer functioning. Factors to consider include the nature, extent, and results of prior tests; the value and sensitivity of data and systems; and changes to systems, policies and procedures, personnel, and contractors. For example, network vulnerability scanning on high-risk systems can occur at least as frequently as significant changes are made to the network.

7.3   The Open Source Security Testing Methodology Manual

According to Pete Herzog, Managing Director of the Institute for Security and Open Methodologies [1], the Open Source Security Testing Methodology Manual (OSSTMM) was developed to set forth a standard for external security testing. Focused more on the skills and techniques of the testers than on the marketing brand of the examiners, OSSTMM is a solution to the problem of inconsistency in both the qualitative and quantitative aspects of a security test. Herzog maintains that any network or security tester who meets the outline requirements described in the OSSTMM is said to have completed a successful security test with more lasting worth than just a snapshot of the current posture. The following paragraphs have been contributed directly by Mr. Herzog:

> Security testing has an impressive and glamorous modern history, from the Navy Seals commissioned to break into American bases and armories to validate defensive measures to the hackers and con men hired to break into secured data stores to verify points of weakness or failure. Security testing is a profession full of megalomaniacs and "lone wolves" attracted to the hacker image, as it is often portrayed. But it's also a profession full of team players, business-minded consultants, and information officers who have a daily job to do in keeping usability, safety, and privacy high on their agenda while reducing security risks and liabilities.
>
> Security testing is also often compared to the parable of the Emperor's New Clothes. The story is about two con artists who sell the king the most glorious clothing made from cloth that is invisible to idiots. Of course, the king, afraid to be thought of as an idiot who can't see the clothes, never questions the con men and buys the clothing. During a parade, the townspeople, also afraid of being thought of as idiots, praise the new clothing. It is a child who then speaks up, "Why is the king naked?"

Like that child in the parable, the security tester must question the world as they see it. They see what is to be seen and then probe, poke, and otherwise test what they see and take note of what occurs in an unbiased way. Anything else would taint the results. For this reason, it's important that beginning security testers see themselves as mad scientists—pariahs with unconventional means, experimenting on what no one else dares. Mad scientists, as we're told from the movies, approach their subjects with great knowledge and curiosity under a strict, repetitive methodology, but are creative as hell where the methodologies end. It's no wonder, then, that security testing appeals to both the good and the bad. The security industry is incredibly wide and therefore, just as wide, is the industry of those to test that security.

An Internet security test is no more than a view of a system at a single moment in time. As we have stated previously, periodic, frequent reviews of security, or multiple snapshots over time, will likely increase the security posture of an organization dramatically. However, the caveat to this increased security posture is an assumption that the vulnerabilities found in security testing are acted upon in a timely manner. OSSTMM provides more than a just a snapshot, if followed correctly. Herzog advocates a more holistic approach, which he refers to as the scattershot effect. This effect is seen when security practitioners execute various tests on the less dynamic components in an organization (e.g., PBX systems, automated door locks, etc.) that offer a longer security value than a simple snapshot, because the degradation of security for those components and the recommended cycle of testing is much longer than for other components. For instance, it may be necessary to scan ports every eight days to remain in a 10% risk level, where testing the PBX is only necessary once every six months to remain in the same 10% risk level. So where a security test of the hosts may last a week, the test of the communications systems may last much longer. This approach deals with the issue of organizational security in a holistic approach, rather than the conventional treat-the-symptom approach used by many organizations.

OSSTMM strives to become a central standard for security testing. Herzog believes that by following an open-source, standardized methodology, participants can make a valuable contribution to Internet security. We tend to agree with him.

7.4   Monitoring and Updating

Organizations should continuously gather and analyze information regarding new threats and vulnerabilities, actual attacks on the organization or others, and the effectiveness of the existing security controls. They should then use that information to update the risk assessment, strategy, and implemented controls. A static security program provides a false sense of security and will become increasingly ineffective over time. Monitoring and updating the security program is an important part of the ongoing cyclical security process. Organizations should treat security as dynamic with active monitoring; prompt, ongoing risk assessment; and appropriate updates to controls.

7.4.1   Monitoring

Effective monitoring of threats includes both nontechnical and technical sources. Nontechnical sources include organizational changes, business process changes, new business locations, increased sensitivity of information, or new products and services. Technical sources include new systems, new service providers, and increased access. Security personnel and organization management must remain alert to emerging threats and vulnerabilities.

This effort could include the following security activities:

- Senior management should give support for strong security policy awareness and compliance. Management and employees must remain alert to operational changes that could affect security and actively communicate issues with security personnel. Business line managers must have responsibility and accountability for maintaining the security of their personnel, systems, facilities, and information.

- Security personnel should monitor the information technology environment and review performance reports to identify trends, new threats, or control deficiencies. Specific activities could include reviewing security and activity logs, investigating operational anomalies, and routinely reviewing system and application access levels.

- Security personnel and system owners should monitor external sources for new technical and nontechnical vulnerabilities and develop appropriate mitigation solutions to address them. Examples include the following:

- ▪ Establishing an effective configuration management process that monitors for vulnerabilities in hardware and software and establishes a process to install and test security patches
- ▪ Maintaining up-to-date antivirus definitions and intrusion detection attack definitions
- ▪ Providing effective oversight of service providers and vendors to identify and react to new security issues

- ■ Senior management should require periodic security self-assessments and reviews to provide an ongoing assessment of policy compliance and ensure prompt corrective action of significant deficiencies.

- ■ Security personnel should have access to automated tools appropriate for the complexity of the organization systems. Automated security policy and security log analysis tools can significantly increase the effectiveness and productivity of security personnel.

7.4.2 Updating

Organizations should evaluate the information gathered to determine the extent of any required adjustments to the various components of their security program. The organization will need to consider the scope, impact, and urgency of any new threat. Depending on the new threat or vulnerability, the organization will need to reassess the risk and make changes to its security process (e.g., the security strategy, the controls implementation, or the security testing requirements). Organizational management confronts routine security issues and events on a regular basis. In many cases, the issues are relatively isolated and may be addressed through an informal or targeted risk assessment embedded within an existing security control process.

For example, the organization might assess the risk of a new operating system vulnerability before testing and installing the patch. More systemic events, such as mergers, acquisitions, new systems, or system conversions, however, would warrant a more extensive security risk assessment. Regardless of the scope, the potential impact and the urgency of the risk exposure will dictate when and how controls are changed.

7.5   Hardening Systems

Many organizations use commercial off-the-shelf (COTS) software for operating systems and applications. A COTS system generally provides more functions than are required for the specific purposes for which it is employed. For example, a default installation of a server operating system may install mail, Web, and file-sharing services on a system whose sole function is a Domain Name Server (DNS). Unnecessary software and services represent a potential security weakness. Their presence increases the potential number of discovered and undiscovered vulnerabilities present in the system.

Additionally, system administrators may not install patches or monitor the unused software and services to the same degree as operational software and services. Protection against those risks begins when the systems are constructed and software is installed, through a process that is referred to as "hardening" a system. When deploying off-the-shelf software, management should harden the resulting system. Patching issues are discussed in further detail later in this chapter.

System hardening is important because file and database servers used to store an organization's critical information resources must be kept strictly confidential. Servers also store information used for management decisions or customer billing, which demands a high level of integrity. Authentication servers store information about user accounts and passwords. Any disclosure from an authentication server could compromise **all of the information** on a network. Public servers (such as Web servers) are used by an organization to represent itself to the public. The integrity of the information on those servers is critically important to maintain the image desired by corporate management and to satisfy customers. Web servers used by customers for electronic commerce must be available and reliable to prevent loss of revenue. Servers that provide essential services for employees of your organization must be reliably available; otherwise, people could be unable to work. As you can see, the reasons for hardening systems are many, and all are quite valid. Hardening includes the actions shown in Figure 7.1.

After deployment, the COTS systems may need updating with current security patches. Additionally, the systems should be periodically examined to ensure the software present on the systems is authorized and properly configured.

7.5.1 Management of the Hardening Process

Most organizations today require an environment that is highly secure, available, scalable, and manageable. One of the first steps in achieving this optimum environment is to implement security hardening services for your corporate servers. This involves some key activities and the generation of certain deliverables that will be used by administrators on an ongoing basis. The first step is a full review of the existing server configurations. It is useful to interview IT staff for the purpose of identifying security requirements, such as the following:

- Access control

- Authentication and authorization

- Privacy

- Obtain the patch from a known, trusted source

Figure 7.1
Tasks undertaken in the hardening process.

- Determining the purpose of the system and minimum software and hardware requirements

- Documenting the minimum hardware, software and services to be included on the system

- Installing minimum hardware, software, and services necessary to meet the requirements

- Using a documented installation procedure

- Installing necessary patches

- Installing the most secure and up-to-date versions of applications

- Configuring privilege and access controls using "deny all, grant minimum" approach

- Configuring security settings as appropriate, enabling only allowed activities

- Enabling logging

- Creating cryptographic hashes of key files

- Archiving the configuration and checksums in secure storage prior to system deployment

- Testing the system to ensure a secure configuration

- Using secure replication procedures for identically configured systems

- Making configuration changes on a case-by-case basis

- Changing all default passwords

- Testing the resulting systems

Next, capture the needs and uses for all applications and services intended to be run on the server. For each server, it is good practice to formally design the operating system build, including procedures and handling recommendations. A "deny all, add essential" philosophy should be taken to adding any features to the operating system builds to prevent unnecessary services from running. All configuration information for the build should be fully documented and put into a change control process. Any future changes to the specification should go through a change control and approval process.

For every server used in the organization, implement the server according to a designated, change-managed, build specification. Test the server implementation to ensure it is properly hardened. There are many documents and resources available on the Web to show how to configure particular operating systems, such as Windows, Linux, Solaris, and so on, for a hardened configuration. A good starting point is the CERT© Coordination Center Web site [2]. Once properly configured, the hardened server is ready for the installation of the business-essential applications it will support. These applications should be carefully scrutinized, as many applications install with default settings that enhance performance rather than security. After the necessary applications have been installed, it is important to develop a "run book" documenting the "how to" actions needed to sustain the hardened server in proper configuration. When the server is ready for production, and all items have been fully documented in the "run book," the final step is to deliver a hardening build specification document to the IT administration group to ensure the server is managed according to organizational security standards.

7.6   System Patches

Software support should incorporate a process to update and patch operating system and application software for new vulnerabilities. Frequently, security vulnerabilities are discovered in operating systems and other software after deployment. Vendors often issue software patches to correct those vulnerabilities. Organizations should have an effective monitoring process to identify new vulnerabilities in their hardware and software. Monitoring involves such actions as the receipt and analysis of vendor and governmental alerts and security mailing lists. Once identified, secure installation of those patches requires a process for obtaining, testing, and installing the patch. Patches make direct changes to the software and configuration of each system to which they are applied. They may degrade system performance. Also, patches may introduce new vulnerabilities, or reintroduce old vulnerabilities. The considerations shown in Figure 7.2 can help ensure patches do not compromise the security of systems.

Figure 7.2
Operating System Patch process considerations.

- Obtain the patch from a known, trusted source
- Verify the integrity of the patch using cryptographic hashes
- Apply the patch to an isolated test system and verify that the patch:
    1. Is compatible with other software used on systems where patches will be applied
    2. Does not alter system security posture unexpectedly, e.g., altering log settings
    3. Corrects the pertinent vulnerability prior to applying the patch
- Back up production systems prior to applying the patch
- Apply the patch to production systems using secure methods
- Update the cryptographic checksums of key files as well as that system's software archive
- Test the resulting system for known vulnerabilities
- Update the master configurations used to build new systems
- Create and document an audit trail of all changes
- Seek additional expertise as necessary to maintain a secure computing environment

7.7   Auditing Fundamentals

Computer security is of increasing importance to private and government sector entities in minimizing the risk of malicious attacks from individuals and groups. These risks include the fraudulent loss or misuse of resources, unauthorized access to release of sensitive information such as tax and medical records, disruption of critical operations through viruses or hacker attacks, and modification or destruction of data. According to a recent General Accounting Office (GAO) publication [3], the risk that information attacks will threaten vital interests increases with the following developments in information technology:

- Monies are increasingly transferred electronically between and among organizational agencies, commercial enterprises, and individuals.

- Organizations are rapidly expanding their use of electronic commerce.

- National defense and intelligence communities increasingly rely on commercially available information technology.

- Public utilities and telecommunications increasingly rely on computer systems to manage everyday operations.

- More and more sensitive economic and commercial information is exchanged electronically.

- Computer systems are rapidly increasing in complexity and interconnectivity.

- Easy-to-use hacker tools are readily available, and hacker activity is increasing.

- Paper supporting documents are being reduced or eliminated.

Each of these factors significantly increases the need for ensuring the privacy, security, and availability of state and local government systems. Although as many as 80 percent of security breaches are probably never reported, the number of reported incidents is growing dramatically. For example, the number of incidents handled by Carnegie-Mellon University's CERT® Coordination Center (CERT/CC) has multiplied more than 86 times since 1990, rising from 252 in 1990 to 21,756 in 2000. Furthermore, CERT® received 3,784 vulnerability reports and handled more than 137,529 incidents during 2002, according to their annual report [4]. Similarly, the Federal Bureau of Investigation (FBI) reports that its caseload of computer intrusion–related cases is more than doubling every year. The fifth annual survey conducted by the Computer Security Institute in cooperation with the FBI found that 70 percent of respondents (primarily large corporations and government agencies) had detected serious computer security breaches within the last 12 months, and that quantifiable financial losses had increased over past years.

7.8   Auditor's Role in Developing Security Policies

According to Alan Oliphant, in his series of articles about computer auditing [5], policy and standards are of critical importance to an information systems security (ISS) auditor. Organizations should define their aims and objectives clearly in order to support their business strategies. This is often expressed in strategic plans and policy statements. When they lack a clear statement of direction, organizations can lose focus and become ineffective. They rapidly find themselves performing well below expectations. Organizations with clearly defined aims and objectives tend to be more successful organizations.

Oliphant contends that because the IT facilities of any organization have become vital to the functioning of the organization, clear policy statements regarding all aspects of IT have become a necessity. The computer auditor should conduct auditing from precisely this point of view. Policies should be reviewed to ensure they are comprehensive and support control and security concepts. This provides an auditor with the necessary foundation essential for reviewing the computing standards implemented in the organization. Such standards are the means used to effect policy. Without standards to base an audit opinion against, any audit opinion can be construed as pure conjecture. Thus, management's duty lies in defining standards and implementing them in the form of policy.

As an auditor, your role is to assess the adequacy of organizational standards and look for compliance with such standards. Computer auditors should examine the policies of IT and the level of security and privacy required, including rights of access to specific types of information, ownership of information, and processes and policies referring to employment in sensitive areas. Once each of the organization's specific policies have been scrutinized, the standards of the organization should also be reviewed to determine whether or not they actually help to mitigate the organization's identified risks (identified from a risk analysis). The standard may implement all facets of a policy for an organization, but if the policy does not serve the purpose for which it was intended, all the standards in the world cannot help fix the problem. The point here is that policies should be focused on addressing specific risks. They should define the tasks that need to be done to prevent the risk from becoming a problem. Standards, on the other hand, are used to implement the "how-to" portion of the policy.

All work performed in an IT organization should be done in a controlled and standardized manner. This ensures the objectives of the organization are met. The computer auditor should be acquainted with the relevant IT standards prior to conducting the audit, in order to perform the work adequately. The work performed by an auditor should be able to withstand review by objective third parties.

Generally accepted standards for IT security are available and should be used where possible. The use of widely accepted standards can form a strong base against which audit work can be carried out, and prospective computer auditors are urged to read such standards. For example, policies and standards are essential in the software systems development life cycle, including:

- Analysis and programming

- Data structures

- Security

- Data controls

- Documentation

- User procedures

- User programming

Policies and standards can quickly become outdated in a highly technical environment, so documenting change management is strongly recommended. The cost of not implementing this change management process should be considered in light of the fact that without strong policy and standards statements, anarchy can quickly take hold of an organization. The computer auditor must remember that **policies should be relatively static**, while **standards can change quickly**, especially in areas such as client/ server applications, where developments are increasingly rapid.

7.9   Auditing Standards and Groups

There are many standards and groups available for you to consult. Several large-body organizations exist to provide general guidance to auditors and to enable certification of auditors for a standardized method of looking at IT security issues in an organization. Certifications are available for professional auditors from many of these groups. For those who wish to learn more about the field of auditing, we provide a brief overview of some of these standards bodies and groups below.

7.9.1 Information Systems Audit and Control Association (ISACA)

ISACA provides information on generally applicable and accepted standards for good information technology security and control practices. The association's Web site also provides a global information repository to help members keep pace with technological change. Additional details on ISACA can be found on the Internet at http://www.isaca.org.

7.9.1.1 ISACA CISA Certification

The Certified Information Systems Auditor (CISA) is the primary ISACA certification. The CISA exam tests applicants in the areas of IS auditing, control, and security. CISA has grown to be a globally recognized and widely adopted worldwide certification standard. According to the ISACA Web site, there are more than 29,000 CISAs worldwide. More than 10,000 individuals took the CISA exam in 2002 alone! The CISA designation is awarded to individuals with an interest in Information Systems auditing, control, and security who have met and continue to meet stringent requirements, outlined below:

- Candidates must demonstrate at least five years of experience working in the field of information systems auditing, control, or security. Such experience must have been gained within the ten-year period preceding the application date for certification or within five years from the date of initially passing the examination. Retaking and successfully passing the examination will be required if the application for certification is not submitted within five years from the passing date of the examination. All experience must be verified independently with employers.

- All candidates must agree to adhere to a Code of Professional Ethics to guide professional and personal conduct.

- Candidates must participate in continuing education programs. This helps maintain an individual's competency by requiring the update of existing knowledge and skills in the areas of information systems auditing, management, accounting, and business areas related to specific industries. It provides a means to differentiate between qualified CISAs and those who have not met the requirements for continuation of their certification, and it is a mechanism for monitoring information systems audit, control, and security professionals' maintenance of their competency. Continuing education can aid top management in developing sound information systems audit, control, and security functions by providing criteria for personnel selection and development. Candidates are required to pay maintenance fees and have a minimum of 20 contact hours of continuing education annually. In addition, a minimum of 120 contact hours is required during a fixed three-year period.

- Candidates agree to adhere to the Information Systems Auditing Standards adopted by the ISACA as a condition of receiving the CISA credential.

- Successful completion of the CISA examination, consisting of six major areas, is chief among these requirements. The examination areas, according to the ISACA Web site, include those shown in Figure 7.3.

Figure 7.3
CISA examination areas.

1. **Management, Planning, and Organization of IS.** Evaluate the strategy, policies, standards, procedures and related practices for the management, planning, and organization of IS.

2. **Technical Infrastructure and Operational Practices.** Evaluate the effectiveness and efficiency of the organization's implementation and ongoing management of technical and operational infrastructure to ensure that they adequately support the organization's business objectives.

3. **Protection of Information Assets.** Evaluate the logical, environmental, and IT infrastructure security to ensure that it satisfies the organization's business requirements for safeguarding information assets against unauthorized use, disclosure, modification, damage, or loss.

4. **Disaster Recovery and Business Continuity.** Evaluate the process for developing and maintaining documented, communicated, and tested plans for continuity of business operations and IS processing in the event of a disruption.

5. **Business Application System Development, Acquisition, Implementation, and Maintenance.** Evaluate the methodology and processes by which the business application system development, acquisition, implementation, and maintenance are undertaken to ensure that they meet the organization's business objectives.

6. **Business Process Evaluation and Risk Management.** Evaluate business systems and processes to ensure that risks are managed in accordance with the organization's business objectives.

7.9.2 FISCAM

The General Accounting Office's publication entitled *Federal Information System Controls Audit Manual* [6] (FISCAM) describes computer-related controls auditors should consider when assessing the integrity, confidentiality, and availability of computerized data. It is not an audit standard. Its purposes are to *inform auditors about computer-related controls and related audit issues* so they can better plan their work and to *integrate the work of information systems (IS) auditors with other aspects of a financial audit*. FISCAM can provide guidance to IS auditors on the scope of issues that generally should be considered in any review of computer-related controls over the integrity, confidentiality, and availability of computerized data associated with federal agency systems.

The manual lists specific control techniques and related suggested audit procedures. However, the audit procedures provided are stated at a high level and assume some expertise about the subject to be effectively performed. As a result, more detailed audit steps generally should be developed by the IS auditor, based on the specific software and control techniques employed by the auditee, after consulting with the financial auditor about audit objectives and significant accounts.

7.9.3 CobIT®

The Control Objectives for Information and related Technology (CobIT®) group, part of the ISACA, was introduced in 1996 and tasked to produce a framework of generally applicable and accepted IT guidance and control practices [7]. The primary purpose of CobIT® is to provide clear policy and good practice for IT guidance throughout organizations worldwide. It is intended to help senior management understand and manage risks associated with IT. CobIT® accomplishes this task by providing an IT guidance framework and detailed control objective guides for management, business process owners, users, and auditors.

CobIT® starts with a simple and pragmatic premise: to provide the information needed to achieve its objectives, an organization should manage its IT resources through a set of naturally grouped processes. The CobIT® framework groups processes into a simple, business-oriented hierarchy. Each process references IT resources, quality, fiduciary, and security requirements for related information.

7.10 Audit Oversight Committee

It is always a good idea to have executive oversight of the audit function. This accomplishes several things. First of all, such high-level oversight demonstrates management commitment to the audit process. Second, it allows the audit team to operate with a fairly high degree of independence, preventing undue influence to affect the outcome of any audit. Finally, the oversight committee can ensure the audit function serves the business needs, focusing on the areas of risk most relevant to the business.

When the oversight group selects the information systems security audit team leader, one of his or her first tasks will be to determine the format of the audit strategy. Options for this strategy include the production of a single strategy document, scrutinized under a regular review process, or the production of a strategy in the form of a corporate audit manual or a series of corporate audit policy documents (which can be separately reviewed and amended as necessary). Whatever format is chosen for the strategy, it should be disseminated to all members of the audit group under audit committee oversight.

The composition of the audit oversight committee is a significant factor of organizational success in the use of audits as a tool for ensuring adherence to policies and standards. Representation should come from every major group in an organization, such as Finance, Human Resources, Service and Support, Sales, Administration, etc. Cross-representation ensures adequate coverage of IT issues related to each of these organizations, and is healthy for the organization overall. Reciprocally, for audits of organizations other than IT, the same principles as stated above should apply.

7.11 Auditing and Assessment Strategies

An audit strategy defines the strategic approach that guides an information systems security audit team leader (ISSATL). The ISSATL should try to manage the audit team in a way that facilitates periodic reporting to the security manager covering the organization's risk management posture and policy adherence. This is accomplished through periodic audit plans. The ISSATL is responsible for providing management with specific recommendations resulting from any audit work. Other ISSATL responsibilities include the identification of audit resources required to deliver an audit service that meets the needs of the organization; establishment of effective cooperation with external auditors and other review bodies functioning in the organization; and the provision of assurance and consultancy services by internal audit to the organization. Regardless of the format chosen for the strategy document, the documented audit strategy should, at a minimum, define the items shown in Figure 7.4.

- How does an internal audit relate to management's risk analysis?
- What elements of the risk analysis are essential for annual review?
- What methods provide reasonable assurance of adherence to the audit compliance standard?
- What is needed to provide risk mitigation assurances to the security manager/audit committee?
- What areas of change in the organization are being subjected to a systems security audit?
- How/to what extent will the internal audit rely on other assurance work to develop an opinion?
- What range of approaches does internal audit plan to employ in conducting the audit?
- How will the internal audit communicate the results of its work?
- What resources are required for the audit, including identification of any specialist skills required?
- How will internal audit and specialist resources be recruited and utilized?
- What methods of recruiting/training/continuing professional development will be used for internal audit staff?
- How will internal audit measure its performance?
- How will internal audit implement quality assurance and seek continuous improvement?
- What are the risks for the audit unit in delivering a strategy and what are the plans for controlling these risks?

7.11.1 Prerequisites for Developing an Audit Strategy

There are a number of knowledge-based prerequisites for developing the audit strategy. All members of the audit team require a thorough understanding of the organization's objectives and performance targets, risk analysis procedures (including the risk priorities of the organization), and persons with key ownership of these risks. The audit team needs to fully understand the processes used by the security manager to establish his or her assurance that risk management, IT security controls, policies, and standards issues have been adequately and properly addressed. This includes a solid understanding of the current response plans for potential risks to the organization, as well as an understanding of the senior management structures of the organization. Gaining this knowledge will be an important issue for any external audit service providers. When a new contract is made, it will be important for all internal audit services to have a mechanism in place to ensure their knowledge remains current and comprehensive.

It is important to realize risk analysis belongs to the management team, often directly assigned to the chief financial officer or the chief accounting officer. It is not the responsibility of the internal audit team to perform risk analysis. They are, however, held accountable by the organization's audit oversight committee for the efficiency and effectiveness of the risk management controls and policies. For this reason, it is essential that an audit strategy be based on *management's risk priorities*, not on the outcome of a separate audit analysis of risk.

Whenever the audit team discovers that a complete management analysis of risk has already been completed, internal audit should leverage preliminary work to enhance the audit strategy. To be effective, the risk analysis should be audited on a systematic basis. This serves two purposes:

1.   It provides the Cheif Security Officer (CSO) with an opinion about the organization's strategic approach to the analysis of risk.

2.   It provides internal audit with assurance that the risk analysis is a sound basis for planning future audit work. This audit should seek evidence of the validity of the risk strategy as shown in Figure 7.5.

If internal audit is dissatisfied with any of the items in Figure 7.5, those issues identified should be discussed with the CSO and/or the security manager. If, after such a discussion, the internal audit finds material deficiencies in the risk analysis, the perceived deficiencies should be reported to the audit oversight committee with a request that they either record in writing their acceptance of the deficient risk analysis or direct to have it revised.

When a complete management analysis of risk is not in place, internal audit should first consider what help management needs to develop an appropriate risk analysis. This effort will later help define the audit process itself. Without an adequate risk analysis, internal audit cannot proceed with its strategy. Where it is appropriate for internal audit to provide consultancy

Figure 7.5
*Audit validation
checklist.*

- Completeness of the risk identification process
- Identification of criteria for evaluation of risk in respect to both impact and likelihood
- Appropriate application of these criteria to the identified risks
- Appropriate consequent prioritization of risks and identification of key risks
- Appropriate relationship between organizational objectives and prioritized risks
- Assignment of ownership of risks at an appropriate level, having authority to assign resources in responding to the risks
- Regular review and revision of the risk analysis

advice, and when it can be done without prejudicing objectivity and independence, internal audit should emphasize that they need to work in partnership with management to develop the risk analysis. They should ensure that risk analysis will be owned by management, not internal audit. Internal audit's role in the development of the risk analysis does not prevent consequent revision of audit opinion on the adequacy of the analysis or guarantee freedom from error in the analysis.

7.11.2 Identifying Audit Coverage Necessary

The next stage in developing the audit strategy is consideration of the depth of coverage needed for the risk management, policy, and procedures. This consideration is required in order to provide the CSO with an audit opinion. Consideration of the coverage necessary has to be based on business need. It will not be necessary to audit every aspect of risk, policy, and procedure every year, but certain factors will be relevant to considerations at this stage, as outlined in Figure 7.6.

Remember, the most effective audit coverage is gained by a combination of strategic audits and operational audits. The audit coverage should aim to address both the question of how well the security process is planned and how well it operates in practice. In addition to considering existing risk, consideration should be given to the extent of change taking place or planned to take place in the organization. Any planned projects or developments that will have an impact on risk, policy, and procedures should be encompassed in the strategy. Changing processes can be inherently more risky than established and known processes. Identification of weaknesses in

Figure 7.6
*Audit coverage
considerations.*

- The organization's risk analysis should be reviewed every year to gain assurance that it continues to be appropriate.

- Within the risk analysis, policy, and procedures, there may be certain high-risk systems or processes that will need to be reviewed annually to deliver the assurance level required.

- Determine whether such systems and processes need to be fully and systematically audited every year or whether techniques such as key security control testing or compliance testing in some years will be adequate.

- The overall coverage will need to encompass the whole range of risks the organization has identified as key to the achievement of its objectives.

- An adequate range of nonkey risks needs to be included in any year's coverage to give credibility to the comprehensiveness of the opinion.

- Risks not defined as key still need to be given attention to gain assurance that material adverse impacts are not arising.

- Current knowledge of the organization's risk management, policy, and procedures will inform assessment of the likelihood of there being (material) deficiencies that will mitigate for greater audit coverage.

developing areas is more economical to correct during development rather than after the process has been put in place.

In addition to the considerations above, internal audit should discuss the level of assurance required with the CSO and the audit committee to help determine the coverage level required. The extent of assurance they require, with respect to non-key risks, will be important. If the assurance required is specified as less than what is felt to be positive and reasonable by the audit team leader, implications of this should be discussed and recorded. Conversely, if it is likely that internal audit will be unable to deliver such assurance for some reason, this should also be discussed with the audit oversight committee. These considerations, along with the organization's risk analysis, will allow a broad template for future audit work to be done, leading to better development of periodic audit plans.

7.11.3   Audit Schedule and Resource Estimates

It is important to create an accurate estimate of the number of staff days that will be required to conduct the audit work for each risk element identified. Allow adequate time for work to be done professionally and for the proper acquisition and evaluation of evidence. The best resource for making these estimates is historic experience of how long audit work takes to do. The audit strategy and risk analysis should be used to determine the depth of coverage and resources that are projected as necessary. This data should be summarized in the internal audit strategy and made available for future use.

7.11.4   Establishing Audit Baselines

Figure 7.7

Areas to consider for establishing a baseline for audit.

- Corporate Security Program
- Planning and Management
- Access Control
- Application Software Development and Change Control
- System Software
- Segregation of Duties
- Service Continuity

Establish a baseline for each area of work completed during the audit process by identifying strengths and weaknesses for each specific information systems security control. Doing so will help your organization further determine how best to proceed. In many instances, this process will determine what is practical to implement within given time and budget constraints. Baselines are often developed from the organization's standards and policies. A list of areas to consider for establishing a baseline is shown in Figure 7.7. Each of these areas is discussed later in this chapter.

7.11.5   Concept of Time-Based Security

Your organization becomes more vulnerable to security threats over time. It is possible to decrease the security threat level when an organization is capable of quickly detecting and reacting to threats. Winn Schwartau, an information security expert who has testified before the U.S. Congress and has served as an expert witness in U.S. courts, has developed a security model called the time-based security model. This model advocates that organizations evaluate their security threats using the following equation:

```
Exposure time = Detection time + Reaction time (Et=Dt+Rt)
```

According to Schwartau's model, the longer an organization is exposed to a threat (a virus such as Nimda, for example) the greater the security threat becomes. To eliminate the threat of the virus, it is imperative to quickly detect and remove that vulnerability from your network. Schwartau claims the $43 billion spent on information security worldwide over the last thirty years has been spent on systems with flaws that are so bad that they can't be fixed with technology. He believes policies that handle **how long it takes** to detect and respond to a security breach are far more crucial than the vast number of preventative technologies available.

the(451), an analyst firm specializing in technology, examined Schwartau's time-based security model in an article [8] and declared that Schwartau's model addresses the fact that no one knows how to secure a computer with complete certainty. As a result, IT security vendors can never provide 100% assurance about the effectiveness of their products. This, in turn, makes evaluating the success of security systems very difficult.

Schwartau contends security should be an automated, reactive chain of events that reduce the amount of time computer systems are available to attack. Based on the equation above, exposure time (**E**) of the system equals detection time (**D**) plus reaction time (**R**). This model always assumes the possibility of systems being exposed for some period of time when an attack occurs. Schwartau's approach requires building a reaction plan to various known problems and scenarios. Classifying data, evaluating assets, and choosing appropriate responses will assist an organization to create a policy for responding to threats in the shortest possible time. Such a policy, if its procedures are followed, would outweigh any technology put in place, according to Schwartau.

7.11.6   The Mind of an Auditor

Consummate skeptic is a positive description of an auditor. The *question everything* mentality should be pervasive in the conduct of an auditor's daily work. The auditor should always present a positive attitude toward the work itself. He or she should conduct every facet of the audit process with the utmost professionalism and respect for the work people have accomplished. Even if the work being audited is of such poor quality that it makes the auditor cringe, the auditor should remember that he or she is there to provide guidance, in the form of reviews and recommendations for improvement, to help the problem go away. Question everything, but be nice about it.

7.12   Basic Audit Methods and Tools

Operational assurance is the process of reviewing an operational system to see that security controls, both automated and manual, are functioning correctly and effectively [9]. To maintain operational assurance, organizations use two basic methods: system audits and monitoring. These terms are used loosely within the computer security community and often overlap. A system audit is a periodic event used to evaluate security. An audit conducted to support operational assurance examines whether the system is meeting stated or implied security requirements, including system and organization policies. Some audits will also examine whether security requirements are appropriate for an organization, based on the risks identified in a risk analysis process. Less formal audits are sometimes called security reviews.

Audits can be self-administered or performed by independent parties (either internal or external to the organization). Both types of audit can provide an organization with excellent information about their technical, procedural, managerial, and other related aspects of security. The essential difference between a self-audit and an independent audit is objectivity. Reviews done by system management staff, often called self-audits or self-assessments, have an inherent conflict of interest. The system management staff may have little incentive to say the computer system was poorly designed or is sloppily operated. On the other hand, they may be motivated by a strong desire to improve the security of the system. In addition, they are knowledgeable about the system and may be able to find hidden problems.

The independent auditor, by contrast, should have no professional stake in the system. The independent auditor has nothing to gain from the outcome (good or bad) of an audit. An independent audit should be performed by a professional, reputable audit firm, and done in accordance with generally accepted auditing standards. Many methods and tools, some of which are described below, can be used to audit a system.

7.12.1   Automated Tools

For small multiuser computer systems, it is a big job to manually review security features. Using automated tools makes it possible to review computer systems, small or large, for a variety of security flaws. Generally, there are two types of automated tools used by an auditor:

1.   Active tools, which find vulnerabilities by trying to exploit them

2.   Passive tests, which examine the system and infer problems from the state of the system

Automated tools can be used to help find many threats and vulnerabilities, like improper access controls or weak access control configurations, weak passwords, lack of integrity of the system software, or not using proper software updates and patches. These tools are very successful at finding vulnerabilities and are sometimes used by hackers to break into systems. Systems administrators are encouraged to use automated tools as much as possible. Frequent use of such tools allows for early detection and remediation of problems and should be a part of the daily routine for an administrator.

Passive testing can assist an auditor in the review of controls put in place in an IS organization and help determine whether they are effective or not. The auditor will often need to analyze both the computer and noncomputer-based controls. Techniques used to accomplish this task include inquiry, observation, and testing (of the controls and the data). The audit can frequently detect illegal acts, errors, irregularities, or a lack of compliance with laws and regulations. Security checklists and penetration testing, discussed below, may also be used to assist in the audit.

7.12.2 Security Checklists

An organization's site security plan outlines the major security considerations for a system, including management, operational, and technical issues. One advantage of using a computer security plan is that it reflects the unique security environment of the system, rather than a generic list of controls. Checklists should be developed using the security plan as the framework for the depth and breadth of the audit. Other checklists can also be developed that include organizational security policies and practices. Lists of "generally accepted security practices" obtained from outside sources can also be used. When using standardized or best-practice checklists, it is important to review them with some consideration of the fact that deviations from their prescribed standards may not be considered wrong. They may be appropriate for the system's unique environment or technical constraints. Checklists can also be used to verify that changes to a system have been reviewed from a security perspective. A general audit should examine the system's configuration to validate whether or not any major changes have occurred that have not yet been analyzed from a security point of view.

7.12.3   Penetration Testing

Penetration testing is used to attempt a system break-in for the purpose of discovering vulnerabilities in the protection controls in place at an organization. Penetration testing often is done using automated tools, but it can also be done *manually*. Security experts advocate penetration testing that mimics methods that would be employed by a real hacker making intrusion attempts against a system. For host systems on the Internet, this would certainly include automated tools. For many systems, poor security procedures or a lack of internal controls on applications are common vulnerabilities that penetration testing can target.

7.12.4   Monitoring Methods and Tools

Security monitoring should be an ongoing activity. Its purpose is to look for vulnerabilities and security problems that may exist in the security controls implemented by the organization. Many monitoring methods are similar to those used for audits, but monitoring is performed on a more frequent basis. In some instances, monitoring uses automated tools and is performed in real time on a continual basis.

7.12.4.1   Review of System Logs

A periodic review of system-generated logs can detect security problems, including attempts to exceed access authority or gain system access during unusual hours. It is a good practice to have log-checking integrated into the daily routine for systems administrators. The chances of detecting intrusions are much greater with a better log-checking program put into operation within an organization.

7.12.4.2   Automated Monitoring Tools

Several types of automated tools can be used to monitor a system for security problems. Some examples are shown in Figure 7.8.

Figure 7.8
*Some automated
tools used in the
audit process.*

- Virus scanners, which are programs that test for the presence of viruses in executable program files.

- Checksumming, which works under the assumption that program files should not change between updates. Checksumming is a process whereby a mathematical value based on the contents of a particular file is generated. To verify the integrity of the file, the checksum is generated on demand for a specific file and compared with the previously generated value for that file. If the two values are equal, the integrity of the file is verified.

- Password crackers, tools that check passwords against a known list of "bad or weak" passwords. Crackers can also check passwords against common permutations of the user ID.

- Intrusion detectors, programs that analyze a system audit trail, especially logons, connections, operating system calls, and various command parameters, for activity that could represent unauthorized activity. Intrusion detection is covered in Chapter 6 of this book.

- System performance monitoring, which analyzes system performance logs in real time to look for availability problems, including active attacks (such as the Slammer worm) and system and network slowdowns and crashes.

7.12.5 Configuration Management

From a security point of view, configuration management provides assurance that the system in operation is the correct version (configuration) of the system, and that any changes to be made are reviewed for security implications. Configuration management can be used to help ensure that changes take place in an identifiable and controlled environment and that they do not unintentionally harm any of the system's properties, including its security. Some organizations, particularly those with very large systems, use a configuration control board for configuration management. When such a board exists, it is helpful to have a computer security expert participate. In any case, it is useful to have computer security managers participate in system management decision making. Changes to the system can have security implications because they may introduce or remove vulnerabilities and because significant changes may require updating the contingency plan, risk analysis, or accreditation.

7.13   General Information Systems (IS) Audit Process

Security auditing is the formal examination and review of actions taken by system users. This process is necessary to determine the effectiveness of existing security controls, to watch for system misuse or abuse by users, verify compliance with current security policies, capture evidence of the commission of a crime (computer or noncomputer related), validate that documented procedures are followed, and detect anomalies or intrusions. Effective auditing requires that the correct data be recorded and that it undergo periodic review. To provide individual user accountability, the computing system must be able be correctly identify and authenticate each user. This is the distinguishing factor between system log data and user audit data.

System log data is typically generated by system processes and daemons that report significant events or information. It does not correspond to specific user actions, nor is it directly traceable to a specific user. It simply indicates that activity and/or resource consumption has occurred at a given time and date for a *named process*. System logs do not generate data that is specific enough to correlate to the activities of a given user.

Audit data, however, is generated by the system and corresponds directly to recorded actions taken by identifiable and authenticated users, associated under a unique audit identifier (audit ID). All processes associated with any user must inherit the unique audit ID assigned when authentication took place. If the user assumes a role for additional privileges, those actions must also be tracked using the same audit ID. All the audit information gathered must be sufficient for a postmortem investigation. Audit data is the complete recorded history of a system user. Once audit data has been recorded, it must be reviewed on a regular basis in order to maintain effective operational security. Administrators who review audit data should watch for events that may signify misuse or abuse of the system and user privileges or intrusions. Some examples that may signify misuse or abuse of the system and user privileges or intrusions are shown in Figure 7.9.

As part of a corporate IS audit process, there are six major areas that we have identified as critical to organizational function. Each of these six areas is, in and of itself, a foundation for a set of specific security controls the organization should consider in developing a protection profile. These six areas, each of which will be discussed further in the following sections, are:

Figure 7.9
*Some examples of
misuse or abuse of
system privileges.*

- Accessing files requiring higher privilege
- Killing system processes
- Opening another user's files, mail, etc.
- Probing the system for vulnerabilities
- Installing unauthorized, potentially damaging software (e.g., viruses, Trojan horses)
- Exploiting a security vulnerability to gain higher privileges
- Modifying or deleting sensitive information

- Corporate security program planning and management
- Access control
- Application software development and change control
- System software
- Segregation of duties
- Service continuity

7.13.1 Corporate Security Program Planning and Management

Several key factors should be included in any security planning process. It is important to perform periodic risk assessments to ensure the company responds to changes in business and environmental factors. The security manager must document a corporate security program plan that will be used by the rest of the organization to guide their activities. Establish a security management structure and clearly assign security responsibilities to those assigned to the security team. Work with the Human Resources department and implement effective security-related personnel policies to ensure your security staff are properly suited to the formidable tasks presented in a security work environment. As a security manager, it is essential that you continually monitor the security program's effectiveness and make changes as needed.

7.13.2 Access Control

This is perhaps the most crucial aspect of your security planning. You may have conducted some of the best planning in the world, but if proper access controls are not established, you may as well post all your company information on the open Internet. You must begin this process by having employees follow a policy that classifies information resources according to their criticality and sensitivity. You must maintain a current list of authorized users and their authorized access levels. Establish physical and logical controls to prevent or detect unauthorized access and frequently monitor such access logs. When appropriate, investigate apparent security violations, and take remedial action to prevent future reoccurrences.

7.13.3 Application Software Development and Change Control

It is crucial to have an auditor or evaluator independent of the development group evaluate processing features and program modifications by means of a formal code review to ensure what is coded is properly authorized and there are no "surprises" (e.g., Trojan horses, virus infections, etc.) in any software released to production environments. It is a good idea to thoroughly test and approve all new software placed into operation in your environment. Any revised software should also be tested before being released onto your network. For all software, you should establish and maintain control of software libraries, ensuring proper versions and licenses are maintained at all times. This is a formidable task and often requires people's full-time attention in larger organizations. Not taking these precautions can be very risky to an organization. Sometimes, it can even bring about litigation in cases of license infringement or negligence (for example, releasing a software product on the open market that contained a virus).

7.13.4 System Software

The software that runs your systems is analogous to the engine that powers an automobile. Just as you would not let just anyone under the hood of your car, you should also limit access to system software to "trusted" individuals. When you do allow access, monitor such access to ensure only proper and authorized actions take place. This may require having one well-qualified administrator looking over the shoulder of another well-qualified administrator. While it may seem overly cautious, keep in mind the fact that approximately 80% of hacks occur from *within* the organization. Ensure all system software changes fall under a managed change control process. It is always a good idea to have such changes tested in a "sandbox" environment before being placed in production. This prevents problems from occurring in a production environment. If your systems are going to fail from a software problem, better to have them grind to a halt in a controlled test environment than a production environment where every minute of downtime can cost thousands, if not hundreds of thousands, of dollars to the organization.

7.13.5 Segregation of Duties

In most corporate environments today, the infrastructure is so complex and difficult to maintain that it would be a huge risk for one individual to have access to all components of that infrastructure. It is important to segregate incompatible duties and establish related policies to properly protect the organization. For example, you would not give the person responsible for building maintenance the keys to the IT server room. His or her duties would be considered incompatible. Similarly, your firewall team has no need to know what the systems-level password is for all applications and database servers. Once again, incompatible duties should drive the decision-making process to segregate those duties. Establish access controls to enforce segregation of duties. Do not make it easy for systems administrators or network administrators to share device passwords. Establish controls that maintain the integrity of the segregation policies. Control your personnel activities by establishing formal operating procedures, maintaining good supervision, and conducting frequent, recurring reviews.

7.13.6 Service Continuity

To keep an operation running in today's 24/7 business environment, it is important for a security manager to assess the criticality of computerized operations and identify supporting resources. Take steps to prevent and minimize potential damage and interruption by working to develop and document a comprehensive contingency plan, and periodically testing and adjusting it as appropriate. Having proper contingency plans in place can often save an organization from sure disaster, because personnel are able to make the right responses at the right times. In a crisis situation, there is little chance of recovery if no one knows what to do.

7.14 Perimeter Audits

As networks have become mission-essential to the business needs of an entity, the network becomes a critical resource that must be protected, both from activities at the perimeter and within, from unwanted intrusions, runaway applications, eavesdropping operations, network protocol architecture(s) lack of security provisions, and many other potential security problems. Further, as network resources increase in size and as more users consume network resources and abuse the network in various ways, virus infiltration and spread, worms, and other network contaminants that would negatively affect the performance of the network and the systems on it become an all-too-real probability.

Some computing sites, due to the nature of their business, require continual network monitoring. Other sites require network security monitoring due to information access reporting laws, audit requirements, guarantees of access (ensuring that only the proper entity is accessing the proper items), protection of competitive information, laws requiring the guarantee of restricted access to personal information, general electronic security (e.g., e-mail access, document transfer), electronic funds exchange, monitoring of exchange or transaction data volume between systems, and many other items related to the security issue. Regardless of the purpose for such monitoring needs, it all begins at the perimeter (i.e., routers and firewalls). Now, let's take a look at what is necessary in an audit of a router. For our purposes, we will be discussing the use of Cisco™ routers.

7.15 Using Nmap

Nmap ("Network Mapper") is an open source utility for network exploration or security auditing. It was designed to rapidly scan large networks, although it works fine against single hosts. Nmap uses raw IP packets in novel ways to determine what hosts are available on the network, what services (ports) they are offering, what operating system (and OS version) they are running, what type of packet filters/firewalls are in use, and dozens of other characteristics. Nmap runs on most types of computers, and both console and graphical versions are available. Nmap is free software, available with full source code under the terms of the GNU General Public License (GPL).

7.15.1 What Is NLog?

NLog is a set of scripts written in the PERL scripting language for managing and analyzing Nmap log files (Nmap Version 2.0 and above). NLog allows one to keep all of their scan logs in a searchable database. The CGI interface for viewing your scan logs is completely customizable and easy to modify and improve. The core CGI script allows you to add your own extension scripts for different services, so all hosts with a certain service running will have a hyperlink to the extension script.

Basically this is a multipurpose Web-based Nmap log browser. The extension scripts allow you to get detailed information about specific services like NETBIOS, RPC services, finger services, and BIND version data from a DNS server. It is extremely easy to create extensions for things like an snmpwalk wrapper, a popper vulnerability check, and so on. NLog provides a standard database format to build your own scripts for any purpose. Included with the NLog distribution are example CGI scripts, the Nmap-log-to-database conversion tool, a sample template for building PERL scripts, and couple of scripts used for dumping IPs from a domain and performing similar reporting operations. Another use of NLog is for network administrators who desire a scan of their local network on a regular basis. This is desirable in order to make sure none of the machines are listening on weird ports and that they are running only authorized services. A cron script can be used to scan the internal network, convert log files to the NLog database format, and store them on a Web server, sorted by time or date. The administrator could then load the NLog search form page and run comparisons between databases collected on different dates or at different times from anywhere. If the Web server is on a gateway machine, the administrator could run RPC or finger requests on the internal hosts through the CGI interface, thus removing any need to be on the (possibly) firewalled or masked network to check a host's status.

7.15.2 Downloading Nmap

Use http://www.insecure.org/nmap/nmap_download.html as the official site for obtaining a copy of the Nmap tool. It is freely available for download from this URL. The Nmap product is officially maintained and managed from the above location. The following data, obtained from the official Nmap Web site, explains some of the major features of Nmap.

7.15.3 Nmap Features

Nmap is a tool used for security auditing. The newest version improves performance and stability and adds more features. At the time of this writing, the latest version of Nmap is 3.0 for all platforms (Windows, Linux tarball, Linux RPM). Some of the new features of Nmap are:

1. Fast parallel pinging of all hosts on a network to determine which ones are active. Use the ICMP echo request (ping), TCP ACK packet, or TCP SYN packet to probe for responses. By default, Nmap uses both ACKs and ICMP pings to maximize the chance

of infiltrating packet filters. There is also a connect() version for underprivileged users. The syntax for specifying which hosts should be scanned is quite flexible.

2. Improved port scans can be used to determine what services are running. Techniques available include use of the SYN (half-open) scan, FIN, Xmas, or Null stealth scans, connect scan (which does not require root), FTP bounce attack, and UDP scan. Options exist for common filter-bypassing techniques such as packet fragmentation and the ability to set the source port number (to 20 or 53, for example). Nmap can also query a remote *identd* for the usernames the server is running under. You can select any (or all) port number(s) to scan, since you may want to just sweep the networks you run for one or more services recently found to be vulnerable.

3. Remote OS detection via TCP/IP fingerprinting. This feature allows you to determine what operating system release each scanned host is running. In many cases, Nmap can narrow the OS information down to the kernel number or release version. A database of approximately 100 fingerprints for common operating system versions is included with Nmap.

4. TCP ISN sequence predictability lets you know what sequence prediction class (64K, time-dependent, "true random," constant, etc.) the host falls into. A difficulty index is provided to tell you roughly how vulnerable the machine is to sequence prediction.

5. Decoy scans can be used with Nmap. The idea of using a decoy scan is that for every packet sent by Nmap from your address, a similar packet is sent from each decoy host you specify. This is useful due to circumvent stealth port scanning detection software. If such software is used, it will generally report a dozen (or however many you choose) port scans from different addresses at the same time. It is very difficult to determine which address is actually doing the scanning, and which are simply innocent decoys.

7.16 Mapping the Network with Nmap

Ports provide capability for interactive communications and services on a computer and they are generally assigned an address in order to make them available to other applications and computers. There are 65,535 available ports assigned on any given system, with applications and devices registered to use these ports for communication purposes. *Because ports are the points of access for a system, they are also the points that are most often scanned by an attacker and tracked by the system administrator.* Over the years, port scanners have continually evolved from primitive to highly stealthy software. Because time is on the side of the attacker, stealth scanning can be achieved by a combination of spoofing and the type of packet sent. Information is retrieved and collected to form the basis for how an attack will be planned.

Typically, the process for a hacker is to first scan to determine which operating system, ports, and protocols are run on a target. For each of the above, a matrix can be established and used later for specific penetration activities. For example, if port 20 is detected as an open port and FTP traffic is detected, the hacker can tailor an attack for penetration of an FTP server. They may use a technique known as "hammering" to find a password that allows the FTP server to grant them privileged access. Once the hacker penetrates the FTP server, he or she has access to everything the FTP server can see in a network segment. As you can see, it does not take a lot of information to aid an attacker in his or her work.

7.17 Analyzing Nmap Scan Results

The result of running Nmap is usually a list of interesting ports on the machine(s) being scanned (if any). Nmap always gives the ports "well-known" service name (if any), number, state, and protocol. The state is either **open**, **filtered**, or **unfiltered**. Open means the target machine will accept connections on that port. Filtered means that a firewall, filter, or other network obstacle is covering the port and preventing Nmap from determining whether the port is open. Unfiltered means the port is known by Nmap to be closed and no firewall/filter seems to be interfering with Nmap's attempts to determine information. Unfiltered ports are the most common case, and are only shown when most of the scanned ports are found to be in the filtered state. Depending on which options are used, Nmap may also report the following characteristics of the remote host: OS in use, TCP sequenceability, usernames running the programs that have been bound to each port, the DNS name, whether the host is a Smurf address, and so on. Nmap comes with myriad configurations that allow a scanner to fine-tune the scanning process to obtain necessary data. It is important to check logs from perimeter devices to check for such repeated scanning and take steps to prevent hacks.

7.18 Penetration Testing Using Nessus

The Nessus Security Scanner is another robust security auditing tool. Once Nmap has found what may appear to be possible chinks in the armor, Nessus makes it possible for auditors to directly test those chinks using security modules to find vulnerable spots that should be fixed. It is made up of two parts, a server and a client. The server/daemon is named **nessusd** and the client is **nessus**. A plug-in architecture allows each security test (module) to be written as an external plugin. In this manner, one can easily add his or her own tests to Nessus without having to modify the source code of the **nessusd** engine. The main features of the Nessus Security Scanner are explained below.

- **Nessus Attack Scripting Language (NASL).** The Nessus Security Scanner includes NASL, a language designed to write security tests quickly and easily (the security checks can also be written in the C programming language). Nessus comes with a fairly current security vulnerabilities database. The security checks database is updated on a daily basis, so all the newest security checks are available from the Nessus Web site, http://www.nessus.org.

- **Nessus client/server architecture.** The Nessus Security Scanner is made up of two parts: a server, which performs the attacks, and a client, which is the front-end. You can run the server and the client on different systems. That is, you can audit your whole network from your personal computer, whereas the server performs its attacks from another system. There are several clients available for Nessus: one for X11, one for Win32, and one written in Java. Nessus can test an unlimited number of hosts at the same time, depending upon the power of the system you run the Nessus server component on.

- **Smart service recognition**. Nessus does not believe the target hosts will respect the Internet Assigned Numbers Authority (IANA) assigned port numbers. This means that it will recognize a FTP server running on a non-standard port (31337, say), or a Web server running on port 8080.

- **Multiples service support**. Imagine a situation where an organization runs two Web servers (or more) on their host, one server assigned to run on port 80 and the other assigned to run on port 8080. Nessus will successfully test both of them, even though they are running on the same host. It makes no assumptions about specific services being tied to specific hosts.

- **Test cooperation.** The security tests performed by Nessus are designed to cooperate with services detected on the host so that useless information is not reported. For example, if an FTP server does not allow anonymous logins, then Nessus is intelligent enough to determine that any anonymous-related security checks need not be performed.

- **Complete, exportable reports.** Nessus will not only tell you what's wrong on your network, but will, most of the time, tell you how to prevent crackers from exploiting the security holes found, and will give you the risk level of each problem found (risk levels are categorized from Low to Very High). The UNIX version of the Nessus client can export Nessus reports in ASCII text, LaTeX, HTML, "spiffy" HTML (with pies and graphs), and an easy-to-parse delimited file format.

- **Full SSL support.** Nessus has the ability to test SSL-type services such as https, smtps, imaps, and more. You can even supply Nessus with a certificate so that it can be integrated into a PKI-like environment.

As you can see, the features available in Nessus allow the auditor many capabilities to perform audit checks. By varying configurations, the auditor can vary the depth of the checks to meet the specific needs of the organization. It is not uncommon for an auditor to maintain a suite of plug-in modules that test most common vulnerabilities. Usually, these tools have been refined by auditors over numerous audits and provide excellent information. As a security manager, it is a good idea to start the use of such a process in your organization so the auditors can perform their tasks in a more automated fashion and do their work in shorter and shorter time frames. For more information on Nessus, the reader is encouraged to visit their Web site, http://www.nessus.org.

7.19　Training Staff for the Business Recovery Process

Managing the training process is crucial to establishing an effective BC program. To accomplish this, the BC team must develop objectives and define the scope of training. They must determine what training needs to be conducted and what materials should be used for the training. A schedule should be prepared for all organizational personnel involved in BC activities, and that schedule should be announced in formal communications to the organizational staff. The BC team should prepare a budget for each training phase, and part of this should include a recurring training program. The following sections will provide more detail about training considerations.

7.19.1 Develop Objectives and Scope of Training

The objectives and scope of the BCP training activities are to be clearly stated within the plan. The BCP should contain a description of the objectives and scope of the training phase. This will enable the training to be consistent and organized in a manner where the results can be measured, and the training fine-tuned, as appropriate. The objectives for the training could be as follows: *To train all staff in the particular procedures to be followed during the business recovery process.* The scope of the training could be along the following lines: *The training is to be carried out in a comprehensive and exhaustive manner, so that staff become familiar with all aspects of the recovery process. The training will cover all aspects of the Business Recovery activities section of the BCP, including IT systems recovery.* Consideration should also be given to the development of a comprehensive corporate awareness program for communicating the procedures for the business recovery process.

7.19.2 Training Needs Assessment

The plan must specify which person or group of persons requires which type of training. It is necessary for all new or revised processes to be explained carefully to the staff. For example, it may be necessary to carry out some processes manually if the IT system is down for any length of time. These manual procedures must be fully understood by the persons who are required to carry them out. For larger organizations, it may be practical to carry out the training in a classroom environment; however, for smaller organizations the training may be better handled in a workshop environment. This section of the BCP should identify, for each business process, the type of training required and which persons or group of persons need to be trained.

7.19.3 Training Materials Development

Once the training needs have been identified, it is necessary to specify and develop suitable training materials. This can be a time consuming task, and unless priorities are given to critical training programs, it could delay the organization in reaching an adequate level of preparedness. This section of the BCP contains information on each of the training program with details of the training materials to be developed, an estimate of resources, and an estimate of the completion date.

7.19.4   Prepare Training Schedule

Once it has been agreed who requires training and the training materials have been prepared, a detailed training schedule should be drawn up. This section of the BCP contains the overview of the training schedule and the groups of persons receiving the training.

7.19.5   Communication to Staff

Once the training is ready to be delivered to the employees, it is necessary to advise them about the training programs they are scheduled to attend. This section of the BCP contains a draft communication to be sent to all members of the staff to advise them about their training schedule. The communication should provide for feedback from the staff member if the training dates given are inconvenient. A separate communication should be sent to the managers of the business units, advising them of the proposed training schedule to be attended by their staff. Each member of staff will be given information on their role and responsibilities applicable in the event of an emergency.

7.19.6   Prepare Budget for Training Phase

Each phase of the BCP process that incurs a cost requires that a budget be prepared and approved. Depending on the cross-charging system employed by the organization, the training costs will vary greatly. It has to be recognized that, however well justified, training incurs additional costs, and these should be approved by the appropriate authority within the organization. This section of the BCP will contain a list of the training phase activities and a cost for each. It should be noted whenever part of the cost is already incorporated within the organization's overall budgeting process.

7.19.7   Feedback Questionnaires

It is vital to receive and assess feedback from the persons managing and participating in each of the tests. This feedback will hopefully enable weaknesses within the Business Recovery Process to be identified and eliminated. Completion of feedback forms should be mandatory for all persons participating in the process. The forms should be completed either during the tests (to record a specific issue) or as soon after finishing as practical. This will enable observations and comments to be recorded while the event is still fresh in the person's mind. This section of the BCP should contain a template for a Feedback Questionnaire for the training phase. The individual BCP training programs and the overall BCP training process should be assessed to ensure effectiveness and applicability.

7.19.8 Exercise the Training

You should consider developing a comprehensive training exercise program to evaluate policies and procedures, ensure that personnel are properly trained, and verify that resources and equipment are capable of supporting operations. Each element of the plan should be evaluated through exercises and a procedure established to remedy any deficiencies in the plans. At a minimum, you should:

- Conduct orientation and training for BCP planning committee members

- Periodically test alert and notification procedures; update rosters and notification checklists

- Exercise operational plans, alternate facilities, and interoperable communications; plan joint agency exercises

- Develop a schedule to evaluate and test equipment

- Develop a remedial action plan with timelines for completion of assigned tasks

- Update plans and procedures as necessary or on an annual basis

7.20 Chapter Summary

This chapter has discussed basic diligence efforts needed to keep a security program healthy, and several areas needed to mitigate risks in an organization. It has explained that the objective of a security audit is to assess the quantity of risk and the effectiveness of the organization's risk management processes as they relate to the security measures instituted to ensure confidentiality, integrity, and availability of information, and to instill accountability for actions taken on the organization's systems.

We have covered the fundamentals of auditing from the perspective of a manager implementing security in an organization. We discussed the auditor's role in developing security policies and how those policies should be implemented with an audit frame of mind. We discussed several audit standards and organizations you can use to obtain further information and covered the basic auditing and assessment strategies needed for making audits successful. The audit process itself was discussed, explaining the six major areas every audit should cover and why. We looked at the need to evaluate organizational perimeters, namely firewalls and routers, and some tools auditors can use to accomplish those tasks.

The latter part of this chapter covered the need for training staff for the business recovery process. This training process begins by having the training team develop objectives and determine the scope of training that will be needed. Next, they must conduct a training needs assessment and begin the work of developing the needed training materials. After the training materials development has begun, it is necessary to prepare training schedules and develop means to get the word out to all of your employees. The importance of proper communication to staff was discussed. When getting ready to train, it is a good idea to prepare a budget for the training phase and to develop feedback questionnaires that will be used to assess feedback. When you actually conduct the training, these will be used to help you evaluate the effectiveness of the training. In the next chapter, we will discuss how you can maintain the BCP once you have it completed.

7.21 Endnotes

1. Herzog, Pete, *Open Source Security Testing Methodology Manual*, February 26, 2002. http://isecom.org

2. http://www.cert.org/security-improvement/#Harden

3. National State Auditors Association and the U.S. General Accounting Office (joint initiative), *Management Planning Guide for Information Systems Security Auditing.* December 10, 2001.

4. CERT Coordination Center. (2005).CERT® Coordination Center2003 Annual Report. Retrieved June 23, 2005 from http://www.cert.org/annual_rpts/cert_rpt_03.html#intro.

5. Alan Oliphant, "An Introduction to Computer Auditing—Part 2," October 1998. http://www.theiia.org/itaudit.

6. GAO/AIMD-12.19.6, *Federal Information System Controls Audit Manual*. January 1999.
    http://www.gao.gov/special.pubs/ai12.19.6.pdf

7. GAO/AIMD-12.19.6, *Federal Information System Controls Audit Manual*. January 1999,
    http://www.gao.gov/special.pubs/ai12.19.6.pdf

8. Anonymous (April 27, 2001). "IT Security Is All Wrong, Says Expert," the(451).

9. National Institute of Standards and Technology, *Special Publication 800-12: An Introduction to Computer Security: The NIST Handbook*. October 1995. Ch. 8.

8

Maintaining a Business Continuity Plan

8.1 How to Maintain the Business Continuity Plan

Environmental changes, new products, policies, new procedures, personnel forgetting or losing interest in critical parts of the plan, or departing from the company—any of these situations may make a BCP obsolete or in need of revisions. Periodic testing of the BCP is required for verification and validation purposes. This stage is to preplan and coordinate plan exercises. It is also to evaluate and document the results of the plan exercise. Develop processes to maintain the currency of continuity capabilities and the plan document in accordance with the organization's strategic direction. Verify that the plan will prove effective by comparison with a suitable standard, and report results in a clear and concise manner.

Tasks to perform:

- Preplan the exercises
- Coordinate the exercises
- Evaluate the exercise plans
- Exercise the plans
- Document the results
- Evaluate the results
- Report results and/or evaluation to management
- Understand strategic directions of the business

- Attend strategic planning meetings
- Coordinate plan maintenance
- Assist in establishing audit program for the business continuity plan

A BCP is a "living" document, changing in concert with changes in the business activities it supports. The plan should be reviewed by senior management, the planning team or coordinator, team members, internal audit, and the executive management team at least annually. As part of that review process, the team, or coordinator should contact business unit managers throughout the institution at regular intervals to assess the nature and scope of any changes to the institution's business, structure, systems, software, hardware, personnel, or facilities. It is to be expected that some changes will have occurred since the last plan update. Software applications are commercially available to assist the BCP coordinator in identifying and tracking these organizational changes so the BCP can be updated.

All such organizational changes should be analyzed to determine how they may affect the existing continuity plan, and what revisions to the plan may be necessary to accommodate these changes. The agencies expect that BCP updates will be documented to show that the plan reflects the institution as it currently exists. Lastly, the financial institution should ensure the revised BCP is distributed throughout the organization.

The plan itself is always changing to reflect changing conditions in the business, the environment, and the community itself. It is necessary for the BCP updating process to be properly structured and controlled. As a living document, the organization should implement a change control process for managing the BCP. Periodic reviews should be conducted and the responsibilities for maintenance of each part of the plan should be clearly delineated. Whenever any change is made to the plan, it is important to test that change to ensure it adequately satisfies all requirements. Also, when changes are made, it is important to notify the training group of those changes so they can be reflected in future training. Whenever changes are made to the BCP they should be fully tested. This will usually involve the use of formalized change control procedures under the control of the BCP Team Leader. Four areas need to be addressed in this process:

1.   Use change control procedures for updating the plan
2.   Assign responsibilities for maintenance of each part of the plan

3.   Test all changes to plan

4.   Advise person responsible for BCP training

8.1.1   Use Change Control Procedures for Updates to the Plan

It is important to recognize the factors that may change the business continuity plan such as:

- Procedural changes

- Organizational structure changes

- Personnel changes/turnover

- Physical changes (e.g., facilities)

- Technology changes

- Recovery requirements changes

- Testing issues

Change management and control policies and procedures should appropriately address changes to the operating environment. Just as all program changes should be fully authorized and documented, business continuity considerations should be included in the change control process and implementation phase. Whenever a change is made to an application, operating system, or utility that resides in the production environment, a methodology should exist to ensure all backup copies of those systems are updated to reflect the new environment. In addition, if a new or changed system is implemented and results in new hardware, capacity requirements, or other technology changes, management should ensure that the BCP is updated and the recovery site can support the new production environment.

It is recommended that formal change controls be implemented to cover any changes required to the BCP. This is necessary due to the level of complexity contained within the BCP. A Change Request Form/Change Order Form should be prepared and approved in respect of each proposed change to the BCP. This section of the BCP will contain a Change Request Form/Change Order to be used for all such changes to the BCP.

8.1.2   BCP Data Synchronization

Data synchronization can become a challenge when dealing with an active/backup environment. The larger and more complex an institution is (i.e., shorter acceptable operational outage period, greater volume of data, greater distance between primary and backup location), the more difficult synchronization can become. If backup copies are always produced at the close of a business day and a disruption occurs relatively late the next business day, all the transactions that took place after the backup copies were made would have to be recreated, perhaps manually, to synchronize the recovery site with the primary site.

Management and testing of contingency arrangements are critical to ensure the recovery environment is synchronized with the primary work environment. This testing includes ensuring software versions are current, interfaces exist and are tested, and communication equipment is compatible. If the two locations, underlying systems, and interdependent business units are not synchronized, there is the likely possibility that recovery at the backup location could encounter significant problems. Proper change control, information backup, and adequate testing can help avoid this situation. In addition, management should ensure the backup facility has adequate capacity to process transactions in a timely manner in the event of a disruption at the primary location.

8.1.3   Assign Responsibilities for Maintenance of Each Part of the Plan

Each part of the plan will be allocated to a member of the BCP Team or a senior manager with the organization, who will be charged with the responsibility of updating and maintaining the plan. The BCP team leader will remain in overall control of the BCP, but business unit heads will need to keep their own sections of the BCP up-to-date at all times. Usually, the corporate HR team will be responsible for ensuring that all emergency contact numbers for staff are kept up-to-date. It is important that the relevant BCP coordinator and the business recovery team are kept fully informed regarding any approved changes to the plan.

8.1.4   Test All Changes to Plan

The BCP team will nominate one or more persons to be responsible for coordinating all the testing processes and for ensuring that all changes to the plan are properly tested. Whenever changes are made or proposed to the

BCP, the BCP testing coordinator will be notified. The BCP testing coordinator will then be responsible for notifying all affected units and for arranging any further testing activities. This section of the BCP contains a draft communication from the BCP coordinator to affected business units and contains information about the changes that require testing or retesting.

8.1.5 Advise BCP Training Staff of Plan Updates/Changes

A member of the BCP team (the BCP training coordinator) will be given responsibility for coordinating all training activities. The BCP team leader will notify the BCP training coordinator of all approved changes to the BCP so that training materials can be updated. An assessment should be made as to whether the change necessitates any retraining activities.

8.2 BCP Maintenance

BCP maintenance helps to provide the framework in which your business continuity plans can be reviewed, both on a regular basis and in response to major changes in your business environment. BCP maintenance can help you maintain the accuracy and currency of your BCPs and maximize the effectiveness of your recovery operations. The benefits of BCP maintenance are that it helps ensure that your plans are maintained in a way that is consistent with your changing business processes, keeps your plans as current as possible with our structured maintenance programs that are validated and refined by internal use within our own organization, and maximizes the effectiveness of your recovery operations by formalizing the BCP change management process.

The average life of a BCP plan is quite short. In as little as six to twelve months after being put into use, a plan may have lost much, if not all, of its value. These plans quickly become outdated because of changes in the organization, purchase and installation of new systems, new procedures, and new personnel. BCP plans are living documents that must grow and change along with the businesses that they protect. An outdated business continuity plan can negatively impact the recovery capabilities and timelines of an organization. Accordingly, it is critically important to implement adequate maintenance policies and procedures.

8.2.1 Maintenance Frequency

The recovery procedures for each team should be updated at minimum on a yearly basis and should also be updated following major organizational changes. Telephone lists and other inventories should be updated at least quarterly. The plan should also be reviewed and updated when there are major changes in technology. A plan maintenance form (as described below) can be used to record and control all maintenance changes, additions or modifications to the plan.

8.2.1.1 Develop Plan Maintenance Procedures

Maintenance procedures consist of two general categories: scheduled and unscheduled. Scheduled maintenance is time-driven; unscheduled maintenance is event-driven. In most organizations, changes in personnel, responsibilities, processing and communications equipment, and the like are common. In a dynamic organization, changes in business processes, facilities and the like might be common.

8.2.1.2 Scheduled Maintenance

Scheduled maintenance occurs as the result of a scheduled review of the business continuity plan. Reviews are predictable (based upon established requirements) and are scheduled at decided time intervals (weekly, monthly, quarterly, etc.). The purpose of the review is to determine what changes are required. Initiate scheduled plan reviews. Ensure the necessary updates are made to the plan. Team leaders are responsible for reviewing their assigned portions of the plan. The review should address any events that have occurred within each team's area of responsibility that may affect the organization's response, resumption, recovery, or restoration capability. The review will expose any updates or changes that are needed.

8.2.1.3 Unscheduled Maintenance

Certain maintenance requirements are unpredictable and cannot be scheduled. The majority of these unscheduled plan changes occur as the result of major changes to the organization, business operations, processes, functions, hardware configurations, (voice/data) networks, etc.

Stay on top of all changes to the plan resulting from unscheduled maintenance. The team leader whose area of responsibility is affected may submit changes.

8.2.2 **Maintenance Responsibilities**

Maintenance responsibilities should be clearly defined in both the plan and in the individual position descriptions for those with maintenance responsibilities. Examples of maintenance responsibilities may include:

- Business Continuity Planner directs and controls plan maintenance
- Team Members are responsible for maintaining their respective team sections
- Department Heads are responsible for the detail relating to their department
- Board of Directors and Senior Management are responsible for review and approval of the plan

Internal Audit is responsible for examining the plan to determine if it satisfies the recovery objectives of the organization and is accurate and up-to-date. Update methods include:

- Page replacement
- Section replacement
- Plan replacement
- Old materials should be returned and destroyed

It is also possible to use paperless business continuity plans. Such plans are often developed in a specialized software package for business continuity planning, and are available electronically over the Internet or intranet. Electronic plans are easier to maintain and distribute.

8.3 **BCP Distribution Issues**

To facilitate maintenance, it is important to monitor and track each copy of the plan. A distribution log, as illustrated below, can be used to record and control all copies of the business continuity plan issued to various personnel.

A Business Continuity Plan (BCP) usually contains information that is confidential to the organization. Accordingly, the BCP should be a restricted document and classified as confidential, given the nature of the contents. Each individual with a copy of the plan is responsible for security and control of the document in accordance with policies for the protection of proprietary information.

The business continuity planner is responsible for the authorized distribution of the BCP and should maintain a master distribution list. Each authorized copy of the plan should contain a version identification number, and the recipient should be recorded on the distribution list.

Full copies of the plan are usually provided to all team managers. Partial copies of the business continuity plan may be distributed to other members; these would reflect plan details associated with the responsibilities of their assigned team(s). Additionally, the business continuity planner should maintain master copies onsite and copies at the offsite storage location—both printed and electronic versions.

8.4   Awareness and Training Programs

Preparing a program to create corporate awareness and enhance the skills required to develop, implement, maintain, and execute the business continuity plan is half the battle. You may have a business continuity plan; however, if no one knows about it or knows what to do in case of an emergency, then the best-laid plan will be of little use. Training programs are essential for recovery processes to flow smoothly and gain support of all affected departments. Some things you can do:

- Establish objectives and components of the training program.
- Identify functional training requirements.
- Develop training methodology.
- Develop awareness program.
- Acquire or develop training aids.
- Identify external training opportunities.
- Identify vehicles for corporate awareness.

BCP training should be provided for personnel to ensure all parties are aware of their responsibilities should a disaster occur. Key employees should be involved in the business continuity development process, as well as in periodic training exercises. The training program should incorporate enterprise-wide training as well as specific training for individual business units. Employees should be aware which conditions call for implementing all or part of the BCP, who is responsible for implementing BCPs for business units and the institution, and what to do if these key employees are not available at the time of a disaster. Cross-training should be used to anticipate restoring operations in the absence of key employees. Employee training should be regularly scheduled and updated to address changes to the BCP. The requirements for team training will vary from plan to plan and by the category of team (e.g., operations, support, and technology). The complexity of the environment and the time-sensitivity of the functions will guide the project team in the development of training. Training materials should cover all steps of disaster readiness planning.

Corporations should consider developing an awareness program to let customers, service providers, and regulators know how to contact the institution, and who will communicate with the media, government, vendors, and other companies and provide the information to be communicated.

8.5   Monitor and Review

The objective of the final step in the risk management process is to monitor risks and the effectiveness of controls over time to ensure changing circumstances do not alter risk priorities or weaken the operation of controls. Many organizations integrate risk assessment into their corporate and annual business planning processes. This ensures regular, periodic review of both strategic and operational risks. Review of controls, to ensure they operate as management intended, has traditionally been the major role of the internal audit function. However, the major drawback is that it may lead operational managers to conclude that internal audit, not the operational manager, is responsible for the system of control. In some cases, organizations will implement corporate governance programs that highlight managers' responsibilities for controls. The use of control "sign-offs" and the introduction of control self-assessment are two useful initiatives in this area.

8.6   Roles and Responsibilities for Maintaining the BCP Plan

Individual recovery team plans must be continually maintained to provide support for business continuity. Administrative procedures and guidelines should be developed to provide for periodic testing and documentation maintenance of the service area recover plan(s) and ongoing training.

Responsibilities for various aspects of BCP maintenance are also established. Ongoing responsibilities should be defined to ensure appropriate BCP maintenance. The groups shown in Table 8.1 have specific BCP maintenance responsibilities.

8.7   Chapter Summary

In this chapter, we discussed the importance of maintaining a business continuity plan. The process of maintaining the business continuity plan includes the use of change control procedures to make updates to the plan

Table 8.1   *Roles and Responsibilities of Recovery Team Participants.*

Role	Responsibility
Recovery Coordinator	Manages BCP, coordinates recovery teams, provides updates to Executive Management. Should ensure the following on a semi-annual basis: ■ Schedule and coordinate BCP training and testing ■ Coordinate BCP document reviews, changes, and approvals from relevant parties ■ Ensure BCP is disseminated to all parties concerned ■ Maintain alternate processing site contracts, maintenance, and service level agreements
Recovery Team	Execute documented steps in the BCP to recover downed systems. Annually, the team should: ■ Maintain team-specific procedures ■ Update reference information pertinent to team procedures ■ Train and test in relevant BCP sections
Users	■ Identify and ensure key information needed to perform job function is stored offsite ■ Undergo awareness training ■ Participate in BCP training/testing

and keep the plan current with BCP data synchronization. You should assign responsibilities for maintenance of each part of the plan and test all changes that are made to it. We recommended that you implement a process to advise BCP training staff of plan updates/changes and conduct periodic BCP maintenance. The maintenance frequency is often a matter unique to each business, but we recommend at least a semi-annual review.

When you develop plan maintenance procedures, ensure that scheduled maintenance and unscheduled maintenance activities are included. It is important to designate maintenance responsibilities to someone or to some group who will can adequately manage the task. BCP distribution issues will need to be addressed by this team. They should also develop and conduct regular awareness and training programs. It is necessary to monitor and review the program to ensure it is effective. For the team maintaining the plan, it is necessary to outline each member's roles and responsibilities for maintaining the BCP plan; follow up to ensure they live up to those roles and responsibilities.

This book has provided you with the information fundamental to development of a solid BCP for your organization. There are abundant resources readily available to help you review, improve, and exercise your plans once you get them developed and ready to test. Should the need arise to move from a test to an actual event, the knowledge and insight you have gained from this book will, we hope, assist you in your recovery and restoration process. Remember, every day, potential disasters happen. You have the knowledge now to be prepared and make the process manageable if you are ever in that situation. Good luck.

BCP/DR Glossary

ABC Fire Extinguisher: A chemically-based device used to eliminate ordinary combustible, flammable liquid, and electrical fires.

Activation: When all or a portion of the recovery plan has been put into motion.

Alert: Notification that a disaster situation has occurred—stand by for possible activation of disaster recovery plan.

Alternate Site: A location, other than the normal facility, used to process data and/or conduct critical business functions in the event of a disaster. *Similar terms: alternate office facility, alternate communication facility, alternate processing facility.*

Application Recovery: The component of disaster recovery dealing specifically with the restoration of business system software and data after the processing platform has been restored or replaced. *Similar term: business system recovery.*

Assumptions: Basic understandings about unknown disaster situations the disaster recovery plan is based on. A set of basic facts or premises, provided to each business unit or established in the course of continuity planning sessions. These premises eliminate the need to consider certain elements during the building of continuity plans.

Back Office Location: An office or building that is used by the organization to conduct support activities, but that is not located within an organization's headquarters or main location.

Backlog Trap: The effect on the business of a backlog of work that accumulates when a system or process is unavailable for a long period—a backlog that may take a considerable length of time to reduce.

Backup Agreements: A contract to provide a service that includes the method of performance, the fees, the duration, the services provided, and the extent of security and confidentiality maintained.

Backup Position Listing: A list of alternative personnel who can fill a recovery team position when the primary person is not available.

Backup Power: Generally, diesel generators used to provide sufficient power to operate equipment normally when commercial power fails.

Backup Strategy: Alternative operating method (e.g., platform, location) for facilities and systems operations in the event of a disaster. *See also Recovery Strategy.*

Base Parameters: These are the key guidelines, which include assumptions. Base parameters establish a foundation on which continuity plans are built.

Business as Usual: Operating under normal conditions, i.e., without any significant interruptions of operations as a result of a disaster.

Business Continuity Plan: A plan of action detailing how to react to and recover from a disaster or crisis that threatens to disrupt normal business activities. The plan steps outline the way in which the company restores operations to core business processes. (A continuity plan is also referred to as resumption plan or contingency plan.)

Business Continuity Planning (BCP): An all-encompassing "umbrella" term, covering both disaster recovery planning and business resumption planning. *See also Disaster Recovery Planning and Business Resumption Planning.*

Business Continuity Program: The advanced planning and development of a Business Continuity Plan(s) and any guidelines that, when implemented, will ensure the timely and orderly resumption of the company's core business processes.

Business Function: The most elementary activities, e.g., calculating gross pay, updating job descriptions, and matching invoices to receiving reports.

Business Impact Analysis (BIA): The process of analyzing all business functions and the effect that a specific disaster may have upon them.

Business Interruption: Any event, whether anticipated (e.g., a public service strike) or unanticipated (e.g., a blackout), that disrupts the normal course of business operations at a corporate location.

Business Interruption Costs: The costs or lost revenue associated with an interruption in normal business operations.

Business Recovery Coordinator: *See Disaster Recovery Coordinator.*

Business Recovery Plan: A document containing corporate-wide policies, test-validated procedures, and action instructions developed specifically for use in restoring company operations in the event of a declared disaster.

Business Recovery Planning (BRP): A "near synonym" for contingency planning. It implies that the plan includes the tasks required to take the organization from the immediate aftermath of a disaster through the return to, or resumption of, normal operations. *See also Disaster Recovery Planning.*

Business Recovery Process: The common critical path that all companies follow during a recovery effort. There are major nodes along the path that are followed, regardless of the organization. The process has seven stages: (1) immediate response, (2) environmental restoration, (3) functional restoration, (4) data synchronization, (5) restoration of business functions, (6) interim site, and (7) return home.

Business Recovery Team: A group of individuals responsible for maintaining and coordinating the recovery process. *See also Disaster Recovery Teams. Similar term: recovery team.*

Business Unit: Any logical organizational element of a company, agency, or other entity.

Business Unit Recovery: The component of disaster recovery which deals specifically with the relocation of key organization personnel in the event of a disaster and the provision of essential records, equipment supplies, work space, communication facilities, computer processing capability, and so on. *Similar terms: work group recovery.*

Certified Business Continuity Planner (CBCP): CBCPs are certified by the Disaster Recovery Institute, a not-for-profit corporation that promotes credibility and professionalism in the disaster recovery industry. This certification originally was known as Certified Disaster Recovery Planner (CDRP).

Checklist Test: A method used to test a completed disaster recovery plan. This test is used to determine whether the information in the plan, such as phone numbers, manuals, equipment, and so on, is accurate and current.

Cold Site: An alternate facility that is void of any resources or equipment except air conditioning and raised flooring. Equipment and resources must be installed in such a facility to duplicate the critical business functions of an organization. Cold sites have many variations, depending on their communication facilities, UPS systems, and mobility. Plans employing a cold site provide a time period when teams procure and install equipment prior to the need to use the facility. *See also Portable Shell, Uninterruptible Power Supply. Similar terms: shell-site, backup site, recovery site, alternate site.*

Command Center: A designated location where business disruptions are reported, damage assessments are forwarded, and from which, if the crisis escalates, management decisions will be generated in response.

Command and/or Control Center: A centrally located facility having adequate phone lines to begin recovery operations. Typically, it is a temporary facility used by the management team to begin coordinating the recovery process and used until the alternate sites are functional. *Similar term: emergency operating center.*

Communications Failure: An unplanned interruption in electronic communication between a terminal and a computer processor, or between processors, as a result of a failure of any of the hardware, software, or telecommunications components comprising the link. *See also Network Outage.*

Communications Recovery: The component of disaster recovery that deals with the restoration or rerouting of an organization's telecommunication network, or its components, in the event of loss. *Similar terms: data communications recovery, telecommunication recovery.*

Computer Recovery Team: A group of individuals responsible for assessing damage to the original system, processing data in the interim, and setting up the new system.

Consortium Agreement: An agreement made by a group of organizations to share processing facilities and/or office facilities, if one member of the group suffers a disaster. *Similar term: reciprocal agreement.*

Contingency Plan: A predefined collection of procedures and documentation designed to assist an organization to respond to any of a set of disasters, disruptions, or emergencies. The plan provides a mechanism for management and employees to use routine, calm periods of time to carefully consider what actions should be taken under emergency conditions. A contingency plan should contain and describe sufficient management thought and preplanning such that any employee can implement management's specific directions in an emergency, whether or not the manager is present. *See also Disaster Recovery Plan.*

Contingency Planning: The process of establishing, in advance, strategies and procedures to minimize disruptions of service to an organization and its customers, minimize financial loss, and ensure the timely resumption of critical business functions in the event of an unforeseen or unexpected event, disaster, or other interruption. The process and act of planning for contingencies. *See also Disaster Recovery Planning.*

Continuous Availability Services: Data processing disaster recovery services that provide up-to-the-minute recovery capability. Generally, these services involve sophisticated telecommunications networks to capture data continuously during normal operations, to prevent loss of any transactions.

Cooperative Hot Sites: A hot site owned by a group of organizations that is available to a group member should a disaster strike. *See also Hot Site.*

Core Business Process: Critical business activities or functions that (if interrupted or unavailable for a sustained period of time) could jeopardize the business's ability to operate. These activities are what make our business run. (Core Business Processes are also known as Critical Business Functions.)

Crate and Ship: A strategy for providing alternate processing capability in a disaster, via contractual arrangements with an equipment supplier to ship replacement hardware within a specified time period. *Similar terms: guaranteed replacement, quick ship.*

Crisis: A critical event that, if not handled in an appropriate manner, may dramatically impact an organization's profitability, reputation, or ability to operate. Also, a circumstance, event, or series of episodes that has the potential to affect the way an organization conducts business. The event and its aftermath may significantly damage the organization's employees, products, services, profitability, and reputation. A crisis can escalate and become a disaster.

Crisis Management: The overall coordination of an organization's response to a crisis in an effective, timely manner, with the goal of avoiding or minimizing damage to the organization's profitability, reputation, or ability to operate.

Crisis Management Team (CMT): A group of senior managers who set policy, create strategies, and make decisions that minimize the impact of business interruptions. These decisions can be made before, during, and after a crisis.

Crisis Simulation: The process of testing an organization's ability to respond to a crisis in a coordinated, timely, and effective manner, by simulating the occurrence of a specific crisis.

Critical Business Functions: Vital business functions, without which an organization cannot operate for long. If a critical business function is nonoperational, the organization could suffer serious legal, financial, goodwill, or other losses or penalties.

Critical Records: Records or documents that, if damaged or destroyed, would cause considerable inconvenience and/or require replacement or recreation at considerable expense.

Damage Assessment: The process of assessing damage, following a disaster, to computer hardware, vital records, office facilities, etc., and determining what can be salvaged or restored and what must be replaced.

Data Backup: The process of copying the essential elements of a data processing function, programs, data, databases, procedures, documentation, and so on. Data backup to support any recovery effort must include a storage strategy that physically separates the backup data from the original data, such that there is an absolutely minimal chance the same event could destroy both copies. Offsite storage in a secure environment is the generally accepted solution.

Data Center Recovery: The component of disaster recovery that deals with the restoration, at an alternate location, of data center services and computer processing capabilities. *Similar term: mainframe recovery.*

Data Center Relocation: The relocation of an organization's entire data processing operation.

Data Synchronization: A process during recovery of a data system. The conditions that existed at a specific point in time prior to the interruption must be reconstructed so the processing functions can restart. Multiple databases or copies of data must be restored to the same or a consistent point in time. Unsuccessful synchronization of data may result in processing functions restarting using databases from multiple points in time. The products of the processing functions may not reflect an accurate picture, and critical functions may produce serious errors.

Database Shadowing: A data backup strategy in which a full copy of the user's database is maintained at a remote data center, often a vendor's facility. "Writes" to the primary database also trigger a transmission and a similar "write" to the remote database. A disaster or interruption at the primary data center may also impact the database. A successful recovery, very near to the point of failure, is possible using the shadow database.

Declaration: A formal statement that a state of disaster exists.

Declaration Fee: A one-time fee, charged by an alternate facility provider, to a customer who declares a disaster. Note: Some recovery vendors apply the declaration fee against the first few days of recovery. *Similar term: notification fee.*

Dedicated Line: A preestablished point-to-point communication link between computer terminals and a computer processor, or between distributed processors, that does not require dial-up access.

Departmental Recovery Team: A group of individuals responsible for performing recovery procedures specific to their department.

Dial Backup: The use of dial-up communication lines as a backup to dedicated lines.

Dial-Up Line: A communication link between computer terminals and a computer processor, which is established on demand by dialing a specific telephone number.

Disaster: Any accidental, natural or malicious event that threatens or disrupts core business processes for a sufficient time to affect the business significantly, or to cause its failure. Impacts may affect lost revenue, life, or both. Outside resources will be needed to respond and potentially recover from this event. Also, any event that creates an inability on an organization's part to provide critical business functions for some predetermined period of time. *Similar terms: business interruption, catastrophe, outage.*

Disaster Management: The function of controlling the activities of an organization taken in response to a disaster situation. The functions of an emergency management team in an emergency operating center are functions of disaster management. Disaster management continues through the recovery stages until normal business function resumes.

Disaster Prevention: Measures employed to prevent, detect, or contain incidents that, if unchecked, could result in disaster.

Disaster Prevention Checklist: A questionnaire used to assess preventative measures in areas of operations such as overall security, software, data files, data entry reports, microcomputers, and personnel.

Disaster Recovery: The ability to respond to an interruption in services by implementing a disaster recovery plan to restore an organization's critical business functions.

Disaster Recovery Administrator: The individual responsible for documenting recovery activities and tracking recovery progress.

Disaster Recovery Coordinator: The disaster recovery coordinator may be responsible for overall recovery of an organization or unit(s).

Disaster Recovery Life Cycle: Consists of (1) Normal Operations—the period of time before a disaster occurs; (2) Emergency Response—the hours or days immediately following a disaster; (3) Interim Processing—the period of time from the occurrence of a disaster until temporary operations are restored; and (4) Restoration—the time when operations return to normal.

Disaster Recovery Period: The time period between a disaster and a return to normal functions, during which the disaster recovery plan is employed.

Disaster Recovery Plan: The document that defines the resources, actions, tasks, and data required to manage the business recovery process in the event of a business interruption. The plan is designed to assist in restoring the business process within the stated disaster recovery goals.

Disaster Recovery Planning: The technological aspect of business continuity planning. The advance planning and preparations necessary to minimize loss and ensure continuity of the critical business functions of an organization in the event of disaster. *Similar terms: business interruption planning, business resumption planning, contingency planning, corporate contingency planning, disaster preparedness.*

Disaster Recovery Software: An application program developed to assist an organization in writing a comprehensive disaster recovery plan.

Disaster Recovery Teams: A structured group of teams ready to take control of the recovery operations if a disaster should occur. *See also Business Recovery Team.*

Distributed Processing: The use of computers at various locations, typically interconnected via communication links, for the purpose of data access and/or transfer.

Downloading: Connecting to another computer and retrieving a copy of a program or file from that computer.

Due Diligence: The practice of gathering the necessary information on actual or potential risks so that a well-formulated decision may be reached regarding the potential for financial loss.

Electronic Vaulting: Transfer of data to an offsite storage facility via a communication link rather than via portable media. Typically used for batch/journal updates to critical files to supplement full backups taken periodically.

Emergency: A sudden, unexpected event requiring immediate action due to potential threat to health and safety, the environment, or property.

Emergency Management: The discipline that ensures an organization's or community's readiness to respond to an emergency in a coordinated, timely, and effective manner. *Similar terms: crisis management, disaster management, emergency preparedness.*

Emergency Operations Center (EOC): An operational center, located in close proximity to the crisis or disaster, staffed to carry out event management decisions and directives.

Emergency Preparedness: The part of the overall contingency plan or related activities that occurs prior to the disaster or event and is focused on the safety of personnel and the protection of critical assets. The contingency plan may reference the emergency preparedness program of the safety office or some other responsible organization.

Emergency Procedures: A plan of action that must be commenced immediately to prevent the loss of life and minimize injury and property damage.

Employee Relief Center (ERC): A predetermined location for employees and their families to obtain food, supplies, financial assistance, and so on in the event of a catastrophic disaster.

Emergency Response Planning: The portion of contingency planning that is focused on the immediate aftermath of a disaster or event. Emergency response planning includes the activities required to stabilize a situation and to protect lives and property.

Emergency Response Teams (ERT): Employees trained to protect the lives of the building's occupants by responding to an event (e.g., fire evacuation, injuries resulting from falling objects in an earthquake, and so on).

Escalation Procedures: The procedures that define the conditions or criteria under which a plan, or a portion of a plan, will be activated. For most incidents, the initial escalation procedures may call for the staff on duty to handle the incident and notify their supervisor. Escalation procedures for a data processing plan with a commercial hot site will include the conditions under which the hot site vendor is to be notified and identify who is authorized to make the official declaration of an emergency condition that warrants expending company and vendor resources.

Event: An occurrence of something that elicits a response. A circumstance that causes some action to ensue in response to the situation that has occurred. An unexpected event is an exception to the rule and poses a condition or set of conditions that can escalate in severity if an appropriate and timely response does not take place. For the contingency planner, a disaster, interruption, or any other occurrence that causes the contingency plan to be activated or considered for activation.

Event Management: The process of managing a business's preparation, response, restoration of the work environment and recovery from a crisis or disaster. The guidelines for managing an event are detailed in the recovery plan.

Executive Succession: The part of the contingency plan that defines the order in which executives will assume operational control of the organization in the absence of the primary executive.

Exercise: An activity, announced or unannounced, that provides an opportunity for participants to validate their business continuity plans, practice their crisis management skills, and strengthen team and organizational performance in a crisis. This activity will identify areas of needed improvement in a safe environment.

Exposure: A state of condition of being unprotected or vulnerable to harm or loss. In the business sense, exposure is the condition of having agency assets and/or resources subject to risk.

Extended Outage: A lengthy, unplanned interruption in system availability due to computer hardware or software problems, or communication failures.

Extra Expense Coverage: Insurance coverage for disaster-related expenses that may be incurred until operations are fully recovered after a disaster.

Facility: A location containing the equipment, supplies, voice, and data communication lines to conduct business under normal conditions. *Similar terms: primary office facility, primary processing facility, primary site.*

File Backup: The practice of dumping (copying) a file stored on disk or tape to another disk or tape. This is done for protection in case the active file gets damaged.

File Server: The central repository of shared files and applications in a computer network (LAN).

File Recovery: The restoration of computer files using backup copies.

Financial Impact: An operating expense that continues following an interruption or disaster, which, as a result of the event, cannot be offset by income and directly affects the financial position of the organization.

Foreign Corrupt Practices Act: An act of Congress mandating that corporate officers and responsible managers ensure the appropriate degree of control to effectively protect organizational assets.

Forward Recovery: The process of recovering a database to the point of failure by applying active journal or log data to the current backup files of the database.

Full Recovery Test: An exercise in which all recovery procedures and strategies are tested (as opposed to a partial recovery test).

Generator: An independent source of power, usually fueled by diesel or natural gas.

Halon: A gas used to extinguish fires; effective only in closed areas. Currently being phased out due to environmental concerns.

Hazard: An event or physical condition that has the potential to cause fatalities, injuries, property damage, infrastructure damage, interruption of business processes, and other types of harm or loss. A dangerous situation or event that may or may not lead to an emergency or a disaster.

Hazardous Material: The term used to identify any material or substance that may pose a threat to health or safety.

Hazardous Material Team (HAZMAT): A team of professionals trained in handling, storage, and disposal of hazardous material.

High-Priority Tasks: Activities vital to the operation of the organization. *Similar term: critical functions.*

Hot Site: An alternate facility that has the equipment and resources to recover the business functions affected by the occurrence of a disaster. Hot sites may vary in type of facilities offered (such as data processing, communication, or any other critical business functions needing duplication). Location and size of the hot site will be proportional to the equipment and resources needed. *Similar terms: alternate processing site, backup site, recovery site, recovery center.*

Human Threats: Possible disruptions in operations resulting from human actions (i.e., disgruntled employee, terrorism, etc.).

Impact: Impact is the cost to the enterprise, which may or may not be measured in purely financial terms.

Incident Command System: An organizational structure used to direct, control, and manage a disaster incident. The incident command center and the commander are located at the scene of the disaster and are responsible for activities in the immediate physical area. There may be another management center in another location with overall responsibility for the disaster activities.

Incident Commander: The person designated to direct and control the activities at the site of an incident.

Infrastructure: The technology, facilities and other support services needed to create a sustainable company work environment.

Interagency Contingency Planning Regulation: A regulation written and imposed by the Federal Financial Institutions Examination Council (FFIEC) concerning the need for financial institutions to maintain a working disaster recovery plan.

Interim Organizational Structure: An alternate organization structure that will be used during recovery from a disaster. This temporary structure will typically streamline chains of command and increase decision-making autonomy.

Interim Processing Guidelines: Procedures that outline how specific activities will be performed until normal processing capability is restored.

Interim Processing Period: The period of time between the occurrence of a disaster and the time when normal operations are restored.

Internal Hot Sites: A fully equipped alternate processing site owned and operated by the organization.

Interruption: An outage caused by the failure of one or more communications links with entities outside of the local facility.

Journaling: Keeping a journal. A journal for a computer includes a record of changes made in files, messages transmitted, etc. It can be used to recover previous versions of a file before updates were made, or to reconstruct the updates if an updated file gets damaged.

Leased Line: Usually synonymous with dedicated line.

Line Rerouting: A service offered by many regional telephone companies allowing the computer center to quickly reroute the network of dedicated lines to a backup site.

Line Voltage Regulators: Also known as surge protectors. These protectors/regulators distribute electricity evenly.

Local Area Network (LAN): Computing equipment in close proximity to each other, connected to a server that houses software users can access. This method does not use a public carrier. *See also Wide Area Network (WAN).*

Local Area Network (LAN) Recovery: The component of disaster recovery that deals specifically with the replacement of LAN equipment in the event of a disaster, and the restoration of essential data and software. *Similar term: client/server recovery.*

Loss: The unrecoverable business resources that are redirected or removed as a result of a disaster. Such losses may be loss of life, revenue, market share, competitive stature, public image, facilities, or operational capability.

Loss Reduction: The technique of instituting mechanisms to lessen the exposure to a particular risk. Loss reduction is intended to react to an event and limit its effect. Examples of loss reduction include sprinkler systems, insurance policies, and evacuation procedures.

Lost Data: Data entered into a computer between the time of last backup and the event occurrence. This data needs to be reentered or it will be permanently lost.

Magnetic Ink Character Reader (MICR) Equipment: Equipment used to imprint machine readable code. Generally, financial institutions use this equipment to prepare paper data for processing, encoding (imprinting) items such as routing and transit numbers, account numbers and dollar amounts.

Mainframe Computer: A high-end computer processor, with related peripheral devices, capable of supporting large volumes of batch processing, high-performance online transaction processing systems, and extensive data storage and retrieval. *Similar term: host computer.*

Maximum Acceptable Outage (MAO): The maximum period of time a given resource or function can be unavailable before the business sustains unacceptable consequences (e.g., financial losses, lowered customer service levels).

Media Transportation Coverage: An insurance policy designed to cover transportation of items to and from an electronic data processing center, the cost of reconstruction, and the tracing of lost items. Coverage is usually extended to transportation and dishonesty or collusion by delivery employees.

Minimum Acceptable Levels of Service: The minimum amount/level of outputs and service expected by our customers and regulators. Going below this established level may result in the ceasing of some other business functions, effecting unacceptable consequences.

Mission: In a government environment, the mission is the organization's reason for existing.

Mitigation: Any measure taken to reduce or eliminate the exposure of assets or resources to long-term risk caused by natural, manmade, or technological hazards. Any measures taken to reduce frequency, magnitude, and intensity of exposure to risk, or to minimize the potential impact of a threat.

Mobile Hot Site: A large trailer containing backup equipment and peripheral devices delivered to the scene of the disaster. It is then hooked up to existing communication lines.

Mobilization: The activation of the recovery organization in response to an emergency or disaster declaration.

Modulator Demodulator Unit (MODEM): Device that converts data from analog to digital and back again.

Mutual Aid Agreement: An agreement between two departments, divisions, or agencies, wherein each agrees to provide backup data processing support to the other in the event of a disaster. These require a substantial degree of hardware and software compatibility between the supporting and supported partners. The supporting partners must have the excess capacity to accommodate the sending partner's most critical applications. These agreements are seldom successful, and many auditors do not recognize them as viable disaster recovery strategies.

Natural Threats: Events caused by nature that bring about disruptions to an organization.

Network Architecture: The basic layout of a computer and its attached systems, such as terminals and the paths between them.

Network Outage: An interruption in system availability as a result of a communication failure affecting a network of computer terminals, processors, or workstations.

Node: The name used to designate a part of a network. This may be used to describe one of the links in the network, or a type of link in the network (for example, host node or intercept node).

Nonessential Function/Data: Business activities or information that could be interrupted or unavailable indefinitely without significantly jeopardizing critical functions of an organization.

Nonessential Records: Records or documents that, if irretrievably lost or damaged, will not materially impair the organization's ability to conduct business.

Notification List: A list of key individuals to be contacted, usually in the event of a disaster. Notification lists normally contain phone numbers and addresses, which may be used in the event that telephones are not operational.

Off-Host Processing: A backup mode of operation in which processing can continue throughout a network, despite loss of communication with the mainframe computer.

Offline Processing: A backup mode of operation in which processing can continue manually or in batch mode if the online systems are unavailable.

Offsite Storage Facility: A secure location, remote from the primary location, at which backup hardware, software, data files, documents, equipment, or supplies are stored.

Online Systems: An interactive computer system supporting users over a network of computer terminals.

Operating Software: A type of system software that supervises and directs all of the other software components plus the computer hardware.

Organization Chart: A diagram representative of the hierarchy of an organization's personnel.

Organization-Wide: A policy or function applicable to the entire organization and not just one single department.

Orphaned Data: The data that describes the actions or transactions accomplished via an alternate method during the period between an interruption to the data processing function and the recovery of the data processing functions.

Outage: *See System Outage.*

Outsourcing: The transfer of data processing functions to an independent third party.

Parallel Test: A test of recovery procedures in which the objective is to parallel an actual business cycle.

Peripheral Equipment: Devices connected to a computer processor that perform such auxiliary functions as communications, data storage, printing, etc.

Physical Safeguards: Physical measures taken to prevent a disaster, such as fire suppression systems, alarm systems, power backup and conditioning systems, access control systems, etc.

Plan Maintenance: Periodic and regular review and updating of a contingency plan.

Planning Software: A computer program designed to assist in the development, organization, printing, distribution, and maintenance of contingency plans.

Platform: A hardware or software architecture of a particular model or family of computers (e.g., IBM, Tandem, HP).

Portable Shell: An environmentally protected and readied structure that can be transported to a disaster site so equipment can be obtained and installed near the original location. *See also Mobile Hot Site, Relocatable Shell.*

Preparedness: Actions taken to ready employees before an event that can include training, exercises, and equipment to assist during a disaster (e.g., first aid kits). When an event occurs, this leads to response.

Procedural Safeguards: Procedural measures taken to prevent a disaster, such as safety inspections, fire drills, security awareness programs, records retention programs, and so on.

Processing Backlog: The documentation of work and processes performed by manual or other means during the time the data center was unavailable.

Qualitative Risk Analysis: The relative measure of risk or asset value by using subjective terms such as low, medium, high; 1–10; not important or very important, and so on.

Quantitative Risk Analysis: Using objective statistical data to measure risk, asset value, and probability of loss. *Similar terms: corporate loss analysis, exposure analysis, exposure assessment, impact assessment, risk assessment, risk identification.*

Readiness Audit: The determination whether the resources for business recovery are currently available.

Reciprocal Agreement: A written arrangement between organizations or agencies in which they agree to assist one another upon request, by furnishing personnel and equipment. (Also known as a mutual aid agreement.)

Record Retention: Storing historical documentation for a set period of time, usually mandated by state and federal law or the Internal Revenue Service.

Recovery: The process in which regular business operations and "lost" data are restored. At this point, other technological issues are resolved, enabling the business processes to begin addressing the backlog of work. Lessons learned from each event will build mitigation efforts to prevent future losses.

Recovery Action Plan: The comprehensive set of documented tasks to be carried out during recovery operations.

Recovery Alternative: The method selected to recover the critical business functions following a disaster. In data processing, some possible alternatives would be manual processing, use of service bureaus, or a backup site (hot or cold). A recovery alternative is usually selected following either a risk analysis, a business impact analysis, or both. *Similar terms: backup alternative, backup site.*

Recovery Capability: This defines all of the components necessary to perform recovery. These components can include a plan, an alternate site, change control process, network rerouting, and others.

Recovery Management Team: A group of individuals responsible for directing the development and ongoing maintenance of a disaster recovery plan. Also, the group is responsible for declaring a disaster and providing direction during the recovery process.

Recovery Planning Team: A group of individuals appointed to oversee the development and implementation of a disaster recovery plan.

Recovery Point Objective (RPO): The point in time to which data must be restored in order to resume processing transactions. RPO is the basis on which a data projection strategy is developed.

Recovery Strategy: The method selected by an organization to recover its critical business functions following a disaster. Possible strategies for recovering from an event that degrades or halts scheduled data processing services delivery are: (1) Revert to manual procedures; (2) Temporarily suspend data processing operations to affect recovery onsite; (3) Contract with a service to provide essential data processing operations from that location; and (4) Transfer essential data files and applications from offsite storage to a hot-site facility and begin processing from the hot site.

Recovery Support Plans: (For a larger business that has units.) These plans ensure that the required technology and infrastructure components are in place to allow business units to restore, recover, and resume the core business processes. Recovery Support Plans are organized around designated team members and specific objectives. There are two types of recovery support plans, Infrastructure and Technology. Infrastructure Plans outline guidelines for managing events to assess damage, repair as necessary, and to sustain the work environment. Technology Plans outline how to restore the physical aspects of our business operations, such as our electrical systems, computer networks, and other technology support items. (Also known as disaster recovery plans.)

Recovery Team: *See Business Recovery Team, Disaster Recovery Teams.*

Recovery Time: The period from the disaster declaration to the recovery of the critical functions.

Redundancy: Providing two or more resources to support a single function or activity with the intention that if one resource fails or is interrupted, an alternate resource will immediately begin to perform the function.

Relocatable Shell: *See Mobile Hot Site, Portable Shell.*

Remote Access: The ability to use a computer system, generally a mainframe, from a remote location, generally by common phone lines.

Remote Journaling: The process of recording the product of a computer application in a distant data storage environment, concurrently with the normal recording of the product in the local environment. May be periodic or continuous.

Response: A planned reaction to a crisis or disaster, which provides protection for employees and assets; assesses damage or impacts; and provides notifications or declarations of the event. Response is followed the Recovery process.

Restoration: The process of restoring the work environment or establishing a temporary work area as necessary. This stage focuses on technology recovery efforts to restore platforms and simultaneously directs employees to minimize core business process interruptions due to lack of platform availability.

Resumption: The stage when processing the backlog of work is complete, all related issues have been resolved, and normal core business processes can start up or resume.

Risk: The potential for harm or loss. The chance that an undesirable event will occur.

Risk Analysis/Assessment: The process of identifying and minimizing the exposures to certain threats that an organization may experience.

Risk Management: The process of a business identifying, measuring, monitoring, and controlling its exposures to ensure that risks are understood and tolerances established by upper management/president/board of directors. This process ensures that capital allocation is consistent with risk exposures. The process can align the strategic direction of a business's performance incentives with risk tolerances, which ensures that risks taken are compensated by the expected return. Continuity planning is one of many activities that support a business's risk management program.

Salvage and Restoration: The process of reclaiming or refurbishing computer hardware, vital records, office facilities, etc., following a disaster.

Salvage Procedures: Specified procedures to be activated if equipment or a facility should suffer any destruction.

Sample Plan: A generic disaster recovery plan that can be tailored to fit a particular organization.

Satellite Communication: Data communications via satellite. For geographically dispersed organizations, may be viable alternative to ground-based communications in the event of a disaster.

Scenario: A predefined set of events and conditions that describe an interruption, disruption or disaster related to some aspect(s) of an organization's business for purposes of exercising a recovery plan(s).

Scope: Predefined areas of operation for which a disaster recovery plan is developed.

Secondary Disasters: Disasters that occur as collateral events associated with a primary disaster. For example, earthquakes are primary disasters that may cause subsequent fires, and so on.

Service Bureau (Center): A data processing utility that provides processing capability, normally for specialized processing, such as payroll.

Service Level Agreement (SLA): An agreement between a service provider and service user as to the nature, quality, availability and scope of the service to be provided.

Shadow File Processing: An approach to data backup in which real-time duplicates of critical files are maintained at a remote processing site. *Similar term: remote mirroring.*

Simulation Test: A test of recovery procedures under conditions approximating a specific disaster scenario. This may involve designated units of the organization actually ceasing normal operations while exercising their procedures.

Single Point of Failure: An element of a system for which no redundancy exists. A failure of such a component may disable the entire system.

Skills Inventory: A roster of employees, listing their skills that apply to recovery.

Social Impact: Any incident or happening that affects the well-being of a population and that is often not financially quantifiable.

Stand-Alone Processing: Processing, typically on a PC or midrange computer, that does not require any communication link with a mainframe or other processor.

Stand Down: Formal notification the alert may be called off or the state of disaster is over.

Store/Forward: A preexisting automated system for capturing data, with the capability to transmit the data when systems are restored.

Structured Walk-Through Test: Team members walk through the plan to identify and correct weaknesses.

Subscription: Contract commitment providing an organization with the right to utilize a vendor recovery facility for recovery of their mainframe processing capability. Usually requires a subscription fee.

System Downtime: A planned interruption in system availability for scheduled system maintenance.

System Outage: An unplanned interruption in system availability as a result of computer hardware or software problems, or operational problems.

Table-Top Exercise: A type of test of a contingency plan in which actions are not actually performed. Participants read through the steps and procedures of the plan, in sequence, and evaluate the expected effectiveness of the plan and the interaction between elements of the plan.

Technical Threats: A disaster-causing event that may occur regardless of any human elements.

Temporary Operating Procedures: Predetermined procedures that streamline operations while maintaining an acceptable level of control and auditability during a disaster situation.

Test Plan: The recovery plans and procedures used in a systems test to ensure viability. A test plan is designed to exercise specific action tasks and procedures that would be encountered in a real disaster. *Similar term: test script.*

Testing: *See Exercise.*

Threat: Threats are events that cause a risk to become a loss. For example, a lightning strike could be the trigger that causes a fire that destroys a facility. Threats include natural phenomena and manmade incidents.

Tolerance Threshold: The maximum period of time the business can afford to be without a critical function or process.

Uninterruptible Power Supply (UPS): A backup power supply with enough power to allow a safe and orderly shutdown of the central processing unit, should there be a disruption or shutdown of electricity.

Uploading: Connecting to another computer and sending a copy of a program or file to that computer. *See also Downloading.*

Useful Records: Records that are helpful but not required on a daily basis for continued operations.

User Contingency Procedures: Manual procedures to be implemented during a computer system outage.

User Preparedness Reviews: Periodic simulations of disaster recovery conditions for the purpose of evaluating how well an individual or department is prepared to cope with disaster conditions.

Vital Records: Records or documents, for legal, regulatory, or operational reasons, cannot be irretrievably lost or damaged without materially impairing the organization's ability to conduct business.

Voice Recovery: The restoration of an organization's voice communications system.

Vulnerability: The degree to which people, property, resources, and commerce, as well as environmental, social, and cultural activity, are susceptible to harm or destruction.

Walk-Through: A type of exercise or plan test. The plan or sections of the plan are reviewed in a systematic manner in which each planned step is discussed and described to ensure appropriateness in that scenario. This is an effective method to verify coordination between plan elements.

Warm Site: An alternate processing site that is only partially equipped (as compared to a hot site, which is fully equipped).

Wide Area Network (WAN): Like a LAN, except that parts of a WAN are geographically dispersed, possibly in different cities or even on different continents. Public carriers such as the telephone company are included in most WANs; a very large WAN might have its own satellite stations or microwave towers.

General References

@stake, Inc. Public Web site.
http://www.atstake.com/research/lc/index.html.

Acharya, Soubir and Susan G. Friedman, "Backup Strategies for Networked Storage." *InfoStor*, November 2001.
http://is.pennnet.com/Articles/Article_Display.cfm?Section=
Articles&Subsection=Display&ARTICLE_ID=126595

Availability.com, "IT Availability Checklist."

Barron's Dictionary of Finance and Investment Terms, 5th ed., 1998.

Black's Law Dictionary, 7th ed., 1999.

CERT®, *CERT Coordination Center Annual Report 2002*. February 17, 2002. http://www.cert.org.

———, *CERT® Security Modules: Practices about hardening and securing systems*. http://www.cert.org/security-improvement/#Harden

CobIT®, *Implementation Tool Set*, 3rd edition, July 2000.
http://www.isaca.org/cobit.htm.

Computer Security Institute, *2002 CSI/FBI Computer Crime and Security Survey*. Richard Power, ed., 2002. http://www.gocsi.com.

Corpus Juris Secundum, vol. 19, section 491.

The CPM Group, *Contingency Planning and Management, Master Source 2001, Buyer's Guide Issue* 6 (2001).

———, *Contingency Planning and Management Online* 6, no. 5 (September/October 2001). http://www.contingencyplanning.com.

Disaster Recovery Journal 14, no. 4 (Fall 2001). http://www.drj.com/drj2/drj2.htm.

DRI International. http://www.drii.org/index.htm.

Engelschall, Ralf. "Load Balancing Your Web Site." *Web Techniques*, May 1998. http://www.webtechniques.com/archives/1998/05/engelschall/.

Federal Emergency Management Agency, *The Federal Response Plan*. Washington, DC: U.S. Federal Emergency Management Agency, April 1999.

————, *Federal Preparedness Circular (FPC) 65—Federal Executive Branch Continuity of Operations* (COOP). July 1999.

————, *FEMA 426: Reference Manual to Mitigate Potential Terrorist Attacks Against Buildings*. Washington, DC: U.S. Federal Emergency Management Agency, December 2003.

Federal Financial Institutions Examination Council, *Information Technology Examination Handbook*. Washington, DC: FFIEC, December 2002. http://www.ffiec.gov.

————, *Information Technology Examination Handbook, vols. 1–8* . Washington, DC: FFIEC, August 2004. http://www.fdic.gov/regulations/information/information/FFIEC.html.

Federal Preparedness Circular (FPC) 65, *Federal Executive Branch Continuity of Operations*, July 1999.

Ferraiolo, D. F. et. al., *Proposed NIST Standard for Role-Based Access Control*. Gaithersburg, MD: National Institute of Standards and Technology, November 2002.

Fites, M., P. Kratz, and A. Brebner, *Control and Security of Computer Information Systems*. New York: Computer Science Press, 1989.

Flesher, Tom, "Remote Journaling: A New Trend in Data Recovery and Restoration." *Contingency Planning and Management*, March 2000. http://www.contingencyplanning.com/article_index.cfm?article=243.

Fraud Examiners Manual, 3rd ed., vol. 1, 1998.

Gartner Incorporated, "Fault-Tolerant Networks: Is There Such a Thing?" *Research Note*, June 14, 2001.

————, "Disaster Recovery: Weighing Data Replication Alternatives." *Research Note*, June 15, 2001.

——, "High Availability: A Perspective." *Technology Overview*, June 15, 2001.

——, "Disaster Management Plan for Remote Access." September 20, 2001.

General Accounting Office, *Executive Guide: Information Security Management: Learning From Leading Organizations*. GAO/AIMD-98-68, May 1998.

——, *Year 2000 Computing Crisis: Business Continuity and Contingency Planning*. GAO/AIMD-10.1.19, August 1998.

——, *Federal Information System Control Audit Manual (FISCAM)*. GAO/AIMD-12.19.6, January 1999.

——, *Year 2000 Computing Challenge: Lessons Learned Can Be Applied to Other Management Challenges*. GAO/AIMD-00-290, September 2000.

——, *Computer Security: Improvements needed to Reduce Risk to Critical Federal Operations and Assets*. GAO-02-23IT, November 9, 2001.

Handelsmann, Andrew. "Insider Threats to E-Security." Gigalaw.com, December 2001. http://www.gigalaw.com

Herzog, Pete, *Open Source Security Testing Methodology Manual*, February 26, 2002. http://isecom.org/.

Information Assurance Technical Framework Forum, *Information Assurance Technical Framework (IATF)*, Release 3.0. October 2000. http://www.iatf.net/

Information Systems Security Association, Inc., *CISSP Review Course 2002*. Domain 1, "Access Control Systems and Methodology" PowerPoint presentation. August 10, 1999, slide 3.

INT Media Group, Incorporated. *Webopedia*. DATE. http://www.webopedia.com/.

Internet Engineering Task Force, *RFC 2196: Site Security Handbook*. September 1997. IETF NWG, B. Fraser, ed. http://www.ietf.org

Leary, Mark F., CPP, "A Rescue Plan for Your LAN."
Security Management Online,
http://www.securitymanagement.com/library/000496.html.

LoadBalancing.net. "Frequently Asked Questions." http://www.loadbalancing.net/faq.html.

Mangal, Vandana. "Business Continuity Planning Is a Challenge for CIOs." *ComputerWorld*, 7 April 2004. http://www.computerworld.com/printthis/2004/0,4814,91998,00.html

Maxwell, John. "Part II—Storage Virtualization: Beyond the Basics." *InfoStor*, October 2001. http://is.pennnet.com/Articles/Article_Display.cfm?Section=Archives&Subsection=Display&ARTICLE_ID=123539

The Merriam Webster Dictionary, Home and Office ed. 1995.

Miastkowski, Stan, "HassleFree Backups." *PC World Magazine*, October 2000. http://www.pcworld.com/howto/article/0,aid,18040,00.asp

National Computer Security Center, *NCSC-TG-003: A Guide to Understanding Discretionary Access Control in Trusted Systems*. Fort George G. Meade, MD: National Computer Security Center. September 30, 1987.

National Drought Mitigation Center, University of Nebraska at Lincoln. Information retrieved from http://www.drought.unl.edu/plan/plan.htm on March 5, 2005.

National Institute of Standards and Technology, *Special Publication 800-12: An Introduction to Computer Security: The NIST Handbook.* .October 1995.

———, *Special Publication 800-18: Guide for Developing Security Plans and Information Technology Systems.* December 1998.

———, *Special Publication 800-21: Guideline for Implementing Cryptography in the Federal Government.* November 1999.

———, *Special Publication 800-26: Security Self-Assessment Guide for Information Technology Systems.* August 2001.

———, *Special Publication 800-27: Engineering Principles for IT Security.* June 2001.

———, *Special Publication 800-30: Risk Management Guide.* June 2001.

———, *Special Publication 800-34: Contingency Planning Guide for Information Technology Systems.* June 2002.

———, *DRAFT Special Publication 800-47: Security Guide for Interconnecting Information Technology Systems.* December 2002.

National State Auditors Association and the U. S. General Accounting Office (joint initiative), *Management Planning Guide for Information Systems Security Auditing*. December 10, 2001.

National White Collar Crime Center and Federal Bureau of Investigation, *IFCC 2001 Internet Fraud Report, January 1, 2001 to December 31, 2001*. Washington, DC: National White Collar Crime Center. http://www1.ifccfbi.gov/strategy/statistics.asp

Office of Management and Budget (OMB), *Circular A-130: Management of Federal Information Resources*, Appendix III. Washington, DC: Office of Management and Budget, November 2000 or February 8, 1996.

Oliphant, Alan, "An Introduction to Computer Auditing—Part 2," *ITAudit*, October 1998. http://www.theiia.org/itaudit/index.cfm?fuseaction=forum&fid=188

Parr v. Security Nat. Bank, 1984 OK CIV APP 16 680 P.2d 648, Case Number: 59733 Decided: 03/13/1984. Retrieved from http://caselaw.lp.findlaw.com/scripts/getcase.pl?court=ok&vol=/appeals/1984/&invol=9764 on March 11, 2005.

Patterson, D., G. Gibson, and R. Katz, *A Case for Redundant Arrays of Inexpensive Disks (RAID)*. Berkeley: University of California at Berkeley, 1987.

Pfleeger, C., *Security in Computing*. Englewood Cliffs, NJ: Prentice-Hall, 1989.

President, Presidential Decision Directive 62: "Protection Against Unconventional Threats to the Homeland and Americans Overseas." May 1998.

———, Presidential Decision Directive (PDD) 63: "Critical Infrastructure Protection." May 22, 1998.

———, Presidential Decision Directive (PDD) 67: "Enduring Constitutional Government and Continuity of Government Operations." October 21, 1998.

Rittinghouse, John W. and James F. Ransome, *Wireless Operational Security*. New York: Digital Press, March 2004.

Schreider, Tari. White Paper: "The Legal Issues of Disaster Recovery Planning." *Disaster Recovery World IV*, vol. 9, no. 2 (1996): 233–235.

Seagate Technology, "Types of Backups." *Technical Bulletin #4062*. http://www.seagate.com/support/kb/tape/4062.html.

Shimonski, Rob, "Hacking Techniques—Introduction to Password Cracking." *IBM developerWorks*, July 2002. http://www-106.ibm.com/developerworks/security/library/s-crack/

Solinap, Tom, "RAID: An In-Depth Guide to RAID Technology." *SystemLogic.net*, January 24, 2001. http://www.systemlogic.net/articles/01/1/raid/.

Sun Microsystems, Inc., Technical White Paper: "Remote Mirroring." http://www.sun.com/storage/white-papers/remote-mirroring.wp.html.

Tanner, Dan, "Storage virtualization: What, how, and why." *InfoStor*, March 2001. http://is.pennnet.com/Articles/Article_Display.cfm?Section=Archives&Subsection=Display&ARTICLE_ID=94313.

Texas Department of Information Resources, *Business Continuity Planning Guidelines*. September 1999. Austin, Texas.

———, *Business Continuity Planning Guidelines*. December 2004. Austin, Texas.

the(451), "IT Security Is All Wrong, Says Expert." *searchSecurity.com*, April 27, 2001. http://searchsecurity.techtarget.com/originalContent/0,289142,sid14_gci547571,00.html.

U.S. Department of Commerce, National Bureau of Standards, Federal Information Processing Standards Publication (FIPS PUB) 87, *Guidelines for ADP Contingency Planning*, March 1981.

U.S. Dept. of Justice, Press Release: "Former Computer Network Administrator at New Jersey High-Tech Firm Sentenced to 41 Months for Unleashing $10 Million Computer 'Time Bomb.'" February 26, 2002. http://www.usdoj.gov/criminal/cybercrime/lloydSent.htm.

———, Press Release: "Creator of Melissa Virus Sentenced to 20 Months in Federal Prison." May 1, 2001. http://www.usdoj.gov/criminal/cybercrime/MelissaSent.htm.

———, Electronic Citation: 2002 FED App. 0062P (6th Cir.), File Name: 02a0062p.06, decided and filed 20 Feb 2002. http://www.usdoj.gov/criminal/cybercrime/4Pillars_6thCir.htm.

U.S. House of Representatives, H. R. 3210, 107th Cong., 1 November 2001. *Terrorism Risk Insurance Act of 2002.* http://thomas.loc.gov/cgi-bin/bdquery/z?d107:HR03210:@@@L&summ2=m&.

U.S. Public Law 100-235. 100th Cong., 40 U.S. Code 759, 101 Stat. 1724-1730, 8 January 1988. *The Computer Security Act of 1987.*

U.S. Public Law 104-191, 104th Cong., August 21, 1996. *Health Insurance Portability and Accountability Act of 1996.* http://thomas.loc.gov.

U.S. Public Law 106-102, 106th Cong., November 12, 1999. *Gramm-Leach-Bliley Act.* http://thomas.loc.gov.

Sample Recovery Checklist

A.1   Recovery Checklist (Incident Response Team)

Note: Generally, this checklist is in sequential order, but actions can be done in parallel.

Action   BCP Reference

EVENT OCCURRENCE

☐   Incident Detection   Page/Section

☐   Incident Reporting   Page/Section

☐   Emergency Response   Page/Section

Initial Notification Contact   Page/Section

☐   Primary contact:_____

☐   Secondary contact:_____

☐   IRT Member Recall (*use the roster below*)

Incident Response Team Recall Roster				
Name	Title	Home	Office	Mobile

☐ **Assembly** (in the event of building evacuation)   Page/Section

    ☐ Pick assembly point and provide instructions
    ☐ Account for all personnel

☐ **Conduct a Preliminary Assessment**   Page/Section

Determine:

☐ Status of emergency response

☐ Incident analysis

☐ Injuries and fatalities

☐ Areas affected

☐ Security

☐ Building access

☐ Status of the following:

    ☐ Facilities
    ☐ Power
    ☐ Utilities
    ☐ HVAC
    ☐ Environmental conditions
    ☐ Data center
    ☐ Voice communications
    ☐ Data communication

☐ **Designate Command Center**   Page/Section

    (at least 2 possibilities are recommended)

    ☐ On-premise (*if the building is habitable*)
    ☐ Off-premise (*if access to the main offices is denied*)

☐ Conduct Situation Briefing (*as appropriate*)   Page/Section

☐ **Assess Damage**   Page/Section

    ☐ Form team
    ☐ Damage assessment team briefing
    ☐ Assess damage
    ☐ Document damage with video recorder, camera, and forms
    ☐ Analyze damage and impact
    ☐ Identify salvageable equipment

☐ **Conduct Damage Assessment Brief/Debriefing**   Page/Section

□   Provide instructions (*policy/procedure*) for dealing with the press/media

□   Develop a Consolidated Action Plan   Page/Section

□   Review planned recovery strategy

□   Review operational status

□   Assess business impact

□   Develop recovery recommendation

□   Review maximum acceptable outage duration

□   Review recovery timeline(s) and assumptions

□   Finalize recovery recommendation

□   Review disaster declaration criteria

□   Formulate a disaster declaration recommendation

□   Brief executive management

□   Obtain disaster declaration approval

□   Obtain/develop corporate media statement

□   Disaster Decision

□   If Declaration = No

    □   Recover in place, using locally available resources

□   If Declaration = Yes

    □   Implement Disaster Recovery Plan and Consolidated Action Plan

    □   Direct systems and operations team leader to notify hot site

□   **Mobilize Recovery Teams**   Page/Section

    □   Direct team leaders to call, assemble, and brief functional recovery team members

□   **Activate Support Personnel** (*as appropriate*)   Page/Section

    □   Human Resources [name]
    □   Finance and Purchasing [name]
    □   Legal [name]
    □   Office Services (Mailroom, Shipping/Receiving)
    □   Records Management
    □   Distribution
    □   Travel

☐ **Travel**   Page/Section

    ☐ Check travel (airline) schedules
    ☐ Make travel arrangement/reservations
    ☐ Deploy teams to alternate facilities (as appropriate)

☐ **Teams: Implement Functional Recovery Plans**   Page/Section

☐ **Coordinate Recovery Actions**   Page/Section

    ☐ Status reports
    ☐ Periodic briefings (*as required*)

☐ **Initiate Salvage and Site Restoration** (as appropriate) Page/Section

☐ **Return Home/Transition Planning**   Page/Section

☐ **Conduct a Post-Incident Review**   Page/Section

    ☐ Review all activity logs
    ☐ Debrief team personnel
    ☐ Document "lessons learned"
    ☐ Prepare an After-Action Report

☐ **Update Disaster Recovery Plans**   Page/Section

Recovery Checklist (Systems and Operations)

Note: Generally, this checklist is in sequential order, but actions can be done in parallel.

Action   **BCP Reference**

EVENT OCCURRENCE

☐ **Incident Detection**   Page/Section

☐ **Incident Reporting**   Page/Section

☐ **Emergency Response**   Page/Section

☐ Assemble on-duty personnel at the designated assembly area (*as appropriate*)

☐ Account for on-duty personnel (*as appropriate*)

□   Provide Instructions to Assembled Personnel (as appropriate)Page/
    Section

□   Provide support to the incident management team (*as required*)

Team Leader

□   **Report to Designated Location** (*Command Center*)   Page/Section

□   **Participate in IRT Briefing**   Page/Section

□   **Alert Hot Site** (*as appropriate*)   Page/Section

□   **Alert Offsite Storage Facility Maintaining
    Backup Tapes**   Page/Section

□   ___ / ___ - _____

□   **Participate in Damage Assessment**   Page/Section

    (mobilize selected team members, as required)

□   **Attend Damage Assessment Briefing**   Page/Section

□   **Participate in the Consolidated Action
    Plan Development**   Page/Section

□   **Disaster Decision**   Page/Section

	□ If Declaration = **NO**
        Execute standard operational corrections (onsite)

	□ If Declaration = **YES**
        Make disaster declaration to hot site

        Review recovery configuration (equipment/facility) with hot site

        Confirm equipment availability

        Instruct hot site to load appropriate operating system

□   **Mobilize Subordinate Functional Recovery
    Team Leaders**   Page/Section

	□ Systems and operations
	□ Applications
	□ Network/communications
	□ Voice communications

Functional Team Leaders

☐ **Call, Assemble, and Brief Team Members**   Page/Section

    ☐ Make team member assignments
    ☐ Coordinate travel arrangements with the incident manager/IMT
    ☐ Retrieve, inventory, verify, and ship or pack backup tapes
    ☐ Dispatch appropriate team members to alternate facilities (*as appropriate*)

Functional Team Recall Roster				
Name	Title	Home	Office	Mobile

☐ **Participate in Salvage and Clean-up** (*as required*)   Page/Section

☐ **Conduct Secondary Notifications**   Page/Section

    ☐ Corporate
       [name/phone] . . .

    ☐ Vendors/Suppliers
       [name/phone] . . .

    ☐ Key Users
       [name/phone] . . .

    ☐ Initiate technical environment recovery procedures at the alternate facility
    ☐ Receive inventory, and check equipment and backup tapes
    ☐ Install operating system using backup tapes
    ☐ Restore applications and data from backup software
    ☐ Restore applications development machine
    ☐ Conduct system test
    ☐ Synchronize the data
    ☐ Notify users
    ☐ Conduct user acceptance test(s)
    ☐ Obtain user acceptance
    ☐ Schedule "*catch up*" input of accumulated work
    ☐ Resume production processing

☐ Establish a New Tape Library   Page/Section

☐ Operate in Crisis Mode   Page/Section

☐   Implement New Backup Procedures   Page/Section

☐   Assist in Site Restoration   Page/Section

☐   Assist in Return Home Plan Development   Page/Section

☐   Transition from Crisis Mode to Home
    Site Operations   Page/Section

    ☐   Conduct a full system backup
    ☐   Ship backup tapes to the home site
    ☐   Deploy personnel from the alternate site to the new home site
    ☐   Inspect/accept new site
    ☐   Install equipment/inspect new equipment
    ☐   Install operating systems
    ☐   Restore applications and data from backup software
    ☐   Conduct system tests
    ☐   Notify users
    ☐   Conduct user acceptance test(s)
    ☐   Obtain user acceptance
    ☐   Begin production

☐   Return to "Business as Usual"   Page/Section

    ☐   Conduct a postincident review
    ☐   Review all activity logs
    ☐   Debrief team personnel
    ☐   Document "lessons learned"
    ☐   Prepare an After-Action Report

☐   **Update Disaster Recovery Plans**   Page/Section

Physical Facility Questionnaire

Have employees been instructed on how to use hand extinguishers?

Is smoking permitted in the computer or tape library area?

Do employees know the location of the sprinkler shut-off valve and the Halon abort switch?

Are furniture and fixtures made of noncombustible materials?

Are wastebaskets made of metal material with fire retardant tops?

Do you have emergency lighting in stairwells and corridors for the evacuation of personnel?

Do you have emergency lighting in the computer area?

Does the fire alarm sound locally?

Does the fire alarm sound at the guard station?

Does the fire alarm sound at the police and fire departments?

Are there enough audible alarms to alert all personnel?

Are watchmen schooled as to what to do if a fire occurs during nonworking hours?

In case of fire, would access to the computer area be restricted because of an electrically controlled system?

Do you have fire dampers in the air ducts?

Is the air conditioning system dedicated to the computer area?

Is remote air conditioning equipment secured?

Are air intakes located above the street or protected from contamination?

Is backup air conditioning by use of a second compressor or chilled water available?

Are the compressor and related air conditioning equipment serviced on a regular schedule?

Is the air conditioning complete with humidity control?

Are air temperature and humidity in the computer environment recorded?

Are building engineers sensitive to the quick response required for computer operations?

Is air conditioning alarmed in the event of failure?

Are ducts secured to prevent entry or bombing?

Do you require uninterrupted power because of the nature of your business?

If your system requires motor generators, do you have backup?

Have you checked your local power supply as to reliability?

Have you monitored your power source with recorders to assure no electrical transients?

In the event of power failure, do you have emergency electrical power available?

Is emergency electrical power tested at regular intervals?

Are power-operated doors and fire alarm systems provided with emergency power?

Do you have lighting arresters?

Do you have emergency power-off switches at all exits and within the computer center?

Does emergency power-off also shut down the air conditioning/heating?

Are emergency power-off switches protected from accidental activation?

Is a current copy of your cabling/electrical schematics stored offsite?

Are intrusion detection devices operational during a power failure?

Are intrusion detection devices inspected and tested regularly?

Is the area under the floor kept clean of dust and dirt?

Are eating and drinking permitted in the computer room?

Is equipment kept free of dust and dirt inside and out?

Is the computer room cleaned on a regular schedule?

Are employees held responsible for a clean working environment?

Does management or supervision inspect areas for adherence to good housekeeping?

Do you have a scheduled removal of empty paper boxes, waste paper, and trash?

Do you display the location of your computer services area?

Is the computer area visible from the outside of the building?

If the computer area is visible to the general public, are windows of non-breakable material?

If there are windows to the computer area that are made of nonbreakable material, is the fire department aware the windows are nonbreakable in the event of a fire?

Is the installation located in a high crime area?

Would you consider your company vulnerable to vandalism or a target because of the nature of your business?

Do you have a 24-hour guard service?

Do you have a 24-hour guard service for all entrances?

Do you have a 24-hour guard service for the computer area only?

Do you use TV cameras in the computer area?

Is control of access to the computer area adequate to allow only authorized personnel?

Is the number of doors leading into the computer area kept to a minimum?

Do you monitor the status of emergency exits?

Are doors to the computer area locked at all times?

Is access to the computer area controlled by use of key, magnetic card, or cipher lock?

Are access methods changed at regular intervals or after termination of an employee?

Are dismissed computer environment employees removed immediately and necessary guard personnel notified?

Is your center alarmed to notify of intrusion?

Do you have a silent alarm to notify guard personnel of security violations?

Are security personnel notified of employees permitted access during non-working hours?

Do company employees escort visiting personnel while in secure areas?

Are all personnel identified by badge when in the computer area?

Are visitors in the computer center identified by distinct badges?

Are operating personnel trained to challenge strangers without proper identification badges?

Is physical access to the computer room restricted to authorized personnel in accordance with an enforced written policy?

Is physical access to the computer room restricted to authorized personnel, but with no written policy?

Is physical access to the computer room unrestricted?

C

Organizational Security Management

C.1   Organizational Security Management

The exact needs for a security organization can vary widely. Small organizations with little to no presence on the Internet may not require an organization at all, getting by with a knowledgeable systems administrator and decent HR policies. However, the vast majority of business entities today falls outside that category and needs to have a team of dedicated, well-trained security professionals in the organization. What should the composition of such a team look like? Who should they report to? What are their roles and responsibilities? In the next several sections, we will try to answer all of these questions.

C.1.1   Perceptions of Security

"Those security guys are holding up development team progress. We need to forget their recommendations and get this product out the door."

Sound familiar? It is not easy to be the voice of dissent when hype is thrown at you during a meeting. However, many companies have learned the hard way, sometimes at extraordinary cost, that it is far cheaper to take security precautions early on in a development process rather than deal with the issues caused by ignoring them completely. From an individual perspective, some people feel the use of security tools on their equipment is an invasion of privacy. For others, the security team members are lifesavers, coming to the rescue every time they are called. They are the white-hatted rangers of cyberspace, saving the day whenever a distress signal is heard. It all depends on who is asking and what they are asking about. Perception is transient. Advocating strong security measures, in the form of policies and adequate enforcement of such, should remain persistent.

C.1.2   Placement of a Security Group in the Organization

Where does security fit in an organization? Does it belong to the CIO, or should it report to the CEO directly? Should there be a centralized function, or should security be distributed across the organization? These are difficult questions to answer. Much of the data needed to answer these types of questions needs to come from an introspective look at the organization itself. It is necessary to determine what level of management attention the security team should have. That should help with the reporting structure. If security is a big issue, for whatever internal reason, then perhaps the CEO will want to keep it reporting directly to him or her. In very large organizations, it may be distributed in a regional model, with each regional security management leader reporting to a regional business leader or president. Our recommendation, of course, is to place the security organization high enough up the corporate ladder to enable it to effect positive change. It must operate with a high degree of autonomy and it must be led by someone who is respected by the management team as an effective role model with a high degree of integrity. Once a company comes to terms with whom the security team should report to, the next issue is to figure out what it should look like.

C.1.3   Security Organizational Structure

Before putting a security organization in place, there are a couple of considerations that must be addressed. First, is security something that will likely be a public or private issue for your organization most of the time? If the vast majority of security issues in your organization are never raised to the public, then your security team is likely also going to be a low-profile operation. However, for most companies, this is not the case. Any publicly traded company is more likely to fit in the high-profile, rather than the low-profile, category. If that is the case, then the security team should be structured to respond to issues that could increase exposure to risk, and they should be able to contain that risk in such a manner that all legal requirements are met and the public at large can feel satisfied that the management team is adequately protecting the assets with which they have been entrusted.

Structural issues now must include the basic elements of security, such as incident response, policy development, forensics, training and awareness, perimeter security measures, intrusion detection, secure remote access, and so on. There are many, many distinct areas that have to be addressed in a security plan. How the organization is structured is also a reflection of what specifically is emphasized in this site security plan. The security manager entrusted with running this organization must decide where to place his resources to get the most bang for the buck. Speaking of which, that brings up the point that an adequate budget must be set aside for the security team. How much? Once again, it depends on what the structure of the organization will look like and what needs to be emphasized for the particular needs of each organization. There is no "one size fits all" answer to this question. Suffice it to say that the security team needs to have a budget large enough to succeed EVERY time and with EVERY issue they will encounter. The CEO or CFO and the security manager should work together to derive a realistic working budget that is flexible enough to accommodate an ever-changing environment.

C.1.4   Convincing Management of the Need

Only a couple of years ago, business interruption and the associated extra expense, as a result of computer virus or malicious destruction of the data inside the computer system, were viewed in terms of cost. However, with the advent of new, major federal and state laws impacting information access and protection, security professionals are obliged to know how to determine what law and jurisdiction applies to information security. They must be aware of what types of information their companies are required to protect. They have specific legal obligations concerning the use and handling of personal information and the protection of the rights of employers and employees concerning e-mail and other information.

C.1.4.1   Legal Responsibilities for Data Protection

No business that is connected to a network or the Internet today is completely secure from the danger posed by hackers. Hackers can destroy data, release information to competitors, or make the computer system unusable. Liability for losses caused by fraudulent and malicious acts committed by either employees or third parties against a company's computer systems, electronic computer programs, and electronic data and media, including computer virus attacks, is becoming the responsibility of the business management team. Executives and directors are becoming more and more accountable for their actions when they allow their organization to remain exposed to preventable risks. Companies now face liability exposure for any failure of their management to meet legal restrictions and requirements recently enacted. Liability considerations facing corporate security managers include some of the following:

- **Media Liability**: Protection for claims arising from content placed on a Web site. This includes trademark, copyright, defamation, privacy, libel, and slander issues. It is also known as "contextual liability" in the insurance world.

- **Unauthorized Access and/or Denial of Service**: A hacker, cracker, disgruntled employee(s), competitor, terrorist, or prank by an Internet "gangster" can cause this claim to be made by bringing your ability to respond to customers' requests to a halt.

- **Loss of Income from Business Interruption**: Income from a Web site can be interrupted due to various technology perils, such as electrical outage without backup equipment being operational, earthquake, data center floods, and so on.

- **Cyberextortion**: There have been numerous extortion events demanding payment to avoid proprietary information, credit card numbers, and other information from being released to the general public.

- **Data and Software Reconstruction**: Reestablishment of the content of the Web site. The cost associated with rebuilding the total Web site.

- **Cybertheft of Money, Securities and Other Property**: The unauthorized theft of money, securities, and other information, including trade secrets, client lists, proprietary information, and so on.

C.1.4.2   DHS Office of Private Sector Liaison

To emphasize the importance of security in recent months, consider the fact the U.S. government created a new cabinet-level office that, in February 2003, started operations in earnest as the Department of Homeland Security (DHS). Part of the mission Secretary Tom Ridge took on when he assumed leadership of the department was to ensure the DHS would provide America's business community with a direct line of communication to government. The office works directly with individual businesses and through trade associations and other nongovernmental organizations to foster dialogue between the private sector and the DHS on the full range of issues and challenges faced by America's business sector in the world after September 11, 2001. The office was organized to specifically deal with America's critical industry sectors as outlined in the President's National Strategy for Homeland Security, as well as general business matters and concerns related to the DHS. The office serves America's business community as the focal point of contact with the DHS. The DHS gives the private sector one primary contact, instead of many, for coordinating protection activities with the federal government, including vulnerability assessments, strategic planning efforts, and exercises.

C.2   Security Management Areas of Responsibility

This section covers the basic areas that should be addressed as part of any security plan for any organization. It does not go into details about how to configure equipment, develop scripts, or so on; it is strictly a management perspective of the "coverage areas" that need to be addressed to ensure adequate organizational protections are in place. These areas are generally implemented by establishing policy. Consider these areas the basic requirements; policy is used to implement the requirements, and the security team is there to enforce the requirements and adjust as needed to ensure currency with changing business conditions.

When putting together a Site Security Plan, it is important to build a strategy that satisfies the needs of the organization. To accomplish this, of course, you must first determine what the organization's needs are by conducting a needs assessment. The results of this assessment will aid in defining the security program appropriate for your organization. Review the program with senior staff to ensure you have their buy-in on implementing the programs, and set up a process to periodically review these programs to ensure they meet the business needs. The next step is to develop an awareness and training plan, identify the various audiences (or constituencies, as some prefer to call them) and begin training. Let's discuss this program in a bit more detail.

C.2.1   Awareness Programs

Successful computer security programs are highly dependent on the effectiveness of an organization's security awareness and training program. If employees are not informed of applicable organizational policies and procedures, they cannot be expected to properly secure computer resources. The dissemination and enforcement of the security policy is a critical issue that can be addressed through local security awareness and training programs. Employees cannot be expected to follow policies and procedures of which they are unaware. In addition, enforcing penalties may be difficult if users can claim ignorance when caught doing something wrong. Training employees can also show that a standard of due care has been taken in protecting information. Simply issuing policy without follow-through to implement that policy is not enough to get the job done. Many organizations use acknowledgment statements to verify that employees have read and understand computer security requirements. New hires are an especially important audience for security awareness training. It is critical that any new employee receive training on the security policies in place at an organization within the first week or two of employment.

Many employees regard computer security as an obstacle to their job productivity. To help motivate employees to be security-aware, emphasize the ways that security can contribute to productivity. The consequences of poor security should be explained without using the fear and intimidation tactics employees often associate with security. Awareness helps to reinforce the fact that security supports the mission of the organization by protecting valuable resources. If employees view security measures as bothersome rules and procedures, they are likely to ignore them. Managers are responsible for ensuring that their personnel are briefed and understand the role they play in supporting security efforts. By informing all personnel of the statutes and policies surrounding IT security, and by conducting periodic security awareness briefings, managers can accomplish this task.

Security training is most effective when targeted to a specific audience. This enables the training to focus on the security-related job skills and knowledge that people need to perform their duties. Divide the audiences into groups according to their level of security awareness. This may require research to determine how well employees follow computer security procedures or understand how computer security fits into their jobs. Training groups can be segmented according to general job task or function, specific job category, or level of competence and understanding of general computer knowledge.

C.2.2   Risk Analysis

A prime consideration for creating a computer security policy is to ensure that the effort spent on developing and implementing the security policy will yield cost-effective benefits. It is important for a security manager to understand where the most obvious "quick wins" in security will be found. While there is a great deal of information in the press about intruders hacking into computers systems, most security surveys reveal the actual loss from "insiders" is a far greater risk. Risk analysis involves determining what you need to protect, what you need to protect it from, and how you need to protect it. Risk analysis is the process of examining all of the potential risks you may face, then rank ordering those risks by level of severity. This process will involve choosing cost-effective solutions, based on what you want to protect and how it is to be protected. It is important to balance the value of the asset that needs protection against the cost of providing that protection. For example, if you spend $500,000.00 to protect reproducible code assets that originally only cost $180,000.00, it is not likely a sound security investment. Always consider the cost versus worth scenario when selecting your security solutions. Much more on this topic is presented in Chapter 2.

C.2.2.1   Identify Assets

For each asset, the basic goals of security are **availability**, **confidentiality**, and **integrity**. A risk analysis process requires the identification of all assets that need to be protected. Try to determine what potential threats exist for each particular asset. A list of asset categories suggested by Pfleeger [1] includes the following:

- **Hardware**: Keyboards, monitors, laptops, personal computers, printers, disk drives, communication lines, terminal servers, routers

- **Software**: source programs, object programs, utilities, diagnostic programs, operating systems, communication programs

- **Data**: used during execution, stored online, archived offline, backups, audit logs, databases, in transit over communication media

- **People**: users, administrators, hardware maintainers

- **Documentation**: on programs, hardware, systems, local administrative procedures

- **Supplies**: paper, forms, paperclips, ink cartridges, ribbons, magnetic media

C.2.2.2   Identifying the Threats

Once the assets have been identified, it is necessary to determine the potential threats to those assets. Threats can then be examined to determine a loss potential. Loss potential helps to rank the asset and threat against other items in your list. The following are classic threats that should be considered: unauthorized access, unintended disclosure of information, and denial of service. Depending on your organization, there will be more specific threats that should be identified and addressed.

C.2.3   Incident Handling

In this section, we discuss the process of establishing the **incident handling function** in an organization. There are several key issues a security manager must consider when establishing an Incident Response Group. What are the goals the group needs to accomplish? What should this team be relied upon to do in a consistent and professional manner? Who are they providing this service to (i.e., what is the incident handling group's constituency)? It is important to understand the constituency, because what is provided for one audience may be inadequate for another. For example, if your constituency is a distributed data center operation, their incident response needs will be quite different from those of a retail Web site selling T-shirts and such.

Once the constituency is known, the next step is to begin determining what the structure of the incident response group will look like. Should it be a centralized organization or a decentralized, distributed organization? This decision greatly effects the staffing and funding requirements. Once you have determined the structure best suited to the needs of a constituency, your organization's management team must support the decision and agree to the funding requirements.

As you begin to set up the operation, set up a centralized mechanism for the constituency to report incidents or potential incidents. A team must be assembled to respond to those incidents, and the team should operate from a high-level "guidebook" or charter. Creating a charter for the team will get everyone on the team working towards achieving the same goals. How they go about achieving those goals is defined by process and procedures, usually put in place by creating an Incident Response Group Operations Handbook. This handbook is considered the starting point for handling all incidents, and the team members must be instructed to update it, making it a living document as environmental conditions change. Finally, when an incident is reported, investigated, and resolved, there should be a management reporting function in place to let management understand what happened and the impact the event had on the organization.

C.2.4 Alerts and Advisories

Alerts and advisories that detail newly discovered vulnerabilities and other security information are released almost daily. This information may require immediate action on the part of the system administrators, the incident response group, or the users. Advisories come from a variety of sources, such as vendors and product manufacturers. There are also places like the CERT® Coordination Center (CERT®/CC) and the Federal Computer Incident Response Capability (FEDCIRC), now both a part of the new *National Strategy to Protect Infrastructure*. To help develop ways of better protecting our critical infrastructures, and to help minimize vulnerabilities, the U.S. Department of Homeland Security has established Information Sharing and Analysis Centers, or ISACs, to allow critical sectors to share information and work together to help better protect the economy. The IT-ISAC is a forum for sharing information about network vulnerabilities and effective solutions [2]. It is also a forum for sharing threat-related information and ways to protect against those threats. The Operations Center is intended to help achieve a higher level of critical infrastructure protection through the sharing of key security solutions. Regardless of which source agency sends out an advisory, upon receipt of any alerts and advisories requiring action, ensure compliance with the required action. If compliance cannot occur for any reason, obtain a statement of waiver with reasons the actions cannot be implemented. Ensure that any compliance or waiver actions needed are reported to the CSO or information security manager for briefing to other senior management.

C.2.5 Warning Banners

It is good security practice for all systems to display warning banners upon connection to a given system. These banners should display a warning that informs the user logging in that the system is for legitimate use only, is subject to monitoring, and carries no expectation of privacy. The use of warning banners provides legal notice to anyone accessing the system that they are using a system that is subject to monitoring. Users should also be notified of the possible sanctions, such as loss of privileges, employment, or even prosecution, if they misuse or access the network without authorization. System administrators can install the banners quite easily, and the information contained in the banners should be approved by the organization's legal staff. A sample of banner wording is as follows:

```
This is a proprietary computer system that is "FOR
INTERNAL USE ONLY." This system is subject to
monitoring. Therefore, no expectation of privacy is to
be assumed. Individuals found performing unauthorized
activities are subject to disciplinary action,
including criminal prosecution.
```

C.2.6 Employee Termination Procedures

Unfortunately, employee termination often leads to a security incident. This sad fact of life must be dealt with by businesses every day. Security teams have routinely become involved in termination processing to ensure that disgruntled employees cannot take actions detrimental to the company. The termination procedure encompasses those activities that occur when an employee terminates his or her employment with the organization or is terminated by the organization. It is good business practice to require the chief people officer (CPO) or VP of Human Resources to provide the chief information officer (CIO) and chief information security officer (CISO) with a list of terminated employees on a weekly or monthly basis.

C.2.7 Training

All authorized users should be required to attend training on how to fulfill their security responsibilities within 30 days of employment. They should also be required to participate in periodic recurring training in information system security awareness and accepted information system security practices, as appropriate to their job functions and responsibilities. Users who have access to multiple applications should be encouraged to attend training on each application as well as on all general support systems. The system security plan should specify the type and frequency of training required in such circumstances.

IT and security managers should plan and prepare for two types of training, one for users and the other for system administrators. Users should be required to participate in certain training activities, such as awareness training and various application-training classes, which may be offered periodically. The second type of training for the system administrators (SAs) should be in security competency. It is the manager's responsibility to ensure that his or her SAs have been provided with all the security training needed to fulfill the security requirements for which they are responsible.

C.2.8 Personnel Security

Personnel security involves training users to be aware of their responsibilities and the consequences of any failure to abide by security policies for using the computer automation assets. Personnel security should be a part of the overall security training plan. Supervisors should be responsible for coordinating and arranging system access requests for all new or transferring employees, as well as for verifying an individual's need to gain access to any sensitive information in an organization.

Regardless of their position or job function, personnel who have access to the network should read and sign an Acceptable Use policy. They should attend periodic security training sessions. Typically, a user only needs to sign the Acceptable Use agreement once, when his or her e-mail account is issued by the organization. After that, the user should be briefed at least annually on any updates to the Acceptable Use policy. New procedures should be covered and awareness of security concerns addressed.

Quite often, an organization will provide all employees with a Personnel Security Handbook that describes the responsibilities of employees. All persons accessing sensitive computer systems should have a background check prior to being granted access. The handbook should describe minimum requirements for any background investigations. Contractors who design, operate, test, maintain, or monitor systems should be required to undergo background checks as well.

C.2.9   Internet Use

It is a good idea for an organization to require all employees and contractors who use company-provided information systems in their jobs to sign an Internet Use policy. Employees and contractors should be prohibited from accessing systems that are not necessary for the performance of their duties. They should also be restricted from performing tasks on systems they are authorized to access, but which are not related to their job responsibilities. For example, a help desk agent may have access to a payroll computer, but that does not give him the right to go in and use the payroll computer for any purposes. System administrators have the ability to audit network logs and perform periodic checks for misuse, and should do so on a regular basis. This practice will help to ensure compliance among the *masses*.

C.2.10   E-mail

It is a primary responsibility of the IT group and/or the security team to ensure the appropriate use of e-mail systems. Various technical measures can assist in this goal. First of all, e-mail should be used primarily for official business. Persons using company systems for sending e-mail should make the same provisions to ensure confidentiality as those that would be made for sending hard copy correspondence. All activities on a company's information systems are subject to monitoring. Users should have no expectations of privacy. By using a company's e-mail system, users implicitly agree to be governed by that company's acceptable use policy regarding e-mail.

C.2.11   Sensitive Information

All organizational personnel are responsible for the safeguarding and appropriate handling of sensitive corporate information. Sensitive corporate information is defined as information that is critical to the operation of the business, and information for which public release is inappropriate. Ensure your users are trained and briefed on how to handle sensitive corporate information. Maintain adequate access controls and accountability of information. Set specific policies for the use and handling of sensitive information.

C.2.12 System Security

Providing for adequate system security requires advanced planning and effort. Ensure that system administrators have adequate resources to establish and maintain system security levels. Listed below are basic areas for which security managers should ensure adequate security measures are in place:

- **Hardening Systems:** No system should ever be placed on the network without a security configuration setup. "*Hardening*" refers to the process of disabling unnecessary services, installing all the latest fixes and patches, installing adequate security software, tuning the operating system for security rather than performance, and documenting the system on the network. All of this work takes a great deal of effort to accomplish, but should not be taken lightly. It takes only one incorrectly configured system to allow an intruder into your network.

- **Network Architecture:** The way systems (nodes) are placed on a network affects the level of security for that network. It is good practice to keep the internal network separate from the publicly accessible network. Publicly accessible portions include things like Web servers and mail systems. The way administrators go about segregating the two sections of the network varies. In many cases, a firewall is used to create a demilitarized zone (DMZ). This is a separate area of the network where the Web servers and other publicly accessible systems are placed.

- **User Authentication and Identification:** All systems should incorporate proper user authentication and identification methodologies. This includes authentication based on user ID and password, tokens, and/or biometrics. To protect systems and data, a company should require outside entities that need access to the company's systems (whether contractors or other agencies) to use access controls commensurate with those used by the organization. Additionally, these systems should undergo a periodic review of user access privileges to ensure no accounts exist where users are no longer working on the system (not to exceed semiannually). All such "ghost" accounts should be deleted.

C.2.13 Physical Security

Physical security involves safekeeping the systems from theft or physical damage and preventing unauthorized access to those systems. If unauthorized users are given physical access to a system, it is a simple matter for them to break in and then gain access to important business data. All employees and contractors should be held responsible (and accountable) for taking every reasonable precaution to ensure the physical security of their IT hardware and related peripherals, including mobile devices, from theft, abuse, avoidable hazards, or unauthorized use. Company servers, routers, and other communication hardware essential for maintaining the operability of the systems and their connectivity to the Internet should be placed in a controlled-access location (i.e., behind locked doors).

Managers must ensure the nodes that comprise the network (such as file servers, Web servers, mail servers, and any other equipment that forms the basis of the network) will be secured in an area where access is controlled. Only authorized personnel will have access to network equipment. Ensure user's systems are as secure as it is practical to be. This includes securing the systems from casual use by installing password-protected screen savers. Provide the ability for users to lock the workstations when they leave their area. The responsibility to safeguard IT assets should not include company employees or contractors endangering themselves or others by attempting to physically prevent the unauthorized removal or destruction of IT hardware, accessories, or supplies. In such a case, employees should notify law enforcement and follow their guidance.

C.3 Security Policies

A good starting point for understanding the development of security policy is RFC 2196 [3], *Site Security Handbook*. Much of the information toward policy development has evolved from the original RFC 1244, which was rendered obsolete by RFC 2196. The purpose herein is to provide practical guidance to administrators trying to secure their information and services as pertains to their "site." For the purposes of this book, a "site" is any organization that has computers or network-related resources. These resources may include host servers, routers, application and database servers, PCs and PDAs, or other devices that have access to the Internet.

C.3.1   Basic Approach to Policy Development

One generally accepted approach to development of site policy is that suggested by Fites et al. [4], who recommend that one take the following steps:

1. Identify what you are trying to protect.

2. Determine what you are trying to protect it from.

3. Determine how likely the threats are.

4. Implement measures that will protect your assets in a cost-effective manner.

5. Review the process continuously, and make improvements each time a weakness is found.

Most organizations will concentrate their efforts on item four above, but if an effective security plan is to be established at your site, the other steps cannot be avoided. An axiom to remember is that the cost of protecting yourself against a threat should be less than the cost of recovering if the threat were to strike you. Cost in this context should factor in losses expressed in dollars, reputation, trustworthiness, and other less obvious measures. Without reasonable knowledge of what you are protecting and what the likely threats are, following this rule could be difficult. We will briefly review each of the five items in the list above.

C.3.2   Identify What Needs Protection and Why

These two steps are initially accomplished in the Risk Analysis phase. The list of categories suggested by Pfleeger is worth mentioning again. The specific items in the list are less relevant than the categories themselves. For every organization, the inventoried assets will be different, but most will fall into one of the categories. Conduct your asset inventory and list every item, grouped by category. This may help you to determine potential threats for an entire group of assets, versus an item-by-item approach. For example, mandating that all disposable supplies should be locked in a cabinet may be more cost-effective, and equally effective as having separate procedures for ribbons, paper, and so on. Once the assets requiring protection have been identified, an organization should take steps to identify corresponding potential threats for those assets. These threats can subsequently be evaluated to determine whether any potential for loss exists.

C.3.2.1   Determine Likelihood of Threats

A computer security policy is generally created to ensure that efforts spent on security yield cost-effective benefits. Most surveys of computer security show that, for most organizations, the actual loss from "insiders" is a much greater risk than attack by an outsider. We have discussed a process that involves determining what a site needs to protect, what it needs to protect itself from, and how to actually protect it. The process of examining all of the risks associated with each of these three items, to include ranking those risks by level of severity, is what we mean by determining the likelihood of a threat. This process involves making cost-effective decisions on what you want to protect. After all, it does not make good business sense to spend more to protect something than it is actually worth.

C.3.3   Implement Protective Measures

The security-related decisions you make, or fail to make, largely determine how secure your network is. However, you cannot make good decisions about security without first determining what security goals need to be set for your organization. Until you determine what your security goals are, you cannot make effective use of any collection of security tools, because you simply won't know what to check for and what restrictions to impose. Your goals will be largely determined by the following key trade-offs:

1.   **Services Offered versus Security Provided.** Each service offered to users carries its own security risks. For some services, the risk outweighs the benefit of the service, and the administrator may choose to eliminate the service rather than try to secure it.

2.   **Ease of Use versus Security.** The easiest system to use would allow open access to any user and require no passwords. Of course, there would be no security. Requiring passwords makes the system a little less convenient, but more secure. Requiring device-generated one-time passwords makes the system even more difficult to use, but much more secure.

3.   **Cost of Security versus Risk of Loss.** There are many different costs to security: monetary, performance, and ease of use, to name a few. There are also many levels of risk: loss of privacy, loss of data, and the loss of service. Each type of cost must be weighed against each type of loss.

Goals should be communicated to all users, operations staff, and managers through a set of security rules, called a "security policy."

C.3.4 Definition and Purpose of a Security Policy

A security policy is a formal body of the rules by which the people given access to an organization's technology and information assets must abide. It is part of an overall organizational site security plan. Its purpose is to inform members of the organization of their responsibilities under certain circumstances that could pose potential risk to the company.

The main purpose of a security policy is to inform users, staff and managers of their obligatory requirements for protecting technology and information assets. The policy should specify the mechanisms put in place to meet these requirements. Another purpose is to provide a baseline from which to acquire, configure and audit computer systems and networks for compliance with the policy. An Acceptable Use Policy (AUP) should be part of any security policy. The AUP should spell out what users shall and shall not do on the various components of the system, including the type of traffic allowed on the networks. The AUP should be as explicit as possible to avoid any ambiguity or misunderstanding.

C.3.5 What Makes a Good Security Policy?

Characteristics of a good security policy are that it must be implementable through system administration procedures, publishing of acceptable use guidelines, or other appropriate methods. It must be enforceable using security tools, where appropriate, and with sanctions where actual prevention is not technically feasible. Finally, it must clearly define the areas of responsibility for the users, administrators, and management. These three characteristics form the basis of any sound security policy. Additionally, there must be "buy-in" from the legal counsel, the CIO, and HR for the policies developed. Otherwise, they are not worth the paper they are printed on.

C.3.6 Components of a Good Security Policy

What elements make up a good security policy? What needs to be in the policy to make it effective without overloading users on hundreds of security-related items? This section has identified eight key areas that should be addressed in security policies:

- Access

- Authentication

- Accountability

- Privacy

- Availability

- Systems and networking maintenance

- Acquisition guidelines

- Violations reporting

The Access Policy is used to define access rights and privileges necessary to protect company assets from loss or disclosure by specifying acceptable use guidelines for users, staff, and management. The Access Policy should provide specific guidelines for use of external connections, data communications, connecting user-owned devices to a network, and adding new software to systems. It should also specify any required banner messages.

The Authentication Policy is used to establish trust through use of an effective password policy. It also is used for setting guidelines for remote location authentication and use of various authentication devices. It should outline minimum requirements for access to all resources.

An Accountability Policy defines the responsibilities of users, staff, and management. It should specify a periodic, recurring audit capability and provide basic incident handling guidelines. The Privacy Policy defines reasonable expectations of privacy regarding such issues as monitoring of e-mail, logging of keystrokes, and access to user files.

Availability Statements are used to set expectations for the availability of resources. This statement should address redundancy and recovery issues. It should also be used to specify operating hours and maintenance downtime periods. It is important to include contact information for reporting system and network failures as a part of this document.

The Information Technology System and Network Maintenance Policy describes how both internal and external maintenance people are allowed to handle and access technology for routine tasks such as system backup, equipment maintenance, application of upgrades, patches, and so on. One important topic to be addressed here is whether remote maintenance is allowed, and how such access is controlled.

Another area for consideration is outsourcing and how it is managed. Computer Technology Purchasing Guidelines should be used to specify required, or preferred, security features. These guidelines should supplement existing purchasing policies and guidelines.

The Violations Reporting Policy indicates which types of violations (e.g., privacy and security, internal and external) must be reported, and to whom the reports are made. A nonthreatening atmosphere and the possibility of anonymous reporting will result in a greater probability that a violation will be reported if it is detected.

It is a good idea to also provide supporting information that can provide users with contact information for each type of policy violation encountered. Specific guidelines on how to handle outside queries about a security incident, or information that might be considered confidential or proprietary, are a good idea. Include cross-references to security procedures and related information, such as company policies. There may be regulatory requirements that affect some aspects of your security policy (e.g., line monitoring). The policy should be reviewed by legal counsel before being put into effect. Once your security policy has been established, it should be clearly communicated to users, staff, and management. Having all personnel sign a statement indicating that they have read, understood, and agreed to abide by the policy is an important part of the process.

C.3.7 Review and Assess Regularly

Security managers must ensure that the organizational security policy is reviewed on a regular basis (*semi-annual is our recommended review frequency*) to see if it is successfully supporting your security needs. Adapt the plan to meet any changed conditions and distribute change notices to the constituency as needed. Ensure training plans are updated with the changed material and that managers brief their personnel on all security changes.

It is equally important to assess the adequacy of measures implemented by the policies. Ensure the measures taken not only solve the problem, but also help prevent the problem from reoccurring. Have security and IT staffs independently evaluate the effectiveness if possible. Sometimes, it is even a good idea to bring in third-party organizations to perform independent assessments of your processes and procedures. If you make changes here, be sure to go back and update the policy book accordingly.

C.4 Security Personnel

C.4.1 Coping with Insider Threats

According to a Gigalaw report [5], an internal security breach occurs when an employee of a company uses the company's information system without authorization or uses it in a way that exceeds his or her valid authorization. The author states that in 2001, the American Computer Security Institute surveyed a large number of corporations, medical institutes, and government agencies about serious security breaches of their computer systems, such as the theft of proprietary information, financial fraud, denial-of-service attacks, and the sabotage of data or networks. The findings were startling. More than 70 percent of respondents reported these kinds of attacks as having occurred from **inside** the company, while only 25 percent reported system penetration from outsiders.

Employees, who often occupy positions of trust, have the greatest access to information within the organization. They have the greatest potential to exploit information sources or sabotage computer systems for personal gain. Insider acts involve unauthorized viewing or use of information, and the unauthorized entry or alteration of data to produce false transactions and tamper with information systems. Handlesmann [6] advocates that "employers must acknowledge the risks of unauthorized access and computer fraud by employees and put in place monitoring systems and preventative measures that address these risks."

While an employee who commits an attack will often face criminal prosecution, the employee's company may also find itself the subject of a civil lawsuit. A significant danger exists in regard to insider e-security breaches. If an employee misuses a company's data systems to commit electronic fraud or cause damage or loss to third parties, the company may be held (vicariously) liable for the acts of its employee. The standard test for vicarious liability is that the employee's action must have been committed *in the course and scope of the employment*. It is important to note that *in the course and scope of employment* is a broad term for which there is no absolute legal definition. However, case law (in Australia) has established a few guiding principles. Handlesmann cites the following:

- Where an employer authorizes an act, but it is performed in an improper or unauthorized manner, the employer will still be held liable.

- It does not matter that an employee is unauthorized to perform an act, and the mere fact that an act is illegal does not bring it outside the scope of employment.

- Even though unauthorized access or computer fraud by an employee is an act that lies outside the employee's scope of employment, this does not automatically exclude the employer from vicarious liability.

- It is not necessarily an answer to a claim against an employer that the wrong done by the employee was for the employee's own benefit.

Much of the computer fraud committed by employees can be averted if employers implement an effective security policy that puts in place measures targeted at prevention, ongoing monitoring, and recovery strategies in the case of breach. Monitoring may detect problems in progress and allow the possibility of aborting a process before any serious damage is done.

C.4.2 How to Identify Competent Security Professionals

It is always a good idea to understand what areas and applications of security are most in demand when trying to find competent staff. Some of these areas include perimeter management, intrusion detection, forensics, firewalls and VPNs, and internal information security. Sounds like all the basic areas of security, right? Well, it is! Security is a diverse field and it covers a lot of territory. When looking for people for your organization's needs, you need to know as much as possible about the organization before you go headhunting. Then, and only then, will you know what to look for in finding competent people. To find these people, one needs to consider, *What are the basic things people seeking information security jobs should know?*

When hiring entry-level or nonsenior security engineers, education and training play a much bigger role. This indicates a strong level of effort to stand out from the crowd and hone skills in a particular area. Look for certifications and similar indicators of professional training and qualification. However, once you get past six to eight years of experience, when looking for management level security professionals, certifications are less important than experience. This does not mean you should ignore certifications, but they should be considered as a secondary factor. For example, would you rather have a security engineer with a certification less than a year and less than six years of experience of industry experience, or someone without the certification but with twelve years of hands-on, in-the-dirt security consulting experience? It is your call, of course, but we encourage looking at the whole person and not focusing on one specific credential or certification. If someone with eight to ten years of experience also has the certifications, all the better. It is but one factor in the decision-making process.

Security managers should have broad security experience. They should know how to manage and implement data security controls, and understand architecture and strategies. They should possess in-depth knowledge and understanding of international, national, and local legislation affecting information security and be able to develop and implement business plans and policies. That is what you should look for. Other considerations may include (in no particular order) background checks, credit checks, drug screening, membership in "hacker groups," and references from the last job.

When hiring a security professional, be sure to have a job description prepared prior to advertising the position. This helps to identify your firm's needs and the skills candidates must offer. Determine the salary range your firm is willing to pay, and check around to make sure it is competitive. In the security realm, it is true that you get what you pay for. Candidates with in-depth experience supported by formal training and a college degree command top salaries. Those with only on-the-job training may not be as costly. In addition to IT and functional departments, let your candidates' future colleagues interview them. Plan an interview process using several people who employ questions in diverse areas and compare notes when the interview is over. Security isn't just technology; it's a process requiring effective communication. Insist on a background check as a condition of employment. In this specialty, professional qualifications should include a problem-free personal background.

C.4.3   How to Train and Certify Security Professionals

C.4.3.1   The Value of Certifications

We are often asked if security certifications are required to get ahead in security. The answer is "No," but they certainly help. Certification isn't mandatory, but it exposes a professional to key concepts, policies, and procedures for practicing security. If two equal candidates, in terms of experience, are competing for the same job, the one with certification will most likely have the upper hand. It indicates a level of effort expended to stand out in the crowd and perform the job better. To be sure, certification will help anyone break into the security field, but it will not carry you through it.

C.4.3.2   Types of Security Certifications Available

"Which security certifications are the most worthwhile?" The answer depends on an individual's background and career interests. Those with an in interest in firewalls should look at the Check Point Certified Security Administrator, or CCSA certification. CCSA is a foundation-level certification that validates a candidate's ability to configure and manage fundamental implementations of Check Point's flagship product, FireWall-1, as an enterprise-level Internet security solution to protect corporate networks [7]. As a CCSA, security professionals possess the requisite skills to define and configure security policies that enable secure access to information across corporate networks. In addition to these essential skills, CCSAs also have the ability to monitor network security activity and implement measures to block intruder access to networks. For people more interested in auditing and monitoring, perhaps the Certified Information Systems Auditor, or CISA, is more appropriate. The CISA certification is awarded to those individuals with an interest in information systems auditing, control, and security who meet stringent requirements, including the successful completion of the CISA examination; certified information systems auditing, control, or security experience; adherence to a code of professional ethics; participation in a continuing education program; and demonstrated understanding of information systems auditing standards.

More experienced security management professionals may choose to get a Certified Information System Security Professional (CISSP) certification. This is a stringent certification process reflecting the qualifications of information systems security practitioners. The CISSP examination consists of 250 multiple-choice questions, covering topics such as Access Control Systems, Cryptography, and Security Management Practices. It is administered by the International Information Systems Security Certification Consortium, or (ISC)2. (ISC)2 promotes the CISSP exam as an aid to evaluating personnel performing information security functions.

The Global Information Assurance Certification (GIAC) Certified Security Expert (CSE) is a comprehensive, technically oriented certification for security professionals. This certification is very rare, and to date only a very few candidates (less than five at the time of this writing, according to the GIAC Web site) [8] have been considered for inclusion in this elite group. The exam for a GIAC/CSE certification consists of ten different parts. Four sections of the exam consist of **hands-on** assessment and reporting about four distinctly different business plans and network designs implemented in a simulated production environment. Four other sections will test the **knowledge** and the ability of the candidate to gather information and interpret it through 30 to 40 in-depth **essay** questions and 90 accompanying **multiple-choice** questions on various focus areas; that's about 130 questions per section! The candidates are also required to deliver a one-hour (or longer) **technical presentation** to demonstrate their ability to relate technical information to others. The remaining portion of the exam requires the candidate to take a business plan, recommend changes, and implement those changes into a simulated production network, which will then be assessed by GIAC staff and the other candidates. Certainly someone who possesses this qualification would be considered at the very top-tier of qualifications in security.

A more common GIAC certification is the Security Essentials Certification (GSEC). This is a basic- to intermediate-level professional certification targeted to security professionals who want to fill the gaps in their understanding of technical information security. It is a good certification for systems, security, and network administrators who want to understand the pragmatic applications of a common body of knowledge. Managers who want to understand information security beyond simple terminology and concepts may also attain this certification. It is also a good certification for anyone who is new to the field of information security, with some background in information systems and networking. GIAC certification graduates have the knowledge, skills, and abilities businesses need to incorporate good information security practice in any organization. The GSEC tests the essential knowledge and skills required of any individual with security responsibilities within an organization.

GIAC also offers certifications in firewalls, intrusion analysis, incident handling, and more. For security managers, it may be a good idea for an organization to have a designee attend the GIAC Information Security Officer (GISO) Certification program. It is a basic-level program designed for newly appointed information security officers who need to hit the ground running and need an overview of information assurance. It is specifically for managers, information security officers, and system administrators who need an overview of risk management and defense-in-depth techniques. It can be useful to anyone who writes, implements, or must adhere to security policies. Persons involved in shaping the decisions an organization makes regarding the use of emerging and changing information technology would be well served by this program.

Currently, the broader, more policy-focused CISSP (for managers) and the in-depth, hands-on certifications from SANS/GIAC tend to pay the best dividends for professional development, and some employers will often pay extra for them. As your security organization develops, you may find it useful to track the number of certifications held by members of your team. I have even seen organizations strive to attain 100% completion levels for certain types of security certifications. Not only does it pay dividends to the organization in terms of having highly qualified, skill-certified practitioners, but it can provide a means to assure customers of the competency provided by the company. Very few companies can brag that their security team is 100% staffed by certified professionals.

C.4.4 Security Related Jobs

Each security position generally has several common threads required by all employers. The job postings that you may see for security folks also tell you that employers expect a lot from their security personnel. Often, they list 20 or more specific technologies that a security professional must be familiar with and demonstrate competency in for the job to be awarded. It is a tough career field, because the expectations are very high and it takes a huge amount of dedication to attain the level of professional skills employers demand. The rewards, of course, can be very good, but they do not come before security professionals have earned them, both in the trenches and the classroom. Security professionals are considered the cream of the crop in the information technology arena and have to work very hard to meet such demanding requirements. Is it any wonder they are so very hard to find?

C.5   Management of Security Professionals

Managing an information security program in an organization presents significant challenges. Information is typically collected, stored, and processed in all departments and locations of the organization. Diverse types of media, systems, and networks are used for the storage and transmission of confidential information. The confidentiality, integrity, and availability of such information must be protected with consistent, effective measures. Staff members and others who may have access must be informed of the importance of protecting the information and about their specific responsibilities for such information protection. Appropriate techniques and mechanisms to protect the information must be provided and communicated to all users of information.

The information security manager must be alert to continual changes in the organization and the business environment. Legal and accreditation requirements for protecting an individual's privacy are rapidly changing. Security technology is also evolving rapidly. The security manager's job of evaluating risks, determining system and network security requirements, and implementing appropriate controls is challenging, to say the least. The information security manager must be prepared to implement measures for information protection in an environment where these measures are sometimes incorrectly perceived as an impediment to business functions.

The information security manager serves as the focal point for the overall coordination of security policy and procedures for the organization. This responsibility is shared with management and all other information and system users. The information security manager identifies potential exposures and risks to the confidentiality, integrity, and availability of information and makes recommendations to management to mitigate the risks. It is the responsibility of the information security manager to identify the impact on the information security program of changes in the business and computer systems environments. Based on an awareness of the industry and organizational needs, the information security manager should direct and modify (as needed) the information security program. The scope of this responsibility encompasses the organization's information in its entirety.

C.5.1 Organizational Infrastructure

Depending upon the size and complexity of the organization, the information security function may range from a part-time assignment for one person to a unit with a full-time information security manager and multiple information security staff members. The information security unit is typically assigned to the chief information officer, but may be assigned to any senior manager in the organization if that manager will provide the most effective reporting arrangement. The information security function should be perceived to be an organization-wide function, not an entity that is limited to a specific department or person. Therefore, except for system security functions that can be successfully managed by the information systems organization with advice from the information security manager, many of the security administration functions will be distributed throughout the organization. An information security advisory group should be formed to provide advice and support to the information security manager. Typical functions of this group include reviewing proposed policies, standards, procedures, and education programs. The membership of an information security advisory group should include:

- Chief Information Officer
- Risk Manager

- Finance and Accounting Manager
- Human Resources Manager
- Quality Assurance Manager
- Legal Counsel

C.5.2   Reporting Relationships

The information security manager often reports to the chief information officer, having "dotted-line" reporting relationships to Legal, HR, or even a CTO. The dotted-line relationship allows a degree of independence needed to ensure the security manager can make decisions that are best for the company even though, sometimes, they may not be pleasant to all parties involved. The scope of the position should be organization-wide and should involve information on all types of media and in all forms. The information security manager maintains an allegiance to the goals and objectives of the organization's information security program rather than to a specific manager or department. It is important that the security manager be given latitude to make decisions in the absence of the CIO or other executive management. These types of decisions usually revolve around incident containment and management. The CIO and the security manager should work out a plan on how to allow such decisions to be made if an incident occurs and the CIO cannot be reached.

C.5.3   Working Relationships

The information security manager must maintain strong working relationships with key representatives from all functional areas of the organization. These areas include:

- **Chief Executive Officer**: provide status reports, advise, apprise of serious incidents, and recommend policy
- **Chief Information Officer**: direct reporting relationship, as well as support for implementation of information security controls in systems and networks
- **Senior management**: foster awareness, determine responsibility for protection of information assets, and provide advice and ongoing education
- **Internal and external auditors**: report on status of information security measures as requested and respond to audit findings on information security issues
- **Consultants and vendors**: convey information security requirements

C.5.4 Accountability

The information security manager is accountable for successful implementation of the information security program. Therefore the information security manager must:

- Maintain technical knowledge about systems, networks, and telecommunications
- Maintain technical knowledge about information security technology
- Effectively manage staffing and budget
- Ensure a competent, motivated, and knowledgeable staff
- Be able to function effectively in a dynamic environment
- Provide prompt information security support to all users of the systems and networks
- Maintain effective communications with all departments
- Maintain good relationships with appropriate vendor and industry personnel
- Participate in industry events and maintain currency in security skills

C.6 Summary

We have taken a brief look at what is required to put together an effective security function in an organization. Management of a security function requires planning and a deep understanding of the concept of risk management. The interface between the CSO/CISO, HR, and legal counsel cannot be emphasized enough. Their partnership is key to successful implementation of a site security plan. The basic precepts of security, such as incident response, forensics, training and awareness, perimeter security measures, intrusion detection, secure remote access, and so on, have been discussed in terms of establishing functions devoted to those functional areas. Policy development and the role such policies play in an organization's risk management and site security plans have also been covered. We looked at issues regarding staffing and hiring security personnel, and we reviewed the items a security manager should be held responsible and accountable for in performance of his or her duties in an organization. While this introduction does not cover specific policies *per se*, it has covered the reasons why they are important.

C.7   Endnotes

1.   Pfleeger, C., *Security in Computing*. Englewood Cliffs, NJ: Prentice-Hall, 1989.

2.   https://www.it-isac.org.

3.   Internet Engineering Task Force, RFC 2196: *Site Security Handbook*. September 1997. IETF NWG, B. Fraser, ed. http://www.ietf.org.

4.   Fites, M., P. Kratz, and A. Brebner, *Control and Security of Computer Information Systems*. New York: Computer Science Press, 1989.

5.   Handelsmann, Andrew. "Insider Threats to E-Security." Gigalaw.com, December 2001. http://www.gigalaw.com.

6.   *Ibid.*

7.   http://www.checkpoint.com/services/education/certification/certifications/ccsa.html.

8.   http://www.giac.org.

Index

Emergency purchasing team, 123
Emergency services
    external, 129–31
    involvement of, 161–62
    specialists, 162
Employees
    morale, 64
    sabotage, xxvii
    termination procedures, 303–4
Encryption, lii–liii, 104
    defined, 104
    DES, 104
Environmental disasters, 31–42
    droughts, 36–38
    earthquakes, 38–39
    electrical storms, 39–40
    fires, 40–42
    floods, 34–35
    hurricanes, 33
    tornados, 31–33
    winter storms, 36
    See also Emergency Incident Assessment
Environmental threats, 23
Epidemics, 62
Equipment
    backup and recovery, 150
    installation team, 123–24
    new, purchasing, 181–82
    nonproduction, 189
    production, 189
Equipment/system failures, 56–59
    air conditioning, 57
    cooling plant, 58
    internal power, 57
    planning, 57
    probability, 58
    production line, 57–58
    types of, 56–57
    See also Emergency Incident Assessment
Executive management team, 124
Executive Order 12656, 13

Expedited Funds Availability Act, 13
External access controls, lv–lvii
    host-based authentication, lvi–lvii
    port protection devices (PPDs), lv–lvi
    secure gateways, lvi
    See also Access controls
External emergency services, 129–31

Facilities preparation team, 124–25
Facility questionnaire, 291–94
Federal Computer Incident Response
        Capability (FEDCIRC), 302
Federal Financial Institutions Examinations
        Council (FFIEC), 157, 193
*Federal Information System Controls Audit
        Manual* (FISCAM), 213
Feedback questionnaires, 196
FEMA, 163
    Mitigation Division, 44
    Web site, 44
Finance team, 125–26
Financial impact, 84–86
Financial institution fraud, xxiv–xxv
Fire extinguishers, 114
Fires, 40–42
    evacuation drills, 41
    impact, 40–41
    response options, 41–42
    suppression and control systems, 112–14
    See also Environmental disasters
Firewalls, 103–4
    application gateway, 104
    circuit-level gateway, 104
    defined, 103
    packet filter, 103
    proxy server, 104
    See also Preventative measures
Floods, 34–35
    contingent floodproofing, 35
    emergency floodproofing, 35